The Challenge of Counseling in Middle Schools

Editors:
**Edwin R. Gerler, Jr.
Canary C. Hogan
Kathleen O'Rourke**

**ERIC Counseling and Personnel Services Clearinghouse
2108 School of Education
The University of Michigan
Ann Arbor, Michigan 48109-1259**

and

**The American School Counselor Association
a division of the
American Association for Counseling and Development
5999 Stevenson Avenue
Alexandria, Virginia 22304**

LB 1620.5
C453x

ERIC Counseling and Personnel Services Clearinghouse
2108 School of Education
The University of Michigan
Ann Arbor, MI 48109-1259

ISBN 1-56109-030-1

This publication was prepared with partial funding from the Office of Educational Research and Improvement, U.S. Department of Education under contract
no. RI88062011. The opinions expressed in this report do not necessarily reflect
the positions or policies of OERI, the Department of Education, or ERIC/CAPS.

®

Contents

Introduction

At ERIC/CAPS we face questions daily about manuscripts. For example, do they meet our expectations and the high standards we set for our publications? This manuscript has been a pleasure to work with for several reasons. First, the middle school counseling area is comparatively new and unexplored. Therefore, what is written has a special "freshness" and "newness" about it. The authors are not only saying what they do well but are including concepts and ideas that are not "bookworn" by now. Second, the organization of the book strikes a compelling balance between developmental concepts and insights, and pragmatic and useful procedures and interventions. Anyone reading this volume, be they middle school counselors, teachers or just someone who is interested in learning about adolescents, will find the contents personally useful to them. Third, I believe the mix of journal articles, original writing, and ERIC materials is a potent combination. By using the best of the three sources, a monograph has been created which offers both breadth and depth.

In short, I believe that Edwin R. Gerler, Jr., Canary C. Hogan, and Kathleen O'Rourke are to be commended for a truly outstanding job. Whether your goal as a reader is to gain a profile of the middle school student or to acquire some workable and effective techniques for counseling with middle school students, I'm betting this book will meet your highest expectations, much as it did mine.

Garry R. Walz, Ph.D., NCC
Director and Professor

Foreword

The Challenge of Counseling in Middle Schools is the second in a series of books resulting from collaboration between the American School Counselor Association and ERIC/CAPS. The book's editors, Edwin R. Gerler, Jr., Canary C. Hogan, and Kathleen O'Rourke, have assembled a collection of articles that addresses topics of importance to counselors who serve middle school students.

The middle school student is a unique individual who often needs the assistance of adults to feel secure, important, and able. The Carnegie Corporation's Task Force on Education recently reported that middle school students benefit most from being in small group learning communities staffed by individuals who have special skills in working with young adolescents. The Carnegie report noted further that middle schools need to rely on the quality of human interactions to shape the character of young people. School counselors play a significant part in shaping the environment for students who attend middle schools.

Dewey wrote that education should extract from physical and social surroundings "all that they have to contribute to building up experiences that are worthwhile." *The Challenge of Counseling in Middle Schools* provides school counselors and other educators many ideas for creating worthwhile experiences for young people within the surroundings of home, school, and community.

Doris Rhea Coy, 1990 President
American School Counselor Association

Preface

Counselors in middle schools work with young people whose lives are in constant flux. Early adolescence is a time of physical, intellectual, emotional, and social development, during which young people confront the question, "Who am I?" The young adolescent's search for identity involves many challenges which include:

1. The challenge of forming new, less dependent relationships with parents and family at a time when the institution of family is itself experiencing other stresses.
2. The challenge of new pressures from peers that may encourage experimentation with drugs and result later in devastating addictions.
3. The challenge of physical development, particularly sexual maturity and its various effects on the emotional and social lives of young people.
4. The challenge of intellectual development which may have both positive and negative influences on academic performance in the classroom.
5. The challenge of the future and of exploring the question "What do I want to do with my life?"

This book deals with how counselors in middle schools can help youngsters face the various challenges of early adolescence. Early adolescence is a time of moving away from childhood and from elementary school. During the elementary school years children's growth rates are usually gradual and predictable. Developmental needs are identified and met by both the teacher and the counselor through a carefully planned and executed school program. Moreover, during the elementary grades, parents typically maintain close contact with the school in regard to their children's education. As students progress to middle schools, many differences can be noted in the operation of the school and in the philosophy of teachers. Since most middle school teachers have subject matter specialties, these teachers usually have focused academic interests. This means that students in middle schools have different teachers for every period of the school day and also that each teacher may work with 150 or more students per day as contrasted with elementary teachers who may spend all day with the same 20–25 students. It is often the case, therefore, that middle school teachers are unable to develop close bonds with students. Counselors are called upon to plan programs that make middle schools inviting places for young people to learn and grow.

Early adolescence, in addition to being a time of moving away from elementary school, is a period of maturation toward the later teen years and toward high school. There are major differences between middle schools and high schools, differences that cause some students to get lost emotionally and to fail academically. High schools are usually larger than middle schools and demand that students find their way with less and less adult supervision. Middle school counseling programs need to focus on preparing youngsters for the increased independence of life in high school that is typically accompanied by more social pressures and by increased stress. The chapters in this book offer many ideas for helping young people improve their sense of self, their decision-making capabilities, their interpersonal relationships, their academic skills, and their abilities to deal with stress.

Chapters contain articles that have been invited for the book as well as articles that have been published in various counseling journals. The journals included are: *Elementary School Guidance and Counseling, The School Counselor, Journal of Counseling and Development, Journal of Humanistic Education and Development, Journal for Specialists in Group Work*, and the *Vocational Guidance Quarterly*. The book contains articles by recognized authorities, including David Elkind on stress in early adolescence, Paul George on counselors and middle schools, Norman Gysbers on career education for students with disabilities, Dave Capuzzi on preventing adolescent drug abuse, and Richard Nelson on teen-parent relationships. The book also contains articles by well established practitioners and new scholars in the area of middle school counseling. The book concludes with a provocative essay by Sidney Simon, entitled "A View from the 'right': Who needs school

counseling and guidance programs, anyway?" an essay which dramatically illustrates the importance of counselors in the lives of young
people.

The Challenge of Counseling in Middle Schools is a book for counselors who are already working in middle schools and for individuals
who are attending graduate schools in preparation for careers as middle
school counselors. The book will also benefit both elementary school
counselors, who help children make the often difficult transition from
elementary school to middle school, and high school counselors, who
work with youngsters making the important transition from middle
school into high school.

Editors:

Edwin R. Gerler, Jr.
Canary C. Hogan
Kathleen O'Rourke

Chapter 1

The Challenge of Self-Discovery in Early Adolescence

In her poem, "A Fence Rider," published in *The School Counselor*, Burnette (1986) wrote this about early adolescence:

> A transescent is too old . . . too young,
> childish . . . adult,
> dependent . . . self-reliant,
> a groupie . . . a loner,
> sexy . . . sexless,
> frustrated . . . excited,
> rebellious . . . conforming,
> free . . . imprisoned.
>
> A transescent is a fence rider who can
> dismount on either side at any given
> moment. (p. 177)

Early adolescence is difficult for most youngsters, a time for challenging one's self and the ideas brought from childhood. It is the beginning of physical, emotional, social, and intellectual growth which brings excitement, delight, anxiety, and misunderstanding. The child, who in elementary school was obedient and academically motivated, may seem disrespectful and lazy in middle school. Early adolescence begins the transition from acceptance of adult direction to challenging authority and moving toward self direction. The goal of educators who work with young adolescents is to provide a blend of challenge and support that will promote identity development.

Middle school students need the guidance and direction of effective counselors to begin the major developmental task of adolescence which is to achieve a clear sense of self. The confusion that reigns in early adolescence creates a challenging climate for the young person and for those trying to help the youngster manage the difficulties associated with leaving childhood for a new stage of life. This chapter brings together articles that describe some practical strategies for counselors to use in helping middle school students move toward self understanding. These strategies include activities (e.g., maintaining daily journals and reading novels about adolescence) that counselors can implement in conjunction with classroom teachers. The most effective middle school counseling programs offer young people many planned opportunities for self exploration.

About the Editors

Edwin R. Gerler, Jr. is a professor in the Department of Counselor Education at North Carolina State University in Raleigh. He has written extensively, including the books *Counseling the Young Learner* and *Elementary School Counseling in a Changing World*. He has been the editor of two AACD journals in addition to serving on several editorial boards. He is presently the editor of *Elementary School Guidance and Counseling*. He has taught, counseled, and conducted research in elementary and middle schools.

Canary C. Hogan was the 1989–90 ASCA Middle/Junior High Vice President. She has 12 years of school counseling experience with the Metropolitan Public School System, Nashville, Tennessee and serves as an adjunct faculty member at Tennessee State University and Trevecca College. She holds an Ed.D. degree in human development counseling from George Peabody College of Vanderbilt University. She is the author of the *Professional Accountability Log (PAL) for School Counselors*.

Kathleen O'Rourke was the 1989–90 ASCA North Atlantic Regional Vice President. She is the guidance department chairperson for the Altoona Area School District and is adjunct assistant professor of counselor education at Indiana University of Pennsylvania. Dr. O'Rourke has recently coauthored the book *Elementary School Counseling: A Blueprint for Today and Tomorrow*. She has 18 years of school counseling experience and for the past five years has been chairperson of the Elementary/Middle School Committee for the Pennsylvania School Counselors Association.

Correspondence about this book should be sent to:

Edwin R. Gerler, Jr.
520 Poe Hall
Department of Counselor Education
North Carolina State University
Raleigh, North Carolina 27695-7801

Office Phone: (919) 737-2244
Home Phone: (919) 848-3435

Contributors

Jo Ann C. Alexander, counselor in private practice, and former middle school counselor, Winter Park, Florida

Ron Anderson, director of student services, Wake County Public Schools, Raleigh, North Carolina

Miguel Arciniega, assistant professor, Department of Counselor Education, Arizona State University, Tempe

John Arnold, coordinator, Graduate Middle Grades Education Programs, Department of Curriculum and Instruction, North Carolina State University, Raleigh

Darryl Lee Bayer, clinical psychologist, Cumberland River Comprehensive Care Center, Harlan, Kentucky

Ana Bermudez, fellow, Baylor College of Medicine, Houston, Texas

Thelma L. Blumberg, school psychologist, Baltimore City Public Schools, Baltimore, Maryland

Donn E. Brolin, professor, Department of Educational and Counseling Psychology, University of Missouri–Columbia

Rebecca F. Brownlee, executive director, Drug Action of Wake County, Raleigh, North Carolina

Dave Capuzzi, professor, School of Education, Portland State University, Portland, Oregon, and editor, *The School Counselor*

Mariam R. Chacko, assistant professor, Baylor College of Medicine, Houston, Texas

James W. Costar, professor emeritus of educational administration, Michigan State University, Lansing

Nancy Shannon Drew, counselor, North Garner Middle School, Garner, North Carolina

Nancy DeNardo, counselor, Lover's Lane Center, Dallas, Texas

John Eddy, professor of counselor education, North Texas State University, Denton

David Elkind, professor of child study, and resident scholar, Lincoln Filene Center, Tufts University, Medford, Massachusetts

Kathryn T. Foley, Outward Bound instructor, Bethel, Maine

Tanis C. Furst, graduate student in educational psychology, Cornell University, Ithaca, New York

Paul S. George, professor of education, University of Florida, Gainesville

Norman C. Gysbers, professor, Department of Educational and Counseling Psychology, University of Missouri–Columbia

Robert L. Harman, director, Counseling and Testing Center, University of Central Florida, Orlando

Dalva E. Hedlund, associate professor of counseling psychology, Department of Education, Cornell University, Ithaca, New York

Theodore W. Hipple, professor of English education, and head of the Department of Curriculum and Instruction, University of Tennessee, Knoxville

Robert L. Hubbard, senior research social psychologist, Research Triangle Institute, Raleigh, North Carolina

Ed Jacobs, associate professor, Department of Counseling and Rehabilitation, West Virginia University, Morgantown

Jeffrey S. Kaplan, English teacher, Forest High School, Ocala, Florida

Lindy L. LeCoq, vocational counselor, Evergreen High School, Vancouver, Washington

David Lemire, school psychologist, Sweetwater County School District No. 2, Green River, Wyoming

Marsha D. Link, counselor, Riley Children's Hospital, Indianapolis, Indiana

Ernest H. McCray, teacher, Denton Independent School District, Denton, Texas

Christina E. Mitchell, director of counseling and testing, and associate professor, Department of Education and Psychology, University of Texas–Tyler

Phyllis Mohr, counselor, College of Engineering, and doctoral student in counselor education, North Carolina State University, Raleigh

Nancy E. Moore, social worker, Child & Family Services, Inc., Hartford, Connecticut

Stephen Moorhead, curriculum specialist, Drug Action of Wake County, Raleigh, North Carolina

John P. Murphy, coordinator, Alcohol Rehabilitation Unit, V. A. Medical Center, Grand Junction, Colorado

Amalya Nattiv, assistant professor of elementary education, Utah State University, Logan

Richard C. Nelson, professor of counseling and personnel services, Department of Education, Purdue University, West Lafayette, Indiana

Betty J. Newlon, assistant professor, Department of Counseling and Guidance, University of Arizona, Tucson

Emily Garfield Ostrower, guidance counselor, Quincy High School, Quincy, Massachusetts

Sandra DeAngelis Peace, doctoral student, Counselor Education Department, North Carolina State University, Raleigh

Gary F. Render, professor of educational psychology, and associate dean for graduate studies and research, University of Wyoming, Laramie, and editor, *Journal of Humanistic Education*

Kristin E. Render, psychology graduate student, University of Wyoming, Laramie

Natalie Rubinton, assistant dean of students, Kingsborough Community College, Brooklyn, New York

Shelda Bachin Sandler, counselor, Interboro School District, Prospect Park, Pennsylvania

Sidney B. Simon, professor of psychological education, University of Massachusetts, Amherst

Peggy B. Smith, professor, Baylor College of Medicine, Houston, Texas

David Stilson, doctoral student, College of Education, North Texas State University, Denton

JoAnna Strother, assistant professor, Division of Counselor Education, North Texas State University, Denton

Margaret G. Sumner, coordinator, Family Life Enrichment, Child & Family Services, Inc., Hartford, Connecticut

Hershel D. Thornburg was a professor in the Department of Educational Psychology at the University of Arizona, Tucson

Jane H. Yarbrough, instructor, Department of English, University of Wisconsin–Marinette

Mary M. Wellman, assistant professor, Department of Psychology, Rhode Island College, Providence

Natalie Susan Wilson, elementary school counselor, King George County Public Schools, King George, Virginia

A Dialogue With Self: The Journal as an Educational Tool

Dalva E. Hedlund
Tanis C. Furst
Kathryn T. Foley

The act of "talking to oneself" is an important component of learning, and of seeking balance, direction, and meaning in life.

We all talk to ourselves. Who has not? Children speak aloud freely until they are taught that it is peculiar behavior; then they learn silent, mental speech, which denies others access and opportunity to ridicule or eavesdrop. Haven't we all been challenged in the midst of such a "conversation," and felt foolish in responding, "I was just talking to myself— thinking aloud—just thinking"? This common human behavior embarrasses us when we are "caught" at it, and amuses or concerns others. Why do we talk to ourselves, especially once we have learned to communicate with others? Internal dialogue may be necessary because we seek meaning in our world, a place for ourselves, perspective, balance, and direction. The journal is a written dialogue with self, a very personal document and a valuable learning tool.

What Is a Journal

The terms "journal," "diary," and "log" are often used interchangeably, but in our understanding the forms differ. A *diary* typically is continuous, spontaneous, and intimate in nature—generally not for the public's eye. A *log* is an objective record of specific events (i.e., ship's log, or experimental record in a laboratory). As a literary form, the journal falls roughly between the diary and the log (Berman, 1986): it consists of regular, though not necessarily daily, entries by which the writer focuses and reflects upon a given theme, or a series of events and experiences. The organizing theme may be spontaneous, or predetermined (Hettich, 1976; Ramshaw, 1983).

Personal content is essential in a journal. The journal has been defined as "a topical autobiography, a short, discontinuous personal document [that] represents the excerpting from an individual's life of a special class of events." (Hettich, 1976, p. 60). "Journal" and "topical autobiography" are similar labels. Sometimes a distinction between the two is made with regard to focus: an autobiography—topical or comprehensive, guided or spontaneous—tends to emphasize external events in the writer's life, whereas a journal—whatever its specific form and rationale—may be centered more upon ideas, or internal events (Kotzbauer & Ramshaw, 1987). The authors shall use the term "journal" to refer to a personal document primarily focusing upon ideas.

The Journal and Learning

A journal is an interactive instrument (Progoff, 1975). "Interactive" implies interaction with one's self: a metacognitive activity of reflecting upon one's own thoughts. Journal keeping engages the writer in a dialogue with the self (Kelsey, 1980; Progoff, 1975; Ramshaw, 1983). As in any true discourse, this dialogue requires active participation. In choosing to write a journal, one chooses to transcend passivity. Active involvement profoundly affects memory and learning. If individuals become conscious of their personal histories and past experiences, they can better integrate and assimilate new information, more actively weave past memories into a new fabric of the present, and more confidently call upon experiences to validate and make sense of the past, present, and future (Birren, 1987; Linton, 1982; Neisser, 1982). Put another way, journal keeping enriches for each of us the process of creating a personal and accessible "landscape"—the ground against which we make our choices, live, and learn (Greene, 1978). The journal records our purposeful journey through this landscape.

Inherent in the process of human learning are shifts in emotions, changes in goals, and new ideas (Birren & Hedlund, 1987). People write journals, and journal writers (and sometimes others) read and react to what has been written, noting patterns of growth, development and change (Lowry, 1959; Ramshaw, 1987). These patterns have been represented in a variety of ways, but three metaphors recur frequently in the literature: stepping-stones (Crow, 1983; Progoff, 1975), the branching tree (Birren, 1987; Linton, 1982), and the forked road (Grumet, 1980; Progoff, 1975). All of these metaphors image choice: reflection upon choices made or not made, and personal interaction with this reflection. Options not chosen, or omissions in the telling—should writers and readers of journals become conscious of them—may reveal as much as what has been done, or reported (Allport, 1942). "There in the interstices, the spaces where the pieces don't quite meet, is where the light comes through" (Grumet, 1980, p. 12).

A journal can develop spontaneously or be predetermined in its form and purpose, or be guided (Hettich, 1976; Ramshaw, 1983). In an educational setting a student may be asked to write a guided journal related to course content (Birren, 1987). A guided journal helps the writer focus upon facts, themes and concepts that are learned in depth as they become incorporated into personal experience.

A Cognitive View of Learning From a Class Journal

The purpose of any course of instruction involves learning, remembering, and being able to use productively some identified subject matter. Our assertion is that keeping a class journal will improve those learning, remembering, and using processes. How might journal keeping help?

Remembering. New material being learned must be encoded in order for it to be retained in long-term memory. There are various ways of conceptualizing the information storage and retrieval process. A model developed by Anderson (1985) demonstrates that one's declarative knowledge—things one knows, including facts, theories, generalizations, personal experiences, and one's likes and dislikes—is stored in a propositional network. Propositions are, roughly, ideas, each consisting of the smallest unit of information about which it is possible to make a true or false judgement. Declarative knowledge is stored in long-term memory in networks of propositions.

Encoding new information involves incorporating it into propositional networks that store our knowledge in organized ways. Interrelated information is more closely linked than information that is unrelated. Propositions already in memory are activated and new information is connected to them when learners acquire new knowledge. Moreover, as new information is encoded, this encoding may stimulate the generation of new propositions (ideas), which then connect the incoming information to other areas of a person's existing network of ideas. This generative process is called elaboration because it adds new information to the incoming idea (Gagné, 1985). The more completely any new information is elaborated, the more easily that new information will be remembered, retrieved, and used.

One studying method that fosters elaboration involves the deliberate organization of new declarative knowledge (Brown & Day, 1983). We clarify propositions by relating elements of the new material to propositions already in long-term memory when we intentionally organize new information. For example, students implementing Novak's (1977) notion of concept-mapping will organize new knowledge and improve their learning.

Higher-achieving students on standardized achievement tests apparently have more effective strategies for encoding new information (Wang, 1983; Weinstein, 1978). These students seem to elaborate upon new material more efficiently by finding novel ways to connect new ideas with other ideas already in memory (Schmeck & Grove, 1979).

Hettich (1976) postulates that journal writing is a way for students to improve the elaboration of new information. By using their own words, students can relate new concepts to their own current knowledge. A journal entry provides the opportunity to connect new knowledge and previously learned knowledge in unconventional ways. Likewise, journal writing provides an avenue for students' exploration of personal experiences. Connecting new knowledge and memories of personal experiences, likes and dislikes, is an excellent way to elaborate upon material and build propositional networks, or schemata, or facts, or concepts and themes that are personally meaningful.

Hettich (1976) also analyzed the use of journals in teaching psychology. He observed that journal keeping provides a way for instructors to individualize lecture-based courses:

> Consequently, students enhance their understanding of many abstract psychological concepts and forge their thoughts on broader issues, using their own words and experiences as tools. Thus, psychological concepts become anchored to the student's cognitive framework, not just to examples provided by the textbook and the teacher. (p. 61)

Skills. Teachers are not only concerned with having students memorize material, but also with teaching them how to think about a subject matter and to do things with it (McKeachie, 1986). Certainly, writing about what one is learning provides practice in how to think about and use the material being learned. Particular assignments in a class journal can be used to enrich the development of procedural knowledge, which is the knowledge of how to do something. Gagné (1985) has demonstrated that practice with declarative knowledge, such as in class journal writing, leads to the development of procedural knowledge.

Using knowledge. A good teacher hopes that students will develop strategic, or conditional knowledge. Conditional knowledge tells us when and where we may appropriately use our declarative and procedural knowledge. When an individual makes a journal entry, he or she assumes the metacognitive stance of an observer: "This is what I know, and this is how and when I can use what I know."

A "Depth Psychology" View

A Jungian (Jung, 1965), or depth psychology (Progoff, 1975) perspective suggests that individuals each have within themselves sources of wisdom or "knowing" that are accessible primarily through unconscious processes. Progoff (1985) and Kelsey (1980), among others, argued that journal writing is one way to tap these sources of wisdom. Most advocates of journal writing as a tool for personal growth and creativity argue from this point of view. They assert that successful classroom learning is not an entirely cognitive activity, but involves development of the whole person. The journal becomes an arena—a crucible— wherein new learning encounters sources of meaning deep within each individual, and new life meaning is created.

Applications in the Classroom

Journals have been implemented in a variety of classroom settings. Drawing upon the idea that the journal is a focusing tool for themes and concepts, which the writer then learns in greater depth and incorporates into personal experience, an instructor or curriculum designer might elect to include some form of the journal within the total schema of classwork.

Some instructors have required students to keep journals documenting learning activities outside the classroom. In one exercise, a group of teachers taking a professional development course on the process of learning were asked by their instructor to make regular observations of a "familiar" phenomenon—the moon in the sky—and record in journals their own observations of the moon's apparent behavior (Duckworth, 1986). The journalists, who were neither astronomers nor trained observers, developed in their journals a variety of personal theories and intuitive insights about why the moon changes its shape from night to night. During the course of the moon-watching exercise, they shared with one another their preconceptions about the moon, and their thoughts about how these notions came to change. Dilemmas arose and were addressed, observations and comparisons accumulated, and the teachers-cum-students applied *metalearning* (learning about how they learn) to readjust their conceptions of themselves as teachers.

Journals can be used within the classroom structure to broaden students' in-class experiences. Kuhn and Aguirre (1986) implemented a constructivist teaching method in a 10th-grade science classroom, incorporating structured journal entries into the course as a component of conventional laboratory notebooks. In these journals students entered "pre-questions" and "preconceptions"—answers to specific questions already formulated from personal experience, untested, and unverified as empirically "correct"—and then followed their experiments with "assessments" containing the following questions to be answered in the journals:

1. What were some things that you already knew about what you observed?
2. What result(s), if any, surprised you?
3. State some questions that you have that are about what you observed or are related to it.
4. State any everyday examples or applications of what you observed. (p. 5)

This method was also used to explore radiation and nuclear energy from the standpoint of individual students' experiences and conceptions, which were used to interpret the experimental results and construct theoretical explanations. A structured journal is a useful device for ensuring that individual perspective plays a central, rather than ancillary, role in the classroom process.

This process contrasts dramatically with the picture of traditional education painted by Grumet:

Years of banking education and of survival in educational institutions have taught the student to figure out what is expected and to deliver the order as neatly, quickly, and obsequiously as possible. (1980, p. 14)

In Kuhn and Aguirre's case study, students were interviewed to assess their receptivity to learning via the use of journals. When asked about differences between science classes and other classes, or between Grade 9 and 10 science, one student reported the following:

> I think this is better, because in the years before, we used textbooks, and you did the labs right out of the textbook. If you do your experiment wrong or you don't understand it, all you do is turn ahead and find out what was supposed to happen or what you are supposed to have learned. In this one you don't have much [of an] idea, and you sort of figure it out for yourself. By the time he gets around to the debriefing, you end up with a pretty good idea. (Kuhn & Aguirre, 1986, p. 15)

Sometimes a student's personal experience is the basis for problem solving or even the basis for a curriculum. One example of this is programs that have the development of self-discovery and personal change as the educational goals. Instructors in these programs may use journals because they recognize that ideas and understanding can come from "nowhere," given an atmosphere in which to thrive and develop.

One such example may be found in the Outward Bound programs, in which journals are a private place for dialogues and impressions. The act of writing an experience down is in itself an act of reflection (Progoff, 1975). Students may share entries if they choose, or simply reflect upon their interactions with a new world. Past, present, and future are rewoven into the fabric of their lives as they discover new or forgotten aspects of themselves.

Some writing teachers have used the journal as a form of a doodle-pad. One creative writing program teacher for high school students asked instructors to begin every class with 10 minutes of journal writing. This exercise corresponds to what Progoff (1975) described as a sifting of the compacted soil of the mind, to allow seeds of future creativity to sprout.

Other classrooms-outside-classrooms use journals to help people process discoveries within the unfamiliar context of other people's lives. An instructor who favors a holistic approach to education may present factual course material while simultaneously facilitating students' understanding of the impact of their personal backgrounds and insights upon this material (Brown, 1971). These elements, taken together, create a whole learning experience. One college anthropology teacher (Ramshaw, 1987) used the journal as a form of record keeping and review of students' visits to impoverished neighborhoods. Students began their coursework by writing a short educational autobiography. Students recorded settings and occurrences during their field visits, as well as their reactions to spending time in different neighborhoods. This course was designed to help students to reflect upon poverty in the United States by asking them to compare their own life experiences with those of the people they visited. An important course goal was to illuminate the students' impact upon host families, as well as illuminate the visits' impact upon students. Gagné's (1985) idea of elaboration is at work here, as students connect what they see in their visits to what they already know about their own lives.

Published journals can also serve as a reading resource for students, providing the insights of others to similar material or experiences. The reflections of Frederick Douglass (1845), and works such as *Memoir of Old Elizabeth, a coloured woman* (1866) comprise a collection of slave narratives that provide personal accounts of antebellum southern life in the same way as The *Diary of Anne Frank* (Cadrain, 1979) relates the experiences of Jews in hiding during World War II. Reading a published journal may also illuminate responses that are held in common: May Sarton (1980) and Florida Scott-Maxwell (1968) reaffirm the commonalities within the human experiences of loneliness and aging. Students in a women's studies course have learned to understand a feminist perspective on Afro-American women, reproduction, and disease from a uniquely personal viewpoint by examining Audre Lorde's battle with cancer by reading her published journal (1980). Journals may tell stories that no textbook chapters could adequately recount, and students' understanding of subjects can be powerfully stimulated by studying other individuals' personal reflections.

Conclusion

In summary, journals are valuable educational tools that help students make sense of their personal histories, assimilate and integrate new information, learn to think about their knowledge, and learn to use new knowledge. Class journals may be more or less structured depending upon the teacher's intent. Journal writing has proved to be a valuable adjunct to almost any classroom subject, from the sciences to the humanities. The adoption of the journal as a teaching strategy validates a student's personal contribution to his or her own learning achievements.

Finally, reading and reflecting upon others' published journals provides a wealth of uniquely human insights into a wide range of academic topics.

References

Allport, G. W. (1942). *The use of personal documents in psychological science.* New York: Social Science Research Council.

Anderson, J. R. (1985). *Cognitive psychology and its implications* (2nd ed.). New York: W. H. Freeman.

Berman, H. J. (1986). To flame with a wild life: Florida Scott-Maxwell's experience of old age. *The Gerontologist, 26,* 321–324.

Birren, J. E. (1987, May). The best of all stories: Autobiography gives new meaning to our present lives by helping us understand the past more fully. *Psychology Today,* 91–92.

Birren, J. E., & Hedlund, B. (1987). Contributions of autobiography to developmental psychology. In N. Eisenberg (Ed.), *Contemporary topics in developmental psychology* (pp. 394–415). New York: John Wiley & Sons.

Brown, A. L., & Day, J. D. (1983). *Macrorules for summarizing text: The development of expertise.* (Tech. Rep. No. 270). Champaign, IL: Center for the Study of Reading.

Brown, G. I. (1971). *Human teaching for human learning: An introduction to confluent education.* New York: Viking Press.

Cadrain, L. A. (1979). *Diary of Anne Frank.* New York: Pendulum Press.

Crow, E. (1983, March). *Shaping self: Using steppingstones and autobiography to create and discover archetypes in "An Illustrious Monarchy."* Speech delivered at Conference on College Composition and Communications, Detroit, MI.

Douglass, F. (1845). *Narrative of the life of Frederick Douglass, an American slave. Written by himself.* Boston: American Anti-slavery Society.

Duckworth, E. (1986). Teaching as research. *Harvard Educational Review, 56,* 481–495.

Elizabeth. (1866). *Memoir of Old Elizabeth, a coloured woman.* Philadelphia: David Heston.

Gagné, E. D. (1985). *The cognitive psychology of learning.* Boston: Little, Brown.

Greene, M. (1978). *Landscapes of learning*. New York/London: Teachers College Press.

Grumet, M. (1980, October). *Restitution and reconstruction of educational experience: An autobiographical method for curriculum theory*. Presented to Annual Meeting of The American Educational Research Association, Boston, MA.

Hettich, P. (1976). The journal: An autobiographical approach to learning. *Teaching of Psychology, 3*(2), 60–63.

Jung, C. G. (1965). *Memories, dreams, reflections*. New York: Vintage.

Jung, J. (1972). Psychology in action: Autobiographies of college students as a teaching and research tool in the study of personality development. *American Psychologist, 27*, 779–783.

Kelsey, M. T. (1980). *Adventure inward*. Minneapolis: Augsberg.

Kotzbauer, L., & Ranshaw, W. C. (1987). *Notes on keeping a journal*. Unpublished manuscript. Department of Anthropology and Sociology, Colgate University, Hamilton, NY.

Kotzbauer, L., & Ramshaw, W. C. (1987). *Some notes towards a final journal entry*. Unpublished manuscript. Department of Anthropology and Sociology, Colgate University, Hamilton, NY.

Kuhn, K., & Aguirre, J. (1986). *A case study—on the "Journal Method"—a method designed to enable the implementation of constructivist teaching in the classroom*. Victoria, B.C.: University of British Columbia.

Linton, M. (1982). Transformations of memory in everyday life. In U. Neisser (Ed.), *Memory observed: Remembering in natural context* (pp. 77–91). San Francisco: W. H. Freeman & Co.

Lorde, A. (1980). *Cancer journals*. San Francisco: Spinsters/Aunt Lute.

Lowry, R. C. (Ed.). (1959). *The journals of Abraham Maslow, Volume 1*. Monterey, CA: Brooks/Cole.

McKeachie, W. J. (1986). *Teaching tips: A guidebook for the beginning college teacher* (8th ed.). Lexington, MA: D. C. Heath and Co.

Neisser, U. (1982). Memory: What are the important questions? In U. Neisser (Ed.), *Memory observed: Remembering in natural contexts* (pp. 3–19). San Francisco: W. H. Freeman.

Novak, J. D. (1977). *A theory of education*. Ithaca, NY: Cornell University Press.

Progoff, I. (1975). *At a journal workshop*. New York: Dialogue House.

Progoff, I. (1985). *The dynamics of hope*. New York: Dialogue House.

Ramshaw, W. C. (1983). *Notes on keeping an intellectual journal.* Unpublished manuscript. Department of Anthropology and Sociology, Colgate University, Hamilton, NY.

Ramshaw, W. C. (1987). *On writing an educational autobiography.* Unpublished manuscript. Department of Anthropology and Sociology, Colgate University, Hamilton, NY.

Sarton, M. (1980). *Recovering: A journal.* New York: W. W. Norton.

Schmeck, R. R., & Grove, E. (1979). Academic achievement and individual differences. *Applied Psychological Measurement, 3,* 43–49.

Scott-Maxwell, F. (1968). *The measure of my days.* New York: Alfred A. Knopf.

Wang, A. Y. (1983). Individual differences in learning speed. *Journal of Experimental Psychology: Learning, Memory and Cognition, 9,* 300–311.

Weinstein, C. E. (1978). Elaboration skills as a learning strategy. In H. F. O'Neil, Jr. (Ed.), *Learning strategies* (pp. 31–55). New York: Academic Press.

The Effects of Two Methods of Affective Education on Self-Concept in Seventh-Grade Students

Darryl Lee Bayer

Positive self-concept in students has long been a concern of psychologists and educators. Psychologists such as Carl Rogers and Clark Moustakas have asserted that positive self-concept is the most crucial factor for the success of the learning person (Moustakas, 1966; Moustakas & Perry, 1973; Rogers, 1969). Educators have pointed out that enhancement of student self-concept is important both as an educational outcome and for the effects it has on academic achievement (Shavelson, Gubner, & Stanton, 1976).

There is considerable empirical evidence that self-concept predicts and influences achievement in school, from the primary grades through undergraduate education (Wylie, 1961, 1974, 1979). Early research demonstrated a substantial association between self-concept and academic achievement (Brookover, Thomas, & Paterson, 1964; Joe, 1971; Morse, 1964) and revealed that self-concept measures could be used to predict school performance as early as kindergarten (Wattenberg & Clifford, 1964). More recent research continues to confirm the strong relationship between self-concept and scholastic achievement (Primavera, Simon, & Primavera, 1974; Scheirer & Kraut, 1979; Simon & Simon, 1975; Stenner & Katzenmeyer, 1976) and the validity of self-concept measures as predictors of academic performance (Bridgeman & Shipman, 1978; Chang, 1976; Cole, 1974; Ellerman, 1980; Shavelson et al., 1976).

Self-concept also has been found to remain stable over time in the absence of enhancing (or deleterious) experiences (Brookover et al,, 1964; Prawat, 1976), but to change as a function of various experiences and influences. For example, previous success is a major contributor to positive self-concept (Kifer, 1975; Peterson, Burton, & Baker, 1983). Factors with strong experiential components include school variables, such as teacher perceptions of student ability or worth (Covington & Beery, 1976; Eato & Lerner, 1981; Purkey, 1978; Schofield, 1981;

Simpson, 1978; Wolf & Wenzl, 1982), family variables, such as degree of harmony in the home and amount of encouragement to perform well academically (Bowman, 1965; Kifer, 1975; McClelland, 1955; McClelland, Baldwin, Bronfenbrenner, & Strodtbeck, 1958; Parish & Nunn, 1981; Pierce & Bowman, 1960), and peer variables such as acceptance within groups (Bilby, Brookover, & Erickson, 1972; Eato & Lerner, 1981; Hamachek, 1977; Slavin, 1980; Wolf & Wenzl, 1982).

Because variables in relationships and interpersonal interaction occurring in the school environment have been identified as influencing student self-concept, these variables (or the lack of them) can help develop (or undermine) scholastic potential in students (Shaha & Wittrock, 1983). Also, because educational and psychological growth seem to be interdependent (Leamon, 1982; Scheirer & Kraut, 1979), it becomes important to determine and promote the change-producing variables involved in affective experiences that enhance student self-concept.

To date, research on school-initiated affective education experiences reveals mainly that some programs achieve gains in self-concept or academic performance and some do not (Baskin & Hess, 1980; Medway & Smith, 1978). Does the activity or specific curriculum make the difference, for instance, or is it caused by variables in the experience itself that are related to the form or style of promoting learning or experiencing?

This research was an investigation of what kind of affective education experience would lead to maximum gain in self-concept. It was hypothesized that the form of affective education opportunity would influence the degree of self-concept change. The contrast in form was between the facilitated condition and the directed condition, defined in the Procedures section and exemplified in Appendix A. The primary research hypothesis was that the facilitated group would show significantly greater self-concept gain than the directed group. A second hypothesis was that the form of affective education experience would influence how interesting and valuable the student perceived the experience to be. Academic achievement was not a focus in this study.

Method

Participants

The 30 students from a California seventh-grade health class were randomly assigned to two experimental groups. Male and female students were equally distributed so that each group contained 6 boys and 9 girls. The control group consisted of 30 other seventh-grade health students (17 boys and 13 girls) who did not participate in either affective education condition. Almost all (95%) of the students were Caucasian.

Design and Analysis

This study was a matched pretest-posttest control group experiment designed to examine effects on self-concept of two forms of affective education— directed and facilitated—holding constant the classroom topics under discussion and the relationship variables of general warmth, empathic understanding, unconditional positive regard, and genuineness. In both experimental groups the primary goal of the experimenters was to provide an atmosphere in which the students would be aware of the opportunity for affective experience and would be interested in using it. The primary difference between the two groups was whether the person directing the individual's affective experiencing was the experimenter or each student.

The independent variable was the form of affective experience: One form was experimenter-directed; the other, experimenter-facilitated. Affective experience was operationally defined as interpersonal interaction, exploration of personal feelings and conflict, and expression of feelings and attitudes among peers about school, family, peers, or themselves.

The dependent variable was the score on the Self-Appraisal Inventory measure of self-concept (Instructional Objectives Exchange, 1972), an instrument based on research and evaluation by Coopersmith (1967) and Wylie (1961). Test-retest reliability of this measure ranges from .75 to .88; construct validity ranges from .70 to .87 (Instructional Objectives Exchange, 1972).

Two experimenters conducted the research: a Caucasian female and a Mexican-American male. Both were graduate students in psychology with 2 years of experience in client-centered facilitation of groups and in working with adults and children in either teaching or therapeutic settings. To determine whether or not the experimenters were able to convey adequately an interpersonal atmosphere that encouraged affective exploration, students rated the experiments on the relationship variables of warmth, empathic understanding, unconditional positive regard, and genuineness. This was done at the midpoint and end of the project.

To control for potential experimenter bias, differences in relationship ability, or other experimenter effects, the experimenters changed groups at midpoint, after being rated as indicated above. The form of affective education opportunity was thus maintained for each group; the experimenters were required to work with both groups and therefore to change modes (i.e., direct the experience in one group and facilitate it in the other). Each group experienced and rated each of the two experimenters but remained within a single experimental condition, either directed or facilitated.

The three groups (two experimental and one control) were statistically equated for small, initial self-concept pretreatment differences by an analysis of covariance.

Procedures

Each of the two experimental groups met for one 50-minute class period daily for 12 school days over a 3-week period, as half of a 6-week unit in health. The control group studied the standard health curriculum in the traditional way during this time.

In the directed condition, the experimenter led the group in planned activities, directed group discussions, and occasionally taught in the traditional (teacher talking and students listening) manner on affective concerns related to school, family, peers, or self in general. Most discussions took place in an intact group rather than in separate units. Although direction by the experimenter and the degree of structure in the activities resembled that of a traditional classroom, the experimenter avoided judgment and criticism of student expressions.

In the facilitated condition, no class activities were planned. Students were encouraged to interact with one another in ways that were personally meaningful on topics concerning school, family, peers, or self. Verbal exchange and social interaction were high. Students were encouraged to talk in general about their own concerns, interests, and conflicts.

In Appendix A, examples of discussions occurring in each group form illustrate the procedures. Procedural differences also are indicated in the Implications section.

Results

Analysis of covariance revealed that the primary research hypothesis was supported: The facilitated experimental group showed significantly greater self-concept gain than did the directed group ($F = 8.85$, $df = 1, 42$, $p < .01$). Neither the directed group nor the control group showed significant self-concept change (positive or negative) from pretest levels (see Table 1).

The mean student ratings of interest in the affective education experience were 9.0 for the facilitated group and 8.2 for the directed group (on a scale of 0 to 12); mean ratings of value of the experience were 8.0 and 6.3, respectively. These group differences were not statistically significant, indicating that the students in both groups perceived the affective experiences as fairly interesting and valuable, although self-concept increased significantly only for the facilitated group. This finding is consistent with research in psychology that shows similar client ratings of degree of liking for therapists, whether or not therapeutic outcomes differ (Gomes-Schwartz, 1978).

Student group mean ratings for both experimenters on the four relationship variables ranged from 9.27 to 11.18 on a scale of 0 to 12, with no significant differences in ratings of experimenters on any of the four variables. This finding indicates that the experimenters were able to create adequately and equally an interpersonal atmosphere conducive to affective exploration.

There were no significant differences for either group in the amount of self-concept change that occurred between pretest and midpoint and that which occurred between midpoint and posttreatment. This finding indicates that each experimenter was successful in presenting each affective experience mode (directed and facilitated).

Table 1
Pretest, Unadjusted Posttest, and Adjusted Posttest Means

Groups	n	Pretest M	Posttest M	
			Unadjusted	Adjusted
Facilitated	15	56.73	62.73	62.96
Directed	15	52.40	53.60	56.79
Control	30	58.80	60.80	60.72

Each group experienced both experimenters, but only one group demonstrated significant positive change. Sex and race of experimenters apparently made no difference in the amount of self-concept gain, in student ratings of relationship variables within the experiences, or in judgments of interest and value.

Discussion

This research supports and is supported by psychological research demonstrating that behavior change or task completion may occur for several reasons, but psychological growth occurs only through self-involved, personally meaningful experience (Gomes-Schwartz, 1978). It is also consistent with recent findings that, when parents become responsive to their children's feelings, the youngsters' self-esteem increases much more than it does through parent counseling that focuses more on parent and child behaviors (Esters & Levant, 1983).

The major difference between the two experimental conditions in this research was that, in the directed form, someone other than the experiencing individual provided alternatives, made suggestions, or directed activity or feeling toward an affective goal. In this research, however, self-concept improved significantly only through affective experiences that the students themselves chose, developed, and explored. In the facilitated form of affective education, gains seem to have occurred in both affective exploration and self-concept as a result of the open nondirective facilitation style that allowed for self-direction by the individual.

Three basic conclusions emerged from the research:

1. Student self-concept is positively influenced in the classroom through certain affective education experiences.
2. Affective education experiences that are structured and directed by the teacher as facilitator will not significantly increase student self-concept, although students and teacher may enjoy the experiences and believe they are valuable.
3. Affective education experiences that significantly increase student self-concept are those that enhance self-direction through facilitator and student trust in themselves, one another, and the situation—trust that they, the participants, will choose to participate in affective experiences that will be personally meaningful.

Implications for School Counselors

The important implication for teachers and school counselors is that, if self-concept is to be influenced positively by affective education programs, students' focus on their own feelings and attitudes in four areas important to self-concept (school, family, peers, and self) must be self-directed. The findings of this research suggest that school counselors pursue three goals in affective education programs:

1. Foster in teachers trust in their own spontaneity and responsiveness, trust that the affective education situation will be a constructive and productive one, and trust in the motivation and ability of students to grow within the opportunity.
2. Foster in students trust in their own spontaneity and responsiveness, trust that the affective education opportunity will be a constructive and productive one, and trust in the motivation and growth potential of the teacher and their classmates.
3. Foster autonomy and reciprocity in the classroom affective education experiences.

Dimensions of trust and differences in facilitated versus directed experiences that produce these optimal conditions can be examined.

Dimensions of Teacher-as-Facilitator, Trust

These dimensions include trust in the constructive nature of the experience, in one's own immediate and potential contribution to and meaning within the experience, and in the willingness and ability of students to use the experience meaningfully.

Self-trust. The teacher experiences and demonstrates self-trust when she or he interacts with the students spontaneously, rather than with predetermined goals, preplanned activities, and superimposed structure, or with a delayed reaction in which potential responses are first evaluated. The teacher's own positive self-concept is reflected through willingness to be a participant, to be natural and genuine, and to respond spontaneously and honestly to students. The authenticity in this interaction, and possibly the example of self-trust, foster similar self-trust and positive self-concept in students, trust in the teacher, and trust that the affective education opportunity will be meaningful.

Trust in the situation. In a facilitated affective experience, the teacher as facilitator allows a situation to occur that differs from the traditional classroom experience. Interaction between students and teacher is more egalitarian than in the traditional classroom. In this context the teacher does not use roles of expert, authority, or leader, does not feel inclined to "correct" students or to change them or the situation, and permits considerable peer interaction. These ways of showing trust create an atmosphere that is more rewarding, less threatening, and less stifling for participants than is a directed experience. This trust is enhanced by student response (e.g., increased responsiveness to the opportunity). The teacher's trust in this different form of interaction—specifically, trust in this form of affective education—reflects ability to tolerate ambiguity, confusion, tension, expression of strong feelings, and talk about difficult subjects. It implies self-confidence and a willingness to take risks—qualities that are perceived, respected, and responded to by students.

Trust in students. The research reviewed earlier suggests that the trust in students that the teacher shows in a facilitated affective experience may be one of the most significant variables in increasing student self-concept. This trust stems basically from the teacher's belief that human beings are interested in exploring, mastering, and creating their worlds and, therefore, want to use constructive learning and experiencing opportunities. The teacher, therefore, trusts students to be or become in contact with the relevant issues and feelings and to choose to attend to them, rather than trying to direct students or choose for them. Teacher trust that students will competently organize and use their own knowledge and experience significantly restores their sense of autonomy. This trust enables students to perceive the affective education offering as an authentic experiential opportunity and leads to greater participation, risk, and effort. Acceptance by the teacher also increases the students' self-acceptance and fosters greater acceptance of the other participants.

Dimensions of Student Trust

These dimensions include trust in the constructive nature of the experience, in one's own immediate and potential contribution to and meaning within the experience, and in the intent and ability of the teacher and classmates to participate meaningfully in the experience.

Self-trust. An interpersonal learning context, in which the teacher facilitator neither approves nor disapproves of students' words, feelings, or actions and simply accepts the students as they are in the moment, increases their willingness to experience, as well as their creativity, flexibility, and openness to concepts, perceptions, and personal meaning. A student can think, feel, and be what is real within himself or herself rather than try to anticipate and produce responses he or she believes are expected by others. Increasing investment in this authenticity, and the accompanying feelings of validation, lead to increasing self-acceptance and self-trust.

Trust in the situation. The teacher's trust in herself or himself, the situation, and the students is one factor that fosters student trust in the affective education opportunity. An interpersonal learning context of reciprocity and autonomy (see below) is another factor; increasing use of the affective education experience by other students is a third. Increased sensitivity, acceptance, genuineness, and empathy develop among the participants, enhancing and reflecting positive feelings and closeness as well as behavioral and verbal content changes. Increased acceptance by others and increased self-trust through more participation lead to more trust in the situation and, therefore, involvement in the experience. The personal meaningfulness (e.g., increased understanding, validation, resolution, and interaction) that results from greater involvement in the situation further enhances trust in self, others, and the situation, making this pattern cyclical and continuous and of maximum benefit.

Trust in the teacher and in classmates. In a facilitated rather than directed experience, students do not mistakenly believe that the teacher as facilitator is unaware of what could productively be done or talked about. They perceive that she or he is sufficiently aware, secure, and self-controlled to provide an affective education opportunity in which they can attend to their own thoughts and feelings, and that she or he believes this will happen. Student trust in the teacher increases with this recognition of the teacher's attitude, genuineness, and trust in self, situation, and students. The new relationship possibilities in the changed classroom atmosphere encourage increased trust in others. New ways of understanding and relating to others in the affective education experience also affect the students' expectations and priorities and increase their interpersonal and affective abilities. Consequences of these changes increase trust in the other participants as well.

Facilitated Versus Directed Experiencing

Research reviewed earlier has shown that the interpersonal context of learning is a variable of influence on the learner. A difference in interpersonal context—whether something is learned through listening to a teacher, through doing it, or through interaction with peers or others—often makes a difference in the consequences of learning. The major finding of this research is that affective experiencing that is self-selected and self-directed significantly increases self-concept. Self-direction of affective education opportunities is a different process in the interpersonal learning context from the process typical in the traditional, teacher-directed classroom experience.

This process change in the interpersonal context (from teacher-direction to self-direction with teacher facilitation) makes possible, and is made possible by, the trust students and teacher feel in themselves, one another, and the situation. The process change is not merely a change from lecturing-listening to experiencing and interacting with one another. Significant improvement of student self-concept occurs when the affective education experiences are self-directed by the students and facilitated, not directed, by the teacher. The affective experiences the students have in this mode of affective education increasingly stimulate, and are stimulated by, trust of the teacher in herself or himself, in the situation, and in the students, and by student trust in the situation, themselves, and the teacher.

The way in which the growth in self-concept takes place as a function of this interaction between self-direction of experiencing and trust in self, others, and the situation, and not simply as a function of changing the classroom interpersonal context to one of involving students in teacher-directed experiences, seems to relate to two central variables: reciprocity between and among individuals in the situation and autonomy in the individual.

Interactional reciprocity. One difference between learning by listening to a teacher and learning through experience or interaction is the considerable difference in reciprocity. Student responses influence the experience and interaction much more than they influence a lecturing teacher (because students are not permitted to respond much while a teacher is lecturing), or a teacher directing the learning situation, even if she or he is requesting student response (because she or he is not allowing student response to alter the learning situation). In contrast, both the learning situation and the classroom interaction are constantly changing in reaction to feedback from the students when the participants feel trust in themselves, others, and the situation. These changes occur because this reciprocal influence is both sought and allowed.

Presumably, through constant adaptation in response to student input, both the experience and interaction in a facilitated experience become increasingly relevant to and usable by each student. Experiencing the deep, personal meaningfulness and relevance of this facilitated affective education experience precedes the increase in positive self-concept. The experiences make sense cognitively, they feel accurate affectively, and they enable self-expression behaviorally. Student participation in the affective education experience also improves self-concept through increased validation brought about by the development or enhancement of psychological and interpersonal competencies, such as increased willingness to take affective risks, better understanding of self and others, sharing oneself more fully or openly, and more skilled articulation.

Autonomy. The teacher as facilitator creates an atmosphere fostering individual autonomy by not initiating, directing, or structuring content or behaviors; by accepting silences or what seems to be chaotic content or irrelevancies; by listening in order to understand (and not mentally preparing a response instead of listening); by attending nonverbally as well as listening; by reflecting emphatically when possible; by facilitating sharing and exploring by others as appropriate; and by checking the accuracy of what she or he thinks others are expressing or feeling, and amending perceptions as necessary to reflect what students are actually feeling and saying.

This greater responsiveness of the teacher to the students' actual words and feelings, the consequences of the interactional reciprocity, and the nurturance of feelings and self-expression are perceived by students as a release from traditional role behaviors and expectations and as support for individual autonomy and responsibility.

The greater acceptance the students experience increases their comfort in the student-teacher relationship, which encourages investment in the affective education experience. The absence of external evaluation decreases anxiety, resentment, and defensiveness, which further encourages affective risking.

Under these conditions, students perceive the teacher as available to but not directing them. The teacher is the source of special experience and knowledge, a person with a particular way of thinking and organizing knowledge and experience that may sometimes be relevant and useful. This availability without imposition implies a trust in the student to choose constructive use of what the teacher offers as relevant to the student's affective concerns and self-direction. The students recognize that this trust supports their individual autonomy.

The more students believe themselves to be participating in classroom experiences in a meaningful way, the better able they are to use the learning and exploring opportunities within the experience. They have more desire to do so and take more responsibility to do so.

Perhaps a sequence exists or becomes possible: The interpersonal context change allowing self-direction leads to student perception of the new situational opportunity (a personal context change) and of the greater acceptance by the teacher (a relationship or interpersonal context change). These changes lead to a greater trust in self, others, and situation, which leads to greater openness to, recognition and acceptance of, and behavior congruent with authentic thoughts and feelings. These changes lead to a more fully functioning person and a more positive self-concept.

Summary

Affective experiences have been shown to influence student self-concept as well as to influence and predict academic achievement. In this research, two groups of seventh-grade boys and girls participated in either a facilitated or a directed affective education experience in which they explored personal feelings and attitudes toward school, family, peers, and themselves. A control group did not participate in an affective education experience. The facilitated group demonstrated significantly more positive self-concept change than did the directed group or the control group. Descriptions and examples of the forms of affective education experiences are given and implications for school counselors are offered and explained.

References

Baskin, E. J., & Hess, R. D. (1980). Does affective education work? A review of seven programs. *Journal of School Psychology, 18,* 40–50.

Bilby, R., Brookover, W. B., & Erickson, E. L. (1972). Characterizations of self and student decision-making. *Review of Educational Research, 42,* 505–524.

Bowman, F. H. (1965). Family role in the mental health of school children. In E. F. Torrance & H. D. Strom (Eds.), *Mental health and achievement* (pp. 20–27). New York: Wiley.

Bridgeman, B., & Shipman, V. C. (1978). Preschool measures of self-esteem and achievement motivation as predictors of third-grade achievement. *Journal of Educational Psychology, 70,* 17–28.

Brookover, W. B., Thomas, S., & Paterson, A. (1964). Self-concept of ability and school achievement. *Sociology of Education, 37,* 271–279.

Chang, T. S. (1976). Self-concepts, academic achievement, and teachers' ratings. *Psychology in the Schools, 13,* 111–113.

Cole, J. L. (1974). The relationship of selected personality variables to academic achievement of average-aptitude third-graders. *Journal of Educational Research, 67,* 329–333.

Coopersmith, S. A. (1967). *The antecedents of self-esteem.* San Francisco: Freeman.

Covington, M., & Beery, R. (1976). *Self-worth and school learning.* New York: Holt, Rinehart and Winston.

Eato, L. E., & Lerner, R. M. (1981). Relations of physical and social environment perceptions to adolescent self-esteem. *Journal of Genetic Psychology, 139,* 143–150.

Ellerman, D. A. (1980). Self-regard of primary school children: Some Australian data. *British Journal of Educational Psychology, 50,* 114–122.

Esters, P., & Levant, R. F. (1983). The effects of two parent counseling programs on rural low-achieving children. *School Counselor, 31,* 159–165.

Gomes-Schwartz, B. (1978). Effective ingredients in psychotherapy: Prediction of outcome from process variables. *Journal of Consulting and Clinical Psychology, 46,* 1108–1132.

Hamachek, D. E. (1977). Towards developing a healthy self-image. In D. E. Hamachek (Ed.), *Human dynamics in psychology and education* (3rd ed.). Boston: Allyn & Bacon.

Instructional Objectives Exchange. (1972). *Measures of self-concept.* Los Angeles: Author.

Joe, V. C. (1971). Review of the internal-external control construct as a personality variable. *Psychological Reports, 28,* 619–640.

Kifer, E. (1975). Relationships between academic achievement and personality characteristics: A quasi-longitudinal study. *American Educational Research Journal, 12,* 191–220.

Leamon, J. L. (1982, August). *Effects of two treatments on anxiety, self-concept, and locus of control.* Paper presented at the meeting of the American Psychological Association, Washington, DC.

McClelland, D. S. (1955). *Studies in motivation.* New York: Appleton-Century-Crofts.

McClelland, D. S., Baldwin, A. L., Bronfenbrenner, U., & Strodtbeck, F. L. (1958). *Talent and society.* Princeton, NJ: Van Nostrand.

Medway, T. J., & Smith, R. E., Jr. (1978). An examination of contemporary elementary-school affective education programs. *Psychology in the Schools, 15,* 260–269.

Morse, W. C. (1964). Self-concept in the school setting. *Childhood Education, 41,* 195–198.

Moustakas, C. (1966). *The authentic teacher.* Cambridge, MA: Howard A. Doyle.

Moustakas, C., & Perry, C. (1973). *Learning to be free.* Englewood Cliffs, NJ: Prentice-Hall.

Parish, T. S., & Nunn, G. D. (1981). Children's self-concepts and evaluations of parents as a function of family structure and process. *Journal of Psychology, 107,* 105–108.

Peterson, K., Burton, G., & Baker, D. (1983). *Geometry students' role-specific self-concept: Success, teacher, and sex differences.* (ERIC Document Reproduction Service No. ED 229 219)

Pierce, J. V., & Bowman, P. H. (1960). *Motivation patterns of superior high school students* (Report on Cooperative Research Project No. 208). Washington, DC: U.S. Office of Education.

Prawat, R. S. (1976). Mapping the affective domain of adolescence. *Journal of Educational Psychology, 68,* 566–572.

Primavera, L. H., Simon, W. E., & Primavera, A. M. (1974). The relationship between self-esteem and academic achievement: An investigation of sex differences. *Psychology in the Schools, 11,* 213–216.

Purkey, W. W. (1978). *Inviting school success.* Belmont, CA: Wadsworth.

Rogers, C. R. (1969). *Freedom to learn.* Columbus, OH: Merrill.

Scheirer, M., & Kraut, R. (1979). Increasing educational achievement via self-concept change. *Review of Educational Research, 49,* 131–150.

Schofield, H. L. (1981). Teacher effects on cognitive and affective pupil outcomes in elementary school mathematics. *Journal of Educational Psychology, 73,* 462–471.

Shaha, S. N., & Wittrock, M. C. (1983). *Cognitive and affective processes related to school achievement: Implications for assessment* (NIE Report No. CSE-R-195). Los Angeles: California State University, Center for Study of Evaluation. (ERIC Document Reproduction Service No. ED 288 272)

Shavelson, R. J., Hubner, J. J., & Stanton, G. C. (1976). Self-concept: Validation of construct interpretations. *Review of Educational Research, 46,* 407-441.

Simon, W. E., & Simon, M. G. (1975). Self-esteem, intelligence, and standardized academic achievement. *Psychology in the Schools, 12,* 97–100.

Simpson, R. D. (1978). Relating student feelings to achievement in science. In M. B. Rowe (Ed.), *What research says to the science teacher* (Vol. 1, pp. 40–54). Washington, DC: National Science Teachers Association.

Slavin, R. E. (1980). Cooperative learning. *Review of Educational Research, 50,* 315–342.

Stenner, A. J., & Katzenmeyer, W. G. (1976). Self-concept, ability, and achievement in a sample of sixth-grade students. *Journal of Educational Research, 69,* 270–273.

Wattenberg, W. W., & Clifford, C. (1964). Relationship of self-concept to beginning achievement in reading. *Child Development, 35,* 461–467.

Wolf, T. M., & Wenzl, P. A. (1982). Assessment of relationship among measures of social competence and cognition in educable mentally retarded-emotionally disturbed students. *Psychological Reports, 50,* 598–700.

Wylie, R. C. (1961). *The self-concept: A critical study of pertinent research literature.* Lincoln: University of Nebraska Press.

Wylie, R. C. (1974). *The self-concept.* Lincoln: University of Nebraska Press.

Wylie, R. C. (1979). *The self-concept: Vol. 2. Theory and research on selected topics.* Lincoln: University of Nebraska Press.

Appendix A

Experimental Condition Examples

Example of Directed Discussion Regarding Schools

Question: What's so bad about school? (Response: numerous immediate complaints.) Which of these can you do anything about? (Numerous reasons why nothing can be done about anything.) What if you requested _____ from a teacher or suggested _____? (Stories of disastrous attempts to participate in school decision making.) How can any of this be changed? (Replies like parental intervention and other authoritarian solutions.) Do the teachers and principal care about the students at all? (Many negatives; a few stories about "nice" teachers.) Would those teachers be interested in your ideas? (Discussion of the possible teachers and possible ideas.) What do you think might happen? (Discussion of the "maybes.") Which of these possibilities we've discussed would you like to try out, just to see? (Heightened discussion.)

Example of Facilitated Discussion Regarding School

A tough homework assignment being completed during this period attracts student attention. Students ask questions about it and make animated complaints about homework, teachers, and school in general. The experimenter occasionally reflects how a student seems to be feeling about what she or he is relating. This brings up others' feelings—mainly of resentment, pressure, frustration, and giving up. A "what's the use" attitude is explained by one student, who believes "you can't win" because of the many requirements, the constant assignments, and the common practice of deducting points from grades for nonconforming behavior. Someone asks what sense it all makes if a student already knows what she or he wants to be and it does not involve college. The traditional reasons for a good academic preparation are brought up by some but not given much credibility. Someone mentions what competition and pressure for grades can do to friendships; another mentions no time for fun; another brings up pressure to cheat for higher grades. The experimenter reflects the feelings of individuals and the group and encourages continuing discussion.

Example of Directed Discussion Regarding Family

Question: What do you do when you're angry with someone or something at home but you can't do very much about it? (Responses: Yell, scream, kick the dog, slam doors, turn on a record player really loud.) Those are some alternatives. How do they make you feel better? (Discussion.) What are other alternatives that might give you more choice in the resolution of the situation? (Responses: When you both cool down, you can talk about it. . . . Sometimes you can talk your way out of whatever trouble you're in. . . . You can sometimes get a different punishment traded for the one you got. . . . You can tell your best friend;

that makes you feel better. . . . You can try to understand, if it's someone like your little sister, that she doesn't know any better—but it's hard to understand sometimes. . . .

Example of Facilitated Discussion Regarding Family

A girl is upset with her mother for "screaming" at her for leaving her sweater in the kitchen. Question: How do you feel about that? (Downcast silence for a moment.) Another student breaks in: What does your mother do about it? (Reply: She says she's going to give it to Goodwill.) Some understanding responses and some irritation are expressed: I know how that feels if you like your sweater. . . . I'd just let her give the sweater to them; she'll just have to buy you another one. . . . I'd leave something I didn't want in the kitchen so she'd have to give that to Goodwill and I wouldn't even care. . . [laughter] I'd leave my mother [more laughter] Similar "suggestions" are made by other students. The girl is laughing with the other students at all the comments. The experimenter makes no attempt to suggest possible responses or solutions or to summarize alternatives.

Facilitating the Not-So-Trivial Pursuit of Identity in Adolescence

Christina E. Mitchell

If there is ever a time when individuals can be expected to undergo change or to experience a major transition it is during adolescence. This is a phase of discontinuity from the latency period with the stability of being a well-established child to the series of stages of becoming an increasingly mature adult (Marcia, 1980). Periods of transition are recognized for their lack of comfort, and this discomfort may provide not only the motivation to conquer the discomfort but the drive to overcome weaknesses and improve the self.

The Importance of Personal Identity

Erikson (Engler, 1979) proposed that humans meet crises in development at predictable points in the life span and that during adolescence the crisis is either to establish a clear self-identity or to experience role diffusion. Marcia calls this identity a "self-structure—an internal, self-constructed, dynamic organization of drives, abilities, beliefs, and individual history" (Marcia, 1980, p. 159). He stated that the "better developed this structure is, the more aware individuals appear to be of their own uniqueness and similarity to others and of their own strengths and weaknesses in making their way in the world" (p. 159). He suggested that a poorly developed self-structure results in lack of awareness of uniqueness and a greater reliance on external influence.

The self-structure is continuously under revision and refinement. Although the self-structuring identity process is a greater issue during adolescence, it begins in infancy with self-object delineation and ends in old age when the individual either recognizes the integrity of his or her life experiences or feels despair over them.

Adolescence: The Time to Search

Through physical development, cognitive skills, and social expectations, the adolescent period provides the elements for transforming oneself as a child into oneself as an adult who will undergo transitions throughout life. Structuring the self is a dynamic process. Some issues during adolescence for this structuring include sexual orientation, ideological position, and vocational development and choice. Adolescence is a time for sorting out what one likes and does not like, what one already has, and what is desired for the future.

Because adolescence is a time of at least periodic discomfort, counselors expect to have students coming to them with a wide range of concerns, all which directly or indirectly serve to work toward resolution of the sense of self (personal identity) and what he or she will "be" in adult life.

Rationale

Conformity and concern for what is "in" is a hallmark of adolescence (Marcia, 1980, p. 408). Currently, the game Trivial Pursuit (1981) is popular among people of all ages and especially young people. The game is built around the players answering blocks of questions in a given content area—history, geography, entertainment, sports and leisure, art and literature, and science and nature. It requires answering all of the questions in each segment or wedge (e.g., history) with the goal of earning the entire "pie" (winning the game).

Making use of a format similar to the trivia game can provide the adolescent with an attractive vehicle for getting a clearer picture of who he or she was as a child, who he or she is now, and who he or she will become as an adult.

Procedure

The counselor will introduce during regularly scheduled group guidance or homeroom time the rationale for and concept of the "trivial" type identity game. The students may need to be instructed or reminded of the value of gaining a current sense of self—one's personal history, abilities, interests, "style" (personality), values, goals—all related to what one becomes in adult life (Feather, 1980). They should be told that self-esteem is dependent on a stable sense of self or self-consistency, which are of great importance as motives for guiding human behavior (Rosenberg, 1979). Thus, to facilitate this sense of self-consistency, a survey of each student's developmental history (past) and current status on various contributors to awareness of self (present) as well as the establishment of goals (future) should provide them with objective data for use with their own subjective material concerning self in establishing a sense of identity.

Students should be asked to collaborate in establishing specific rules and in individualizing various components of the "game." This will aid in increasing their interest and personal involvement in playing the game.

Game Components

The following categories could serve as wedges of the adolescent's identity pie:

1. The individual's past: history
2. Present: abilities and interests
3. Present: achievements
4. Present: social style and personality
5. Present: beliefs and values
6. Future: goals

Each counselor or other facilitator may, however, feel free to design a specific plan based on a particular setting or on individual need.

Game Plan

A general game plan includes the following tasks: Each of the six categories will be introduced in a scheduled weekly group session. A second session should be scheduled for guided sharing and discussion of information the students have gained about themselves in session one as well as before the second session, and how that information affects their beliefs and feelings about themselves. A total of 13 sessions will be scheduled with an introduction and at least partial completion of the assignment in the first session and a discussion and sharing in the following session. A total of 12 weekly sessions will be scheduled with two sessions to be spent on each of the six categories. A final wrap-up session will follow for sharing self-awareness gains make during the period the game was played.

For example, the first session, which deals with personal history, will be spent with the counselor introducing the questionnaire, the group revising it if necessary, and each student completing his or her questionnaire. If the student is unable to provide information, he or she will gather it before the second session.

The second session will be spent on history. Divided into groups of three, the students will be asked to share their findings and insights about their personal history (i.e., who they have been.) At the end of this session, the counselor will guide a brief discussion in large group(s) of 10 to 15 students. The primary focus of these discussions will be on developing students' awareness of strengths and attributes of their early lives of which they have been unaware. Sharing of course would be voluntary.

The third and fourth sessions would be spent on abilities and interests, the second category of identity pursuit, and so on. No board, dice, or other paraphernalia will be used; however, each student will receive a colored paper wedge (labeled by category) to be affixed to a blank Identity Pursuit game sheet.

Wedges are given at the second session of each segment (e.g., history) to each student who has completed the tasks involved in the category and who has attended the two group sessions allotted for that category. A "pie rim" outlining the six wedges is given to each student who has earned all six wedges and to all students on completion of the 13th (final) session. This session is set aside for students to share in groups of three and in a large group summaries of their identity pursuits. They may want to discuss the degree of success each had in gathering information, self-discoveries each has made, how they are using their self-awareness, and additional goal setting or other areas needing further exploration.

The accrual of all six wedges and the outer rim of the pie form a complete identity pie, thus the game is won. Each student who completes the game wins; that is, every player can win.

No attempt is made to establish a specific scoring procedure because the scoring may have an encumbering effect on the students. If students

Figure 1
Adolescent's Identity Pie

prefer to use actual scoring, however, one method is to allow one point per item requested in each segment. A tally of the student's completed items then would be made and when it equals the possible points (items) requested in that segment, that wedge has been earned.

For students who are delayed in completing a wedge, a paler colored wedge may be provided. Because the purpose of the game is to encourage the students to have a greater sense of self, a penalty (no wedge) for delay in completion would defeat the purpose.

Besides increased self-awareness and self-regard, an additional incentive for winning the game could be the members' eligibility for counselor-led "identity groups" (or other group names such as "Pursuit" and the "ID" group). In these groups, the students are privileged to meet for guidance-related discussions during a period in the school day in which they otherwise would not be allowed to leave study hall. Other possibilities would be that such a group would be allowed to take a guidance-related field trip or serve as an advisory body to the administration.

Identity Categories

History

This requires the student to gather the type of information that is compiled on a pediatrician's data sheet (i.e., birth place, birth weight, condition at birth) by consulting with his or her parents or other primary caregivers (grandparent, foster parent, elder sibling). Other requirements include a collection of early childhood photos and a listing of milestone events such as age of walking, first words, early temperament, and what they did or said that was smart, cute, or funny. At this group session, the counselor will distribute to each student a blank personal data sheet with extra space for additional early childhood information. The student must complete this assignment with help from relatives to win the history wedge of the identity pie.

Standardized Measures of Abilities and Interests

Included in this segment are standardized ability, aptitude, and achievement tests, interest inventories, and computer-assisted career exploration; that is, any of the tests or inventories that are routinely used in the individual school and that are already available to the student. Group interpretation or review of the results of these measures may be indicated. Examples of some of the tests used include intelligence tests such as the Cognitive Abilities Test (Thorndike, Hagan, & Lorge, 1974), achievement tests such as the Science Research Associates (SRA) Achievement Test (Thorpe, LeFever, & Naslund, 1969), aptitude tests such as the Differential Aptitude Test (Bennett, Seashore, & Wesman, 1972), interest inventories such as the Kuder General Interest Survey (Kuder, 1970), and computer-based career exploration programs such as Discover (American College Testing Program, 1983) or the System of Integrative Guidance Information (Educational Testing Service, 1983).

Personal Achievements

Students will be required to compile a list of their academic achievements, such as completion of required subjects, grades earned, honor roll or other recognition, and school and community activities (e.g., sports and clubs) in which they have participated. A partial checklist, with additional space for other achievements, might consist of the following:

honor roll, scholarships, athletics (participation, team member, awards), club member or officer (4H, Future Farmers of America, Future Homemakers of America, Girl Scouts or Boy Scouts, Campfire Girls, Young Republicans or Young Democrats), church (member, regular attender, special group involvement, leadership role), and jobs held (duration, raises, promotions).

Social Style and Personality

Inventories of personality (such as the Rotter [1950] Incomplete Sentence Blank), self-concept (such as Offer [1974] Self-Image Questionnaire for Adolescents), self-esteem (such as Coopersmith [1981] Self-Esteem Inventory), and type (Myers-Briggs Type Indicator, Myers & Briggs, 1976) could be used. If personality tests are not routinely administered, an exercise designed to focus on one's personality and social style could be used instead. One such exercise requires each individual to write a six-line personal ad including positive but accurate self-descriptive characteristics, as if for a classified section of a magazine for teenagers (Atwater, 1983).

Beliefs and Values

This segment can be achieved through use of such instruments as the Rokeach (1967) Value Survey; Allport, Vernon, and Lindsey's (1970) Study of Values; or even a simple rank ordering of the student's 10 major beliefs or values. The use of typical social situations in which behavior is determined by one's values with discussion between counselor and student alone or in groups is recommended.

Goals

Establishment of goals that are measurable, realistic, achievable, observable, and suitable to breaking into subgoals or units of progress is mandatory. Goals may be set in a variety of areas, such as career, marriage or singleness, one's contribution to society, or any other socially acceptable achievement. By establishing goals based on individual values, the student is aided in developing a clear-cut, positive plan for his or her adult life. Thus, the student is given assistance not only in preparing for individual life satisfaction but in achieving a better awareness of his or her own personal identity.

One exercise for goal setting is to have the students identify what they want to achieve in areas such as education, career, income, and family, in the next 5 and 10 years, and to list yearly markers designating how much progress should have been made at each point. Additional ideas for this segment can be found in career and life planning books such as *Where Do I Go from Here with My Life* (Crystal & Bolles, 1974).

Evaluation

After the game has been played, the counselor will need to evaluate it for its general worth and for possible revisions. Any of a number of evaluations could be used. A few examples are:

1. A Likert scale evaluation sheet of the game made by the counselor and administered at the final session. Examples of this are (a) I enjoyed playing the identity game; (b) I would recommend it to other students; (c) I know more about myself now than I did before playing the game.

2. Student self-report on pre-post questions created by the counselor. The students respond by filling in the blank in the statements with one of the following: *very well, well, somewhat, not well, not at all.* The statements might include (a) I am _____ informed about my early childhood (history), (b) I am _____ aware of my present intellectual ability (abilities and interests), (c) I am _____ aware of my present occupational interest (abilities and interests).

3. Equal or greater numbers of students participating the following year (by those who had not participated) might be interpreted to mean positive word-of-mouth reports by former players. The counselor may ask students for assistance in improving it for future players.

Conclusion

The identity pursuit concept was developed to encourage adolescents to become active in discovering themselves. If playing the game facilitates a greater sense of adolescents' self-continuity, from past to present to future, thus helping them to gain a positive direction toward an integrated adult life during this transitional period, that purpose will have been served.

References

Allport, G. W., Vernon, P. E., & Lindsey, G. (1970). *Study of values.* Boston: Houghton Mifflin.

American College Testing Program. (1983). *Discover for microcomputers.* Hunt Valley, MD: Author.

Atwater, E. (1983). *Psychology of adjustment.* Englewood Cliffs, NJ: Prentice-Hall.

Bennett, G. K., Seashore, H. G., & Wesman, A. G. (1972). *Differential Aptitude Test.* New York: Psychological Corp.

Coopersmith, S. (1981). *Coopersmith Self-Esteem Inventories.* Palo Alto: Consulting Psychologists Press.

Crystal, J. C., & Bolles, R. N. (1974). *Where do I go from here with my life?* New York: Seabury Press.

Educational Testing Service. (1983). *System of Interactive Guidance and Information.* Princeton, NJ: Author.

Engler, B. (1979). *Personality theories.* Boston: Houghton Mifflin.

Feather, N. T. (1980). Values in adolescence. In J. Adelson (Ed.), *Handbook of adolescent psychology* (pp. 247–294). New York: Wiley.

Haney, J., Haney, C., & Abbott, S. (Creators). (1981). *Trivial Pursuit.* Bay Shore, NY: Selchow Richter.

Kuder, G. F. (1970). *Kuder General Interest Survey.* Chicago: Science Research Associates.

Marcia, J. E. (1980). Identity in adolescence. In J. Adelson (Ed.), *Handbook of adolescent psychology* (pp. 159–181). New York: Wiley.

Myers, I., & Briggs, K. (1976). *Myers-Briggs Type Indicator.* Consulting Psychologists Press.

Offer, D. (1974). *Offer Self-Image Questionnaire for Adolescents.* Chicago: Institute for Psychosomatic & Psychiatric Research Training.

Rokeach, M. (1967). *Rokeach Value Survey.* Sunnyvale, CA: Halgren Tests.

Rosenberg, M. (1979). *Conceiving the self.* New York: Basic Books.

Rotter, J. (1950). *Rotter Incomplete Sentence Blank.* Cleveland: Psychological Corp.

Strong, E. K., Campbell, D. P., & Hansen, J. (1981). *Strong-Campbell Interest Inventory.* Cleveland: Harcourt Brace Jovanovich.

Thorndike, R. L., Hagan, E., & Lorge, I. (1974). *Cognitive Abilities Test.* Boston: Houghton Mifflin.

Thorpe, L. P., Lefever, D. W., & Naslund, R. A. (1969). *SRA achievement series.* Chicago: Science Research Associates.

Twenty Adolescent Novels (and More) That Counselors Should Know About

Theodore W. Hipple
Jane H. Yarbrough
Jeffrey S. Kaplan

Although bibliotherapy may not have been the panacea that its staunchest advocates boisterously proclaimed it would be, few practitioners in the helping professions deny that reading problem-centered fiction has considerable value for some people in some settings. One such setting is the secondary school, where severely troubled or merely anxious youth have more questions than answers and more problems than solutions. Fortunately for these youth, there exists a substantial body of literature—adolescent novels—that explores answers and solutions and that gives teenagers vicarious opportunities to examine the lives of other teens who may be confronting troubles similar to their own.

Adolescent novels have dramatically changed in the last 10–15 years. Today, they are written specifically for adolescent audiences and usually feature teenaged characters who encounter significant and realistic contemporary problems. These novels are a useful source of help for junior and senior high school students. But these youth must know these novels exist and know of the issues they illuminate. Counselors can help convey this knowledge if they themselves are familiar with the books.

To this end, this article provides what amounts to a list of novels. They are categorized according to problems, one novel for each problem is annotated, and others are mentioned simply by title. Because some of these novels are helpful for a variety of problems, they have been mentioned more than once. It is hoped that counselors will read these books (at least skim them) and, when appropriate, suggest them to their students. Whenever possible, paperback publishers are included in the reference list because teenagers are more apt to read paperbacks than hardbacks.

Alienation and Identity

The Chocolate War (Cormier, 1980). Jerry Renault, a freshman at a parochial high school, has a poster in his locker that reads: "Do I dare disturb the universe?" For Jerry, the question is much more than a stimulus for philosophical musing; he has, in fact, disturbed the social core of his school—a secret society called the Vigils. As a pawn in a Vigils' prank, Jerry is supposed to refuse to participate in Father Leon's fund-raising chocolate sale; for reasons of his own, he continues to refuse past the prescribed 10 days. The leader of the Vigils, Archie Costello, is outraged and brings his full power to bear on squashing the rebel who dares to act on his own—an act of defiance to Archie and to the system.

Adolescents who find themselves pressured by peers, confused about their own beliefs, and lacking confidence in their power to affect events will cheer for Jerry's impact on the school. A caveat is in order, however; Jerry does indeed disturb the universe, but he loses the war and possibly his spirit. Also: *Catcher in the Rye* (Salinger, 1977); *Home Before Dark* (Bridgers, 1977); *One Fat Summer* (Lipsyte, 1977); *Breaktime* (Chambers, 1979).

Athletics

Winning (Brancato, 1978). Gary Madden, the star of the high school football team, suffers a near fatal blow when he is paralyzed from the shoulders down by a simple tackle. Angered and depressed, Gary lashes out at his parents, relatives, and friends until he is sincerely helped by a young, understanding English teacher, Mrs. Treer, who is also recovering from her own personal tragedy. Brancato has written an honest and compelling novel about the importance of winning and surviving in our daily lives. Also: *Zanbanger* (Knudson, 1979); *Vision Quest* (Davis, 1981).

Close Friend or Sibling Rivalry

A Separate Peace (Knowles, 1962). This powerful novel presents a reflective look at an adolescent's feelings of rivalry against the background of the global rivalry of World War II. It is Gene's story of his love for and envy of his best friend Phineas, for whom success in athletics, friendship, and adventure seems so effortless.

Phineas, always seeking to enliven events in the prep school, forms the Super Suicide Society. Gene, constantly looking for signs of competitive feelings in his friend, chooses to view the frequent meetings of the secret club as his friend's attempt to wreck his (Gene's) grades. But he cannot be certain, and in fact he comes to doubt that Phineas ever acts on such motives. Phineas remains a hero; Gene remains the thinker who never quite accepts his own feelings of rivalry. Also: *Jacob Have I Loved* (Paterson, 1981); *The Outsiders* (Hinton, 1980a).

Death and Dying

Bridge to Terabithia (Paterson, 1979). Ten-year-old Leslie creates Terabithia, a secret place in a nearby woods where she and her friend Jess will reign as King and Queen. Here, these two lonely fifth graders build an imaginary and secluded world where they can lock out their worst fears and nightmares. All goes well in their loving friendship until an unexpected tragedy shatters their lives. This is a perceptive, beautifully crafted novel about the anger, frustration, and loneliness that accompany any death. Also: *Hold Fast* (Major, 1981); *Tiger Eyes* (Blume, 1981); *A Day No Pigs Would Die* (Peck, 1972); *A Summer To Die* (Lowry, 1979).

Divorce

Breaking Up (Klein, 1982). Ali Rose's parents are divorced and now fighting bitterly over who should raise Ali. To complicate matters, Ali's father upsets his daughter by implying that her mother's friendship with a woman is more than a friendship. Ali is torn emotionally between her parents as she tries to decide on her own what to do. This is a realistic and provocative portrayal of the tensions felt by any teenager whose parents divorce. Also: *It's Not the End of the World* (Blume, 1982b); *Like Mother, Like Me* (Schwartz, 1978); *Mom, the Wolf Man, and Me* (Klein, 1977b).

Drugs and Alcohol

Go Ask Alice (Anonymous, 1982). Thousands of teenagers die from drug overdoses each year, while parents, teachers, and fellow students wring their hands and wonder what they can do. A possible step for arriving at a solution is to read this powerful account of a 15-year-old girl who turns to drugs in a desperate search to find a better world, and, perhaps, herself. Harsh language and shocking episodes complete this honest portrayal, which is based on the actual diary kept by "Alice." Also: *The Late Great Me* (Scoppettone, 1980); *The Peter Pan Bag* (Kingman, 1971); *Angel Dust Blues* (Strasser, 1979); *That Was Then, This Is Now* (Hinton, 1980b).

Ethical Dilemmas

Justice Lion (Peck, 1981). Set in rural Vermont during the Prohibition, this novel is the story of a young man torn between his love for a girl and her family and his love for his father. Muncie Bolt and his father Jesse have been friends with the Lions, good country folk who make fine moonshine, for many years. Then Justice Lion, the head of the family, is arrested by federal agents, and Jesse Bolt is appointed prosecuting attorney. Muncie is deeply hurt by his father's acceptance of the appointment and leaves home. The ending, though violent, brings about a reconciliation of Muncie's conflicting loyalties. Also: *Ellen Grae* (Cleaver & Cleaver, 1978); *The Kissimmee Kid* (Cleaver & Cleaver, 1981); *Gentlehands* (Kerr, 1981a).

Handicapped Youth

Deenie (Blume, 1974). Deenie was born beautiful. Her mother took her to modeling auditions. She tried out for the junior high school cheerleading squad. But she failed at both; something was wrong with her posture. Suddenly, she learns that she has adolescent idiopathic scoliosis and must wear a brace for the next four years.

Other physically handicapped teenagers, especially those who become handicapped suddenly and unexpectedly, may see, through Deenie's eyes, that friends can be tremendously supportive. They may also, after reading this novel, better understand their parents' sometimes confusing reactions to the new circumstances. Also: *Winning* (Brancato, 1978); *Me Too* (Cleaver & Cleaver, 1975); *Lester's Turn* (Slepian, 1981); *Little Little* (Kerr, 1981b).

Homosexuality

Happy Endings Are All Alike (Scoppettone, 1979). Jaret Taylor and Peggy Danziger are both high school seniors, both good students from good solid homes, both bound for good colleges, and both in love—with each other. Lesbianism in a small town like the setting for this novel is dangerous; others may inevitably find out, which would create problems for all. In addition, and worse, a deranged friend of Jaret's younger brother learns the girls' secret, brutally rapes Jaret "to teach her a lesson," then tries to blackmail her into keeping the rape silent, or he will divulge the love affair to the entire town. Also: *Trying Hard to Hear You* (Scoppettone, 1981); *The Man Without a Face* (Holland, 1980).

Mental Illness

Lisa, Bright and Dark (Neufeld, 1970). Lisa is 16-years old, and she knows she has a problem. She is losing her mind. What makes matters worse is that nobody believes her. Her parents think she is faking, and her friends regard her as weird. Gradually, a few perceptive friends realize that Lisa might be schizophrenic, and they struggle valiantly to find her help. This book shows how adolescents can become terribly isolated through mental illness. Also: *I Never Promised You a Rose Garden* (Green, 1964); *All Together Now* (Bridgers, 1980); *I Am the Cheese* (Cormier, 1977).

Parents

Ordinary People (Guest, 1977). As this novel opens, Conrad Jarrett has returned to his home in the wealthiest suburb of Chicago after four months in a mental institution, where he was sent after a suicide attempt. The suicide try came as a result of his remorse over his supposed role in his older brother's accidental drowning and the subsequent changed relationship with his parents, especially his socialite mother who, Conrad thinks, loved the dead older brother far more than him.

This story is of a troubled adolescent in a troubled family—just "ordinary people" despite all their material advantages. Among its useful features is a sensitive portrayal of a most effective adolescent psychologist. Also: *Summer of My German Soldier* (Greene, 1974); *The Pigman* (Zindel, 1980); *Dinky Hocker Shoots Smack* (Kerr, 1978); *The Cat Ate My Gymsuit* (Danziger, 1974).

Prejudice

The House on Prague Street (Demetz, 1980). This autobiographical novel is a story of a young woman's experiences growing up amid the ravages of outrageous prejudice. It also presents an unusual and moving perspective on the Holocaust. Helene Richter is a "mongrel"—the daughter of a gentile-German father and a Jewish-Czech mother—who witnesses the gradual but relentless accumulation of horrors heaped on her mother's people and yet falls in love with a young Nazi soldier. The stunning ending clearly brings out the terrible truth: prejudice is a two-sided sword. When victims become victors, reversals in the recipients of horrors occur, but the horrors seem to go on. Also: *Chernowitz* (Arrick, 1981); *Durango Street* (Bonham, 1972).

Rape

Are You in the House Alone? (Peck, 1977). High schooler Gail is raped. The rape is an aftermath to obscene notes, filthy telephone calls, suggestive messages, and leers—all from the boyfriend of Gail's best friend. Then that boyfriend rapes her. Because he is from the wealthiest and most powerful family in town, he escapes a trial, leaving Gail, like so many contemporary rape victims, friendless among the punished innocents even as the guilty go free. Also: *Happy Endings Are All Alike* (Scoppettone, 1979).

Religious Pressures

God's Radar (Arrick, 1983). Sixteen-year-old Roxie and her family move from Syracuse to small-town Georgia, where a huge, fundamentalist Baptist Church is in power. They live in a house next door to a family active in this church, who immediately take it as their challenge to bring Roxie and her family to Stafford Hills Baptist Church and its charismatic minister, Dr. Caraman.

Having grown up in Syracuse with dating, rock and roll, movies, and even an occasional beer or cigarette, Roxie finds the taboos on her behavior unacceptable and the pressures intolerable. Although Roxie begins in the public schools, soon all are persuaded that, for her soul's sake, she should transfer to the Stafford Hills School. Is a mindless devotion to the church her next step? Also: *Blinded by the Light* (Brancato, 1979).

School

The Cat Ate My Gymsuit (Danziger, 1974). Marcy Lewis, or "the blimp" as she calls herself, hated school and hated herself—until Ms. Finney came along. Finney, an innovative ninth-grade teacher, brings adventure and excitement to her classes; more significantly, she helps the students—especially Marcy—understand and feel good about themselves. Because her methods and beliefs are unusual and controversial, she is suspended. Marcy, during the process of organizing a protest with her friends against the firing of Finney, grows in confidence, and her growth triggers a corresponding growth in her mother. Also: *The Chocolate War* (Cormier, 1980); *Catcher in the Rye* (Salinger, 1977).

Sex

Forever (Blume, 1982a). "Sybil Davisson has a genius I.Q. and has been laid by at least six different guys." So begins this novel—one that is enormously popular with teen and preteen girls who are wondering about their past, present, or future first sexual relationship.

The protagonist Kathy, a high school senior, a virgin although not terribly hung up about remaining one, meets Michael at a party at Sybil's house. Michael is also a senior, is not a virgin, and terribly hung up about Kathy's not remaining one. The novel treats in graphic detail their developing sexual relationship that is part of a love that will last forever—or at least until summer comes. Also: *It's OK If You Don't Love Me* (Klein, 1977a); *Up in Seth's Room (Mazer, 1981); Steffie Can't Come Out to Play* (Arrick, 1978).

Social Responsibility

Bless the Beasts and Children (Swarthout, 1971). The "Bedwetters," six boys who are ages 12 to 16 and rejected by parents and peers alike, set out from their summer camp—a rustic but expensive dude ranch—in a stolen jeep to save the buffalo. They want to liberate the beasts from the annual buffalo kill—an event in which penned buffalo are released three at a time and shot in cold blood.

The boys sympathize—in fact, identify—with the plight of the innocent beasts. The ending, although not a happy one, nevertheless transcends the harsh facts because for the Bedwetters, "It was the finest moment of their lives. They awed themselves." Also: *Lord of the Flies* (Golding, 1959); *I Am the Cheese* (Cormier, 1977); *All Together Now* (Bridgers, 1980).

Suicide

Tunnel Vision (Arrick, 1980). Anthony Hamil died at the tender age of 15. Why? He committed suicide. So begins this novel about a problem that has reached epidemic proportions in American life: teenagers who take their own life. Because he leaves behind no visible clues as to the reason for his death, Anthony's parents and friends must piece together their own solution and come to grips with their own personal grief. Also: *Ordinary People* (Guest, 1977).

Teenage Crime

Killing Mr. Griffin (Duncan, 1978). "That Griffin's the sort of guy you like to kill," Jeff mumbled. Mark replied, "Why don't we then?" Mr. Griffin is Mark and Jeff's strict and autocratic high school English teacher, and what starts out as a prank by them to frighten him turns into a nightmare of unparalleled dimensions. This novel deals carefully and thoughtfully with some of the hidden reasons why some teenagers commit murder and turn to a life of crime. Also: *I Know What You Did Last Summer* (Duncan, 1975); *The Magician* (Stein, 1975).

Teenage Pregnancy

Mr. and Mrs. Bo Jo Jones (Head, 1971). Although a bit dated by now—things were a little different in 1967—this novel still appeals to students who are pregnant or worried about pregnancy and its consequences. July is from the right side of the tracks, a cheerleader type. Bo Jo is a high school football hero, and one night after the big game, they have sex. Just this once causes them remorse, guilt, and pregnancy.

Abortion is not even thought of, nor is giving the baby up for adoption. Instead, they get married and in a somewhat romanticized but nonetheless fairly realistic treatment of their troubles, try to adjust as a couple of high school kids who are married—and not always too happy about it. Also: *Phoebe* (Dizenzo, 1979); *He's My Baby Now* (Eyerly, 1977); *Sharelle* (Neufeld, 1983); *My Darling, My Hamburger* (Zindel, 1971); *Don't Look and It Won't Hurt* (Peck, 1973).

References

Anonymous. (1982). *Go ask Alice.* New York: Avon.

Arrick, F. (1978). *Steffie can't come out to play.* New York: Dell.

Arrick, F. (1980). *Tunnel vision.* New York: Dell.

Arrick, F. (1981). *Chernowitz.* Scarsdale, NY: Bradbury Press.

Arrick, F. (1983). *God's radar.* Scarsdale, NY: Bradbury Press.

Blume, J. (1974). *Deenie.* New York: Dell.

Blume, J. (1981). *Tiger eyes.* New York: Dell.

Blume, J. (1982a). *Forever.* New York: Pocket Books.

Blume, J. (1982b). *It's not the end of the world.* New York: Dell.

Bonham, F. (1972). *Durango Street.* New York: Dell.

Brancato, R. F. (1978). *Winning.* New York: Bantam.

Brancato, R. F. (1979). *Blinded by the light.* New York: Bantam.

Bridgers, S. E. (1977). *Home before dark.* New York: Bantam.

Bridgers, S. E. (1980). *All together now.* New York: Bantam.

Chambers, A. (1979). *Breaktime.* New York: Harper & Row.

Cleaver, V., & Cleaver, B. (1975). *Me too.* New York: New American Library.

Cleaver, V., & Cleaver, B. (1978). *Ellen Grae.* New York: New American Library.

Cleaver, V., & Cleaver, B. (1981). *The Kissimmee kid.* New York: Lothrop.

Cormier, R. (1977). *I am the cheese.* New York: Dell.

Cormier, R. (1980). *The chocolate war.* New York: Dell.

Danziger, P. (1974). *The cat ate my gymsuit.* New York: Dell.

Davis, T. (1981). *Vision quest.* New York: Bantam.

Demetz, H. (1980). *The house on Prague Street.* New York: St. Martin.

Dizenzo, P. (1979). *Phoebe.* New York: Bantam.

Duncan, L. (1975). *I know what you did last summer.* New York: Archway.

Duncan, L. (1978). *Killing Mr. Griffin.* New York: Dell.

Eyerly, J. (1977). *He's my baby now.* New York: Harper & Row.

Golding, W. (1959). *Lord of the flies.* New York: Capricorn.

Green, H. (1964). *I never promised you a rose garden.* New York: New American Library.

Greene, B. (1974). *Summer of my German soldier.* New York: Bantam.

Guest, J. (1977). *Ordinary people.* New York: Ballantine.

Head, A. (1971). *Mr. and Mrs. Bo Jo Jones.* New York: New American Library.

Hinton, S. E. (1980a). *The outsiders.* New York: Dell.

Hinton, S. E. (1980b). *That was then, this is now.* New York: Dell.

Holland, I. (1980). *The man without a face.* New York: Dell.

Kerr, M. E. (1978). *Dinky Hocker shoots smack.* New York: Dell.

Kerr, M. E. (1981a). *Gentlehands.* New York: Bantam.

Kerr, M. E. (1981b). *Little little.* New York: Bantam.

Kingman, L. (1971). *The Peter Pan bag.* New York: Dell.

Klein, N. (1977a). *It's OK if you don't love me.* New York: Fawcett.

Klein, N. (1977b). *Mom, the wolf man, and me.* New York: Avon.

Klein, N. (1982). *Breaking up.* New York: Avon.

Knowles, J. (1962). *A separate peace.* New York: Dell.

Knudson, R. R. (1979). *Zanbanger.* New York: Dell.

Lipsyte, R. (1977). *One fat summer.* New York: Harper & Row.

Lowry, L. (1979). *A summer to die.* New York: Bantam.

Major, K. (1981). *Hold fast.* New York: Dell.

Mazer, N. F. (1981). *Up in Seth's room.* New York: Dell.

Neufeld, J. (1970). *Lisa, bright and dark.* New York: New American Library.

Neufeld, J. (1983). *Sharelle.* New York: New American Library.

Paterson, K. (1979). *Bridge to Terabithia.* New York: Avon.

Paterson, K. (1981). *Jacob have I loved.* New York: Avon.

Peck, R. N. (1972). *A day no pigs would die.* New York: Knopp.

Peck, R. (1973). *Don't look and it won't hurt.* New York: Avon.

Peck, R. (1977). *Are you in the house alone?* New York: Dell.
Peck, R. N. (1981). *Justice lion.* New York: Little.
Salinger, J. D. (1977). *Catcher in the rye.* New York: Bantam.
Schwartz, S. (1978). *Like mother, like me.* New York: Bantam.
Scoppettone, S. (1979). *Happy endings are all alike.* New York: Dell.
Scoppettone, S. (1980). *The late great me.* New York: Bantam.
Scoppettone, S. (1981). *Trying hard to hear you.* New York: Bantam.
Slepian, J. (1981). *Lester's turn.* New York: Macmillan.
Stein, S. (1975). *The magician.* New York: Dell.
Strasser, T. (1979). *Angel dust blues.* New York: Dell.
Swarthout, G. (1971). *Bless the beasts and children.* New York: Pocket Books.
Zindel, P. (1971). *My darling, my hamburger.* New York: Bantam.
Zindel, P. (1980). *The pigman.* New York: Bantam.

Chapter 2

The Challenge of Family Relationships in Early Adolescence

As young people begin to seek their own identities, they face the challenge of leaving much of their early dependence on home and family. Parents and family members, however, should continue to provide structure and support during the difficult moments adolescents face in growing away from complete dependence on home. The so-called traditional family, however, has virtually disappeared in America. Divorce, single-parent homes, and step-families are a fact of life confronting youngsters. In the climate of changing families, middle school counselors need to be prepared to help youngsters and their parents understand one another and to work together in making the difficult choices that occur during adolescence. As Richard Nelson and Marsha Link note in the lead article of Chapter 2,

> The special needs and characteristics of adolescents speak loudly for the development of enriched interactions with parents, even as bodily changes and peer pressures create in them a drive toward independence.

Substance abuse is also widespread in families, another difficulty confronting many students. Middle school counselors need to be aware of dysfunctional aspects of students' families in order to develop counseling strategies and guidance programs that help young adolescents find themselves. As John Murphy states in his article in Chapter 2,

> The consequences of not treating a family that has become dysfunctional by the substance abuse of a family member can be disastrous for that family, the chemically dependent individual, or both. . . . The dysfunctional family is usually unable to accomplish the most basic of family tasks without considerable difficulty and upheaval.

Finally, and perhaps most important, counselors need to be aware of cultural differences that students bring from their homes into middle school life and into the search for personal identities. This chapter presents counselors with the implications of family diversity for developing effective middle school guidance programs.

Teen-Parent Relationship Enrichment Through Choice Awareness

Richard C. Nelson
Marsha D. Link

Since 1973 the Choice Awareness system has been applied to a variety of populations. To the present, outcome data resulting from Choice Awareness experiences suggest that as a result of their exploration of this system elementary school children have made more and better choices (Nelson, 1980; Zimmerman, 1979), married couples have gained in a number of variables involved in their relationships (Fenell, Shertzer, & Nelson, 1981; Friest, 1978; Nelson & Friest, 1980), and CETA participants have come to see themselves as choosers (Nelson, 1981). These successes have encouraged the writers to ask whether or not there is value in using the concepts of Choice Awareness to improve relationships between teens and their parents.

The special needs and characteristics of adolescents speak loudly for the development of enriched interactions with parents, even as bodily changes and peer pressures create in them a drive toward independence. Enhanced teen–parent relationships and increased individuality are not mutually exclusive goals. On the contrary, it is likely that a high proportion of mentally healthy, individualistic adults benefited from open dialogue with their parent in their teenage years. Teens too seldom really talk about their needs for independence; parents too seldom share their concerns and hopes for their teenagers; and these matters may be discussed only in the heat of conflict. Furthermore, effective personality development for teens, and positive self-image development for adults in the area of parenting, depend at least in part on the teen-parent relationship.

Effectiveness in close relationships of all kinds involves such elements as maintenance of communication links; development of trust; mutual sharing of joys, fears, aspirations, and successes; and willingness to make changes in interpersonal choice patterns when the situation demands them. Relationships between a great number of teens and their parents are woefully inadequate in these characteristics; however, it seems likely that appropriate intensive experiences might set many of these relationships in motion in new directions.

Relationship enhancement efforts in the past have been focused primarily on the institution of marriage. Communication-based enrichment approaches have included Marriage Encounter (Gallagher, 1975; Genovese, 1975; Regula, 1975), and the Minnesota Couples Communication Program (Nunnally, Miller, & Wackman, 1975); other approaches have focused on teaching partners behavioral learning approaches (Tsoi-Hoshmand, 1976). A more general cognitive-affective-behavioral relationship enrichment approach based on Choice Awareness theory (Fenell, 1979; Friest, 1978; Nelson & Friest, 1980) has been used recently. Research on the effectiveness of these relationship enrichment processes has yielded inconsistent findings; however, self-report data and the continued growth of these programs indicate that many people strongly desire experiences that may enable them to grow within their significant relationships.

The purpose of this paper is to describe a process through which counselors may help to enrich relationships between teens and their parents. To this end, the system called Choice Awareness is discussed, a Choice Awareness workshop process for enriching teen–parent relationships is described, and outcomes of an experience with the workshop process are reported on a case-by-case basis. Perhaps this initial effort will spur professionals to give further consideration to Choice Awareness as a process for enhancing this significant relationship.

The Choice Awareness System

Choice Awareness is a system designed to help individuals make more constructive cognitive, affective, and behavioral choices. In the Choice Awareness system, the term *choice* is defined simply as any behavior over which persons have some reasonable degree of control. Thus, what we say, nearly all that we do, most of our facial expressions and gestures, and many of our feelings are choices.

Choice Awareness workshops present this system through a structured group process in which pairs of individuals, in this instance parents and teenagers, work together to enrich their relationships. The 16 basic concepts of Choice Awareness are developed through the workshop process; these concepts enable group members to explore their interactions, to examine alternatives, and to try out new choices. In the following paragraphs the concepts are listed and briefly related to teens and their parents.

We make many choices. Teens and parents need to understand that they make many interactive choices daily and should accept responsibility for their words and actions.

In each choice we have many options. Parents and teenagers may be helped to understand that they can exercise nearly every choice in a great variety of ways, and to practice making the kinds of choices that will contribute positively to their relationship.

We have an instant to choose. Choice Awareness helps parents and teenagers understand that after a stimulus confronts them they have a brief moment in which to choose their response; and in that moment they can bring their choice under their own control.

Our relationships affect our choices. Many teens and parents allow their relationships to become unnecessarily habitual, acting in stereotypical ways because "he's my dad," or "she's my daughter." Relationship enrichment can expand the range of choices for both individuals.

Our goals affect our relationships. Instead of acting on their long-range goal of closeness and warmth, many teens and parents focus on immediate annoyances, acting on short-range goals. They each need to learn to make the kinds of positive choices they wish to receive; that is, to send warmth and love and care if they hope to experience those choices from one another.

Our choices may be OK or OD. One way of looking at choices is to consider them either as OK or OD. Some OK choices are minor: saying good morning, taking out the trash, cleaning up. Other OK choices are major: a hug, a very positive compliment, a helpful action. For choices to be truly OK they must be acceptable to both sender and receiver. OD choices, on the other hand, are those that are overdone, as in cooking; an overdose, as in drug use; or an overdraft, as in banking. Some OD choices are minor: not listening, a thoughtless comment. Other OD choices are major: a scolding, a shout, a slap, or biting criticism. Parents and teenagers generally need to increase their OK choices and reduce their OD choices with one another, and most can do so if they commit themselves to improved relationships.

We have five kinds of choices. Another way of looking at choices is to consider the five categories that form the heart of the Choice Awareness system. Nearly all choices can be classified as Caring, Ruling, Enjoying, Sorrowing, Thinking/Working, or some combination of these. The acronym CREST is useful as a reminder of the five choices. Choices may overlap, and the same behavior under different circumstances may be classified in different ways. A hug is a caring choice if it responds to a need; it is an enjoying choice if given spontaneously and freely.

1. *We make Caring choices.* Caring includes choices that are designed to be helpful; they range from holding, reflecting feelings, and guiding, to guarding and defending. Most parents and teenagers need to develop more skill in initiating and responding to caring choices in ways that strengthen the relationship.

2. *We make Ruling choices.* Ruling choices demonstrate leadership: from requesting, suggesting, and asserting, to ordering, scolding, and forbidding. Most parents need to learn to reduce the frequency of their OD ruling choices, while most teens could learn to make more OK self-ruling choices.

3. *We make Enjoying choices.* Enjoying includes such choices as acting in fun, being joyful, loving, creating, and teasing. Teens and parents may think of enjoying choices as events and forget how little time it takes to give a compliment, smile, touch someone, or say, "You made my day."

4. *We make Sorrowing choices.* Sorrowing includes being sad, worrying, feeling hurt, crying, even being angry, and fighting. It is a tenet of Choice Awareness that we will do something with the sadnesses we encounter so frequently in our daily lives. If we do not find OK ways to handle our hurts, we may externalize them through meanness or internalize them and exhibit miserableness. Parents and teenagers alike often try to hide their sadnesses from the other, but the hurt or trouble affects the relationship anyway, and both should learn effective ways in which they might make their sorrows explicit.

5. *We make Thinking/Working choices.* Thinking/Working choices range from wondering, considering, asking or answering questions, planning, and doing, to intellectualizing, procrastinating, and redoing. Parents and teenagers need to develop skill in making OK thinking/working choices and in balancing these suitably with enjoying, caring, ruling, and sorrowing choices.

We can choose to listen, give feedback, and get involved. Parents and teenagers can be helped to enrich their relationships by improving their skills in listening, giving feedback, and demonstrating involvement: the thoughtful and active sharing of ideas, feelings, hopes, and fears.

We influence consequences. Parents and teens alike may deny responsibility for their actions, saying: "I have no other choice. They [You] made me do it" [forced me to this action]. Both need to consider the consequences of their behaviors and to be deliberate about attempting to influence consequences positively.

We choose our feelings in the moment. We are complex creatures. Our feelings are often complicated. A person's actions may seem to make us furious, but the very fact that we are furious shows that we care about that person. When a teenager is very late coming home, the parent may feel concerned, frustrated, annoyed, disappointed, angry, and, in the moment of the child's arrival, relieved. Both can learn that their feelings do not control their choices; both can learn to choose more often to act on their positive feelings with one another.

We choose how we feel about ourselves and others. We can continue to assume or assign to others old labels from long ago: clever, slow, bossy, helpful, tomboy, sissy, bully. Teenagers and parents need to acknowledge the importance of each to the other and to do what they can to help one another take on positive labels.

Choice Awareness and the Teen-Parent Workshop Process

The objectives of using Choice Awareness with teenagers and parents are to help each person explore the choices he or she is making, to develop a broader range of choice-making behaviors, and to foster improved understanding and communication between parents and teens. Members of the contemporary American family seem less and less to do things together as a unit: Each goes his or her separate way, each is involved in myriad individual activities. Some families are so busy that they jokingly say they need to schedule time to see each other, not to mention arranging extended time together. Especially in the teen years, when there are many developmental issues facing adults and adolescents, finding quality time for face-to-face, uninterrupted interaction and communication is important and necessary for both. Participation in Choice Awareness workshops can provide a setting for teens and parents to spend quality time together so that they might enhance their relationships. Single parent and two-parent family units alike can benefit from these relationship-building experiences.

Choice Awareness relationship enrichment workshops are organized in 16 one- to two-hour sessions, held over a number of weeks in an intensive group experience, or in a number of other scheduling arrangements. Content materials and structured activities are presented through the *Choice Awareness Workshops Guidebook* (Nelson, 1979a), the *Choice Awareness Workshops Leader Manual* (Nelson, 1979b), and the *Choice Awareness Workshops Audiotapes* (Nelson, 1979c), which are played during the workshop session. These materials can be supplemented through the use of the book *Choosing a Better Way to Live* (Nelson, 1977).

A step-by-step workshop process is presented in the materials specified above. Workshop leaders are afforded a variety of activities from which they may choose. Suggestions for a typical session might be as follows:

1. **Warm-up activity.** Conduct an activity as a means of encouraging participation, following up the previous concept, or setting the stage for the concept to be developed in the current session. Example: In Session 7, "A Variety of Responses" calls for one group member to leave the room, then return; the other (or others) then demonstrates the variety of things they can say to a person who has just arrived.

2. **Follow-up.** Take time for sharing observations, successes, and failures in applying the Choice Awareness ideas developed in previous sessions.

3. **Audio presentation.** Play a two- to five-minute tape segment to present the next context for consideration.

4. **Goal, key points, reactions.** Call attention to the goal for the session, review the key points on the tape, and provide a brief period for members to make any notes they might wish to write in their guidebook.

5. **Initial activity.** Direct the group members to the initial activity and have members complete it, then discuss it. Example: In Session 7, CREST Goals, members are asked to mark the CREST choice they would like to make more often, and the one they would like to make less often with their partner, and to explain why for each choice circled.

6. **Additional activities.** As time permits, complete additional activities and leave others for partners to complete on their own.

7. **Recycling with new content.** Repeat Steps 3, 4, 5, and 6 on the basis of the new content presented in the second tape segment. In some sessions a third segment is also presented.

8. **Change of pace activity.** In each session an activity is available for use at any time when the atmosphere needs to be changed. Example: In Session 7, CREST Cube, members throw a cube marked C.R.E.S.T., or CREST on each of the six sides. They demonstrate their developing understanding of the CREST choices by making a choice of the kind that

appears on top of the cube. If CREST appears they may make any of the five choices and label it.

9. **Five minutes a day.** Encourage workshop members to spend at least five minutes a day in discussing an idea presented, in continuing or starting an activity from the guidebook, or in some other way continuing toward their goals for the relationship.

10. **Closing activities.** Note the goal for the session and ask members to indicate whether they are beginning to make progress toward it. Clarify suggestions made during practice sessions; use change of pace activity if not completed previously; allow for expression of "now" feelings; and take care of any unfinished business. These activities are designed to leave members feeling good about the group and to encourage them to apply what they are learning outside the workshop session.

Through the workshop experiences, teens and parents are encouraged to explore their relationships specifically and positively, in a setting in which they may be assisted in interacting more effectively. The focus of the sessions is on interactions between the teen and parent; however, the group process may contribute in at least three ways: individuals are helped to see that others experience similar concerns, members frequently learn specific and valuable approaches from their peers, and the leader is able to monitor progress while serving a number of families simultaneously.

A Choice Awareness Workshop Experience with Teens and Parents

The particular teen-parent Choice Awareness group described here consisted of six persons: three pairs of parents and teenagers, plus a leader, who met for seven weekly 3-hour sessions. All of the teens were male; all the parents were female. The three pairs were from a middle class community in Southern California.

Following is a description of each parent–teen pair, their objectives for the group experience, and their comments regarding the gains made. Included also is material abstracted from their feedback about the workshop.

At the time of the workshop Don was 13, his mother Terry in her mid-30s. Terry's interest in participating in the workshop was to increase communication between herself and her son; Don willingly participated in the experience, although initially he had no clearly defined objective for himself.

Both Don and Terry were struggling with Don's newly found independence and Don often interpreted his mother's choices as OD ruling, dictatorial, and domineering. A case in point was Don's desire to attend an X-rated movie. Don perceived his mother as making her habitual OD choice in the matter. Through the workshop activities and group discussion, Don and Terry learned that other parents and teenagers experience similar conflicts, that the issues are not always as simple as they may seem at first, and that they could find alternative choices to make. They both learned to make choices not based solely on habit.

In an activity dealing with habits, Don remarked that he liked the fact that his mother cares for him, but disliked her habit of displaying affection through hugging and kissing. Terry, a very demonstrative person, did not realize Don felt so strongly about this. In fact, Don wished for an alternative means of expressing caring, mainly through spending private time together. He felt troubled because his sisters, one younger and one older, had much more opportunity to be with his mother than he did. He sometimes thought that his mother favored the girls. He expressed a desire to spend some time alone with his mother, without interference from his sisters. Together, Terry and Don planned specific times to spend with each other, quality time in which caring for and enjoying each other's company could be demonstrated to the satisfaction of both. In the feedback section Terry wrote, "I'm sure I will be more conscious of all my CREST choices!...My partner wanted more private time together and I feel I have made an honest attempt to supply this." Don indicated that the workshop helped him to identify different kinds of choices and to make better choices.

Another teen-parent pair was Sandy and Jane. Jane was in her mid-30s and Sandy was 15 years old and the eldest of three children. The two younger siblings are both girls. Jane and Sandy each hoped that the workshop experience would bring them closer together. Beginning in Session 1 of the workshop, Sandy and Jane both worked on improving their thinking/working choices as a way of reducing conflict. Specific problem areas included eating habits, study routines, and household chores. The initial activity in Session 1 in the guidebook, in which each person drew a cartoon to depict his or her early morning behavior, led Sandy and Jane to a discussion about their conflict over breakfast. Jane perceived Sandy's choice as eating "junk food"; Sandy stated a dislike for the food his mother prepared. By the end of the session, Sandy and

Jane negotiated a plan for Sandy to cook his own food two mornings a week and eat what the family eats on the other mornings. At the end of Session 7 they both reported that the breakfast concern no longer existed and that the plan continued to be effective.

Sandy, a busy teenager, often seemed to have difficulty finding time for some of his responsibilities. Both his parents thought Sandy procrastinated and misjudged the amount of time needed for studying and for household chores, and conflict often existed between them and Sandy. Through the Choice Awareness process, Sandy and Jane made plans for more effective working choices. One result was that Sandy made more constructive choices in situations at home and in the relationship with both parents as well. Even though only one parent and teenager participated in this workshop setting, there was evidence of benefit to the relationship of the teen and the nonparticipating parent.

As a result of the workshop process Sandy and Jane became closer, and each reported that the group experience seemed to draw the whole family together. Among Sandy's comments were the following:

> The experience brought my Mother and me closer together. One of the major strengths of the workshop was that it got me thinking about things that I never really thought about before.

Jan evidenced her own interpersonal and intrapersonal growth when she wrote:

> I made some definite changes in the way I approach my son with regard to OD caring and OD ruling choices. I really felt that my relationship with my son was enriched by these sessions. I also became very much aware of the choices [or control] I have over my relationship with others in my family, my friends, or even people I bump into on the street.

The third teen-parent pair was Isaac, age 18, and Esther, his aunt and guardian, a woman in her late 30s. Isaac is from Jerusalem and had been in this country for 1-1/2 years. He had lived with his aunt and her family since that time, but still had many cultural, social, and educational adjustments to make. He worked on accepting and expressing sorrowing choices and increasing his enjoying choices. Esther worked toward decreasing the frequency of her ruling choices with Isaac in an effort to allow him to make his own self-ruling choices.

While Isaac was perhaps the least verbal member of the group, he participated fully. He became aware of his negative feelings and his inability to express them. In an activity in the guidebook entitled *Negative Feelings I Choose*, he became aware of the negative feelings that were influencing current situations. The leader and group members encouraged him to express his feelings and his aunt assured him that he would not offend her if he did so.

Isaac also spent time learning to increase his frequency of enjoying choices, since he experienced difficulty in initiating contact with others beyond an initial "hello." Although Isaac's feedback form indicated he probably would not use Choice Awareness concepts frequently in his everyday life, on a day some time after the group ended, he called the leader on the phone to ask about another matter and shared the pleasure he felt as a result of making enjoying choices. He had decided to go skiing with some friends over the weekend. For Isaac that was a major breakthrough!

Both Isaac and Esther indicated that they had achieved their objectives as a result of the workshop experience. Esther's written comments included the following:

> Choice Awareness is a good way to gain some personal insight in general and the way to improve communication with your partner in particular. It has a no-nonsense, common sense approach that I like.

Some general comments related to the format of this particular parent-teen Choice Awareness workshop were:

1. More time was needed in general; seven 3-hour sessions seemed too short.
2. All participants felt that the group experiences and discussions were extremely beneficial and wished for more. This was interesting in the light of an initial preference stated by members for dyadic activities.
3. The participants' reactions to being asked to write their feelings and observations in the guidebook were mixed. Some liked it, others did not.
4. Group members described the Choice Awareness concepts and materials as being new to them, but significant, relevant, helpful, clear, and concise.
5. All participants indicated that overall the workshop was growth-producing.

Summary

Choice Awareness is a cognitive, affective, and behavioral system that goes beyond both communication training and behavioral contracting in enriching the teen-parent relationship. The Choice Awareness workshop format provides a means for participants to explore their relationship in some depth in a constructive group atmosphere. Each participant in the workshop who is described in this paper not only learned to use the theory and language of Choice Awareness, but made positive changes and realized growth in the relationship with his or her partner. It is clear from this experience that Choice Awareness workshops can be used effectively for the enrichment of teen-parent relationships.

References

Fenell, D. L. (1980). The effects of a choice awareness marriage enrichment program on participants' marital satisfaction, self-concepts, accuracy of perception of spouses, and choosing behaviors. (Doctoral dissertation, Purdue University, 1979). *Dissertation Abstracts International, 40,* 4894A. (University Microfilms No. 8005872)

Fenell, D. L., Shertzer, B., & Nelson, R. C. (1981). The effects of a marriage enrichment program on marital satisfaction and self-concept. *Journal of Specialists in Group Work, 6,* 83–89.

Friest, W. P. (1978). An analysis of the differential treatment effects of a marriage enrichment handbook. (Doctoral dissertation, Purdue University). *Dissertation Abstracts International, 39,* 5323A-5324A. (University Microfilms No. 7905722)

Gallagher, C. (1975). *The marriage encounter.* Garden City, NY: Doubleday.

Genovese, R. J. (1975). Marriage encounter. *Small Group Behavior, 6,* 45–56.

Nelson, R. C. (1977). *Choosing: A better way to live.* North Palm Beach, FL: Guidelines Press.

Nelson, R. C. (1979a). *Choice awareness workshops guidebook.* North Palm Beach, FL: GuideLines Press.

Nelson, R. C. (1979b). *Choice awareness workshops leader manual.* North Palm Beach, FL: GuideLines Press.

Nelson, R. C. (1979c). *Choice awareness workshops audiotapes.* North Palm Beach, FL: GuideLines Press.

Nelson, R. C. (1980). The CREST program: Helping children with their choices. *Elementary School Guidance and Counseling, 14,* 286–298.

Nelson, R. C. (1981). *Choice awareness employment program.* Project Report. Purdue University, Lafayette, Indiana.

Nelson, R. C., & Friest, W. P. (1980). Marriage enrichment through choice awareness. *Journal of Marriage and Family Therapy, 6,* 399–407.

Nunnally, E. W., Miller, S., & Wackman, D. B. (1975). The Minnesota couples communication program. *Small Group Behavior, 6,* 57–71.

Regula, R. R. (1975). The marriage encounter: What makes it work? *Family Coordinator, 24,* 153–159.

Tsoi-Hoshmand, L. (1976). Marital therapy: An integrative behavioral-learning model. *Journal of Marriage and Family Counseling, 2,* 179–191.

Zimmerman, D. J. (1980). CREST: Choice, responsibility and effective skills training with elementary school children. (Doctoral dissertation, Purdue University, 1979). *Dissertation Abstracts International, 40,* 4906A–4907A. (University Microfilms No. 8005966)

Support Group for Children of Divorce: A Family Life Enrichment Group Model

Nancy E. Moore
Margaret G. Sumner

The high incidence of divorce has a serious impact on adults and children. The statistics of divorce in this country are familiar to everyone. Nearly one in two marriages end in divorce each year. It is estimated that more than 45% of today's children under 18 will spend some of their lives in a single-parent family, due primarily to divorce. Statistics only begin to reflect the devastating impact the marital disruption has on each family member. During the divorce process, both parents and children are bombarded by a wide range of feelings, including isolation, hurt, anger and guilt. It is a time when family members may have difficulty communicating with each other or completing even the simplest task. Relationships with others may become tenuous and demand extraordinary effort to maintain, particularly for people in such a vulnerable state. Due to this, divorce has been called "crazy time" by those who have gone through the process.

Traditionally, divorce has been recognized as a crisis for adults and many services exist to meet their special needs at this time. While its impact on children has been acknowledged, few services have been developed to specifically address youngsters' needs at the time of their parents' divorce.

Approximately half of the children experiencing divorce have school problems resulting from home problems. While the remainder do not exhibit long-term adjustment problems affecting school performance, they generally experience the same painful feelings of anger, confusion, betrayal and isolation as their counterparts. Few services have been available to all of these children to help them deal with the trauma relating to their parents' divorce.

Parents participating in educational and support groups on separation/divorce and parenting children of divorce at a family service agency recognized the lack of similar support services for their children and requested a group be offered to them. School personnel also indicated a growing need for help with this segment of their student population.

In response to this need, a structured, short-term group has been designed to enable children whose parents are in the process of divorce, or already divorced, to meet other children in similar circumstances, to recognize they are not alone, to express their feelings relating to their parents' divorce, and to identify an adult from whom they can seek ongoing help. This group was initially offered at a social service agency but this setting was found to be too isolated from the rest of the child's life. Now the group is held in the school environment which is a more conducive setting for enabling the children to fulfill their needs.

The group is designed to be an enjoyable experience as well as a supportive and educational one. This is achieved through stories, games, role play, drawing activities and discussion. The members learn how to express their feelings in a safe neutral environment, learn coping skills, skills to express themselves to others, and develop ongoing contact with peers in the group as well as with the school professional acting as facilitator.

The designers of the group, social workers in the family life enrichment department of a family service agency, developed a training program for school personnel in the use of the model so that the curriculum can be used in a wide number of school districts. So that each district receives the full benefit of the training provided, each workshop member is expected to train at least one other school professional. In this way, the training is passed on so that many children can benefit from any one training session.

This paper will discuss how social workers from the private, non-profit sector can cooperate with school professionals to serve the concerns of the child whose parents are divorcing.

The group's curriculum will be presented and descriptive material from children attending the group as well as comments from workshop participants will illustrate how the curriculum addresses the needs of children of divorce and enables them to function better in school.

Program Description

Due to the large numbers of people affected locally by divorce, two of the most popular groups offered by the Family Life Enrichment program at Child & Family Services, Inc., Hartford, Connecticut for the past eight years have been for individuals who are separated and/or are in the process of obtaining a divorce and for parents who want to better understand the effects of divorce on their children and want to learn ways to better deal with these effects. Approximately 650 adults have been served in these two groups. Many of the members who were parents found the groups helpful, and requested that a group be offered for their children. Teachers and social workers reinforced the idea that services were needed for the children they worked with, who were experiencing divorce in their families. To respond to these requests, the authors of this paper collaborated with a child therapist in the agency's child guidance clinic to develop a curriculum, *Children of Divorce,* for a time-limited structured group for children which focused on the issues of separation and divorce. (See Appendix A.)

The first group was given at the agency for six boys ages 9–11, whose mothers had been participants in our divorce groups. While the group experience was described as positive by members, parents and leaders, the one drawback observed was that it was not possible for the boys to continue the relationships established within the group because they lived in different towns. Since ongoing support was intended to be one of the benefits for the participants, it was obvious that this issue needed to be addressed in any future groups. The most effective way to accomplish this was to offer the groups in school settings where children could continue contact with others they met in similar situations. In addition, in the school-based groups, members would have the opportunity to establish rapport with the school professional who led the group. This would facilitate future contacts between student and leader, who would be available when the student felt the need for some individual support or when the leader noted some area in which the student might need help.

Pilot groups in two elementary schools and one middle school were arranged through the auspices of the social work consultant for the Connecticut Department of Education; the authors co-led groups with school social workers in three different school systems. The original premise that the group members would benefit from having the opportunity to make friends with others in the same situation was borne out by observing the children having interaction with other group members at different times of the day. In addition, the school social workers in several instances were available both to reach out to some who needed it and to help in specific individual situations after the group had ended.

Having received positive feedback from the school social workers, other school personnel, and the children, the next step was to determine how best to make the curriculum available to as many schools as possible, to benefit the greatest number of children. Again, the social work consultant became the intermediary, writing a proposal for the curriculum *Children of Divorce* to be used as a model for training school professionals throughout the state. An expectation of those participating in the workshop series was that each person would in turn co-lead the group with someone else in his/her school system so there would be a statewide ripple effect of those trained in the use of the model, dissemination of the curriculum, and ultimately in the number of children served. To date, approximately 140 school social workers, psychologists, guidance counselors, nurses, and other school professionals have participated in the training workshops.

Model

The theoretical framework for this group is based on the model used for the adult Family Life Enrichment workshops. Family Life Enrichment is defined as a supportive group process that combines experiential and didactic learning with mental health concepts of recognizing and utilizing feelings to build and refine life skills. The time and emphasis of the group is divided equally among three focal points, facts, feelings, and experiential exercises, each building on the other in an interrelated fashion.

Children experiencing divorce deal with some of the same issues faced by their parents, as well as other issues unique to them. This model addresses a number of the children's concerns by: recognizing the wide range of feelings experienced by the children, demonstrating the "normalcy" of these feelings for this particular time in their lives, teaching ways to express these feelings, providing support for those who feel isolated and different, recognizing changes in the family structure, and helping members to accept this as reality.

Starting the Group Within a School System

This group is appropriate primarily for children who currently and/or previously have been within a normal developmental range, with good peer relationships, minimal amounts of anxiety, and stable academic functioning, but who may also have episodic feelings of being out of control and may think they are going "crazy" because of the divorce situation. The group is not appropriate for children who have two or more of the following characteristics: excessive need for individual attention, too much aggression, difficulty sticking with a task to completion, difficulty following a thought (so that thoughts become tangential), or poor reality testing. If the group includes a child who is clearly not appropriate, the other group members may be reinforced in their doubts about their own normalcy.

Another important consideration in the composition of the group is the need to minimize differences of any outstanding characteristic such as race, sex, or age. Such differences only intensify the members' feelings of being atypical.

While groups are often formed by social workers identifying appropriate children from their case loads, recruitment can take other forms: teachers can be requested to provide referrals; or announcements or letters to all parents can publicize the group, often providing referrals from parents who have not previously identified themselves as being divorced or separated. In all referrals, parents must be notified of the group and their permission obtained before their child can be invited to join. Once the leader makes known the availability of the group, there generally is little difficulty in filling it with the recommended maximum of six children. Rather, as children and parents learn of its existence, there tends to be a waiting list.

Scheduling is one of the key problems in establishing the group, as time is always a limiting factor. The group is designed to run for six sessions of 75 minutes each, but due to the realities of school systems, that time frame may need to be altered. A number of variations are possible. This group has been given over the lunch hour with extended time granted by teachers, during last period when optional subjects are often scheduled, after school when most children can walk home, at a latch-key after-school program, and before school. The curriculum is offered as a model for leaders to use as a guideline, to adapt and to use in whatever time-frame is available. For example, if each session is shortened, the total number might be extended. When the leader has determined a convenient timetable, it should be announced prior to starting the group and the schedule maintained for that series. Doing so provides a consistent structure for the members.

When the idea of groups for children experiencing divorce in their families was first proposed, it met with resistance from some school administrators and parents. Administrators' concerns were that schools should focus on academics, while parents had questions about discussing private family matters in a school setting. This occurred in spite of the fact that school social workers and teachers dealt with these issues daily when children shared their concerns at school. To help deal with these concerns, school staff had frequently requested consultation on this matter. With a curriculum in hand, the potential group leaders were able to dispel many of the major concerns of administrators and parents. In addition, when the initial groups were designated as a pilot project, the group members' enthusiasm and the teachers' positive feedback did a great deal to insure the success of the program. Teachers observed that children who had been performing poorly in the classroom often showed marked improvement after participating in *Children of Divorce* where they were able to address some of their personal issues in a safe environment. After three years of offering this program to school personnel on a statewide basis, who, in turn, are offering it in their own school systems, it appears to be widely accepted by everyone concerned.

The development of a trusting relationship between leader and children begins during the recruitment process and continues throughout the period the group meets and afterward. Prior to the start of the group, an important role of the leader is that of introducing potential members to the idea of the group and assessing their appropriateness for the group. Essential to this process are individual interviews which attempt to lower the anxiety that the child may feel about coming to the group. As he/she meets the leader, sees the room where the group will take place, gets some concrete understanding of what will happen in the group and how the group will be run, the child's fantasies begin to dissipate and his/her integration into the group becomes easier. During this brief session (15–20 minutes), the leader can also begin to assess the child's motivation, how much and what he/she wants out of the group for him/herself and how much is pushed by the parent, what the child's interests are, what the child likes to do, what things will be fun for him/her in the group, how appropriate the child is for the group, and his/her ability to relate to others. Finally, the leader can provide information to the child regarding the length, frequency, dates, and content of group meetings, as well as deal with the child's resistances to coming.

The leader can gain an understanding of how the child feels about the group by asking such questions as: How did you hear about this group? How did you feel about coming to the group? What made you decide to come? What are you hoping to gain? What will you miss out on by coming? During the interview, the leader should note how the child's thoughts relate to each other, whether or not his/her anxiety level goes down as the interview proceeds, and how the child relates to the interviewer.

The role of the leader in the group is one of a facilitator, enabling members to make connections with each other, to express feelings, and to master skills for coping. The leader helps the members recognize that in divorcing families there are many similarities of feelings and experiences, but the leader also acknowledges the uniqueness of each family's situation.

While many leaders prefer to do the group alone, certain advantages accrue from co-leading. Co-leaders can react to and learn from each other, more time can be spent observing and responding to group members, and co-leadership is helpful to someone with no previous group leadership experience. There are also disadvantages: co-leadership may not be practical or possible due to time and staff constraints, the relationship between leader and children may be diluted, styles and personality may not be complimentary, and extra time needs to be allocated for planning. These considerations need to be weighed in determining whether or not to co-lead.

Content

Children of Divorce is designed to be highly visual. When the children enter the meeting room for the initial session, the walls will be bare. As art work is completed, it should be hung on the walls. (A useful technique is to hang paper for drawings on the wall, then have the children use the wall as an easel). Games with visual components are also left on the wall after they have been used in a session. This growing accumulation of visuals fosters group cohesiveness by changing a previously barren room into the group's own room, and fosters a sense of group history by allowing members to view quickly what they have discussed and accomplished over the life of the group. The less movement there is from room to room the better.

Each session involves a variety of activities reflecting the divorce experience of the child's family. While a variety of activities is essential to maintain high interest, the structure of the group should remain consistent. Therefore, the group is designed so that one activity involves something that the child does alone and then shares with other members, and at least one activity is done with the total group.

This assortment of activities includes games, role-playing, drawings, stories, sculpting, writing, and discussion. Each was developed for the curriculum as a specific way to help children cope with the separation/divorce in their families, the feelings they have about it, the changes it has brought into their lives, and their need to communicate with others about it.

An illustration of how an activity helps children explore their feelings and the changes in their lives is in the use of books and/or movies. When children see their own feelings and experiences in print or on film, their feelings are validated and their experiences are normalized. The difficulty in using these audio-visual aids is that many of them portray idealized situations in which parents are shown always putting the best interests of the child before all else. This is often different from what group members are experiencing. The value of using books and films comes from the fact that similarities and differences between the children's situations and those portrayed fictionally can be used as a focus for discussion. This, in turn, often highlights the many similarities between their own concerns and those of other members, resulting in increased group support and cohesiveness and increased feelings of normalcy.

An example of how communication skills are taught is in the use of an art project in which the group members draw two people they know well, one with whom they can talk comfortably, and one with whom they would like to be able to talk more easily. Children then are encouraged to identify the communication skills used with the first person in order to utilize them in breaking down the communication barriers with the second person.

One technique is used throughout all the sessions to focus on the central issues of separation and loss in the children's lives. This is a calendar, used at the beginning and end of each session to remind the children how many sessions remain. This emphasizes the aspect of endings which parallels their struggles within their families. Other activities included in this model also enable the children to express feelings, master skills for coping, and make connections with each other while focusing on the issue of divorce in their families.

Adaptations

Although this curriculum was designed principally for groups of children in the fourth, fifth, and sixth grades, there have been a variety of adaptations for use with different age levels. With younger children there is more of an emphasis on stories, drawings, and games and less on activities requiring reading and writing. For older children verbal activities and audio-visual materials are accentuated. Another adaptation has been to use many of the activities in individual work with children. This has been found to be an effective way of enabling a reticent child to begin discussing concerns and feelings about his/her parents' marital disruption. Parts of the curriculum have also been used with children, either in groups or individually, who are not facing the divorce of parents, but who could benefit from learning the communication skills and how to identify and express feelings.

This model for group work with children affected by divorce achieves its effectiveness for a variety of reasons: it enlists professionals already working with children in a congenial setting; it presents a focused and coherent curriculum; it recognizes the value of emotional concerns and reactions; and it takes cognizance of the realities of group process in starting and running the groups. The model has the added advantage of flexibility. It can be adapted to a variety of ages, settings, and problem definitions. As one response to the needs of children involved in the divorce process, it provides for the amelioration of negative effects and builds strengths that facilitate coping.

Appendix A

The Training and Consultation Institute of Family Life Enrichment

Child & Family Services, Inc.
Hartford, Connecticut

Offers Training and Consultation Utilizing the Workshop Model for....

Children of Divorce: A Support Group

A one-day workshop includes:

- A detailed six-session curriculum with games, activities, and discussion topics
- Training in use of workshop model
- Adopting the curriculum for different age groups
- Starting groups in school system
- Handling of group process issues
- Marketing the program to administration and parents
- Follow-up ideas with children, parents and teachers

Appropriate for: Social Workers, Guidance Counselors, Psychologists, Teachers, Nurses and other Professionals working with children

Child & Family Services, celebrating 175 years of service to children and families, offers experience in training and consultation programs, designing and publishing curricula, Family Life Enrichment groups, Plays for Living and extensive counseling services for children, individuals, couples and families.

For further information on the Training Workshop for *Children of Divorce* and other Family Life Enrichment training and consultation programs contact:

Margaret G. Sumner, A.C.S.W., Director
The Training and Consultation Institute
Child & Family Services, Inc.
1680 Albany Avenue
Hartford, CT 06105   Tel. (203) 236-4511

Substance Abuse and the Family

John P. Murphy

The consequences of not treating a family that has become dysfunctional by the substance abuse of a family member can be disastrous for that family, the chemically dependent individual, or both. If the chemically dependent member returns to a family system that, through lack of treatment, remains dysfunctional and chaotic, he or she will be faced with two choices: (1) to return to abusive drinking or drug use or (2) to leave the family. These choices may seem extreme, but these are the alternatives available to the chemically dependent person who tries to return to an untreated family.

Functional Versus Dysfunctional Families

Any examination of a family system suffering from chemical dependency should begin by contrasting this system with a healthy, functional, family system. At the positive end of the family continuum are the nurturing or optimal families. These families, as characterized by Lewis (1981), enjoy high levels of closeness, as well as considerable individuality for various family members. Clear communication exists, and verbal invasiveness is kept to a minimum. The parents share power. The family outlook is optimistic and warm and encourages the expression of feelings. The family exists mostly problem-free. When conflicts arise, they are handled quickly and openly, using negotiation as the primary problem-solving technique.

Below the nurturing family on the continuum, but still within the confines of "normality," are the families of lesser competence (Lewis, 1981). These families may seem healthy and are as effective as optimal families in providing support for family members. There is still security and love, but on occasion, complaints may occur concerning remoteness of a family member, particularly the husband/father. Wives may suffer from depression or anxiety. Family strengths include investment in children, allowance for individuality, clear communication, and reasonably effective problem solving. Levels of closeness may be moderate to low, and there is less expression of optimism and warmth.

At the lower end of the continuum are the dysfunctional families. There are two basic types of dysfunctional families: the dominant-submissive and the chronically conflicted (Lewis, 1981). These are the types of families that may suffer from chemical dependency and whose members may attempt to escape from pain by assuming maladaptive roles.

Control is assumed by one parent in the dominant-submissive family system. The other parent assumes a passive, child-like role. The submissive parent may resent powerlessness and respond with passive-aggressive behaviors or with covert support of the acting out of a rebellious child. Children may also seem inhibited, affectively muted, and subdued. Closeness is minimal. Problem solving is the prerogative of the dominant parent, with little concern for the wishes of other family members. The family mood is characterized by lack of enthusiasm and depression. There is usually little overt friction between parents because of the complementary roles, however.

The chronically conflicted family is identified by unceasing conflict between the parents for dominance and power. Every decision, no matter how minor, becomes a crisis and a struggle for control. Family members relate to each other via manipulative behavior prompted by survival. When the family dysfunction becomes acutely severe, the family system is totally chaotic. Family members perceive their environment as danger-ous and hostile. Communication is minimal, problems are denied, and the family mood is hopeless and cynical.

The dysfunctional family is usually unable to accomplish the most basic of family tasks without considerable difficulty and upheaval. Domestic violence, particularly battering by the husband/father, may occur.

Dysfunctional Family Phases

The dysfunctional family with a member suffering from substance abuse will progress through four phases. These phases, identified by the Johnson Institute (1979), are (1) the learning phase, (2) the seeking phase, (3) the harmful phase, and (4) the escape phase.

Family members experiment with various defensive behaviors in the **learning** phase, to learn what works best for them in times of stress or crisis. They may not identify chemical dependency as the cause of family unrest, but they do realize that stress is present and that they need something to defend themselves against it.

In the **seeking** phase, the family begins asking "What is the problem?" and may look for solutions. Members may begin to suspect that the substance abuse is part of the problem but may also quickly rationalize away this position and unite in a process of family denial. By so doing, they avoid confronting the problem and allow the substance abuse to progress.

The **harmful** phase witnesses the family's behavior becoming compulsive and defensive. The defensive behavior may result in individual family members assuming maladaptive roles and identifying these roles as necessary for survival in this painful family system. These roles are harmful and destructive. The family may accept this way of living as "normal" until the pain becomes unbearable.

Then family members may begin looking for ways of escape, moving logically to the **escape** phase. When family members finally arrive at this point, where they are emotionally exhausted and all their efforts have failed, they may leave. If the wife is the substance abuser, the husband and children may reorganize as a family unit, excluding her. They may take with them, however, a number of unhealthy emotions that were used as defenses in their maladaptive roles acquired for survival prior to the time the escape phase occurred and the family disintegrated.

Emotions Found in Dysfunctional Families

Before examining various maladaptive family roles, it is useful to identify some of the emotions family members may experience in these roles, including:

1. **Fear**. Family members are afraid of continuing arguments, loss of income, domestic violence, and general family disruption.
2. **Anger.** Family members are angry with the substance abuser because of what he or she is doing to them.
3. **Shame.** The substance abuser's actions embarrass the family.
4. **Guilt.** Family members blame themselves and each other for their painful experiences.

5. **Resentment.** Family members resent having to live these painful experiences.
6. **Powerlessness and inadequacy.** No matter what the family members do, the substance abuser continues to abuse.
7. **Fragility.** Family members may be extremely vulnerable and unable to withstand one more traumatic event.
8. **Loneliness and isolation.** There is a breakdown in normal family communication. Family members may be too ashamed to develop relationships outside the home.
9. **Insecurity.** The family is unable to furnish its members the usual love and warmth experienced in the normal family.
10. **Confusion.** Children particularly may not be able to identify a sense of self or an appropriate role.
11. **Rejection.** In a dysfunctional family, members reject one another and reject themselves.

Maladaptive Roles

Several maladaptive roles exist that may be assumed by members of a dysfunctional family to survive. Not all families have every role at any given time, and roles may be interchanged from time to time. If a role becomes vacant, for whatever reason, another family member may try to fulfill that role. The distinction among roles in a given family may be distinct or diffused and blurred, depending on the family's reaction to the individual maintaining the role. Wegscheider (1981) identified several roles that may be assumed in dysfunctional families.

The Enabler

The enabler is sometimes called **the compensator**. The enabler's function is to adjust things in the family relationship when crisis arises and to provide responsibility. The enabler is most often the spouse or a parent—the family member on whom the substance abuser is most dependent. As the illness grows, so does the involvement of the enabler. As the abuser continues to lose control, the enabler accepts more and more responsibility, makes more and more decisions, and compensates for the abuser's lack of power and control. The enabler sets up a rescue mission, allows the substance abuse to continue and become worse, ignores the basic problem, and saves the abuser from crisis. The enabler's actions stem from good intentions; it can be a loving thing to do. The enabler's defenses include fragility, self-pity, and manipulation (and he or she tries everything). An enabler usually attempts to maintain some control and, in so doing, he or she may become superresponsible.

The enabler is a very serious individual. There is not much fun in this person's life. Moreover, enablers discover that they are powerless. No matter what they do, the substance abuser continues to abuse. Enablers suffer from repressed emotions, hurt, anger, fear, guilt, and pain. They are hurt because, no matter what they do, the substance abuse does not stop. They get angry at the abuser because he or she continues to abuse. They are afraid. If the enabler is the wife/mother and the chemical dependent is the husband/father, she may fear that he will lose his job and the family will be without income. Enablers feel guilt and powerlessness. They work hard to interrupt the abuse process, and, no matter what they do, it does not stop. They feel pain; they are suffering.

The Family Hero

The **family hero** is usually an adult but can be the oldest child. The family hero's function is to provide self-worth for the family. This is the individual whom other people observe and say: "Yes, there are some good things going on in that family." The family hero understands more than anyone else what is happening in the family and how to remedy it, but the rest of the family refuses to listen. The hero works hard to improve the situation, but as the chemical dependency progresses, the hero is always losing ground and feeling more inadequate.

The family hero's defenses include working hard for success and being superresponsible. This individual puts forth the front of being an "all-together," solid person. The hero is the rallying point for the family when a crisis arises. The principal repressed emotion suffered by the family hero is inadequacy. No matter how great the effort, things get worse, not better, and this is confusing. Family heroes are lonely. They resent their role and become angry at the individual who has forced this role on them.

The Scapegoat

The function of **the scapegoat** is to distract the family focus away from the substance abuser. Often, the scapegoat will be a male child, though not always. The scapegoat defends him or herself with strong peer identification and withdraws as much as possible from the family. Family experiences are painful, and he or she can receive recognition and reward from the peer group. At home, the scapegoat reacts with sullenness, defiance, and acting-out behavior. He or she may reject the family, and the family may reject him or her in return.

A male scapegoat with a chemically dependent mother often becomes involved in substance abuse. A female scapegoat with a chemically dependent father, on the other hand, may act out sexually. Scapegoats suffer from repressed emotions such as loneliness. The home is not a pleasant place to be, and scapegoats cannot be on the street all the time. Scapegoats also suffer from fear, hurt, anger, and resentment.

The Lost Child

This is a child by definition. The function of the **lost child** is to offer the family relief. The family does not have to worry about the lost child. This child is quiet, aloof, puts distance between him or herself and others, withdraws from the family, and is superindependent. Super-independence can sometimes cause poor schoolwork because this child will not ask teachers for help. The lost child feels rejected. He or she neither gives nor receives much attention. The lost child has learned not to make close connections in the family to avoid being hurt. He or she may spend a lot of time alone, being very busy and very quiet. This is safe because it causes no problems.

The lost child suffers from repressed emotions such as loneliness. He or she has not made personal contact in this family and by not making contact in the family, the lost child has not practiced making friends with other people. Because of his or her inadequacy, the lost child may have no friends outside the family and is unsure about how to develop these friendships. The lost child is hurt and angry because of the isolation forced on him or her by the family and the substance abuser.

The Family Clown

The **family clown** is usually the youngest female child, mostly because nobody else in the family could get away with it. The family clown's function is to provide fun and humor for the family and, by so doing, reduce tension. The family clown's defenses include being supercute and fragile. In their constant effort to alleviate tension, family clowns may become hyperactive, particularly if their efforts are unsuccessful. The family clown suffers from insecurity, confusion, loneliness, fear, and, at times, resentment. The family clown uses charm and humor to survive in a painful family system.

Therapeutic Issues

There are two distinct therapeutic issues to be addressed when attempting to counsel the dysfunctional family whose dysfunctions are the result of chemical dependency. The first issue is the substance abuse. Little can be done for the family until the abuse is interrupted and the chemically dependent member has entered treatment. This will occur when the pain and suffering experienced by the substance abuser outweigh the perceived satisfaction that continued abuse may bring. Ostracism or the threat of ostracism from the family may be sufficient to force the chemically dependent individual into treatment.

The usual treatment paradigm includes three components. The first is detoxification or removing the addictive substance from the substance abuser's body. Detoxification is followed by treatment, the therapeutic process through which the abuser deals with problems causing the chemical dependency and the problems resulting from the abuse. Finally, the after-care and follow-up phase assist the abuser to maintain a chemically free condition.

The second issue is therapy for the family unit. Family intervention can begin while the chemically dependent member is undergoing treatment, and many treatment facilities have staff members whose primary function is to accomplish this. The desired outcome of this family therapy is the reorganization of the family unit to include the former substance abuser in such a way that the family can address problems in a functional, normal manner.

Phases in Family Therapy

There are four phases encountered in family therapy that may lead to a therapeutic relationship and regeneration of the family unit (Rosenberg, 1981–1982). During the **random** phase, the family may act in an unstructured manner and express hostility. Few, if any, attempts may be made to communicate problems, and there may be denial that interpersonal problems exist.

In the **recrimination** phase, the family involves itself in accusations and counter-accusations. Family members may try to involve the therapist in consensus rather than counseling and have the therapist take one side or the other. Horror stories from the years past may be resurrected to convince the counselor who is right and who is wrong.

From this point, the family quickly enters the **policing** phase, testing the limits the counselor has established, particularly the limits to refrain from references to substance abuse. Therapists who are unable to avoid the traps of the policing phase will lose control of the sessions, and the family will be fixated at this phase and make no further progress.

Finally, in the therapeutic **realization** phase, the chemically dependent individual and the counselor develop a positive relationship, and the family and the substance abuser begin communicating more effectively without reference to drugs/alcohol and their abuse. Attention is focused on family problems and solutions to these problems. During this final phase, the family's task is to develop a positive self-image or an expanded frame of reference. To do this, the family and its individual members will have to deal with a number of feelings and emotions such as confusion, anxiety, frustration, fear, anger, hostility, and resentment. Effective resolution of these emotions is opposed by such conditions as isolation, denial, resistance, and the balance of the status quo. The force field generated by the latter conditions mitigates against the family's attempts to accomplish its task.

The change/growth process for the family is analogous to climbing a flight of stairs and is schematically represented in Figure 1. The task of the counselor is to assist the family to progress from a baseline, consisting of a poor self-image, up the emotional stairway, through the traps of comfort, relief, and satisfaction, to the goal of an expanded frame of reference.

The climb will be difficult to accomplish. The family that has been in a state of disarray and pain for many years may find it difficult to muster the energy required to continue beyond the point of comfort and relief. Failure to do so, however, could result in recidivism by the substance abuser and a return to the baseline by the family.

Guidelines for Counselors

Because every family situation is unique and each therapist is different, there are no "guaranteed" solutions to these intricate family problems.

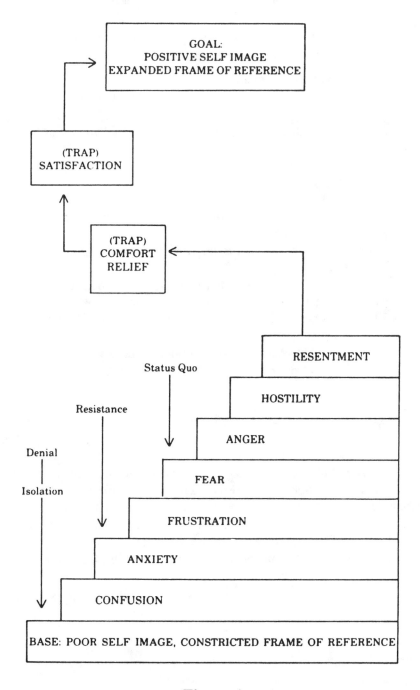

Figure 1
Family Change/Growth Process

There are, however, some guidelines that the counselor can follow when confronted by the chemically dependent family (Wilson, 1981):

1. Listen to all family members.
2. Be aware of other family members' reactions to what is being said.
3. Recognize that chemical dependency is *a* problem, but probably not the only problem.
4. Do not be trapped into validating the chemical dependency as the *only* problem.
5. Do not take sides.
6. Require the family to examine the dynamics in their lives— which roles who assumed.
7. Get each family member to tell how they see themselves and the family.
8. Be constantly looking for rewards and payoffs that family members get from assuming maladaptive roles.
9. Do not assume that the family wants the chemically dependent to stop abusing the drug.
10. Do not project your value system onto the family.
11. Use common sense.

Conclusion

Substance abuse is a family disease. It is a disease that can be treated and reversed, but only when the therapist treats the whole family. Counselors should not become discouraged if, after the first attempt at therapy, nothing much changes. Family members may have a considerable investment in their dysfunctional roles because, for them, these roles have worked. Counselors can assist the family to identify more appropriate roles and more positive problem-solving techniques that allow the family unit to become functional again.

References

Johnson Institute. (1979). *Chemical dependency and recovery are a family affair*. Minneapolis: Johnson Institute.
Lewis, J. M. (1981). *The family, stress, and coping*. Philadelphia: Smith Kline.

Rosenberg, D. M. (1981–1982). Holistic therapy with alcoholism families. *Alcohol Health and Research World, 6,* 30–32.

Wegscheider, S. (1981). *Another chance: Hope and health for the alcoholic family.* Palo Alto: Science and Behavior Books.

Wilson, W. B. (1981, June). *Through troubled waters.* Paper presented at the University of Utah School on Alcoholism and Other Drug Dependencies, Salt Lake City.

A Theoretical Rationale for Cross-Cultural Family Counseling

Miguel Arciniega
Betty J. Newlon

Increased technology and shared world problems have forced people to become more involved with each other and to assume a greater responsibility to live together cooperatively. As our society has moved toward the American dream of democracy (If you just work hard you can share in the results afforded by money and achievement), many groups have demanded personal, social, economic, and political equality. As early as 1946 Dreikurs predicted "that women, Blacks and other minority groups would progressively demand equality." These minority groups have become increasingly aware of their rights and privileges and more importantly have become conscious of dominant societies' exclusionary practices.

One result of this increased awareness is that school counselors and mental health workers have become aware of the rights of minorities to have equal access to counseling and psychological care. The community health movement of the 1960s promulgated the philosophy that counseling and mental health are a right and privilege of all citizens, not just the wealthy and the middle class. LeVine and Padilla (1980) state, "the need for culturally relevant therapy has developed and 'pluralistic counseling' is becoming a must for the therapist who intends to provide service in our technological age."

School counselors need to understand not only the culture of the clients they are serving but their history, beliefs, values, and behaviors in a holistic sense. School counselors can no longer operate in a vacuum with individual clients but need to see the totality of a cultural group and its interacting systems. Counselors also need to have an understanding of the process of acculturation along with the individual and family interpretation of the process.

Minority Cultures

Minority cultures, by their very nature, operate from a cohesive psychological family structure in order to maintain their sense of identity. The single most important influence in a person's life is the family. The family socializes children in their own cultural milieu with cultural values imparted to the children through the significant adults and siblings in the family. Children are reared to identify with family, community, and cultural group. In many instances the history of the family is tied to the history of the cultural group and its interaction with other groups. Arciniega, Casaus, and Castillo (1978) have labeled this phenomenon "psychological identity survival and collective cultural identity." When any cultural group experiences oppression, the tendency is to band together and identify more closely with the family and cultural group in order to ensure survival. The sense of self and others becomes very distinct.

Unless we as school counselors assume a posture that integrates certain beliefs about working with minority families, our intervention processes are doomed to fail. The school counselor must understand the differences that exist between the "culture of poverty" and the uniqueness of the culture itself. It is easy to confuse the two because many minority members experience the commonalities manifested by poverty, which consequently become cultural stereotypes.

Minority Processes

The school counselor must be cognizant of the process of acculturation that occurs when minority and majority cultures come in contact. Historically the major culture has viewed the minority culture as inferior and has labeled problems that occur as minority problems rather than problems of interacting cultures. Gordon (1958) indicated that, while individuals may become acculturated, they do not assimilate but retain much of their identity as members of their ethnic group. When the minority culture comes in contact with the majority culture, the belief and value systems of the minority culture are not supplanted but added to in a creative manner. In order to cope with this phenomenon, families are forced to provide survival mechanisms for their members. It is important that school counselors understand that there is no single definition for any cultural minority family. The acculturation process is unique for each. A large degree of cultural variability exists in minority families who are at various points on a continuum of acculturation dictated by environment, socioeconomic status, and education.

In order to work more effectively with minority families and their variability, it is essential that school counselors move toward working with the system that most influences the development of the individual— the family. The family is where individuals develop a sense of belonging and security, testing their sense of separateness. School counselors cannot hope to effect change unless they can understand the interaction of the individual family, cultural group, and institutions. Understanding alone, however, cannot effect change. Effective intervention requires a belief system that undergirds the family counseling intervention.

Most family counseling interventions are based on the premise that it is not desirable to view a child's problem outside the context of the child's interactions within the family and other networks. These interventions share the ideology that change can best be realized and maintained if modification of the beliefs, attitudes, and behaviors of significant persons or institutions occurs simultaneously with modification of the beliefs, attitudes, and behaviors of the so-called problem child (Okun & Rappaport, 1980).

Counseling Approaches

The major approaches to family counseling are: (a) social learning, including the operant-conditioning and Adlerian approaches; (b) client-centered approaches; and (c) the communication and structural approaches based on systems theory.

While each of these approaches offers viable methods for working with families, most are specific problem-centered approaches with very little attention paid to the sociocultural contact and the system that affects them. The underlying assumption in most counseling approaches requires a "fixing" of the family interpersonal systems. Little note is taken of how the external systems operate on the family and the subsequent cultural interpretations. Of the various counseling approaches that have been examined and analyzed in terms of their applicability to counseling minority families, it is our opinion that Adlerian counseling comes closest to providing a belief system plus a rationale for behavior that encompasses the necessary understanding of minority families in this society.

Adlerians have worked with family dynamics ever since Adler's demonstrations in the child-guidance clinics of Vienna in the 1920s. Adlerians see all problems as social problems, and they assign greater importance to the relationships between people and groups than to what is going on within the individual (interpersonal versus intrapersonal approach). Although family therapy may result in changes in the personal life-style of the various family members, such change is not the primary goal. Adlerian family therapy is aimed at teaching family members how to deal effectively with one another and how to live together as social equals. This aim is accomplished by sharing with the family group the principles of democratic conflict resolution, by reorienting the family members away from destructive modes of communication, and most importantly by teaching all members of the family to be agents of encouragement (Dinkmeyer, Pew, & Dinkmeyer, 1979).

The counseling process in Adlerian theory is an educational process (dysfunctional behavior is seen as a loss of information rather than pathology). The counselor, therefore, includes information regarding sociocultural variables, racism, and economic and acculturation factors when counseling minority families.

Definition of Cross-Cultural Pluralistic Counseling

Levine and Padilla (1980) propose the following definition for counseling in a cross-cultural setting: "Pluralistic counseling is defined as therapy that recognizes the client's culturally based beliefs, values and behaviors that is concerned with the client's adaptation to his or her particular cultural milieu." They go on to say that a pluralistic therapist considers all facets of the client's personal history, family history, and social and cultural orientation. Although this definition implies a one-to-one counseling situation, the definition can be extended to include the whole family and provide a more comprehensive counseling view. Therefore, we propose the following basic Adlerian premises (axioms) of behavior for the cross-cultural, pluralistic counselor working with minority families.

Adlerian Cross-Cultural Premises

1. **Behavior is best understood in a social context.** In order to understand behavior one has to observe the behavior in the context of all

social interactions and systems in which it operates—beginning with the family. The minority family relies heavily on social interaction to survive, and this interaction provides meaning to the activity of the family. The larger social systems of the community affect the family economically, socially, and politically and give impetus to socialization processes that enhance its survival and continuance. Unless the family, and ultimately the individual, is viewed in light of its operation in larger social systems, we cannot hope to understand behavior in a minority family.

Adler believed that human beings had a basic inclination toward being a part of the larger social whole, a need to belong, with a willingness to serve for the betterment of a whole group. Adler called this *Gemeinschaftsgefuel*, social interest (Ansbacher & Ansbacher, 1967).

Minority families in the same sense are striving to belong, to be part of the greater whole. Many minority groups such as Native Americans, Mexican Americans, and Blacks already operate under this framework of social interest within their family value structure.

2. **Behavior is understood in terms of striving for significance.** Adlerian psychology recognizes the family as the first social group in which each individual strives to find a significant place. Once this significance is established, the individual moves toward the goals of significance and recognition as a part of the whole society. Any inferiority feelings are generally the result of "faulty" self or group evaluation.

The striving for significance is in essence a movement toward the achievement of a unique identity. This movement toward significance is the master force behind all individual and collective human activity. For minority families this master force takes on a greater import as the striving for identity is more pronounced and the search for significance is sought in different and unique ways for each individual, family, and cultural group. Although the process is unique for each minority-group family, there is a generic process. Members of the dominant society do not have to strive for significance as an equal group; this contrasts markedly with members of minority groups who give priority to the struggle for equality.

3. **Each individual is considered equal and has value.** The notion of equality in Adlerian psychology is one of the basic tenets of the belief system. "There is an ironclad law of social living—all people are equal" (Dreikurs, Corsini, Lowe, & Sonstegard, 1959). All people are of equal value; therefore, the family and the cultural group have inherent rights to mutual respect and equal treatment. The effect of this egalitarian concept has been evident in minority families. Minority families no longer

tolerate inequality from the dominant society. Traditional counseling approaches have reflected the dominant society's views and as a consequence inadvertently treat minority clients in a patronizing manner under the guise of understanding their problems. Counselors working with minority families need to become aware of this subtle, but still depreciating, approach.

4. **Working with behavior is an educational process.** A basic premise made in this approach is that maladjustment or dysfunctional behavior is based on lack of information or lack of awareness and, given insight and action-oriented information, a family can learn to operate more effectively. The counselor and the family are involved in a mutually beneficial egalitarian process in which the counselor and the families assume a posture of mutual learning.

It is incumbent on the counselor to have some prior understanding of systems interaction in order to impart information about systemic problems so the family can arrive at decisions more effectively and with a greater degree of comprehension. Merton (1957) alludes to this when he emphasizes that it is the individual's relationship to the larger social system that begins to affect the family in developing adaptive coping mechanisms to deal with prescribed goals and behavioral expectations. When a dominant social system prescribes the same goals for all people without consideration of distinctiveness or location of the individual and groups within the social structure, society labels individual responses as maladaptive. Counselors are trained in institutions that are usually microcosms of the dominant society, and they are trained to see maladaptive behavior from one perspective when in fact the responses may be normal for that group's situation. As counselors, we may seek inadvertently to help a minority family move towards a dominant normative tractive response that would be ultimately detrimental for that minority family. A counselor must be prepared to be an advocate for minority families in interpreting and managing the system.

5. **Behavior is a function of perception.** Individuals perceive life subjectively. This view includes the cultural interpretations families make and pass on to their children. This is not to negate each child's own subjective view but to expand the view to include all nuances that are inherent in any cultural group. Therefore, interpretations that are made regarding the systems that affect a particular cultural group and its families are a reality and must be dealt with as such. In order to understand a people's behavior, it is necessary to recognize the significance of the inner, subjective experience of a particular group. It is essential that

the counselor be involved in a continuing process of attempting to see a minority family's collective view and hear the messages the family is hearing. Faulty perceptions are mutually examined, analyzed, and placed in a perspective that provides the family with a more comprehensive and realistic view.

6. **Idiographic versus nomothetic interpretation of behavior.** Behavior is best understood in terms of concrete laws that apply characteristically to specific individuals in relationship to their lifestyles and cultures rather than laws that apply generally but include many exceptions. The nomothetic approach assumes that counseling will have meaning only insofar as it postulates a theory that helps the client to live in a manner that is personally satisfying and socially acceptable (Dinkmeyer et al., 1979). The idiographic view requires the counselor to understand how a minority-group family acquired its beliefs and value system and how the family presently uses this system within its own cultural group and the dominant society. In this way the counselor can understand the way the minority family processes decisions, establishes goals, and sets the values its members live by.

The premise allows the counselor to understand a family's behavior from a particularistic point of view and not to make it fit a particular mold.

7. **Behavior is viewed in terms of use rather than possession.** Behavior is used to reach a person's perceived goal. "One will do that which is most useful or which best accomplishes one's purpose and striving; that which interferes with one's goal is not done" (Dinkmeyer et al., 1979). The important issue is what individuals do with what they have rather than what they possess. Often minority groups are stereotyped and labeled; they come to believe this fiction and use it in counterproductive ways.

Heredity and environment are not static but are combined in a dynamic process. The use that is made of heredity and environment, in a productive manner, is what a counselor needs to emphasize when working with minority families rather than reviewing these aspects as static entities. A family lifestyle is not determined by heredity or environment, but these are simply factors one uses. The counselor is more interested in the family's motivational process than on concrete definitions. Again, the counselor engages in an educational process rather than in a clarification of where the family is at a given moment.

8. Behavior is seen as a unified whole with unity and patterns. Behavior cannot be understood unless seen as a unified whole. Although we have designated specific axioms for the purpose of explaining separate parts, these axioms are intertwined and cannot be seen as separate. The relationship of one aspect of behavior to another provides the counselor with insight into individual and family patterns. All behavior must be seen in light of the individual family's cultural life-style and more importantly its creatively chosen subjective view. This is why a family's cultural history, values, and beliefs are necessary to understanding the dynamics of the minority family.

Conclusion

We have posed these axioms of behavior from Adlerian theory applied to minority families because we feel they most approximate the belief structure necessary when working in a cross-cultural setting. Specific techniques and approaches would serve no purpose unless the proper belief structure undergirded their implementation. For this reason, we have avoided the traditional "bag of tricks" in favor of proposing a theoretical rationale that we have found effective in working with minority families in schools and counseling centers. We selected this particular theory because of the basic premise of equality that it postulates. It is the only counseling theory that uses this as a basis for counseling.

Some studies have shown that the ethnicity of counselors is not always the significant variable in determining the efficiency of counseling (Atkinson, Maruyama, & Matsui, 1978; Jones, 1978; Ramos, 1981), while other studies have found that ethnicity is a significant factor (Carkhuff & Pierce, 1967; Grantham, 1973; Miranda, Andujo, Caballero, Guerrero, & Ramos, 1976). The conflicting evidence points out the inconclusiveness of research in this area. More importantly, this confusing evidence suggests there are effective counselors who are not of similar ethnic makeup as their clients. Perhaps what is needed is an exploration of counselor effectiveness with minority clients.

Some counselors appear to have enough skill and understanding of minority clients and their backgrounds to be effective. This seems to indicate the existence of a process and an attitudinal mind set, a belief system that projects certain assumptions. We contend that this belief structure and process of understanding are the intervening variables that constitute viable counseling for minority families.

We propose that the process involve the following: (a) confronting and challenging personal stereotypes held about cultural groups; (b) acquiring knowledge and appreciation of a group's culture and, more importantly, the heterogeneous response of the group; (c) understanding of traditional, institutional, dominant society's interaction with minorities and vice versa; (d) first-hand experience with target minority groups; (e) understanding racism and stereotypes; (f) challenging traditional counselor approaches and ability to understand the use of cultural implications; (g) using a culturally pluralistic model in counseling and (h) understanding an underlying set of theoretical assumptions.

Although this process does not necessarily guarantee an effective counseling approach, it does provide the counselor with a foundation that can be used with minority family clients. The use of a pluralistic model with its inherent beliefs will affect not only your minority client families, but also yourself as a person, and the people with whom you are involved.

References

Ansbacher, H. L., & Ansbacher, R. (Eds.). (1967). *The individual psychology of Alfred Adler.* New York: Harper & Row.

Arciniega, M., Casaus, L., & Castillo, M. (1978). *Parenting models and Mexican Americans: A process analysis.* San Diego: California School Finance Project, San Diego State University.

Atkinson, D. R., Maruyama, M., & Matsui, S. (1978). Effects of counselor race and counseling approach on Asian Americans: Perceptions of counselor credibility and utility. *Journal of Counseling Psychology, 25,* 82.

Carkhuff, R., & Pierce, R. (1967). Differential effects of therapist role and social class upon patient depth of self-exploration in the initial counseling interview. *Journal of Counseling Psychology, 31,* 632–634.

Dinkmeyer, D. C., Pew, W. L., & Dinkmeyer, D. (1979). *Adlerian counseling and psychotherapy.* Monterey, CA: Brooks/Cole.

Dreikurs, R. (1946). *The challenge of marriage.* New York: Hawthorn Books.

Dreikurs, R., Corsini, R., Lowe, R., & Sonstegard. M. (1959). *Adlerian family counseling: A manual for counseling centers.* Eugene, OR: University Press, University of Oregon.

Gordon, M. (1958). *Social class in American society.* Durham, NC: Duke University Press.

Grantham, R. J. (1973). Effects of counselor race, sex, race and language style on Black students in initial interviews. *Journal of Counseling Psychology, 20(6),* 558.

Levine, E., & Padilla, A. (1980). *Crossing culture in therapy: Pluralistic counseling for the Hispanic.* Monterey, CA: Brooks/Cole.

Merton, R. K. (1957). *Social theory and social structure.* New York: The Free Press.

Miranda, M. R., Andujo, E., Caballero, I., Guerrero, C. C., & Ramos, R. A. (1976). Mexican American dropouts in psychotherapy as related to level of acculturation. In M. R. Miranda (Ed.), *Psychotherapy with the Spanish-speaking: Issues in research and service delivery.* Los Angeles: Spanish Speaking Mental Health Research Center, UCLA (Monograph No. 3).

Okun, B. F., & Rappaport, L. J. (1980). *Working with families: An introduction to family therapy.* North Scituate, MA: Duxbury Press.

Ramos, L. (1981). *The effect of ethnicity and language on Mexican American students' perceptions of counselors.* Unpublished doctoral dissertation, University of New Mexico, Albuquerque.

Chapter 3

The Challenge of Peer Pressure and Drug Abuse in Early Adolescence

Early adolescence is a time of experimentation with new behaviors and of reliance on peers for guidance and direction. This combination can have devastating effects on young people's lives if it results in experimentation with alcohol and other drugs. Young people who begin to use alcohol and other mind altering substances during their middle school years may be especially prone to the problem of addiction later in adolescence and into adulthood.

Most middle schools are not prepared to offer adequate prevention programs to help youngsters challenge the social pressure to experiment with drugs. In fact, the current status of drug education in schools throughout the United States is ambiguous at best. Many of the programs offered to counselors for implementation in middle schools, for instance, have not been tested thoroughly and are not well grounded in human development theory. Theory-based prevention programs that have been tested or that are currently being tested offer hope that drug abuse prevention programs will improve over the next few years. Assertiveness training programs, for example, that are designed to help adolescents resist peer pressure, seem to offer middle school counselors intriguing ideas for program development. In addition, cognitive-development programs that are intended to raise the psychological maturity of youngsters and improve their decision-making offer considerable hope for middle school counseling programs.

This chapter (a) helps middle school counselors understand the relationship between peer pressure and substance abuse and (b) presents educational strategies that are designed to prevent drug abuse by helping young adolescents deal with the pressures to use drugs. The chapter offers two articles that focus on education and prevention. Emily Ostrower's article, *A Counseling Approach to Alcohol Education in Middle Schools*, is particularly noteworthy since alcohol continues to be the most accessible and most commonly abused substance during adolescence. Lindy LeCoq and Dave Capuzzi advocate a broad-spectrum approach to drug education offering elements of effective assertiveness training and decision-making programs.

The concluding article in this chapter presents a comprehensive look at drug information which middle school counselors can use to inform themselves and their students about the dangers inherent in the most commonly abused substances. As noted in the article, if counselors elect to present this information to students, they must do so in the context of comprehensive drug education programs that offer students opportunities to explore thoughts and feelings about drug use.

Initiation of Alcohol and Drug Abuse in the Middle School Years

Robert L. Hubbard
Rebecca F. Brownlee
Ron Anderson

The evidence of initiation of abuse of alcohol and drugs early in adolescence (Rachal et al., 1980) supports the need for prevention programs for middle school students. More recent findings suggest that children are beginning to experiment with drugs at a younger age. Only 1.1% of graduating seniors in 1975 reported using drugs as early as 6th grade, but 4.3% of seniors in 1985 reported drug use at this age (Johnston, O'Malley, & Bachman, 1985). Surveys for specific drugs also showed regular patterns of use and heavier use among younger age groups in recent years (Johnston, O'Malley, & Bachman, 1985; Newcomb, Maddahian, Skager, & Bentley, 1987).

The younger adolescent or preadolescent who begins to use alcohol and drugs may be at an even greater risk for regular use and related-problem use than those who initiate use later in adolescence. For example, early use may extend the period of involvement with drugs for the typical adolescent and allow for greater levels of involvement before drug use declines in the early 20s. Early use may increase opportunities to be exposed to more substances during ages when experimentation with drugs is high (Kandel, 1975). In addition, early initiation to drugs, especially before the age of 25, has been linked to a variety of adverse outcomes occurring later in life including increased levels of drug use (Welte & Barnes, 1985; Kandel, 1982), involvement with more substances (Kandel, 1982), and alcohol and drug related problems (Kandel, 1982; Rachal et al., 1980).

Despite the importance of learning more about initiation of alcohol and drug abuse in the middle school years, most of the available data on initiation is based on retrospective reports of youth interviewed later in adolescence. Few studies have examined the nature and extent of alcohol and drug abuse during middle school years; even fewer have included data on youth in the sixth grade. The purpose of the current study is to present a prospective assessment of the nature and extent of alcohol and drug abuse among middle school youths. This assessment was the first stage of a comprehensive study of community-and school-based prevention programs for middle school students.

Method

The study involved students in 13 middle, junior high, and elementary schools in a rapidly growing southeastern county of 300,000. The schools participating in the prevention served approximately two-thirds of the middle school students in the county public school system. Eight of the schools served the urban and adjacent suburban populations of the major city of 150,000. Another five schools served a population from rural and mostly suburban areas of the county.

The initial data were collected in the fall of 1985 for urban/suburban schools and in the fall of 1986 for the rural/suburban students. Information forms explaining the study, offering to answer any questions and requesting cooperation, were printed on school stationery and signed by school and prevention program administrators and the principal investigator. A copy was mailed to the students' home. Parents were asked to sign and return forms if they did not want their child to participate.

The data collection procedure was a classroom administration of self-report questionnaires. The procedures were originally developed for a national survey of 7th- to 12th-grade students (Rachal et al., 1980) and is similar to those currently used in national (Johnston et al., 1985) and state (Welte & Barnes, 1985) studies. Trained survey interviewers, who were monitored by a field supervisor, administered the questionnaire. All questionnaire administration sessions were scheduled for a single day. All students in attendance electing to participate had the opportunity to complete questionnaires; those students whose parents had denied consent were excused from the sessions before the questionnaires were distributed. Questionnaires with preassigned numbers were distributed to each student listed on the class rosters; names were never entered on the instruments. Upon completion, questionnaires were placed in an envelope. Neither survey administrators nor school personnel saw the students' responses to any question. Class rosters were retained by the field supervisor to identify students absent at their scheduled session. One return visit was made to each school to conduct sessions in libraries or study halls for students absent from earlier sessions.

A total of 7,562 youth in grades 6, 7, and 8 completed the baseline questionnaire. The initial session resulted in a 90.3% rate of completion. A makeup session yielded another 5%, for a final completion rate of 95.3%. Parents of approximately 1.5% of the youth did not wish to have their children participate in the study and another 1% of the students chose not to participate. The remaining 2.2% of students were not present for both administrations. Participation rates were similar for all the schools in the study.

The questionnaire used in the prevention research was based on the instruments used in the 1974 and 1978 National Surveys of Adolescent Drinking (Rachal et al., 1980). The questionnaire focused on major prevention concepts: a) the invitation of experimentation, b) the transition to patterns of abuse, c) the exposure to school and community prevention efforts, and d) the effects of these efforts on invitation and transition. The key questions on usage were the following: "About how old were you when you first tried (type of drug)" and a follow up, "How many times have you *ever* used (type of drug)?" A question on maximum amount of alcohol ever consumed was also included. Data on basic sociodemographic characteristics and risk factors for drug abuse were also collected.

Results

The reports by youth attending 6th, 7th, and 8th grade showed dramatic increases in the level of initiation of abuse and negative consequences through the years of early adolescence. Few youths attending 6th grade reported alcohol or marijuana use; 13% said they had never had more than two drinks at a time, 4% reported having been drunk, and 7% had tried marijuana. Neither current nor frequent use of alcohol or marijuana was common. In 7th grade these rates were double and in 8th grade they doubled again. Among youth in 8th grade, experience with alcohol and marijuana use was much greater: 38% reported at least one episode of drinking two or more drinks, 29% reported being drunk at least once, and 27% had tried marijuana. For 8th graders, some behavior indicating risks of abuse is reported: 7% were having problems with their families because of their alcohol use in the past year, 12% had been drinking until they were drunk in the past month, 8% had used marijuana ten or more times, and 9% had gone to school while drunk or high in the past year.

It is also important to note the nature of initiation of alcohol and drug abuse for different types of youths. To describe the nature of initiation in middle school, three levels of abuse were defined. The first level was *drinking 2 or more full drinks (at least 2 ounces of pure alcohol) at one time*. A second level was *progression to trying marijuana*. The third level was *trying drugs in addition to alcohol and marijuana* (such as cocaine, uppers, downers, or psychedelics). The levels form a hierarchy of initiation of increasingly more serious levels of abuse. This description also provides a way to compare the nature and extent of abuse among different types of youths. For example, girls are often assumed to be at a lower risk of involvement in alcohol and drug abuse. The data in Table 1 support this assumption for youths in 6th grade. By 8th grade, however, the level of initiation is similar for boys and girls.

To further test some of the assumptions about the types of youths at the greatest risk for initiation of abuse in middle schools, multivariate analyses were conducted. A logistic-regression model was used to predict whether youths had initiated abuse of any type: alcohol, marijuana, or other drugs. The regression equation included variables controlling for sex, grade level, race, school location (urban/suburban or rural/suburban), family structure (single parent or two-parent family), and other risk factors.

After these other factors are statistically identified in a multivariate analysis, rates of initiation of abuse often do not differ significantly across sex, race, and urban/rural groups. Although demographic differences do not seem to be important correlates of abuse, some types of behavior seem to indicate major risks of abuse. The major risk factors are (a) poor school performance, (b) early initiation (before the 11th birthday) of regular smoking, (c) having friends who do not disapprove of alcohol or marijuana use, and (d) involvement with older teenagers or adults. The comparative odds ratios are 6.13 ($x^2 = 18.42$ $df = 1$ $p < .0001$) for regular smoking before 11 years of age, 3.71 ($x^2 = 47.32$ $df = 1$ $p < .001$) for friends who don't disapprove of alcohol use, 3.11 ($x^2 = 118.62$ $df = 2$ $p < .001$) for grades below a C average, and 2.38 ($x^2 = 59.66$ $df = 1$ $p < .001$) for hanging around with older teenagers or adults. These results indicate that youths who start smoking regularly before the age of 11 are 6 times more likely to initiate alcohol and drug abuse in middle school than similar students who do not start smoking. Compared to students of the same age, race, sex, and other characteristics who have grade averages of As and Bs, students with grades

Table 1

Level of Initiation of Alcohol and Drug Abuse by Youth in Different Years of Middle School

Level of Abuse	Males			Females		
	6th n =	7th n =	8th n =	6th n =	7th n =	8th n =
	%	%	%	%	%	%
Drank 2 or more drinks (1 oz of AA) at one time	11.6	16.5	18.3	6.4	11.7	14.5
Tried marijuana in addition to 2 or more drinks	5.2	10.8	17.9	3.8	7.0	14.7
Tried other drugs (uppers, downers, cocaine, psyche-delics) in addition to marijuana and/or alcohol	3.9	7.0	11.5	1.9	6.5	11.9
TOTAL INITIATING ABUSE	20.7	35.0	47.7	12.1	25.2	41.1

averaging below C are three times more likely to initiate abuse in early adolescence.

Discussion

The results of this study demonstrate the rapid escalation in the initiation of alcohol and drug abuse among youths through the middle school years. To reduce this escalation, prevention programs are needed both before and during middle school. Programs in the elementary schools can help provide the foundation for knowledge, skills, and attitudes and can help young adolescents make healthy decisions about alcohol and drugs. This foundation, however, may not be sufficient. The programs in the elementary schools may be too abstract for preadolescent youth, most of whom have not been exposed to drugs. Thus, prevention messages may need to be reinforced by programs in the middle school years focusing on situations in which most adolescents face the concrete decision on whether to use or not use. Prevention programs during the middle school are needed to help youths reject any initial use and to help support their decision not to use.

The findings in the current study also suggest that additional prevention programs need to be provided to those youths with a high risk of abuse; those whose school performance is low and those who have begun to smoke regularly. Because many youths will make the initial decision to abuse, prevention programs must also discourage further abuse without excessive stigmatization or alienation. Intervention to identify students with alcohol and drug abuse during the middle school years may be of limited use. Given this limited extent of use and the lack of immediate detectable negative consequences, it would be extremely difficult to identify youths who have initiated some type of alcohol or drug abuse. More general interventions for high risk youth, which include alcohol and drug abuse prevention components, have the potential to become effective. Including effective alcohol and drug prevention components in programs targeted for these high risk youths may help prevent or delay initiation and reduce the long-term consequences associated with early initiation.

References

Johnston, L. D., O'Malley, P. M., & Bachman, J. G. (1985). *Use of licit and illicit drugs by America's high school students 1975–1984* (DHHS Pub. No. ADM 85–134). Rockville, MD: National Institute on Drug Abuse.

Kandel, D. B. (1975). Stages in adolescent involvement in drug use. *Science, 190,* 912–914.

Kandel, D. B. (1982). Epidemiological and psychosocial perspectives on adolescent drug use. *Journal of the American Academy of Child Psychiatry, 21*(4), 328–347.

Newcomb, M. D., Maddahian, E., Skager, R., Bentler, P. M. (1987). Substance abuse and psychosocial risk factors among teenagers: Associations with sex, age, ethnicity, and type of school. *American Journal of Drug and Alcohol Abuse, 13*(4), 413–433.

Rachal, J. V., Guess, L. L., Hubbard, R. L., Maisto, S. A., Cavanaugh, E., Waddell, R., & Benrud, C. H. (1980). *Adolescent drinking behavior—Volume I. The extent and nature of adolescent alcohol and drug use: The 1974 and 1978 national sample studies.* Research Triangle Park, NC: Research Triangle Institute. (NTIS No. PB–19267).

Welte, J. W., & Barnes, G. M. (1985). Alcohol: The gateway to other drug use among secondary-school students. *Journal of Youth and Adolescence, 14*(6), 487–498.

A Counseling Approach to Alcohol Education in Middle Schools

Emily Garfield Ostrower

Alcohol abuse in the United States is a pervasive problem affecting many children and their families. There are 100 million drinkers in the United States, and 10 million are chronic abusers; drunk drivers kill 28,000 people each year on the nation's highways; alcohol is associated with about 69% of all drownings; it is a factor in approximately 70% of all deaths and 63% of all injuries from falls; and $19 billion a year is lost to business, government, and industry because of decreased work productivity caused by alcohol abuse (Channing L. Bete Co., 1984). Of course, behind these numbers are the despair and anguish suffered by millions of individuals and families because they or others in their lives are alcoholics. A counselor who works with youngsters in a public school often sees the reality of alcohol abuse translated into school problems for children, such as poor academic performance, low self-esteem, truancy, school phobia, aggressive or disruptive classroom behavior, withdrawal, depression, or difficulty relating to peers.

Because of concern for the pervasiveness with which I was seeing problems caused by alcoholism, I developed a curriculum and program, specifically for middle school youngsters (Grades 6–8), to focus on alcohol and the personal problems associated with alcoholism. The program, titled "What We Need To Know About Alcohol," had three objectives:

1. To provide correct information on the subject, so that students can begin to make informed and reasoned decisions about their own drinking.
2. To offer an educational process that fosters the development of decision-making skills, so that students will be able to make responsible choices when confronted with situations involving alcohol.
3. To develop a counseling and referral system to help specific youngsters cope with personal and family difficulties that occur

and to enable them to admit that they or someone in their family is abusing alcohol.

Throughout the program these three objectives were carefully integrated so each contributed to the importance of the other. Presentation of a program that imparts only the facts about alcohol abuse is like teaching youngsters to swim without providing practice time in the water. Similarly, students who study alcohol need exercises in which they can apply their knowledge to potential situations in real life. In fact, offering information alone has the effect of reducing youngsters' concerns about alcohol use. Moreover, I believe that simple alcohol awareness programs, in their effort to impart the basic facts, can be quite dangerous.

Students also need help to understand the great dangers of alcohol abuse and require a controlled environment in which to act out ways of preventing those dangers. Consequently, the decision-making component is crucial if students are to learn responsible drinking behavior. Finally, those who run the program must interface it with a readily available counseling and referral system for those students who have personal issues related to alcohol abuse.

The Program

An Overview

The program consisted of eight 50-minute sessions structured sequentially to meet each course objective. Given its strong emphasis on the physiological aspects of alcohol and alcohol abuse, the program usually was offered as part of the middle school science curriculum, but it also was integrated into social studies classes. Involvement in the program was voluntary and was determined by teachers' willingness to include it as part of their instruction. Participants consisted of heterogeneous groupings of students enrolled in preexisting science or social studies classes. The average class size was 22 students. In the two years the program was offered (1982–84) approximately 160 students from Grades 6, 7, and 8 participated.

In general, the educational objectives were achieved in the first three sessions, when students were provided with facts about the effects of alcohol use and abuse. This discussion extended to an exploration of the disease of alcoholism. In sessions 4 and 5 the program changed from an objective, factual presentation into a more personal and affective one with speakers from Alcoholics Anonymous and Alateen. In this way, these sessions not only provided further information as part of the educational objective, but began to focus on rehabilitation and sources of help as part of the counseling objective. Once the educational stage had been set, Sessions 6 and 7 focused on developing decision-making skills by using specially designed activities. The last session emphasized the counseling objective of the program with a detailed discussion of sources of help. The counselor skillfully introduced channels through which students could reach out for help at any time.

Session 1

The first meeting was crucial in establishing the purpose and the tenor of the program. Special care was taken to avoid appearing either moralistic or judgmental. A candid and straightforward presentation of the facts and the attendant dangers of alcohol abuse were underscored. Statistics were shared to illustrate the magnitude of alcoholism in the United States today and to emphasize the prevalence of drinking and drunk driving accidents among the nation's teenagers. To put these numbers into clearer focus, the counselor pointed out that several youngsters in every classroom suffer from the emotional stress of living with an alcoholic.

The three course objectives were then listed and specifically discussed. The need to develop decision-making skills that are based on facts was stressed, as was the availability of help for those who wish it. At this juncture the issue of confidentiality was raised, so that ground rules could be established about sharing personal information. A bibliography for further reference, including resources such as Alcoholics Anonymous, Alanon, and Alateen, and a glossary of words they would be hearing in the coming meetings, was shared. The students kept a folder in which they placed these and other handouts. In addition, they were asked to collect magazine and newspaper clippings related to alcohol to help them become more cognizant of the ways alcohol affects their daily lives. Finally, the class took a true or false quiz that covered information that would be taught in the coming weeks.

Session 2

The second meeting was essentially factual and was the basis of the course's educational component. The students were shown a film, *Route*

One (General Services Administration, National Audiovisual Center, 1976), which deals with the science of alcohol and the effects of beverage alcohol on the human body. Particular emphasis is placed on the effect alcohol has on the brain. This general introduction was developed in greater depth through the use of several handouts I prepared for the program on the following topics: *How Alcohol Is Made, How Alcohol Is Metabolized in the Body, Alcohol's Effect on the Brain,* and *The Stages of Intoxication.* Three key points were made through the use of these handouts.

1. Alcohol is not digested the way food is, and, therefore, it enters the bloodstream much more rapidly, causing an immediate "high."
2. In an average 150 lb person, the liver can only break down 1 oz of alcohol in 1-1/2 hours, returning the unoxidized alcohol to the bloodstream to again wash over the brain.
3. The correlation between the amount of alcohol and its effect on certain brain functions explains the reasons for both the physiological and psychological changes related to alcohol use.

Once students understood these three points, several basic facts were presented:

- The faster one drinks, the faster one gets drunk.
- The bigger one is, the slower one gets drunk.
- Eating 15 minutes before drinking slows down the intoxication process.
- The alcoholic content of 12 oz of beer equals 1/2 oz of whiskey or 6 oz of wine.
- Carbonated mixers accelerate intoxication whereas water dilutes the alcohol.
- Black coffee, cold showers, and exercise do not sober a person up; only time does that.
- Alcohol mixed with other drugs can add up to more than the sum of the two and can lead to death.
- 50% of all children of alcoholic parents become alcoholics themselves.

Armed with these basic facts, students are equipped to begin to make decisions about alcohol use.

Session 3

In the third meeting the effects of long-term drinking were discussed. Alcoholism was introduced as a blameless disease that has medical, emotional, and spiritual consequences for its victims. Students were given a handout I prepared that includes candid information about the medical consequences for the alcoholic, attendant personality changes, and the effects of an alcoholic's drinking on family and friends. Theories of alcoholism were explored. This session was important, for it began to address, in personal terms, the realities of alcoholism for the abuser and for the abuser's family. Clearly, some youngsters will identify with such realities. The counselor must handle this type of information with sensitivity and be alert to youngsters for whom the discussion is particularly provocative.

A 10-question handout (Al-Anon Family Group, 1980), which indicates typical behavior of the alcoholic, was discussed in this session. Many experts believe that if a person can answer "yes" to three or more of the following questions (adapted from the handout), he or she may be an alcoholic.

1. Does the person talk about drinking? Often?
2. Is the amount of drinking increasing?
3. Does the person sometimes gulp drinks?
4. Is the drink used as a way to relax?
5. Does the person drink when alone?
6. Are there memory blanks after drinking?
7. Does the person need to drink to have fun?
8. Have hidden bottles been found?
9. Does the person drink in the morning to relieve a hangover?
10. Does the person miss school or work because of drinking?

This questionnaire often helps to clarify, for some youngsters, whether they are living with an alcoholic. Students in this program were given a homework assignment in which they were to write a description of an alcoholic personality after discussing certain typical traits including denial, obsessive interest in drinking, and an inability to keep promises. At the end of the session, each youngster was invited to write down questions he or she might wish to ask the guest speaker from Alcoholics Anonymous who was scheduled for the next meeting.

Session 4

In the fourth session a speaker presented information about Alcoholics Anonymous, its history, and its purpose as a fellowship for recovering alcoholics. Often the speakers related some aspects of their own experiences with alcoholism. Interaction between the speaker and the class was encouraged through a question and answer period. The questions the students had written in the previous meeting were presented to the speaker. These questions tended to reveal many of the students' own concerns and worries and typically were direct and to the point. For example, students repeatedly wondered how a person becomes an alcoholic and were interested to learn the details of the speaker's personal struggles with alcoholism. Some typical questions included the following:

- What was your behavior like when you were drunk?
- How did you get started drinking? How old were you?
- When did you realize that you were an alcoholic?
- Do you have children of your own? What did they say about your drinking?
- Did you ever beat them when you were drunk?
- What made you stop drinking?

This question and answer period helped students overcome their initial apprehension and freely engage with the speaker. Students were repeatedly surprised to see attractive, well-spoken people in this role, people who could be their mothers, fathers, teachers, or friends.

Session 5

During this meeting the focus shifted from the alcoholic to the child of an alcoholic parent. The session began with a particularly moving and sensitive film, *Lots of Kids Like Us* (Gerald T. Rogers Productions, 1983), which portrays a young boy's personal struggle to deal constructively with his father's alcoholism.

During the rest of the class time, students from Alateen, who also viewed the movie, answered class questions relating to their own experiences with a parent's alcoholism and the impact of Alateen on their lives. Often these youths were quite open in sharing their personal experiences and were articulate in describing the ways in which Alateen had helped them. They served as positive role models for students, especially when they spoke about Alateen gatherings as a place where meaningful friendships develop and grow. For many youngsters, Alateen has taken the place of a gang or youth group. Consequently, it was offered to the class as an example of a viable social alternative. One 13-year-old spoke of the relief he felt to be able to hang around with friends without the pressure of having to drink.

As part of this presentation, a handout printed by Al-Anon Family Group (1980) and titled *Do You Need Alateen?* was shared with the students. Affirmative answers to many of the questions were interpreted as an indication that the student could benefit from Alateen. At the end of the session students talked informally and individually with the Alateen youngsters.

Finally, students were given a homework assignment to write a "Dear Abby" letter. Each youngster was instructed to write a letter to Abby as if they or someone they cared about were alcoholic. They were asked to embellish the letter with details about the drinking from the standpoint of its physical, mental, and spiritual effects. The letter could be fictional or true, and students could indicate truth or fiction at their own discretion. All letters were signed, and the promise of confidentiality was stressed.

This particular assignment was the most significant activity the students were asked to do during the course; many students used this opportunity to reveal how alcoholism was affecting their lives and in so doing took the first step in reaching out for help. The timing of this exercise is crucial for it to be effective. After five sessions of discussion about alcohol and alcoholism, including presentations by people who suffer it and cope with it daily, invariably someone stepped forward through the private, protective cover of the letter to share his or her personal story. At a later session several letters were selected and anonymously read to the students, who were asked to take the role of Abby in answering them.

This activity contributed to achievement of the three course objectives. First, having students describe alcoholism encouraged them to review the basic facts about alcohol use, the core of the educational component of the course. Second, this activity was a decision-making exercise that provided the class with ready-made situations to solve. Third, the activity could be used as a catharsis; that is, a youngster could fantasize a painful situation, real or imagined, and write a letter seeking help. Finally, the letter served as an assessment tool: The counselor could identify those youngsters who indicated through this means, either implicitly or explicitly, that their story was, in fact, true. When an open revelation to the class is emotionally dangerous, especially to students of this age group, a private writing through an assignment may be a much easier means of communicating very real, painful experiences.

As a result of this exercise I began working individually with several youngsters to address the issue of their parents' alcoholism. One sixth grader wrote:

> My mom is an alcoholic. She has been for a long time. She went to AA, but it didn't work. Today she had to go to school [to meet my teachers] but she [woke up] drunk so I told my teacher she was sick. They made another time for her to come. I hope she isn't drunk then.

He ended the letter with a plea: "Please don't tell anybody in my family [that I told you about this]. They would be mad at me. You are the first person I told this to. Please don't tell anyone. P.S. I trust you not to tell anyone."

During a series of six weekly sessions, this sensitive youngster began to unburden himself and found comfort in being able to share and recount the daily, painful experience of his mother's alcoholism. It was particularly significant, however, that he was eventually able to tell his non-alcoholic father, who provided the emotional strength of the family, about his meetings with me. Our sessions ended at the close of the school year with his resolution to begin to attend a local Alateen meeting. It was especially important for him that he had his father's permission to do so.

Another youngster, a sixth-grade girl, revealed that her father was an alcoholic. Writing in the present tense, she described aspects of his behavior and its effect on her mother and siblings. During her first counseling session, she indicated she had not seen her father for three years. Clearly, however, the distress she was experiencing was as severe as if he had never left.

The next several sessions were intense and emotional. During the seventh session, she shared a photograph of her father, handsome and smiling, holding a can of beer. I asked her what she felt when she looked at that picture. She answered that it made her feel angry because "that beer" was a reminder of his drinking and what it did to their family. She added that she hated him for it. I responded, "But you have saved the picture." Her eyes welled up and she looked at me and said, "But I guess

I still love him too." The greatest indication that the sessions were helpful to this shy, quiet young girl was manifested in her report card the next term. She made the honor roll for the first time since entering middle school.

In both cases the students were regarded by their teachers as quiet, well-mannered young people. They were "good kids" who stood out neither academically nor socially. In short, their teachers would never have suspected the level of torment in their daily lives. Thus, the program in general and the "Dear Abby" letter specifically served as significant means of identifying those students who otherwise would never have received the much needed help of a counselor.

In addition to cases such as these, the "Dear Abby" letters uncovered other youngsters who needed different kinds of services. For instance, referrals were made to outside agencies when one student revealed that she was drinking uncontrollably and when another revealed that her alcoholic father was physically abusing her mother and her siblings.

A seventh-grade girl referred herself through a "Dear Abby" letter. In her first session she described how her alcoholic father, when intoxicated, would physically abuse both her mother and her older sister. Although she usually was not the target of his worst beatings, she became terror-stricken when they occurred. Clearly a dangerous situation existed; the proper legal authorities were notified, and an investigation ensued.

An 11-year-old girl was referred to me by the school psychologist, who suspected that the youngster had an incipient problem with alcohol. In my first meeting with her, she proudly boasted that she drank beer with her friends on the weekends. Her attendance, behavior, and academic performance were closely monitored at school. After a New Year's Eve party, she revealed in counseling that she had gotten very drunk and that her friends had rescued her after she vomited and collapsed on a snowbank. At the counseling session it was agreed that this situation was serious, and, with a certain amount of relief, she acknowledged that her parents needed to be informed. With my help she was able to tell her parents, and with their help she was able to seek counseling at a social service agency for alcoholic youngsters.

There was enough information in several other letters, in which students stated that the content was fictional, to lead me to suspect that these youngsters had more than a passing knowledge about the problems of alcoholism. Their progress in school was monitored.

Sessions 6 and 7

In Sessions 6 and 7 the emphasis shifted to the development of decision-making skills. Exercises were designed to encourage students to solve possible real-life problems involving alcohol use. Activities included the Dear Abby Letter described above and trigger films, such as *Drinking Driver: What Could You Do?* (Centron Films, 1978), *Party's Over* (General Services Administration, National Audiovisual Center, 1976), and *Trying Times* (Northern Virginia Educational Telecommunications Association, 1975), which dramatically present situations in which the viewer is left to decide how the characters might solve a problem.

Another useful tool was role playing. Students volunteered to play various roles outlined in a given situation. The following is a sample role play:

> Mike and Al are invited home with Ted after school. Ted's dad is an alcoholic. Ted's mom had thrown his dad out of the house weeks ago. On this particular day, however, as the boys enter Ted's house, they walk in on Ted's intoxicated dad. Ted's mom is screaming at him to leave. Ted's sister is crying.

This activity served several functions; one was catharsis for both participants and observers. As participants, students who were usually victims could play the victimizers; those who often felt helpless to solve the large problems of their families could take the roles of problem solvers. As observers, students were able to maintain some emotional distance as they watched the situation unfold. Lively class discussion was consistently generated through this activity.

In the final session of the course, another film, *Like Father, Like Son* (General Services Administration, National Audiovisual Center, 1976), was shown. This film not only provides a summary of key educational points made in the previous sessions, but, most important, through the dramatization of an alcoholic family, it imparts a hopeful view of the ways in which youngsters can cope with a parent's drinking by offering suggestions for rehabilitation and sources of help.

Students were asked to express their opinions about the program and offer suggestions for improving it. The course ended with the counselor's offer to be available to youngsters at any time.

Role of the Counselor and the Classroom Environment

Throughout such a program, the counselor serves as a teacher and must come to these sessions well-prepared with backup materials in case class participation falters. Moreover, the counselor must be knowledgeable about the long- and short-term physiological effects of alcohol abuse, as well as its social significance as the substance of choice among the current generation of American teenagers. The counselor must understand the psychological and emotional impact alcoholism has on the alcoholic family and, in particular, the special kinds of problems children of alcoholics experience. With this background knowledge, the counselor is ready to use his or her skills to facilitate the realization of the course objectives.

Although this program was presented in course form, it is important in such programs, given their potential emotional and personal content, that sensitivity and care be imparted along with the factual information. The use of group work skills is essential while answering questions and encouraging class discussion. Youngsters need to feel safe to discuss the various aspects of alcohol and alcoholism, and the counselor at all times must be aware that there are a number of students in every class who, without knowledge of school personnel, live daily with the pain and shame of alcoholism. Giving them permission to seek help starts with the counselor's continual attempts to create a nonjudgmental, sensitive, and caring classroom environment.

Students are prone to pass judgments that drinking is evil or, at the other extreme, that if a person does not drink he or she is not one of the crowd. By encouraging students to respond through class discussion to these comments, in an effort to dispel the former notion or expose the elements of peer pressure in the latter, a classroom environment of openness and safety can be established. Therefore, the counselor's role is one in which information is imparted and discussion of ways to improve decision-making abilities is encouraged. The subject matter, although it is the core around which the class is built, must always be secondary to the group process. Ultimately, the goals for the course will be achieved through the group process. For those youngsters who have personal problems with alcoholism, it is often the counselor to whom they will eventually turn if the classroom experience leads them to believe that it is safe to do so.

One particularly important aspect of the group work approach is the way confidentiality is handled. Children of alcoholics simultaneously experience both denial of the problem and shame that it occurs. To protect them, the class must decide that any personal information shared is not to be discussed outside the class. The counselor must stress that sharing of personal information is an act of courage and faith and must be treated with care and compassion. The counselor, therefore, must handle personal information for the benefit of the entire group, improving the understanding of all students while simultaneously offering protection through confidentiality to those who reach out for help. This climate is essential in realizing the third objective of the course.

Conclusion

Alcohol and alcohol abuse is pervasive in American society today. Its impact on the lives of young people has been well documented in tragedies that have had a significant spillover effect on the academic and emotional functioning of children in school. Often poor academic performance, erratic attendance, or inappropriate behavior is, in fact, symptomatic of alcohol abuse either by the student or by a member of the student's family.

Thus, it is imperative that schools offer programs to improve students' understanding of alcohol and alcoholism. Not only must they learn the facts about alcohol and alcohol abuse, but they must be equipped with the skills to make responsible decisions when they confront alcohol in their daily lives. Teaching only the facts without also including a decision-making component has the effect of minimizing students' anxiety while potentially increasing their chances of experimentation. Finally, by their design and intent, effective alcohol education programs must encourage youngsters who have personal experiences with alcohol abuse to come forth, either directly or indirectly, for help. A referral system and sources of help must be readily available.

References

Al-Anon Family Group. (1980). *Al-Anon: Is it for you?* New York: Author.

Al-Anon Family Group. (1980). *Do you need Alateen?* New York: Author.

Channing L. Bete Co. (1984). *What everyone should know about alcohol* (Scriptographic Booklets). South Deerfield, MA: Author.

Drinking driver: What could you do? [Film]. (1978). Lawrence, KS: Centron Films.

Like father like son (Jackson Junior High Series) [Film]. (1976). Washington, DC: General Services Administration, National Audiovisual Center.

Lots of kids like us [Film]. (1983). Skokie, IL: Gerald T. Rogers Productions.

Party's over (Jackson Junior High Series) [Film]. (1976). Washington, DC: General Services Administration, National Audiovisual Center.

Route one (Jackson Junior High Series) [Film]. (1976). Washington, DC: General Services Administration, National Audiovisual Center.

Trying times [Film]. (1975). Annandale, VA: Northern Virginia Educational Telecommunications Association.

Additional Resources

Books for Middle School Children

Channing L. Bete Co. (1984). *Alcoholic in the family* (Scriptographic Booklets). South Deerfield, MA: Author.

Channing L. Bete Co. (1986). *About drinking and driving* (Scriptographic Booklets). South Deerfield, MA: Author.

Englebardt, S. L. (1975). *Kids and alcohol: The deadliest drug.* New York: Lothrop, Lee and Shepard.

Houser, N. W. (1969). *Drugs: Facts on their use and abuse.* New York: Lothrop, Lee and Shepard.

Hyde, M. O. (1978). *Addictions: Gambling, smoking, cocaine use and others.* New York: McGraw-Hill.

Lee, E., & Israel, E. (1975). *Alcohol and you.* New York: Julian Messner.

Marr, J. S. (1970). *The good drug and bad drug.* New York: Evans.

Seixas, J. S. (1979). *Living with a parent who drinks too much.* New York: Greenwillow Books.

Swertha, E., & Swertha, A. (1979). *Marijuana*. New York: Franklin Watts.
U.S. Department of Health and Human Services, National Institute of Alcohol Abuse and Alcoholism. (1977). *Thinking about driving* (pamphlet). Washington, DC: Author.

Resources for Curriculum Development

AA Publications/AA World Services, Box 459, Grand Central Station, New York, NY 10017.
Al-Anon Family Group Headquarters, P.O. Box 182, Madison Square Station, New York, NY 10010.
Alcohol Resource Center, 474 Center Street, Newton, MA 02158.
Mothers Against Drunk Driving, P.O. Box 18260, Fort Worth, TX 76118.
National Clearinghouse for Alcohol Information, P.O. Box 2345, Rockville, MD 20852.
Scriptographic Booklets, Channing L. Bete Co., South Deerfield, MA 01373.
U.S. Department of Health and Human Services, National Institute of Alcohol Abuse and Alcoholism, Washington, DC 20402.

Preventing Adolescent Drug Abuse

Lindy L. LeCoq
Dave Capuzzi

As long as drugs exist, adolescent drug experimentation and social recreational use of these substances are likely to occur. Efforts aimed at eliminating all chemical substance use seem futile. A more realistic program of intervention may be drug abuse prevention. Because drug education programs that primarily dispense information about drugs and their psychological and physiological effects seem to be of questionable value (Horan, 1974; Stuart, 1974; Vogt, 1977), drug use/abuse prevention efforts have shifted toward more indirect methods (Horan, 1974). For example, Kandel (1980) proposed a model of progressive stages of drug involvement with behavior-specific antecedents. By using antecedents as signals, intervention may be aimed at specific use-level groups.

Attempts to intervene antecedently, focusing on fostering attitude and belief structures for responsible drug use and against drug abuse, may achieve better results when aimed at adolescents prior to age 12 or 13 (Jones, 1968, 1971). Developing coping skills, decision-making skills, and positive self-image also seems to be facilitative at this age, as well as with older age groups.

Attitudes toward drug use, however, may prove highly resistant or reactive to change. Those adolescents who endorse nonconventional values and behavior can be expected to resist traditional, values-oriented treatment (Wingard, Huba, & Bentler, 1979). Certain belief structures surrounding drug use seem more reactive than others. Schlegel and Norris (1980) found that beliefs associating drug use with pleasure are especially reactive. Thus, while attempting to dispose adolescents to hold less favorable attitudes toward drug use, persuasion that portrays the activity as unpleasant may increase positive beliefs and strengthen behavioral intention. Appealing to other components in the belief structure, especially perceptions of personal control of actions while intoxicated, may reduce intentions and behavior regarding marijuana smoking (Schlegel & Norris, 1980).

Carney's (1972) longitudinal examination of values clarification programs in public schools indicated that students who participated in these classes had less initial use of alcohol and marijuana than those who did not. As Aubrey (1973) stated:

> The decision-making process....to abuse or not abuse drugs, is inexorably interwoven with the entire fabric of the individual's value system. As a consequence all drug programs must begin and end with recognition of this reality. (p. 5)

Initiation into use of illicit drugs other than marijuana seems to be predicted by poor parent-child relationships, parent and peer licit and illicit drug-using models, and feelings of depression (Kandel, 1980). At this stage of drug involvement, referral for family counseling and individual therapy may be the required intervention. Because drug dependence by any member of a family will create stress and compensatory shifts of behavior within the family unit, developing a treatment plan for every member of the chemically dependent family seems preferable (Wegscheider, 1979). When entire family participation is not achievable, community resources, such as Alcoholics Anonymous, Narcotics Anonymous, Al-Anon, and Al-Ateen, may provide needed support services to family members.

In addition to establishing an attitude of acceptance and caring about all adolescents, the school and guidance department can best serve students by fostering a climate of trust and acceptance toward drug-experimenting youth, without condoning the behavior (Aubrey, 1973). The school guidance department can make a commitment to assist adolescents who are engaging in (or contemplating) licit or illicit drug experimentation by establishing a group counseling program. This article describes an eight-session model for a group counseling program within the school setting for preventing drug abuse.

A Group Counseling Model

This proposed program will help counselors facilitate building those skills that have been identified as being helpful to adolescents who are at the point of making choices regarding initiation of chemical substance use and abuse (Aubrey, 1973; Jessor, Jessor, & Finney, 1973; Jones, 1968, 1971; Kandel, 1980). The program is designed to help adolescents identify and modify personal coping behaviors, learn new communication and interpersonal relationships skills, recognize and build on personal strengths, take responsibility for personal decisions, choices, and behavior, and integrate values, life-styles, and life goals with behavior choice and decision making.

Session I: Developing Awareness of Group Functions and Defining Responsible Chemical Substance Use

The purposes of Session I are to express structure, rules, and processes of the group, to become acquainted with group members, and to define responsible chemical substance use. The materials needed are paper, pens or pencils, chalkboard and chalk, and the handouts "Feedback," "Definition of Self-Disclosure," and "Identifying Environmental Pressures." The "Feedback" handout states:

> Feedback is a way of helping another person to consider changing behavior. It is communication to a person (or group) that gives that person information about how he or she affects others. As in a guided missile system, feedback helps an individual keep behavior on target and thus better achieve goals.

Some criteria for useful feedback are:

1. *It is descriptive rather than evaluative.* By describing one's own reaction, it leaves the individual free to use it or not use it as he or she sees fit. Avoiding evaluative language reduces the need for the individual to react defensively.
2. *It is specific rather than general.* To be told that one is "dominating" will probably not be as useful as to be told that "just now when we were deciding the issue, you did not listen to what others said and I felt forced to accept your arguments or be attacked by you."
3. *It takes into account the needs of both the receiver and giver of feedback.* Feedback can be destructive when it serves only one's own needs and fails to consider the needs of the person on the receiving end.
4. *It is directed toward behavior that the receiver can do something about.* Frustration is only increased when a person is reminded of some shortcoming that is resistant to change.
5. *It is solicited rather than imposed.* Feedback is most useful when the receiver has formulated the kind of question that those observing can help answer.

6. *It is well timed.* In general, feedback is most useful at the earliest opportunity after the given behavior.
7. *It is checked to ensure clear communication.* One way of doing this is to have the receiver try to rephrase the feedback received to see whether it corresponds to what the sender had in mind (paraphrase).
8. *When feedback is given in a training group, both giver and receiver have the opportunity to check with others in the group on the accuracy of the feedback.*

Feedback is a way of giving help. It is a corrective mechanism for individuals who want to learn how well their behavior matches their intentions; it is a means for establishing one's identity.

The "Definition of Self-Disclosure" handout (adapted from Johnson, 1971) states that:

Self-disclosure means expressing your reaction to what is happening right now and bringing in any relevant information from your past experiences that helps someone else understand your reaction. Usually self-disclosure means you express your feelings about what is going on between you and your environment in the present. Self-disclosure can help other people understand your honest and sincere feelings and your reactions, which will help you build stronger, more trusting, and meaningful friendships. Self-disclosing carries with it the responsibility of listening to others and hearing their self-disclosure as well.

The "Identifying Environmental Pressures" handout is a chart that has the following column headings: Who, What Happens, When, Where, How, and Your Response.

There are five activities in Session I. The first is a large-group activity—*introduction of the group.* Instructions to facilitators are: (a) briefly introduce the co-facilitators and group members; (b) discuss the rules of the group (membership, confidentiality, attendance, promptness, participation); and (c) using the "Feedback" and "Definition of Self-Disclosure" handouts, discuss rules for constructive feedback, definition of self-disclosure, and the concept of consensus (time: 20–25 minutes).

The second is also a large-group activity—*getting acquainted.* Instructions to facilitators are: (a) have group members walk around and non-verbally greet one another (handshake, smile, nod); (b) after a few minutes, have them pick a person they would like to know better; (c) instruct them to sit down together and interview each other for five minutes; (d) have pairs introduce each other by sharing information about the partner with the group, telling four or five important things about their partner; and (e) have the person who was introduced add one more important piece of information and describe his or her goals and expectations for the group experience (time: 35–40 minutes).

The third activity is a small-group discussion—*defining responsible substance use.* Instructions to facilitators are: (a) randomly divide the group in half with one facilitator per group; and (b) sit in two separate circles and give both groups the following assignment:

1. As a group, define (a) responsible chemical substance use and (b) chemical substance abuse. Concentrate on alcohol and marijuana use.
2. Choose a recorder and a spokesperson to report your group's definition to the large group.
3. You must reach consensus within your group.
4. Complete the assignment within 10 minutes (time: 15–20 minutes).

The fourth activity is a large-group discussion—*defining responsible chemical substance use.* Instructions to facilitators are: (a) have adolescents return to the large group and have spokespersons report their group definitions; (b) write each definition on the chalkboard; (c) negotiate with the full group and arrive at a consensus about their definitions; and (d) write the final definitions on the chalkboard and instruct group members to make a copy for themselves before leaving (time: 10 minutes). The fifth activity allows the group members to reflect and make comments about their observations, the definitions, and the experience (time: 5–10 minutes).

Other handouts include selected material from Do It Now Publications (Worden & Rosellini, 1981), from the National Institute of Alcohol Abuse and Alcoholism, and from the National Institute on Drug Abuse for group members to use for comparison with their group definitions. Homework involves having members keep a looseleaf journal in which homework assignments, handouts, and behavior change progress will be recorded. Experiences and insights gained during the group sessions also may be included. Confidentiality concerns should be addressed by instructing the group members to use colors, letters, or numbers rather than names when identifying specific people.

The students are instructed to identify, during the next week, environmental sources exerting pressure on them to use or abuse chemical substances and to record how they respond to the pressure. Using the "Identifying Environmental Pressures" handout, they should determine who, what, where, when, and how the pressure occurs, along with their responses.

Session II: Identifying Coping Behaviors

The purposes of Session II are to develop awareness of feelings, thoughts, and how outward behavior flows from inner perceptions and to recognize some personal coping behaviors. Materials needed include pens or pencils, chalkboard and chalk, and the exercise sheets "Good Feelings," "Bad Feelings," and "Behavior Change Planning Guide." The "Good Feelings" worksheet is a chart for listing internal and external sources, good or positive feelings one has every day, and behavior—how one handles these feelings. The "Bad Feelings" worksheet asks for the same things about bad or negative feelings. The "Behavior Change Planning Guide" worksheet asks the following:

1. State your goal. What are you going to change in yourself, and in what situation will this change be occurring?
2. If your goal is complex, what are some smaller subgoals that are steps toward achieving the whole goal?
3. What specific behaviors will be involved in attaining each subgoal?
4. What barriers to achieving your goal(s) have you identified (thoughts, feelings, other people, situations, opportunities)?
5. What could you change antecedently to help yourself achieve your goal(s)?
6. Who could you observe or spend time with and learn from by "imitating"?
7. What specifically will you use to reward and reinforce yourself for achieving your goal(s) (self-praise, things or activities you like)?
8. How will you know you have accomplished your goal(s)?

There are four activities in Session II. The first is a large-group activity—*identifying feelings*. Instructions to facilitators are: (a) give each group member a "Good Feelings" worksheet, a "Bad Feelings" worksheet, and pens or pencils; (b) on the "Good Feelings" sheet, instruct students to list at least five different "good" or positive feelings they have almost every day; (c) on the other, have them list at least five "bad" or uncomfortable/negative feelings they have almost every day; and (d) when students are finished, instruct them to think about each feeling they listed and next to it, write a short, specific description of what they do when they have that feeling (time: 10–15 minutes).

The second is a small-group activity—*identifying sources of feelings*. Instructions to facilitators are: (a) have group members pair into dyads and share their lists with one another; and (b) using the left-hand column of the exercise sheets, instruct them to help each other identify whether each feeling is something that comes from within themselves or is being influenced by someone or something outside themselves (time: 10 minutes).

The third is a large-group activity—*sharing feelings*. Instructions to facilitators are: (a) have students return to the large group and instruct them to choose one positive and one negative feeling and share the feelings and their consequent behaviors with the group; (b) model by recording a feeling and behavior on the chalkboard; and (c) use the exercise to point out how thoughts and feelings lead to actions, how our actions show our ways of coping (including drug use and abuse), and what we tell ourselves are the reasons for our behaviors (time: 35–40 minutes).

The fourth activity is a large-group discussion—*homework assignment*. Instructions to facilitators are: (a) using the homework assignment from the previous session, ask each group member to identify one particular environmental pressure to use or abuse chemical substances from his or her own experience; (b) model by disclosing environmental pressures they experience and go around the circle until each member has shared an experience with the group; and (c) brainstorm alternative coping methods (time: 35–40 minutes).

The homework includes instructions to students to monitor their own and other people's coping methods during the week. Using the "Behavior Change Planning Guide," they should determine what they could do before, during, or after the pressure situation to help themselves. What rewards could they give themselves if they achieved their goals?

Session III: Using Relaxation and Guided Fantasy as Coping Methods

The purposes of Session III are to follow-up on observations about coping methods to provide relaxation training through guided fantasy and to establish a specific behavior change goal. The materials needed are comfortable chairs or pillows in a carpeted room.

There are two activities in Session III. The first is a small-group activity—*behavior change goals*. Instructions to facilitators are: (a) divide into two groups, one facilitator each; (b) model and then ask each group member to use his or her homework assignment to tell the group about one of their behavior change goals, what elements in their environment they will modify in the change process, and what rewards will be used to reinforce themselves (goals and rewards should be specific and attainable); and (c) urge group members to share their suggestions and encouragement, and from the observations group members have made about their own and other people's coping behaviors, help participants reemphasize when they are attributing blame for their own behavior to others and when they may be accepting someone else's responsibility (time: 30–35 minutes).

The second is a large-group activity—*guided fantasy*. Instructions to facilitators are: (a) return to full group, have participants get comfortable, darken the room, and ask group members to close their eyes; (b) use a pretaped guided fantasy or present your own; (c) when everyone is back to the present, turn up the lights and form a circle; and (d) allow participants to share their reactions to the exercise, where they were, and how they felt (time: 45–50 minutes). The following elements should be included in the guided fantasy.

1. Allot five minutes of concentration on deep breathing and "letting go" of tensions with exhalation of breath.
2. Ask participants to think of a special place that is all their own, where they can be comfortable and relaxed.
3. Guide participants through each of the five senses, bringing detail and dimension to their mental picture.
4. Give participants permission to be, alone or with someone, as long as they can be themselves, free from constraint and worry.

5. Have the group slowly return to the present. Tell them that the place they created in their mind is one to which they can return any time they wish. Caution them that their special place is not meant to be used as an escape but rather as a means of getting in touch with their internal selves and relaxing.

The homework includes instructions to students to initiate their behavior change plans and be sure to reward themselves. They should write experiences in their journals and mention times when they did not follow through with their plans. They should also refer to the "Behavior Change Planning Guide" and write down the specifics involved.

Session IV: Accepting Responsibility for Personal Choices

The purposes of Session IV are to reinforce the concepts of personal responsibility as opposed to blaming others, to introduce the concept of controlling one's own behavior as opposed to giving power away, and to recognize self-talk as a behavior shaper. The materials needed are paper and pencils or pens.

There are four activities in Session IV. The first is a large-group discussion—*homework assignment*. The instruction to facilitators is to discuss the homework assignment (time: 15–20 minutes): "Is your behavior change plan working for you? Are you reinforcing yourself? What kinds of responses are you getting from others? How are you feeling about it?"

The second activity is a large-group discussion—*accepting responsibility*. Instructions to facilitators are: (a) using examples, explain the differences between accepting responsibility for our own decisions and attributing blame to others when we are unhappy with the consequences of our decisions; and (b) make sure all members demonstrate a clear understanding of being responsible for their own behavior, of making choices and decisions, of experiencing consequences (both positive and nonpositive), and of projecting or attributing blame to others (time: 10–15 minutes).

The third is a large-group activity—*identifying attributions of responsibility*. Instructions to facilitators are: (a) enact short, emotion-packed adversarial situations; (b) provide dialogue that has statements such as "if it weren't for you…," "if only you didn't…," "you make me feel…," "it's all your fault that I…," and "if they weren't all against me, I'd…"; (c) during role play, have group members identify and write down as many attributions of responsibility as they can; (d) allow three to five minutes; (e) go around the group, asking "How did it feel? Who is responsible for your feelings? Who is in control of your thoughts, feelings, and behavior?"; and (f) explain how we give away power when we let someone else make us think, feel, or behave, and include how we may give our personal power to control our thoughts, feelings, and behavior over to drugs or alcohol and can attribute any problems that occur to them (time: 40–50 minutes).

The fourth is a large-group activity—*accepting responsibility.* Instructions to facilitators are: (a) have group members relax, close their eyes, and breathe deeply for one or two minutes; (b) ask them to be aware of their "here and now" feelings; (c) start by saying "Now I am feeling _____, and I am responsible for that," and each member of the group will then use the same phrase, supplying their own feelings to the sentence; (d) go around three to five times; and (e) end the sequence by saying "Now I am feeling it is time to end our session, and I am responsible for that!" (time: 10–15 minutes).

The homework has students practice being aware of feelings and decisions they make, mentally rehearsing "I am responsible for the way I feel and the choices I make." In their journals, they should outline at least two significant situations during the week—one in which they found that they were attributing blame to someone else and another one in which they felt that they were receiving attributions of blame from someone else. They should write down how they responded and what they were saying to themselves mentally at the time.

Session V: Life Positions and Personal Control

The purposes of Session V are to reinforce concepts of personal responsibility for controlling behavior and to explore ways of coping with receiving attributions of blame. The materials needed are a stopwatch, the handout "Life Positions," and two "OK Corral" squares. The "OK Corral" exercise is a Transactional Analysis technique. The "Life Positions" handout states as follows:

1. "I'm OK; you're OK"—When people look at the world from this point of view they feel good about themselves and about other people. They generally are able to cope with situations positively and accept responsibility for their own behavior.

2. "I'm OK; you're not OK"—People who operate from this point of view are fairly distrustful of other people. Usually they believe that others are to blame for what happens to them. One way they cope with adversity is to shift responsibility from themselves to others.
3. "I'm not OK; you're OK"—People who feel this way generally are depressed a lot of the time. Often they do not think they compare favorably with other people or to their own self-expectations. They see themselves as having little control over their situation and commonly cope with adversity by with-drawing.
4. "I'm not OK; you're not OK"—Life is a "no win" situation from this person's point of view. People who feel this way lose any interest in living because it does not seem worth the effort. In extreme cases, they may commit suicide or kill other people. They blame themselves and the world for the situation they are in and see no way of getting out of it. They feel helpless and hope-less most of the time (adapted from James & Jongeward, 1978).

For the "OK Corral" exercise, the materials needed are large plain paper, like butcherpaper, enough to make two 3-foot by 3-foot or 4-foot by 4-foot squares, and a wide-tip felt marking pen. On each square, make a cross, dividing it into four equal squares. In each corner, write in one of the four life positions, as shown in Figure 1.

There are four activities in Session V. First, briefly discuss progress on behavior change plans. Any participant experiencing difficulty may be referred for additional individual counseling (time: 5 minutes).

The second activity is a large-group discussion—*homework assignment*. Instructions to facilitators are: (a) ask students "How does it feel to take responsibility for your own thoughts, feelings, and behavior? When you notice other people attributing blame to you for their own situations, what did you do, say, think, and feel?; (b) ask group members to share what they wrote in their journals; and (c) ask "What do the group members' responses to the situation say about the way they are coping? How could they change their responses? Would a different response change the behavior of the other people involved? Can we make other people change?" (time: 20–25 minutes).

The third is a large-group activity—*life positions*. Instruction to facil-itators is: using the "Life Positions" handout, explain that what other people say and do toward us influences how we feel and think about

1 "I'm OK; you're OK"	2 "I'm OK; you're not OK"
3 "I'm not OK; you're not OK"	4 "I'm not OK; you're OK"

Figure 1
"OK Corral"

ourselves and that although we cannot always change the circumstances around us, we can change how we feel about ourselves (time: 10 minutes).

The fourth is a small-group activity—*OK Corral*. Instructions to facilitators are: (a) divide into two groups, one facilitator each; (b) using the "OK Corral" square, demonstrate assuming the role written in each square with "Now I am feeling..." statements; (c) have each group member do the same exercise, allowing two to three minutes in each role square; (d) have those group members who are not in the "corral" act as observers and recorders of the speaker's facial and physical gestures, voice inflections, and the statements made; and (e) allow three to five minutes for each speaker to express feelings about being in each "corral" and to receive feedback from group members immediately after his or her turn (time: 65–75 minutes).

The homework has students continue monitoring their thoughts, feelings, and behaviors in difficult situations. They should listen to their self-talk. How does it influence their thoughts, feelings, and behaviors? Who is responsible for that?

Session VI: Building Communication Skills

The purpose of Session VI is to introduce and practice the third type of coping skill—communications skills—for clear understanding and better interpersonal relationships. The material needed is a timing device.

There are seven activities in Session VI. These exercises were adapted from Johnson (1972). The first is the behavior change progress reports (time: 5 minutes). The second activity is a large-group discussion—*homework assignment*. Instruction to facilitators is: ask students "How does your self-talk influence your thoughts, feelings, and behavior? What life positions do you find you are assuming?" (time: 10–15 minutes).

The third is a large-group activity—*communication skills*. Instructions to facilitators are: (a) introduce communication skills as a way to deal with unfair attributions and to develop more productive, rewarding, and new relationships; (b) ask for two volunteers or select two people to role play a conversation; (c) instruct one of the participants to talk about a matter of personal concern or interest without pause, regardless of the partner's response; (d) separately instruct the other participant to respond with irrelevant (noncomprehending or uninterested) statements (the conversation will last two to three minutes); (e) have the group observe the role play; (f) ask the partners to tell their feelings while experiencing this; and (g) ask group members to express their observations and feelings (time: 10 minutes).

The fourth is a continuation of the large-group activity—*communication skills*. Instructions to facilitators are: (a) using two different group members, instruct one to talk about a subject of personal interest or concern and instruct the other to respond by changing the subject to a matter of his or her own concern, allowing two to three minutes for the conversation; and (b) ask participants to discuss what occurred and how they felt about it—"Did the conversation initiator feel listened to and cared about?" (time: 10 minutes).

The fifth is a small-group activity—*paraphrase*. Instructions to facilitators are: (a) demonstrate the skill of paraphrasing; (b) have the group form dyads to practice paraphrasing their partners' "feeling" statements with the facilitators; and (c) return to the full group and ask how that felt—"Did you feel you were being listened to and heard?" (time: 10–15 minutes).

The sixth is a small-group activity—*negotiating for meaning*. Instructions to facilitators are: (a) demonstrate the skill of negotiating for meaning; (b) have the group form dyads and practice negotiating for meaning, with one partner making a personal statement and the other person responding by saying what probably was meant; (c) have the two discuss and negotiate until the originator of the statement can say the respondent has expressed the original meaning, with each person doing this as initiator and respondent two to three times in sequence; and (d) observe and assist the dyads (time: 15–20 minutes).

The seventh activity is a large-group discussion. Instructions to facilitators are: (a) return to the full group and discuss reactions; and (b) ask students "Was it easy or hard to negotiate for meaning? Did you find you really felt 'heard'?" (time: 15 minutes).

The homework involves having the students observe others and monitor their own communication patterns during the week. They should practice communication with the paraphrase and negotiating for meaning methods with at least two different people and write about it in their journals.

Session VII: Enhancing Positive Self-Concept

The purposes of Session VII are to continue building coping and communication skills, to identify strengths, and to foster positive self-concept. The materials needed are prepared 3 x 5 index cards, paper, and pencils or pens. An example of an index card is displayed in Figure 2.

There are four activities in Session VII. The first is the behavior change progress report (time: 5 minutes). The second activity is to share homework assignment experiences (time: 5 minutes).

The third is a small-group activity—*personal strengths*. Instructions to facilitators are: (a) divide into two groups, one facilitator per group; (b) instruct group members to make two lists—one of their past accomplishments and one of their perceived personal strengths; (c) have each person share the list with the group, with a facilitator perhaps modeling by going first; (d) when each member has completed reading his or her list, have the other group members each add one other observed strength to that person's list by writing on the 3 x 5 index cards provided; (e) instruct the person receiving the feedback to remain quiet until all group members have given their positive additional strength statements; (f) when all have completed giving their verbal feedback, have them pass their cards to that person; (g) immediately go to the next person who will read his or her own list of accomplishments and strengths, again with the group providing a round of verbal feedback, accompanied by the 3 x 5 index cards; and (h) after all group members have read their lists and received feedback, ask "Why is it hard to say and hear nice things about yourself? What happens when you like yourself?" (time: 60–70 minutes).

The fourth is a continuation of the small-group activity—*identifying barriers*. Instructions to facilitators are: (a) after discussion, model and have each group member ask the other group members to help them identify attitudes, behavior, or environmental forces keeping them from using their strengths; (b) honest, constructive feedback is essential at this point—wherever drugs infringe on the individual's strengths or his or her use of strengths, acknowledge it; and (c) encourage participants to paraphrase and negotiate for meaning so that the feedback is understood accurately (time: 25–30 minutes).

The homework has students bring to the next group meeting a list of one, two, or three strengths on which they would like to build. They should identify any barriers preventing their use of that strength. How might they overcome those barriers?

NAME

I see you as a person who:

And I believe that because:

YOUR NAME

Figure 2
Index Card Format

Session VIII: Terminating the Group

The purposes of Session VIII are to clear up unfinished business, to express appreciation, to give and receive positive feedback, and to give closure to the group.

There are five activities in Session VIII. The first activity is to discuss progress on strength-building goals. Emphasize that the process of increasing strengths is one that is ongoing and that the same skills can be applied to other behavior change goals (time: 10–15 minutes).

The second is a large-group activity—*life goals*. Instructions to facilitators are: (a) instruct each group member to rank order all the life goals they have listed; (b) then have them select the top one to reveal to the group; and (c) ask "What does the goal say about your values and lifestyle preferences? How will chemical substance use fit into your lifestyle? How could chemical substance use or abuse keep you from achieving your goals?" (time: 55–60 minutes).

The third is a large-group activity—*expression of appreciation*. Instructions to facilitators are: (a) have the group form a circle with one person in the middle; (b) instruct that person to verbally or non-verbally express their positive feelings and appreciation for each person in the circle, with facilitators modeling first; and (c) encourage each group member to take a turn in the center of the circle (time: 15–20 minutes).

The fourth activity is to announce the option of having a follow-up session and to determine a time and date if the option is elected. The fifth activity is to tell everyone to express their own goodbyes for now.

Conclusion

School systems have an important role to play by providing drug use/abuse prevention programs. Program training aimed at helping children and young adolescents develop belief and attitude structures and decision-making and coping skills and providing accurate, timely information about chemical substances may prove to be extremely beneficial. Where long-term chemical substance use/abuse programs are initiated, careful assessment procedures will help ensure that the program goals and subgoals are achieved.

References

Aubrey, R. F. (1973). *The counselor and drug abuse programs*. Boston: Houghton Mifflin.

Carney, R. E. (1972). *Summary and results from 1969–1972 values-oriented drug abuse prevention programs*. Santa Monica, CA: Educational Assistance Institute.

Horan, J. J. (1974). Outcome difficulties in drug education. *Review of Educational Research, 44*, 203–211.

James, M., & Jongeward, D. (1978). *Born to win*. Chicago: Signet.

Jessor, R., Jessor, S. L., & Finney, J. (1973). A social psychology of marijuana use: Longitudinal studies of high school and college youth. *Journal of Personality and Social Psychology, 26*, 1–15.

Johnson, D. W. (1972). *Reaching out*. Englewood Cliffs, NJ: Prentice-Hall.

Jones, M. C. (1968). Personality correlates and antecedents of drinking patterns in adult males. *Journal of Consulting and Clinical Psychology, 32*, 2–12.

Jones, M. C. (1971). Personality antecedents and correlates of drinking patterns in women. *Journal of Consulting and Clinical Psychology, 36*, 61–69.

Kandel, D. B. (1980). Drug and drinking behavior among youth. *Annual Review of Sociology, 6*, 235–285.

Schlegel, R. P., & Norris, J. E. (1980). Effects of attitude change on behaviors for highly involving issues: The case of marijuana smoking. *Addictive Behaviors, 5*, 113–124.

Stuart, R. B. (1974). Teaching facts about drugs: Pushing or preventing? *Journal of Educational Psychology, 66*, 189–200.

Vogt, A. T. (1977). Will classroom instruction change attitudes toward drug abuse? *Psychological Reports, 41*, 973–974.

Wegscheider, S. (1979). *The family trap*. Crystal, MN: Nurturing Networks.

Wingard, J. A., Huba, G. J., & Bentler, P. M. (1979). The relationship of personality structure to patterns of adolescent marijuana substance use. *Multivariate Behavioral Research, 14*, 131–143.

Worden, M., & Rosellini, G. (1981). *Problem drinking continuum: A tool for treatment, training and education*. Phoenix: Do It Now Publications.

Drug Information: The Facts About Drugs and Where to Go for Help

Edwin R. Gerler, Jr.
Stephen Moorhead

Elementary and middle school counselors are concerned about how to prevent substance abuse among young people and about how to identify substance abuse when it occurs. These professionals need to be knowledgeable about various substances and to have quick access to relevant information about drugs and their effects. In many elementary and middle schools, counselors need to concern themselves primarily with students' abuse of cigarettes and alcohol. In other schools, particularly in large urban and inner city areas, counselors must have sophisticated knowledge about a wide range of abuse substances.

Facts About Drugs and Their Effects

Counselors must be aware that drug education should always include more than just facts about drugs. Simply providing students with information may encourage experimentation. Nevertheless, it is important that elementary and middle school counselors have the best possible information themselves about commonly abused drugs. The following is a discussion of facts about various drugs, their effects, and evidence of abuse:

Commonly Abused Drugs

Alcohol. The drug of choice in late childhood and early adolescence is alcohol. Students often have easy access to beer, wine, wine coolers, and liquor at home. The effects of alcohol include decreased heart rate, blood pressure, and respiration, as well as impaired coordination, slurred speech, and fatigue. Long-term health problems related to alcohol abuse are psychological and physical dependence, liver damage, stomach problems, and vitamin depletion. Other hazards related to alcohol use are driving while intoxicated, incurring Fetal Alcohol Syndrome, and combining the use of alcohol with other drugs. Physical evidence of its use and abuse include hidden bottles and the odor of alcohol.

Cannabis. This category includes marijuana and hashish, those products of the plant Cannabis Sativa. Street names for marijuana include pot, grass, herb, weed, and reefer. The substance looks like a weed with stems of various colors, usually brown, green, yellow, or red. Physical evidence of its use include smoking pipes, cigarette papers, clips for holding the cigarette, and rubber tubing. Hashish is more potent than marijuana and is processed from the resin of the plant. Commonly referred to as hash, it comes in the form of small, dense blocks or chunks that are smoked in a pipe or water pipe. Marijuana and hashish can also be cooked with food. The use of cannabis brings about red or glassy eyes, increased appetite, impaired coordination, forgetfulness, reduced attention span, animated behavior, and fatigue. The health effects of long-term use include damage to the respiratory system and possible heart damage.

Stimulants. This category includes various drugs: amphetamines (speed, uppers, bennies, dexies), methamphetamines (crank, crystal, crystal meth), look-alike amphetamines (hearts, crossroads, white crosses), caffeine (coffee, colas, chocolate), and nicotine (cigarettes, snuff, dip, chewing tobacco). Among other things, these substances cause loss of appetite, hyperactivity, and paranoia. The amphetamines, methamphetamines, and look-alike amphetamines in small doses create agitation, anxiety, confusion, blurred vision, heart palpitations, and tremors. Higher doses of these drugs bring about delirium, panic, aggression, hallucinations, psychoses, weight loss, and heart abnormalities. Psychological and physiological dependence are other consequences of abuse. The person will experience severe withdrawal symptoms after curtailing long-term use. Many types of stimulations are readily available to children and young adolescents, and are thus commonly used and abused by this age group.

Inhalants. This category also includes various substances: butyl nitrite (rush, locker room), nitrous oxide (laughing gas, whippets), amyl nitrite (poppers, snappers), aerosol sprays (paint cans, cleaning fluids), correction fluid, and solvents (gasoline, glue, paint thinner). Inhalants usually provide an immediate high. Inhaling these substances causes slurred speech, impaired coordination, drowsiness, runny nose, confusion, numbness, tears, headaches, and appetite loss. With high doses, respiratory depression, unconsciousness, or even death may result. As a result of chronic use, temporary abnormalities have been found in the liver, kidneys, bone marrow. Other problems include gastritis, hepatitis, jaundice, peptic ulcers, and blood abnormalities. Persons who abuse these substances typically put the chemicals on a rag or in an empty bag and then inhale. Physical signs of abuse include empty containers and bags or cloths with odor of the substance.

Cocaine. Also known as coke, snow, lady, blow, and Bernice, this drug creates an immediate high, bringing about feelings of exhilaration, euphoria, high energy, and self-confidence that last for 15 to 30 minutes. After this intense "rush," the user will experience a certain degree of psychological depression, irritability, and nervousness. The chronic user will create a vicious cycle by continuing to use the drug to avoid the consequences of abuse. Serious health problems include heart attack, brain hemorrhage, liver and lung damage, seizures, and respiratory arrest. The drug is ingested by snorting, smoking (freebasing), or injecting. A type of freebase known as "crack" is also used. Physical evidence of cocaine abuse includes bits of white crystalline powder, short straws, mirrors, scissors, glass pipes, and round small screens.

Psychedelics. This category of drugs includes LSD (acid, blotter acid), phencyclidine (PCP angel dust, THC), mescaline and peyote (mesc, buttons), psilocybin (magic mushrooms), and MDA (love drug). The drugs are ingested in various ways: PCP, LSD, and mescaline are taken as pills or in powder form while psilocybin is chewed and swallowed. These substances alter the senses and often cause panic, nausea, and elevated blood pressure. The possible health consequence of LSD, mescaline, peyote, and psilocybin is psychological dependence. The hazards of MDA are similar to those associated with amphetamine use, and large doses of PCP may cause death from brain hemorrhage, heart, and lung failure, or repeated convulsions.

Depressants. These drugs include barbiturates (downers, barbs, yellow jackets), methaqualone (quaaludes, ludes, sopors), and tranquilizers (valium, librium, xanax, serax). They are swallowed as pills or capsules and cause impaired coordination, slurred speech, fatigue, and decreased respiration, pulse, and blood pressure. Persons who use depressants often appear drunk but without the odor of alcohol. When used with other substances such as alcohol, depressants may cause death. Chronic use of depressants results in physical dependence.

Narcotics. These substances include heroin (smack, hose, junk, black tar), codeine (empirin with codeine, Tylenol with codeine, cough medicines with codeine), meperidine (demerol), opium (paregoric) morphine, and various other narcotics. These drugs are typically injected but are also taken in tablet, capsule, or liquid form. Narcotics cause decreased respiration, blood pressure, and pulse rate as well as fatigue, constricted pupils, weary eyes, and itching. They may also result in nausea and vomiting. Coma, shock, respiratory arrest, and death may result from very high doses. When these drugs are injected, AIDS may be spread through the sharing of unsterile needles.

Designer drugs. These substances are analogs of various narcotics and hallucinogens. They are designed to imitate the effects of illegal drugs. Often the effects of designer drugs are greater than the imitated drug. Designer narcotics may result in drooling, paralysis, tremors, and brain damage. Other designer drugs may cause impaired vision, chills, sweating, and faintness.

Sources of Additional Drug Information

Elementary and middle school counselors may wish to have convenient access to drug information that can be shared with parents, teachers, and principals. Numerous drug information organizations throughout the country provide free or inexpensive pamphlets and brochures which contain concise facts about drugs and drug abuse. A few of these centers of information are listed below:

The Drug Education Center
East Morehead Street
Charlotte, North Carolina 28202
(704) 336-3211

Do It Now (DIN) Publications
2050 East University Drive
Phoenix, Arizona 85034
(602) 257-0797

National Institute on Drug Abuse
5600 Fishers Lane
Rockville, Maryland 20857
(800) 638-2045

The Wisconsin Clearinghouse
1954 East Washington Avenue
Madison, Wisconsin 53704-5291
(608) 263-2797

The following is a selected list of useful drug information pamphlets and brochures published and distributed by the previously mentioned organizations.

Anderson, B., & Nash, A. (1987). *Teens and drugs: Information for parents.* Charlotte, NC: The Drug Education Center.

Davis, L. (1981). *All about alcohol.* Phoenix, AZ: DIN Publications.

Dye, C. (1983). *Coke-alikes: A close-up look at lookalike cocaine.* Phoenix, AZ: DIN Publications.

Dye, C. (1985). *ACID: LSD today.* Phoenix, AZ: DIN Publications.

Dye, C. (1985). *Marijuana: Health effects.* Phoenix, AZ: DIN Publications.

Dye, C. (1985). *MDA/MDM: The chemical pursuit of ecstasy.* Phoenix, AZ: DIN Publications.

Dye, C. (1986). *All about smoking: A special report for young people.* Phoenix, AZ: DIN Publications.

Dye, C. (1986). *Psilocybin: Demystifying the "Magic Mushroom."* Phoenix, AZ: DIN Publications.

Dye, C. (1986). *Smoking & health: A special report on the health effects of cigarettes.* Phoenix, AZ: DIN Publications.

Dye, C. (1987). *Cocaine: Waking up to a nightmare.* Phoenix, AZ: DIN Publications.

Dye, C. (1987). *Crack: The new cocaine.* Phoenix, AZ: DIN Publications.

Dye, C. (1987). *Drugs & alcohol: Simple facts about drug & alcohol combinations.* Phoenix, AZ: DIN Publications.

James, J. (1986). *All about marijuana: A special report for young people.* Phoenix, AZ: DIN Publications.

National Institute on Drug Abuse. (1986). *Hallucinogens and PCP.* Washington, DC: U.S. Government Printing Office.

National Institute on Drug Abuse. (1986). *Marijuana.* Washington, DC: U.S. Government Printing Office.

National Institute on Drug Abuse. (1986). *Opiates: Just say no.* Washington, DC: U.S. Government Printing Office.

National Institute on Drug Abuse. (1986). *Sedative-Hypnotics.* Washington, DC: U.S. Government Printing Office.

National Institute on Drug Abuse. (1986). *Stimulants and cocaine.* Washington, DC: U.S. Government Printing Office.

Parker, J. (1983). *Darvon/Darvocet & other prescription narcotics.* Phoenix, AZ: DIN Publications.

Parker, J. (1984). *The second generation lookalikes.* Phoenix, AZ: DIN Publications.

Parker, J. (1985). *Booze: A guide for young people.* Phoenix, AZ: DIN Publications.

Parker, J. (1985). *Heroin: The junk equation.* Phoenix, AZ: DIN Publications.

Parker, J. (1985). *Valium, Librium, and the Enzodiazepine Blues.* Phoenix, AZ: DIN Publications.

Parker, J. (1986). *Downers: The distressing facts about depressant drugs.* Phoenix, AZ: DIN Publications.

Parker, J. (1986). *All about downers: A special report for young people.* Phoenix, AZ: DIN Publications.

Parker, J. (1986). *All about sniffing: A special report for young people.* Phoenix, AZ: DIN Publications.

Parker, J. (1986). *All about speed: A special report for young people.* Phoenix, AZ: DIN Publications.

Parker, J. (1987). *Crystal, crank & speedy stuff: A close-up look at stimulant drugs.* Phoenix, AZ: DIN Publications.

Wisconsin Clearinghouse. (1981). *Alcohol and marijuana: Info for teens.* Madison, WI: Wisconsin Clearinghouse.

Facts About Drug Abuse Prevention and Intervention

Elementary and middle school counselors often coordinate the drug abuse prevention programs for schools. These programs usually involve collaboration between teachers and counselors and are part of the school curriculum. Counselors, however, need to have information available about a wide range of prevention and intervention services to make sure that all segments of the school population are being adequately served. What follows are some information sources counselors may find helpful in the area of drug abuse prevention and intervention.

Selected Sources of Information about Prevention and Intervention

Organizations throughout the country provide free or inexpensive pamphlets and brochures that give helpful information about prevention and intervention. A few of these centers of information are listed below:

Al-Anon Family Group Headquarters, Inc.
P.O. Box 862
Midtown Station
New York, New York 10018-0862
(212) 302-7240

Alcoholics Anonymous General Service
P.O. Box 459
Grand Central Station
New York, New York 10163
(212) 935-7075

Do It Now (DIN) Publications
2050 East University Drive
Phoenix, Arizona 85034
(602) 257-0797

Krames Communications
312 90th Street
Daly City, California 94015-1898
(415) 994-8800

National Institute on Drug Abuse
5600 Fishers Lane
Rockville, Maryland 20857
(800) 638-2045

The Wisconsin Clearinghouse
1954 East Washington Avenue
Madison, Wisconsin 53704-5291
(608) 263-2797

The following is a selected list of brief publications about prevention and intervention distributed by the above organizations.

Al-Anon. (1984). *A guide for the family of the alcoholic*. New York: Al-Anon Family Group Headquarters.
Al-Anon. (1984). *To the mother and father of an alcoholic*. New York: Al-Anon Family Group Headquarters.
Al-Anon. (1986). *So you love an alcoholic*. New York: Al-Anon Family Group Headquarters.
Alcoholics Anonymous. (1979). *Young people and A.A.* New York: Alcoholics Anonymous World Services.

Burkett, M. (1982). *Junk: A look at heroin treatment and alternatives.* Phoenix, AZ: DIN Publications.

Dye, C. (1986). *All about saying "No."* Phoenix, AZ: DIN Publications.

Inskeep-Fox, S. (1986). *Let's make a deal: A recovering parent's guide to winning through family negotiation.* Phoenix: AZ: DIN Publications.

Inskeep-Fox, S. (1986). *Theme song for recovery: A communication guide for recovering alcoholics and families of alcoholics.* Phoenix, AZ: DIN Publications.

Krames Communications. (1986). *Alcoholism in the family: What you can do.* Daly City, CA: Krames Communications.

Krames Communications. (1987). *Marijuana: A second look at a drug of isolation.* Daly City, CA: Krames Communications.

National Institute on Drug Abuse. (1980). *Drug abuse prevention for your family.* Washington, DC: U.S. Government Printing Office.

Parker, C. (1986). *Children of alcoholics: Growing up unheard.* Phoenix: AZ: DIN Publications.

Parker, J. (1986). *Everyday detox: A guide to recovery from almost anything.* Phoenix, AZ: DIN Publications.

Wisconsin Clearinghouse. (1984). *Young children and drugs: What parents can do.* Madison, WI: Wisconsin Clearinghouse.

School counselors and others who want to have the quickest access to current information about prevention and intervention programs will find the following toll-free telephone numbers useful:

(800) COCAINE:	This cocaine hotline provides round-the-clock information and referral services for cocaine abusers. Reformed cocaine addict counselors offer help and referrals to public and private treatment centers.
(800) 258-2766:	The Just Say No to Drugs Foundation provides information on this line to help schools establish "Just Say No" clubs.
(800) 554-KIDS:	The National Federation of Parents for Drug Free Youth provide this number to help with preventing drug addiction among children and adolescents. The number also gives access to information about help for young people who are already abusing drugs. The service is available between 9:00 a.m. and 5:00 p.m.
(800) 662-HELP:	The National Institute on Drug Abuse provides this hotline giving interested persons information about

	cocaine abuse treatment centers. This hotline also supplies requests for free drug abuse materials.
(800) 241-9746:	The "Pride Drug Information Line" provides information on how parents can form groups called PRIDE (Parent's Resource Institute for Drug Education). Persons calling this number can also get consulting and referrals to emergency health centers as well as taped information about substance abuse.
(800) 541-8787:	This "Slam the Door on Drugs" hotline offers parents information on drug abuse prevention.
(800) 424-1616:	The U.S. Department of Education receives requests on this hotline for a free copy of "What Works— Schools without Drugs," a resource that contains much valuable information.

Conclusion

Drug abuse is a societal problem that will not be overcome easily or quickly. Elementary and middle school counselors, however, will not be effective educators and prevention specialists unless they are equipped with the best information possible. Counselors need to be informed in order to consult effectively with parents, school administrators, and professionals in community agencies about matters related to substance abuse. Most importantly, school counselors must be well informed to counsel young people in the area of drug use and abuse.

Chapter 4

The Challenge of Stress and Suicide in Early Adolescence

Students in middle schools frequently complain about the stress they experience in their everyday lives. Typical adolescent complaints include:

> Everyone is watching for me to make mistakes. Parents and teachers should pay more attention to their own mistakes.

> I never have any time for myself. I go to school all week and am busy with what my parents want me to do on weekends—most of which I hate.

> My parents want me to get better grades. What's wrong with my grades? At least I'm passing. I know lots of kids who fail everything.

> Everyone has a boyfriend but me. My face is so awful. No wonder I can't find someone to like me. I wish I were dead.

Adults sometimes have a tendency to discount what adolescents say, believing that most of the stress youngsters experience will pass as maturation occurs. This lack of empathy on the part of adults may leave adolescents feeling misunderstood, or worse, may foster what noted psychologist Harry Stack Sullivan called "the delusion of uniqueness," which leads to feelings of alienation, to despondent behaviors, and sometimes to suicide.

Chapter 4 is about the challenges counselor's face in dealing with adolescent stress and suicide. As David Elkind observes in his article, young adolescents often rely on contemporary music to relieve their anxieties about such matters as sexual behavior and drug use because the music offers simple answers to these complex issues. He notes:

> Middle graders today are under more stress than in the past and are less prepared to cope because they have not been given the time and guidance needed to acquire a healthy sense of self-esteem and self-identity, which is the best defense against stress.

This chapter offers help to middle school counselors who are working to implement programs designed to improve adolescents' sense of worth and belonging.

Stress and the Middle Grader

David Elkind

Psychological stress is pervasive in contemporary American society. But are the middle graders of today really more stressed than this age group was in the past? This question needs to be addressed before dealing with the main issue of this article, namely, how contemporary psychological stress affects middle-grade students.

Technology and Stress

Technology, in many indirect ways, has been the most fundamental cause of the rise of psychological stress in industrial and post-industrial societies. One consequence of the growth of technology has been an exponential growth in the number and variety of our social interactions. The telephone, the automobile, and jet travel have multiplied the number of people who interact on a day-to-day basis. Qualitatively speaking, these interactions are primarily of the superficial variety. For example, an individual typically does not know the operator on the telephone, the person who takes the money at the gas station, or the stewardess on the airplane.

If technology has increased the number and variety of surface interactions between people, it has also decreased the number and variety of deep and intimate interactions with people such as parents, friends, and relatives. Deep interactions give individuals the sense of security, trust, and self-esteem so vital in dealing with stresses of all kinds. Deep interactions also promote intellectual growth; thus, the deep interactions available in small families and small teacher-student ratios at school are more conducive to intellectual growth than the more limited ones available in large families or classes. The smaller the group of people, the greater the potential for more intense and deeper interactions among those involved.

But technology has progressively eroded the deep interactions between individuals; these interactions are the source of psychological strength and a major contributor to healthy intellectual growth. This erosion has not always been a straight line function. For example, technology brought society from the farm to the city and hence contributed to the formation of nuclear rather than extended families. Until World War II, this smaller family size enhanced deep interactions and had the effect of facilitating personality strength and intellectual development.

Following World War II, however, technology increasingly moved members of our society toward an individualistic, self-fulfillment philosophy. For example, the new technology resulted in a post-industrial society in which muscle was no longer a prerequisite for getting a job. The decline in the need for heavy labor and the growth in service and professional occupations helped to pave the way for the reintroduction of women into the work force. As the possibility of pursuing a greater diversity of careers increased for women as well as for men, the ideal that all individuals should "do their own thing" became easier to attain.

In this regard, the psychologies that promote self-fulfillment, such as Maslow's (1964) notion of self-realization, Berne's (1961) concept of being "okay," and the contemporary idea of "looking out for number one" did not produce the self-fulfillment movement. Instead, they reflected trends that were already well under way because of the thrust of technological innovation. The self-fulfillment movement has meant that, even in nuclear families, deep interactions are becoming rare because each person in the family is spending a major portion of his or her time pursuing self-fulfillment and self-realization.

This situation of increased surface interactions and decreased deep interactions highlights the unique stress of the times. The large number of surface interactions is stressful because individuals are dealing with many people on the basis of objective indices of power, status, and ability. In contrast, the individuals in deep interactions are known well and the relationships are determined by personal qualities such as kindness and sensitivity. By increasing the number of surface interactions vis-à-vis the number of deep interactions, technology has effectively made surface appearances more important in social interactions than intimate personal qualities.

This fact has been recognized by a number of recent writers in the business field (e.g., Peters & Waterman, 1982) who have urged the management of large firms to focus on deep interactions. Likewise, sociological writers have talked about the "minimal self." The point is, young people today are confronted with increased surface pressures at the very time when, because of fewer deep social interactions, they are least capable of dealing with these pressures. Divorced parents and two-parent working families need not, but often do, cause decreased deep interactions of the kind that would give the young person the security and self-esteem needed to deal with the stress of surface interactions. In this article I describe the basic forms of surface stress encountered by young people in the middle grades, as well as some typical responses to each form of stress, and provide suggestions to assist counselors in implementing strategies that can help young people cope with stress.

Three Basic Stress Situations

Stress Situations—Type A

Some stress situations are both foreseeable and avoidable. For example, some areas of a city may be known to be dangerous, particularly at night. Such areas clearly present a foreseeable and avoidable danger. If people choose to visit such areas after dark, then they are inviting trouble. Similarly, roller coaster rides and horror movies present both foreseeable and avoidable frightening situations. But as these examples demonstrate, people do not always choose to avoid foreseeable dangerous or unpleasant stress situations.

The stress situation (Type A) is complicated when there are two competing foreseeable and avoidable dangers. For instance, for the young man who is urged by some friends to take part in stealing a car, the potential consequences of this action are clearly both foreseeable and avoidable, yet the dangers of not going along are equally foreseeable and avoidable. If the young man does not go along with his friends, he will be ostracized by them and called a sissy or a coward. In such a situation, the young man is in the difficult dilemma of choosing between two Type A situations. If he avoids one, he encounters the other.

Stress Situations—Type B

If some types of stress situations are both foreseeable and avoidable, others are the reverse, neither foreseeable nor avoidable. The most obvious example of this sort of stress is the sudden unexpected death or endangerment of a loved one. Accidents and illness are examples of stress situations that are neither foreseeable nor avoidable. In the past, stress situations (Type B) were encountered mainly with respect to loved ones; however, as the number of our deep interactions has declined, some surface events become symbols of these deep interactions. Some young people, for example, consider good grades or winning a competition necessary to the maintenance of parental love. If a child loses, through no fault of his or her own, but because of competition, this event is experienced as a stress situation (Type B), as a loss that was neither foreseeable nor avoidable.

Stress Situations—Type C

Type C stress situations are those that are foreseeable but not avoidable. Many stresses are of this kind. Examples include going to the dentist and paying income tax and monthly bills. For middle-grade students homework, reports, and tests are foreseeable but unavoidable stress situations.

Stresses Common to the Middle Grader

Type A Stressors

Middle graders encounter numerous foreseeable and avoidable dangers. Many of these dangers arise out of the increased freedoms granted to many of today's young people. If, for example, both parents work, the middle grader may have the house or apartment to himself or herself for the hours between the time school lets out and the time the parents get home. This provides an opportunity to experiment with alcohol or sex in a relatively protected place. The availability of drugs on most junior high campuses is another example of a foreseeable and avoidable danger.

As suggested earlier, peer pressure may enter into this stress equation. A young person who is aware of the dangers of drugs or sexual experimentation is also aware of the consequences for peer group acceptance if he or she does not conform. This peer group pressure often comes as a shock to middle graders who encounter its intensity for the first time. As children, their parents and their parents' good opinion mattered most. But as part of the social and emotional metamorphosis that middle graders encounter, peer opinion counts for more, or at least as much, as parental opinion. This is a new Type A stressor for middle graders.

Type B Stressors

The prevalence of divorce among American couples is an additional Type B stressor to many middle graders. Although the signs of impending divorce may be evident in family life, most young people tend to deny them as well as the possibility that their parents will ever divorce. Accordingly, when the separation is announced, the young person perceives it as an event that was neither foreseeable nor avoidable. The parting of parents is experienced by middle graders as a loss. One of the losses is the young person's belief in the absolute permanence of the parental relationship. Lost as well is the daily interaction with the parent who leaves the home. In many cases, the absent partner spends less and less time with the middle grader.

Other Type B stressors experienced by today's middle graders also have to do with loss. For example, the moving of many families every five years or so means that many young people have to separate from friends with whom they have grown up. This sort of stress is much less common in many other societies, where a family may live in the same place for generations. Additional Type B stressors faced by today's young people come from the large number of young people who are killed, for example, in substance abuse-related accidents and suicides. Even a single suicide or accidental death in a large junior high school is taken as a serious loss by every student in the school. The impact of such events is multiplied many times both by the large size of the schools and by the publicity of the media.

Type C Stressors

To the usual admonition that one can count on two things in life—death and taxes—can be added a third. For students, this third certainty is tests. Even though they are foreseeable, tests are still stressful because there is always the element of uncertainty about the test's content and format. Academic achievement, a surface interaction, has come to take the place of the qualities of deep interaction (e.g., good character and manners). Test performance, therefore, has taken on added significance as the grounds for the reinforcement of deep attachments.

Tests, of course, are not the only source of foreseeable but unavoidable stress confronting young people. The changes in technology and the occupational structure of the society make the foreseeable and unavoidable entrance into the work force stressful because it makes preparation for a vocation more difficult than it was in the past. With some occupations (e.g., linotype setter and tool and dye maker) disappearing and others (e.g., computer programmer and chip setter) emerging, the vocational picture for youths is unclear. It is possible to prepare for a test but less easy to prepare for occupational choices that are in a constant flux.

Stress Symptoms in Middle Graders

I have suggested that middle graders today are experiencing more stress than that age group experienced in the past. In addition, middle graders are experiencing these stressors at a time when they are more vulnerable to stress than they have ever been. The deep interactions, which are essential for attainment of a sense of security and self-esteem that are so important in coping with stress, have been diminished by changing family styles and the absorption of society in a self-fulfillment philosophy. If both the amount of stress young people are experiencing and their vulnerability to stress are increasing, then their reactions to stress will remain the same but they will increase in intensity and frequency.

Reactions to Type A Stressors

The most common reaction to Type A stressors is anxiety. Type A situations always call for some type of decision making. A person has to evaluate the possible costs against the possible gains. Such assessments are difficult at best for experienced adults. Middle graders, who have had little experience in decision making, may not know what criteria to use, where to look for the right information, and what emotional cues and intuitions to consider.

For example, a 13-year-old girl is being pressured by her boyfriend to have intercourse. On the one hand are the dangers of pregnancy, disease, lost reputation, and impaired self-esteem; on the other hand are the loss of the boy's attentions and the public humiliation that loss can bring. Then, too, there is the pressure from peers who are already sexually active and who treat the girl as immature and unsophisticated. When natural curiosity, the idealized images of romance on television, movies, and teenage romance novels are added to this, the pressures of decision making are evident. How to decide? What to do? Anxiety is a natural consequence of being placed in such a predicament.

Another example is a young man whose friends want him to experiment with drugs. On the one hand, he knows the potential dangers of getting "hooked," being caught, and destroying his future. On the other hand, there is the thrill of the unknown, the belief that he can handle things, the desire to be part of the gang and to share what now seems a mystery and excludes him from full membership in the group. How to decide? What to do? Anxiety is the natural consequence when one is faced with such a situation.

One way of dealing with anxiety is to make a decision. Making the decision does not always solve the problem, however, because some of the concerns remain. "Did I make the right decision?" "How can I get out of it, now that I am into it?" Given the freedoms available to youths today, the prevalence of anxiety over decisions regarding stress situations (Type A) is endemic. Middle graders are torn between former values that still abide in the society, such as church and moral values, and the new permissive values that seem to pervade the society.

Much of contemporary rock music, films, and rock videotapes can be interpreted as speaking to the new freedoms experienced by young people and the difficult decision making associated with such freedoms. Current cinematic productions aimed at young people also can be viewed in this way. In recent movies and television dramas, middle graders frequently are presented as wise and thoughtful, whereas their parents are presented as "nerds" or worse. A recent film, titled *Back to the Future* (Spielberg, 1985), reflects this theme. The parents of a young teenage boy are presented in a very negative light: The father is dull and inept and the mother is an alcoholic. The boy is bright, alert, and intelligent. What such films convey is "what the parents stand for is not worth much, so you are free to do your own thing."

Rock music and rock videotapes move in the same direction. They make sex something one does for fun, and they demonstrate techniques for various activities such as break dancing or disco. Sex, as presented by the media, has become another surface interaction rather than a deep interaction. Sex, therefore, can be engaged in as casually as it is on popular television programs. Violence, too, has become a surface interaction. Violence no longer has to be engaged in against those whom one hates or resents. Rather, it is permissible to hurt people for the sake of hurting them even if they have not done you any wrong. Vandalism, in which the victims are innocent of any provocation, is a good expression of surface interaction violence.

One could argue, then, that a major theme of contemporary music and drama aimed at our young people has either the implicit or explicit function of helping them deal with the anxiety over Type A stressors. By making difficult decisions seem easy and moving deep interaction issues to surface interactions, contemporary music and drama take some of the pressures off decision making and reduce anxiety. Unfortunately, the effects of these influences are at best superficial guides for today's young people, who must deal seriously with deep interaction issues.

For these youths, to whom the "pap" of the music and media is just that, the anxieties associated with freedom are excruciating. Their anxiety can take many different forms. For youths caught up in stress situations (Type A), psychosomatic symptoms are common. Stomach-aches and headaches are frequent reactions among young people caught in situations involving conflicting demands. Some middle graders may repress their feelings and become shallow and superficial, flighty in thought, and sloppy in appearance and action.

Anorexia and bulimia are other reactions to the anxieties of upper middle graders. Many anorexic girls have been "good" girls who were obedient and thoughtful of their parents' wishes and subservient to their values. But when these girls reach the upper middle grades and are confronted with the choice of remaining under parental domination or moving out on their own and taking chances with peer group values and actions, they become very anxious. This anxiety becomes focused on impulse control. If these girls can control their impulse to eat, they can control other impulses as well. The refusal to eat brings the parents under the child's control. In addition, because the anorexic has no shapely curves and has become amenorrheic, she does not have to deal with the issue of whether or not to become sexually active. The increasing number of young women who suffer from anorexia is at least partly a direct consequence of the growing freedom of young girls to become sexually active.

What might be called the "seventh-grade slump" is also exacerbated by the freedoms and anxieties of today's middle graders. For many youths who have done well in elementary school, going to junior high school can be a shock. From being the oldest, biggest, and most mature students in the school, they move to a setting where they are the youngest, smallest, and least mature. Their transition is further complicated by other changes they experience, including rapid transformations in body configurations and functions, new levels of interaction made possible by new levels of thought, and new social awareness, particularly of the other sex. Not surprisingly, then, many seventh graders decline in their studies and work habits and show a slump in interest, motivation, and, inevitably, in grades.

Although this slump was common in previous generations of middle graders, it has become much more widespread as the pressures and freedoms available to this age group have increased. In the past, the slump was bounded and limited by concerned parents and teachers, who recognized that its origins and transience had to be addressed, but they did not call for drastic action. Today, many middle graders who enter the slump period go unnoticed by parents and teachers who are too busy or too overwhelmed to accord the youths individual attention. Left unattended, however, a slump easily becomes an irreversible slide.

These are only a few of the ways in which Type A stressors, the anxiety producers, are handled by contemporary middle graders. Again, it is the combination of additional stress and inadequate preparation that is the culprit in the increase of stress symptoms in this age group.

Reactions to Type B Stressors

The basic response to Type B stressors, painful events that are both unforeseeable and unavoidable, is depression. When individuals lose something in which they have invested emotionally, they experience a sense of loss. Personal investment means, in effect, that the person, place, or thing invested in has become a part of the person. Depression ultimately involves a loss to the self. If middle graders invest too heavily in surface interactions, in what strangers will think or how they will respond to the student's actions, the possibility of loss goes through a manifold increase and middle graders become slaves to public approval.

Middle graders who move into adolescence without a solid base of deep interactions and a good sense of security and self-esteem are the most likely to suffer from an increase in the fear of loss. Such youths can become hypersensitive to peer group approval, elated when they believe they have this approval, and devastated when they perceive it to be lost. The peer group's approval can be fickle. Without warning, a rumor can spread and friends can become enemies, "wimps" become bullies, and a presumed support structure is suddenly viewed as having no more substance than a house of cards. Because so many young people are sensitive to peer group pressure, the possibility of losing peer approval and the inevitable sense of depression that follows is increased.

Other sources of depression have already been mentioned. Today, many middle-class youths, more than in any other generation, come from divorced families. In many of these families the absent parent is never heard from or seen again. Even under the best of circumstances, the noncustodial parent sees the child much less than he or she would if the divorce had not occurred. In any case, the youngster does lose a parent—even if only to a degree—when a divorce occurs. Such a loss is a powerful one and can be a major source of depression.

Depression, of course, is a normal and healthy response to loss. Indeed, one would be suspicious if a young person did not show depression when his or her parents were going through a divorce. But healthy depression has a normal cycle of reactions: initial shock when the fact is learned, subsequent anger at the parties involved, a period of denial that the event actually occurred or will occur, a period of attempts at "deal making" to undo the fact, and eventually, acceptance. Depression becomes unhealthy when the young person does not go through the whole cycle but rather "gets stuck" in one of the phases.

In my clinical practice, for example, I sometimes see young people who simply will not or cannot accept the fact that their parents are divorced or that the father or mother is remarried and has a new life. Although middle graders may intellectually acknowledge their parents' divorce or remarriage, they seem unable to acknowledge it emotionally. Years after the divorce and remarriage they still behave as if the absent parent will come back and the family will be as it once was. Often the custodial parent contributes to the child's fantasy by also refusing to accept the reality.

Other young people get stuck in the anger phase of depression. The anger spreads beyond the parents to adults and the world in general. It is the depressed young person in this phase of anger who is likely to shoot someone or to kill himself or herself if the anger is turned inward. Sometimes, or course, the depression comes from sources other than parental divorce. Some youths turn on their parents when they have been physically abused. They are depressed at the loss of the desired "good parent" and angry at the "bad parent," not only for his or her "badness," but also for destroying the pleasant fantasy of the good parent.

Still other youths never go beyond the bargaining and undoing stage. They seem always to be atoning for someone else's wrongdoing. Youths of this type are likely to get caught up with cults or religious groups that promise that wishes will come true if only one follows the right discipline, believes in the right things, and denies the wrong ones. These children are attracted to systems that offer opportunities for changing the world. Most of them are disillusioned because they realize they have ignored their own needs and personal lives, which at some time will have to be considered.

Reactions to Type C Stressors

The most common Type C stressors for middle graders center around schoolwork and include tests, written and oral reports, and term papers. All of these stresses are foreseeable but unavoidable. Such stresses are compounded today by the great importance that is attached to academic achievement. For many young people, academic success is at the heart of their self-esteem. Getting good grades is, in the Freudian sense, over-determined. Test scores and grades mean much more than that one has worked hard or learned something important. They come to be measures of one's value as a person.

Given this pressure, many young people react with anger, which is the most common emotional response to Type C stressors. Students who are worried about tests may get angry at the teachers for imposing them, at their parents for insisting that they study, and at the whole school system for being "dumb, stupid, boring, and worthless." These young people are really angry at themselves because they fear they cannot succeed academically. They cannot or will not accept that fact and instead project their anger outwardly while frequently denying all responsibility for their behavior.

This pattern of projected anger, finding fault, and avoiding responsibility is most common among school dropouts and so-called in-house truants, who come to school to socialize rather than to attend classes. Such youths are difficult for their parents to handle as well, often refusing to do their share of the household chores, leaving their rooms a mess, and exhibiting hostile and rebellious behavior when asked to do almost anything. Programs such as "Toughlove" (Community Service Foundation, 1980) were devised for youths who react with this "do-nothing response" to Type C stress situations.

Another type of reaction to Type C stressors reflects a different response to anger. When a youth has to come home to parents who are constantly bickering and fighting with one another, this constitutes a foreseeable but unavoidable stress situation. Although anger is the natural response to such a situation, the young person often finds it impossible to express that anger because either the parents are often not willing to listen or the youth believes that he or she is the source of the parents' arguments. The youngsters, therefore, may turn the anger inward.

Many of these youths turn out to be among the increasing number of runaways each year in the United States. Young people today run away for different reasons than they did in the past. Barely a decade ago young people ran away toward something—a new lifestyle, an idealistic political philosophy, a guru. Today they are running away from something, most often an intolerable home situation. Sadly, many youths who run away from home become prostitutes to make a living and in so doing expose themselves to the risks of disease, exploitation, and, in too many cases, early death.

Coping Strategies

Counselors cannot change the pressures on middle graders, nor can they remove any of the factors that prevent middle graders from attaining a healthy sense of self and identity, which would help them deal with these stressors. As health professionals, school counselors often see these young people after much of the damage has been done and after destructive patterns of behavior have been established and reinforced in the children. Is there anything counselors can do? Can counselors be of help in any way? I think so.

Encourage Deep Interactions

Individuals gain a healthy sense of self-esteem and security from deep interactions, from talking and being with people to whom they are attached and who are attached to them. These are the people who support and accept a person as an individual. It is not always easy, nor is there always time, for a counselor to establish this kind of relationship with young people. Counselors, however, should use every occasion to be positive to these youths. Middle graders need to be shown and told that they are lovable and capable, even though they may sometimes act irresponsibly. This support from counselors is particularly needed by young people who have convinced themselves that they are "bad" and who engage in the self-fulfilling prophecy of destructive behavior.

Counselors can also use student support seminars to encourage deep interactions. In these seminars, the counselor meets with small groups of youths and initially tells them stories about some of the young people with whom he or she has worked. The point of the stories is to show middle graders how important it is for them to talk about what is bothering them. Counselors who use this technique typically find that middle graders readily welcome the opportunity to talk about the everyday events in their lives that trouble them. Middle graders also find others in their age group who have had similar experiences; thus, they frequently obtain spontaneous support from several group members.

Through these seminars, counselors can encourage young people to talk on a regular basis with their friends, relatives, or significant others. Counselors do not need to mention the word communication because it is too technical and does not address what middle graders really need (i.e., a chance to talk spontaneously at length about the things that are troubling them). Talking things over on a regular basis is as important as exercising, eating, and resting regularly.

It is also important for counselors to encourage deep interactions by asserting their maturity and authority. Young people need limits, values, and standards, if only to rebel against them. This rebellion can be healthy because it often facilitates the middle grader's developmental task of achieving independence.

Conflicts revolving around standards, values, and limits are healthy, deep interactions. Only someone who cares about the welfare of young people, and who is willing to insist, can convince them to talk or dress in a certain way when they are in school. Similarly, concerned counselors care about what middle graders learn and insist that they take school seriously.

For counselors to assert their maturity and to encourage other educators to do the same does not mean that they are ogres or "bad guys." Educators can set limits with concern, establish standards with hope, and express values with love. They need not be hostile and punishing if middle graders do not go along with established rules, values, or standards; instead, they can be disappointed and sad that middle graders have failed to take an opportunity to better themselves. Young people do not need adults as friends, but they do need adults who can care enough to take the risk of setting and enforcing limits. Middle graders know that adults who let them do as they please really do not care enough about them.

Developmental Guidance Strategies

If counselors are working with middle graders who are not in trouble or whose deep interactions are adequate, there are developmental guidance strategies for each type of stress situation that counselors can teach these students. In each case, it is important to identify the particular type of stress and then explore the appropriate strategies.

Stress Situations—Type A

Decision making is the critical event in stress situations (Type A), and helping young people learn to make decisions in an informed way is most helpful to young people faced with this type of stress situation. One strategy that many professionals have found useful is a three-step, decision-making process. First, identify the decision to be made and express it in a simple sentence. For example, "Should I have sex with my boyfriend?" or "Should I drink beer with my friends?" The next step is to consider as many alternatives as possible. With respect to the sexual question, some of the alternatives are (a) a definite no, (b) a definite yes, (c) postponement ("Not until I am 16" or "Not until we know each other really well and are sure of what we are doing"), or (d) consultation ("I want to talk to my doctor about it first"). Once the alternatives have been outlined, the third step is to take some kind of action.

Stress Situations—Type B

When bad things happen to good people, a typical stress situation (Type B), one has to rely on a set of values, religious or otherwise. At such times the human condition should be appreciated; that everyone is mortal and that no life is free of unhappiness, conflict, and trials. At such times, counselors can help young people change their ideas that somehow they are the only ones to which unforeseeable and unavoidable events happen.

Stress Situations—Type C

The best strategies counselors can impart to middle graders for dealing with stress situations (Type C) are good work habits. It is amazing how few students come to colleges and universities with well-established work habits. Learning to do homework promptly and on a regular basis is an important habit of this kind. Organizing work assignments and keeping a list of things that need to be done are other useful work habits that young people can learn as effective ways of dealing with stress situations (Type C).

Summary

Middle graders today are under more stress than in the past and are less prepared to cope because they have not been given the time and guidance needed to acquire a healthy sense of self-esteem and self-identity, which is the best defense against stress. By recognizing these forms of stress and using the approaches or strategies I have recommended, counselors can help middle-grade youngsters deal with stress.

References

Berne, E. (1961). *Transactional analysis in psychotherapy.* New York: Ballantine.

Community Service Foundation. (1980). *Toughlove.* Sellersville, PA: Author.

Elkind, D. (1984). *All grown up & no place to go.* Reading, MA: Addison-Wesley.

Maslow, A. H. (1964). *Religion, values, and peak experiences.* Columbus: Ohio State University Press.

Peters, T. J., & Waterman, R. H. (1982). *In search of excellence.* New York: Warner.

Spielberg, S. (Producer and director). (1985). *Back to the future* [Film]. Los Angeles, CA: Universal City Studios, Inc.

Adolescent Stress As It Relates to Stepfamily Living: Implications for School Counselors

JoAnna Strother
Ed Jacobs

The stepfamily has emerged as a significant family system in American society. The demographic data reported by Glick and Norton (1979) suggested that there is no longer a typical American family unit. Glick (1979) further indicated that the percentage of children under 18 years of age living with their two natural parents will decline from 73% in 1960 to 56% in 1990. Visher and Visher (1979) wrote that in 1964, there were approximately 8 million children living in stepfamilies, and by 1975, there were 15 million.

Despite the increasing need for investigating stepfamily living, along with training and education for therapists, the amount of empirical research in this area is limited. Lutz (1980) stated, "As the incidence of remarriage following divorce continues to rise significantly, there is an increasing need for clinicians and social scientists to examine the unique characteristics of the remarriage family" (p. 2).

The blending of two families is potentially stressful for all stepfamily members. Much of the stepfamily literature suggests that adolescent stepchildren may experience the greatest difficulty in adjusting to the stepfamily system (Capaldi & McRae, 1979; Rosenbaum & Rosenbaum, 1977; Walker, Rogers, & Messinger, 1977). Visher and Visher (1979) reasoned, "Because adolescents have developed to the point where they have become differentiated from their parents and are cognitively mature enough to observe what is going on around them psychologically, they can figure out that their parents and stepparents are themselves feeling insecure in their new roles" (p. 195). Another aspect of adolescence that may lead to stress for adolescent stepchildren is the need for them to gradually break away from the family to experience autonomy. Stepfamily adjustment may compound this aspect of the adolescent's developmental process.

The purpose of this study was to ascertain what adolescents believe to be the stressful and nonstressful aspects of stepfamily living. This study also attempted to determine whether the level of stress for the adolescent stepchildren diminished over the time spent in the stepfamily when comparing the level of stress reported by individuals living in a stepfamily less than 2 years, 2 to 3 years, 3 to 4 years, and 4 to 6 years.

Method

Participants

To obtain as true a picture as possible of adolescent stress as it relates to stepfamily living, the volunteer participants in this study were 63 male and female high school students, ages 13-18, who had entered their stepfamily during adolescence. For the purpose of this study, *adolescence* was defined as ages 13 to 18. The participants attended high school in the Marion County and Berkeley County school systems in West Virginia.

There were 28 males and 35 females. Eighteen of the participants lived with stepmothers, and 40 lived in stepfather families; five chose not to respond to this question. There were 55 who lived in stepfamilies formed after their natural parents had divorced; eight lived in stepfamilies formed after the death of a natural parent. Further data were compiled from the demographic information reported by the participants. The mean age of the participants was 15.8 years. The average length of time spent in a stepfamily was 2.76 years. Finally, the mean age at which participants became stepfamily members was 13.09.

Questionnaire

The participants provided data for this study by responding to a 41-item questionnaire designed to measure their perceived stress in 12 areas of stepfamily life.

The 12 areas of stress explored via the questionnaire are potentially stressful areas for stepchildren as discussed in much of the current stepfamily literature (Lutz, 1980; Lutz, Jacobs, & Masson, 1981; Roosevelt & Lofas, 1977; Visher & Visher, 1979). The categories are (a) biological parent elsewhere, (b) compounded loss, (c) desire for natural parents to reunite, (d) discipline, (e) divided loyalty, (f) family constellation,

(g) living with one parent before the remarriage, (h) member of two households, (i) pseudomutuality, (j) social attitudes, (k) parent's and stepparent's understanding of the stepchild's feelings about the stepfamily, and (l) unrealistic expectations. Three items were included in the questionnaire for each of the 12 categories. Five filler items were included in the questionnaire, along with three open-ended questions.

The questionnaire provided the participants with four possible choices for responding to each of the 41 items included. These choices were: 1 = not stressful, 2 = slightly stressful, 3 = somewhat stressful, and 4 = very stressful. The results of the responses are reported in mean stress scores for each of the 12 categories. Mean stress scores were also computed for each of the 41 individual questions and for each participant.

Results and Discussion

One finding of this study was that the overall mean stress score (2.12) for the 63 participants fell just above the "slightly" point on the 4-point response scale. Although there was some stress reported by each of the participants, the results indicate that the overall stress for the adolescents related to stepfamily issues was not high. It may be that much of the stress experienced by the adolescent stepchildren who participated in this study is stress related to adolescence and not stepfamily living. For example, for one of the filler items on the questionnaire, "feeling that your opinion as a teenager is not taken seriously," a mean stress score of 2.87 was yielded. This finding is indicative of potential stress experienced by adolescents in general and may not be related to stepfamily life.

Discipline

The category of discipline yielded the highest level of stress (2.52) for the participants (Table 1). Although discipline was not seen as very stressful by the participants, there was some stress reported by them. Lutz (1980) found that discipline was a significantly stressful part of stepfamily living for the adolescent stepchildren that she questioned. One explanation for these findings may be related to adolescents' developmental growth.

Some adolescents may have a particularly difficult time dealing with discipline from their parents and stepparents because of their strong need for autonomy. It is not unusual for teenagers to experience ambivalence and

Table 1
Rank Order of the Categories of Stress by Mean Stress Scores

Category of Stress	Mean Stress Score
Discipline	2.52
Biological parent elsewhere	2.28
Compounded loss	2.27
Parent's and stepparent's understanding of the stepchild's feelings about the stepfamily	2.26
Pseudomutuality	2.22
Living with one parent before the remarriage	2.20
Unrealistic expectations	2.19
Divided loyalty	2.16
Family constellation	2.10
Desire for natural parents to reunite	2.08
Member of two households	2.01
Social issues	1.50

rebellion toward their parents. They are striving for control in their lives, and a change in family structure may threaten this control.

The area of discipline is not only a stepfamily issue; problems with discipline are common in all family structures. A pilot study of 100 high school students living in nuclear families revealed that discipline was also the most stressful area of family life for those adolescents (Strother, 1981). Adolescence is a time of testing, rebelling, and seeking independence. It may be difficult for an adolescent to accept discipline from anyone, especially someone they have not known for a long time and who is not their biological parent. Therefore, the slight stress expressed by the participants concerning discipline may not be totally the result of living in a stepfamily, but stepfamily living may compound the problem for these particular adolescents.

Biological Parent Elsewhere

Another area of exploration was the category of biological parent elsewhere. Although this category was not reported as very stressful for the participants

(Table 1), the participants' responses indicated that they experience more stress in not being able to visit their absentee parent than in feeling excluded from that parent. It may be that these adolescent stepchildren have established a strong relationship with their absentee parent because of a longer history with that parent. If they feel secure in their relationship with the absentee parent, time away from that parent may not pose a significant problem.

A stress response in terms of time spent with the absentee parent could be due to the unwillingness of biological parents and stepparents to cooperate in a manner that facilitates the stepchild's visitation with the absentee parent. One possibility that is often overlooked by counselors as well as stepfamily members is that these adolescent stepchildren may prefer the stepfamily unit to visiting their absentee parent. Therefore, spending time away from the absentee parent may not be stressful for these adolescents.

Social Issues

The area of social issues was found to be the least stressful for the participants. The category of social issues incorporates issues dealing with telling others that you live in a stepfamily, explaining why your name is different from your biological parent's name, and feeling different from your friends because you have a stepparent. Muro and Dinkmeyer (1977) suggested that adolescents set norms and establish values within their peer groups. In light of the importance placed on the socialization of adolescents, the results of this study are important. These results support the Lutz (1980) study, in which social attitudes were also perceived to be the least stressful area of stepfamily living by adolescent stepchildren.

One reason why this category may not be perceived as stressful by the participants is that divorce and remarriage may be acceptable phenomena in today's society. Perhaps these adolescent stepchildren do not feel different as a result of living in a stepfamily because others in their peer group live in similar family structures. Related to this issue is the possibility that any embarrassment observed by counselors, teachers, and parents as a result of the remarriage may be short lived for the participants. It may be that because these adolescents are becoming involved in their lives outside the family unit, family issues play a less significant role in their interactions within their peer group.

Time Spent in the Stepfamily

Another finding of this study dealt with the relationship of time spent in the stepfamily to the perceived stress of the adolescent stepchildren who participated in the study. Current literature suggests that the first few years of stepfamily life may be the most stressful (Lutz, 1980; Visher & Visher, 1978). The results of this study do not support that premise (Table 2). Those participants who had lived in a stepfamily 2–3 and 3–4 years yielded higher mean stress scores than those who had lived in a stepfamily 0–2 years.

Because all the participants in this study were adolescents when they became stepchildren, perhaps the study depicts a truer picture (as compared to most of the literature) of adolescent stress as it relates to time spent in the stepfamily. When stepfamily life improves, it is not because of time spent in the stepfamily, but rather the willingness of family members to cooperate and try to understand one another. Giving false hope to stepfamily members that time alone will "make things better" seems in error for counselors.

Another factor that may be related to time spent in the stepfamily and adolescent stress may be that these stepfamily members entered the stepfamily determined to create an ideal family situation. Their over-zealous efforts to create harmony may have led themselves to a false sense of family unity. After family life settles into a routine, stress may manifest itself in such areas as discipline and the relationship with the absentee parent.

The findings of this study indicate that it is possible that the first two years of stepfamily life are not perceived to be as stressful for the participants as subsequent years because stepfamily members may be "on their best behavior" during the initial stages of the blending process. It seems that stress does not necessarily diminish over time and that the first two years of stepfamily life may not be the most stressful time for adolescent stepchildren. Because the results of this study cannot be generalized to all stepfamilies, further research needs to be done in this area to assist stepfamily members.

Implications for Counselors

Although the results of this study are based on the perceived level of stress of only 63 adolescent stepchildren, there are implications that

Table 2

Mean Stress Scores of Participants According to Time Spent in the Stepfamily and Age

Time spent in the stepfamily (years)	Age (years)					
	13	14	15	16	17	18
0–2 years $\overline{X} = 1.96 (n = 13)$	1.92(3)	1.93(2)	1.89(1)	1.96(5)	2.12(2)	
2–3 years $\overline{X} = 2.49 (n = 16)$		2.17(8)	2.87(2)	2.47(2)	2.45(4)	
3–4 years $\overline{X} = 2.17 (n = 20)$			2.30(7)	2.02(7)	2.19(6)	
4–6 years $\overline{X} = 1.95 (n = 14)$				1.76(4)	1.92(7)	2.17(3)

Note. $\overline{X}$ computed from mean stress scores from individual participants.

merit consideration by school counselors who are counseling adolescent stepchildren, stepparents, custodial parents, and noncustodial parents. The overall stress score for the 63 participants was 2.12. Although the adolescents in this study noted some overall stress, the indications seem to be that these adolescents are adjusting to stepfamily living.

Unfortunately, the bulk of the stepfamily literature has been written by stepparents who entered stepfamily life with little preparation and information and by professionals who have counseled stepfamily members who are experiencing difficulty. Therefore, the literature describing positive stepfamily adjustment is scant. It is important for counselors to convey a message of hope to stepfamily members, along with strategies for coping, that the stepfamily can truly be a family unit that functions for the good of all its members.

Even though this study did not yield results that indicated stepfamily stress to be any higher than stress in nuclear families for the adolescent, counselors *can* be of help to adolescents living in stepfamilies, especially those who are experiencing stress. Because discipline was seen as a stressful area of stepfamily living for some of the participants, it would be valuable for school counselors to teach parents and stepparents more effective ways to interact with the adolescent in terms of rules and guidelines for the family. Counseling for parents and stepparents may also help them understand the complexities of adolescence and the impact that discipline may have on the teenager.

School counselors can also help the stepfamily unit by providing information and assistance regarding the adolescent stepchild's relationship with the absentee parent. Counselors can support the stepchild and the parents in developing a system, agreeable to all, concerning weekends, holidays, and other times when disagreements arise over visitation. Also, the school counselor should serve as a student advocate in these situations, especially when the adolescent is feeling pressure to visit the absentee parent or be kept from visiting that same parent.

The category of social issues has important implications for school counselors. Professionals need to be aware of the possibility that some adolescents may not need an inordinate amount of support in dealing with significant others in terms of becoming a stepfamily member. This is a factor for school counselors to be aware of when counseling adolescent stepchildren. Often, school personnel have a tendency to label an adolescent *stepchild* and decide that the student's problems revolve around that label. This study and the Lutz (1980) study indicate that the adolescent stepchildren who participated are adjusting to society's reactions concerning stepfamilies. In fact, the social stigma attached to stepfamilies may be a myth conceived in the minds of those adults who have had difficulty in their adjustments to stepfamily life.

School counselors can assist parents and stepparents by helping them understand their adolescent's needs and feelings, by encouraging them to make positive changes, and by pointing out their unrealistic expectations for their adolescent stepchild. It may be crucial for school counselors to teach stepfamily members, especially parents, that the expression "time heals all wounds" is a myth. School counselors are in an excellent position to dispel this myth for those stepfamily members who are merely waiting for "things to get better." Time itself does not make the stepfamily unit work; it is what family members do in that time that helps to blend the stepfamily.

References

Capaldi, F., & McRae, B. (1979). *Stepfamilies*. New York: New Viewpoints/Vision Books.

Glick, P. C. (1979). Children of divorced parents in demographic perspective. *Journal of Social Issues, 35*, 170–182.

Glick, P. C., & Norton, A. J. (1979). Marrying, divorcing, and living together in the U.S. today. *Population Bulletin, 32*(5), 1–40.

Lutz, P. (1980). *Stepfamilies: A descriptive study from the adolescent perspective*. Unpublished doctoral dissertation, West Virginia University, Morgantown, West Virginia.

Lutz, P., Jacobs, E., & Masson, R. (1981). Stepfamily counseling: Issues and guidelines. *The School Counselor, 28*, 189–194.

Muro, J. J., & Dinkmeyer, D. C. (1977). *Counseling in the elementary and middle schools*. Dubuque, IA: Brown.

Roosevelt, R., & Lofas, J. (1977). *Living in step*. New York: Stein & Day.

Rosenbaum, J., & Rosenbaum, V. (1977). *Stepparenting*. New York: Dutton.

Strother, J. (1981). *Analyzing stress as it relates to stepfamily living*. Unpublished doctoral dissertation, West Virginia University, Morgantown, West Virginia.

Visher, E. B., & Visher, J. S. (1978). Common problems of stepparents and their spouses. *American Journal of Orthopsychiatry,48*, 252–261.

Visher, E. B., & Visher, J. S. (1979). *Stepfamilies: A guide to working with stepparents and stepchildren.* New York: Brunner/Mazel.

Walker, K. N., Rogers, J., & Messinger, L. (1977). Remarriage after divorce: A review. *Social Casework, 58,* 276–285.

The School Counselor's Role in the Communication of Suicidal Ideation by Adolescents

Mary M. Wellman

Suicide attempts and successful suicides by adolescents have become causes of major concern for school counselors, teachers, parents, and community mental health care professionals. Nationally, the number of reported adolescent suicides has increased 400% in the last 20 years (Maris, 1982). The National Center for Health Statistics (1977) reported that 57 adolescents and young adults attempt suicide each day, and of those, 13 are successfully completed. Prior to 1977, suicide was the third leading cause of death among adolescents, after accidents and homicides. Since then, the incidence of suicides has surpassed that of homicides, to become the second leading cause of death among the 15–19 age group (Mack & Hickler, 1971). This increase may have come about because there is greater professional awareness of this phenomenon in the last few decades; thus a greater number of adolescent suicides is identified and reported.

Those who work with adolescents play a vital role in diagnosing the adolescent's suicidal intent. That intent is communicated through language and action in a progression of events in the youth's life. Of suicide attempters, 80% communicate their intentions verbally prior to their attempt (Rudestam, 1971). Although the other 20% do not verbalize their suicidal ideation, their behaviors can communicate the notion that they are at risk for suicide.

Five-Stage Model of Suicidal Behavior

Jacobs (1980) proposed a five-stage model of suicidal behavior, derived from interviews with adolescents who have attempted suicide. This model is discussed in this article based on the observations of the present author. The first case used to illustrate each stage is that of Vivienne (Mack & Hickler, 1981). Although Mack and Hickler did not discuss

Vivienne's case in terms of Jacob's stages, the parallels are clear. The second two cases—Bill and Michelle—are adolescents known to the present author.

First Stage

The adolescent has a long-standing history of problems stemming from early childhood. The child perceives the parents as unloving and rejecting. There is a sense of powerlessness and loneliness.

Case 1. Vivienne seemed to suffer alienation from her mother by the age of 3. Her mother reported that Vivienne "tuned her out." In elementary school, she was socially isolated from her peers. She dressed differently, and her family was somewhat ostracized for their liberal views.

Case 2. Bill recalled that his parents constantly argued violently for as long as he could remember. His father invariably blamed Bill for every action, however innocuous. Bill was aware of his father's sexual abuse to Bill's sister.

Case 3. Michelle's parents divorced when Michelle was 5. Two years later, her mother remarried. Michelle's stepfather was cold and authoritarian, while her mother became withdrawn. Michelle, who had been an extroverted child in kindergarten and first grade, became sullen and withdrawn in the second grade.

Second Stage

Instead of diminishing or resolving themselves, the problems of the suicidal adolescent escalate at the onset of adolescence. The problems extant since childhood continue to plague the adolescent and are complicated by new difficulties.

Case 1. Vivienne's serious depression began at the onset of adolescence. She began to be more withdrawn socially and had a poor body image because she felt overweight. Her depression was not manifested to everyone. At school, she attempted to mask it by her acidic wit, and she began smoking marijuana to alleviate her symptoms. Her poor self-esteem was shown most poignantly in her diary, in which she wrote, "How can you kill nothing?"

Case 2. Bill was forced to change schools at the onset of adolescence. Failing to make new friends, he became withdrawn, often retreating to his room at home. At school, he did a minimal amount of academic work and ate lunch by himself or with one other person. His teachers barely noticed him; he rarely participated in class and their time was spent on the more vocal and acting-out students.

Case 3. Michelle's mother began drinking heavily at the onset of Michelle's adolescence and was increasingly unavailable to her. Michelle began to act out as a result of these events. She was truant from school and was overtly hostile to her parents. Her stepfather retaliated through the use of physical violence.

Third Stage

The adolescent becomes progressively less able to cope with life stressors and exhibits more social isolation.

Case 1. Vivienne attempted to cope with her life stressors by forming an alliance with her teacher. When that teacher relocated to California and was unavailable to her, she grew more depressed. Vivienne's bond with her sister was also broken when Laurel transferred to a new school.

Case 2. Bill began to abuse alcohol in his retreat from his family and school problems. He rarely spoke to anyone but began reading material connected with death and suicide.

Case 3. Michelle began to avoid going home, often staying at a friend's house overnight. She was engaged in a number of short-lived sexual relationships and was abusing a variety of drugs, using whatever became available to her. Her parents desired to have her removed from the house. The school referred Michelle to a social welfare agency, and she was placed in an adolescent residential center.

Fourth Stage

The adolescent is involved in a series of events that dissolve the remaining social relationships and cause a "last straw" phenomenon. The suicidal youth feels that there is no remaining hope.

Case 1. Vivienne found herself in the middle of her family's upheaval, which involved an imminent move to a new community and her father's professional dislocation. She wrote in her diary, "I am of no use to anyone."

Case 2. Bill had been involved in an auto accident in which he had suffered several broken bones and some internal injuries. He was hospitalized for a week, then released.

Case 3. Michelle ran away from the adolescent residential center where she had been placed. After several meetings with her social worker, it was discovered that Michelle was pregnant.

Fifth Stage

During this final stage immediately preceding the suicide attempt, the adolescent goes through the process of self-justification of the suicide.

Case 1. Vivienne wrote, "Death is going to be a beautiful thing."

Cases 2 and 3. Because no written records (diaries or suicide notes) were left, we have no glimpse at the internal process described in this stage.

Discussion

In these five stages, a steady downward spiral occurs, whereby problems and stressors escalate. The adolescent attempts a variety of coping mechanisms and becomes progressively more isolated. The behavioral pattern follows a predictable course. The acting-out behaviors of alcohol or drug abuse, sexual promiscuity, and running away from home are seen as coping mechanisms. They are methods of escaping from the inner and outer turmoil of the adolescent's existence; they are also manifestations of the depression the adolescent feels. The professional working with adolescents who is cognizant of this series of events and behaviors can more easily identify the adolescent who is at risk for suicide.

Verbal Communication of Suicide Intent

A second method of communicating suicidal notions is through a two-step progression. The first step is characterized by the adolescent's verbal communication with persons he or she trusts, accompanied by experimentation with death, often called a *suicidal gesture*. The second step is a period of silence in which a lethal method of suicide is attempted. Some adolescents proceed immediately to the second step with no verbal warning. Some may never reach the second step because their experimentation with death is accidentally fatal.

First Step

In the first step, methods of experimentation include wrist slashing and medication overdosing. These methods do not usually cause death because the adolescent victim is found and treated in time, but if intervention is not forthcoming, the experiment becomes fatal. Therefore, this type of suicide attempt, often called *the cry for help,* is not to be taken lightly. Many adolescents never reach the second step because they receive adequate ongoing intervention after the first suicide attempt. This type of attempt is usually preceded by verbal remarks by the adolescent regarding his or her lack of self-worth, his or her burdensome nature, and the feeling that he or she will not be around much longer. In addition, the adolescent may write a suicide note and distribute his or her personal belongings.

Second Step

In the second step, after one or several suicide attempts have failed to either resolve the adolescent's life problems or result in death, the attempter takes more drastic measures, such as use of firearms or hanging. At this step, the adolescent is usually silent with regard to his or her intent. To communicate verbally would result in outside intervention, which the adolescent no longer desires.

Case 1. Vivienne told three people of her suicidal intent and attempts. It seems that all three denied the possibility to themselves; none could accept the fact that she really would kill herself. In fact, Vivienne attempted to strangle herself in front of a mirror several times. "I know what my dead face will look like," she wrote. Furthermore, her family was aware that she had attempted to overdose on medication. Finally, in the last stage, she hanged herself in the basement of her house.

Case 2. Bill, at first glance, seems to be one of the adolescent victims who omits the first step and immediately attempts a lethal means. Three weeks before his death, however, he had been hospitalized because of the auto accident mentioned previously. One can speculate that the accident may have been a suicide attempt, as much evidence for this pattern exists (e.g., American Academy of Pediatrics, Committee on Adolescence, 1980). After recuperating at home for two weeks following his hospital discharge, Bill fatally shot himself.

Case 3. Michelle had been living on the street. She refused to remain in any of the placements offered by social welfare, and although she met regularly with her social worker, she was mute during the sessions. Her parents refused to allow her to live at home. She was three months pregnant and elected not to have an abortion. She spent much of her time visiting fellow homeless adolescents in the hospital who had attempted suicide. Although she has not yet made any suicide attempts, she is certainly at high risk. Had recognition of Michelle's problems and intervention begun at Jacobs' (1980) first and second stages, perhaps the downward spiral would have been averted.

These cases illustrate that adolescents do communicate their depression and suicidal thoughts through their conversations with friends, their withdrawal and social isolation, or their acting-out behavior. Recognition of these symptoms by school counselors and teachers could bring about earlier intervention. In addition, because many teachers and counselors are not comfortable dealing with issues of suicide, a series of inservice workshops designed to help school personnel deal with their own feelings about suicide, as well as recognize and respond to students with suicidal depression, would be of great benefit. Ross (1980) reported on such a program instituted in California for high school counselors, teachers, and nurses. In this program, group discussions helped to alleviate anxiety concerning adolescents' suicidal thoughts and quelled fears of precipitating a suicide by broaching the topic with a student.

Summary of Methods of Communication of Suicidal Notions

An adolescent whose life follows the pattern exhibited in Jacobs' (1980) stages and who communicates some of the following verbal or behavioral messages may be considered at risk for suicide:

1. prevailing sadness, lack of energy, difficulty in concentrating, loss of interest or pleasure in usual activities, or atypical acting-out behaviors, anger, belligerence to authority figures, alcohol/drug abuse, sexual promiscuity, and running away from home;
2. academic failure in school, often accompanied by the adolescent's feelings of disinterest or helplessness;
3. social isolation—lack of close friends or confidants—even though the adolescent may have superficial contact with a group of peers;
4. disharmony or disruption in the family, divorce, separation, alcoholism, and physical or sexual abuse;

5. recent loss of or suicide attempt by a loved one or family member and/or break-up with boyfriend or girlfriend;
6. atypical eating/sleeping patterns—either excessive increase or decrease;
7. verbal remarks about sense of failure, worthlessness, isolation, absence, or death and written stories, essays, or art projects displaying the same themes;
8. collecting pills, razor blades, knives, ropes, or firearms;
9. giving away personal possessions and writing a suicide note; and
10. previous suicide attempts.

Intervention

Often a teacher will first identify the adolescent at risk because of daily contact and will bring the matter to the attention of the school counselor. The adolescent should be seen by the counselor immediately. By showing concern for the adolescent and through active listening, the counselor can assess the gravity of the situation. Support for the adolescent should be offered. Inform the student that your concern warrants a team meeting.

The adolescent is referred to the multidisciplinary planning and placement team. The school psychologist, administrator, and parents are notified at once, and the team meets without delay. At the team meeting, parental resistance and denial may be evident. The team needs to hear the fears of the parent, offer support, and be united in the presentation of the need for a thorough psychological evaluation and possible outside referral. If the parents are still resistant, suggesting an evaluation for the purposes of nullifying the gravity of the situation is often a tactic that is successful.

The school counselor, as a member of the team, may also be involved in referring the adolescent and the family to other necessary social service agencies at this time. During this process, the school counselor needs to provide ongoing support and counseling for the adolescent. Parental pressures on the adolescent may escalate at this time, and environmental stress from the assessment by various professionals may make the adolescent more unstable.

The school counselor must help coordinate his or her own efforts with those of the classroom teachers and the school psychologist, so that the adolescent does not receive conflicting messages. The school counselor as part of the team coordinates and reviews reports and input from outside agencies and in-school assessment and helps decide on an appropriate course of action in treating the adolescent, ranging from possible hospitalization to counseling and support services for both adolescent and parents. School counselors and teachers need to know the various ways in which adolescents communicate their suicidal ideation and strategies in intervention to prevent further escalation of the incidence of adolescent suicide.

References

American Academy of Pediatrics, Committee on Adolescence. (1980). Teenage suicide. *Pediatrics, 66,* 144–146.

Jacobs, J. (1980). *Adolescent suicide.* New York: Irvington.

Mack, J. E., & Hickler, H. (1981). *Vivienne: The life and suicide of an adolescent girl.* New York: New American Library.

Maris, R. (1982, August). *Death and suicide: A teenage crisis.* Program presented at the 90th annual convention of the American Psychological Association, Washington, DC.

National Center for Health Statistics. (1977). *Vital statistics of the United States.* Washington, DC: Government Printing Office.

Ross, C. (1980). Mobilizing schools for suicide prevention. *Suicide and Life-Threatening Behavior, 10,* 239–243.

Rudestam, K. E. (1971). Stockholm and Los Angeles: A cross-cultural study of the communication of suicidal intent. *Journal of Consulting and Clinical Psychology, 36,* 82–90.

One Counselor's Intervention in the Aftermath of a Middle School Student's Suicide: A Case Study

Jo Ann C. Alexander
Robert L. Harman

Four young people have died of suicide within the last month in our county. The second of these was Jason, a 13-year-old student in the middle school in which I am a counselor. The first death occurred on Valentine's Day, and Jason's followed by three weeks. The subsequent two deaths occurred in other parts of the county within a week of Jason's death. These events seem like a poignant validation of the "Werther" effect (Phillips, 1985)—the tendency of humans to imitate.

It is important for school counselors to have skills not only in programming for suicide prevention but also for intervening in the aftermath of suicide. Existing literature, however, offers little to prepare counselors—particularly those in school settings—for this role. Researchers (Calhoun, Selby, & Faulstich, 1982; Calhoun, Selby, & Selby, 1982) have reported on the aftereffects of suicide, but few actually (Hill, 1984; Zinner, 1987) have discussed the ways in which a counselor might intervene.

In short, I had little from the professional literature to inform me when I learned of Jason's death. My task, as I identified it, was to help our young people grieve over Jason, to assist them in the process of letting go of him, and to minimize the likelihood of copycat suicides. I did not know what to expect in terms of their response to the news. I was coordinator of guidance in the school, in which we had three counselors, one per grade level, and approximately 1,000 students. I was assigned to the sixth grade, in which Jason had been a student.

Fortunately, I had been a Gestalt therapy trainee for two years. Also, I had some specific training in working with suicidally depressed adolescents and had done considerable reading in this area. It was with this preparation that I began my interventions. The approach described below should not be used by counselors without the support of comparable theory, knowledge, and skill.

After I decided that the most effective use of my time would be to work primarily with those 150 students with whom Jason had daily contact, I met with the faculty to prepare a consistent and appropriate schoolwide response. We agreed not to eulogize Jason but to focus in public on our feelings of grief, shock, loss, fear, and even anger. We would not glorify his act, nor would we ignore that which we would miss about him.

In my work with students, I relied heavily on my knowledge of the theory and practice of Gestalt therapy. My task was to enhance students' awareness of their thoughts, feelings, and sensations about the death of a classmate and also to help them learn to express themselves in ways that might be more nourishing to themselves and to others at this time of trauma. With awareness, students might have more choice about how to respond both to Jason's death and to their feelings of isolation, hopelessness, and despair. My intent was to involve each student in his or her present experience in as many ways as possible; I began by visiting six of Jason's seven daily classrooms. Access to these classrooms was not difficult: Six teachers were delighted and relieved to accept my offer to work with their students; only two remained in the classroom to participate in my one class period intervention. One teacher chose to work with his students himself.

Class-Sized Groups, Individuals, and Groups of Two

Jason chose to die with his goodbyes left unsaid. His act was abrupt and blunt. So as not to deflect from the quality of his act, I entered each classroom and announced, "I'm here today to help you say goodbye to Jason Davis. Jason is dead. He committed suicide. . . . He won't be back. . . . Where did Jason sit?"

Most suicides constitute an unfinished gestalt. In these cases, goodbyes are left unsaid, and the question of why a life was taken is left unanswered. Jason's was no exception. The purpose of my work, then, was to encourage students to say goodbye to Jason as a preface to letting go, to experience the collective and individual responses to his death in the here and now, to open avenues for intimate relating, and to explore constructive ways of coping with the situation.

Students acknowledged sadness and anger. My responses were intended to legitimize their feelings of betrayal and resentment. Those who had been the targets for some of his obscure signals were given the opportunity to cry and to speak to Jason's empty seat to tell him of their anger, resentment, betrayal, guilt, grief, confusion, sadness, and emptiness. Also, they were able to tell him what they would have done for him if they had known he was troubled. Others, as well, were given the opportunity to address Jason's empty seat, telling him what they would like him to know. Each was encouraged to end his or her statement with ". . . and goodbye, Jason."

For some, this experience seemed too threatening or overwhelming, so yet another mode of expression was offered: the nonverbal, subvocal goodbye. Students were invited to look at Jason's seat and imagine saying goodbye to him and to imagine telling him what they would like him to know. If time permitted, some classroom groups were given the opportunity to write their goodbyes to Jason. The exercise was varied in the art class to allow for another avenue of expression, that of artistic representation of feelings.

Whenever a student exhibited strong emotion, I invited classmates to respond directly to that student. The students were exceptionally kind, caring, and supportive in their relating with each other. Many pleaded with their peers, "Please don't leave me. I'll help you." Others said, "I'm afraid I'll kill myself."

As the day progressed, I noticed that some students had been present in previous classes, so I invited them to remain in the classroom or gave them an opportunity to go to the library instead. Only one child, Jason's closest school friend and classmate in all of his seven classes, elected to go to the library. He did, however, choose to participate in five classroom sessions and requested two additional sessions, one of which is described in the section below.

At the conclusion of these classroom sessions, I offered the opportunity for additional counseling. As a result, several students sought individual or dyadic (students in pairs) sessions. Because of an expressed continuing need, I formed a small group that met once and another small group that met weekly for the remaining three months of the school year. The individual and dyadic sessions, as well as the small-group sessions, were similar to the work done in the classrooms but with more intense, focused attention.

Small-Group Sessions

Initial Group

The group sessions proved to be by far the most intense of the counseling sessions that I conducted. I employed with these students a projective technique adapted from that suggested by Oaklander (1978). Students were asked to think for one minute about Jason and his death. When time was called, they each were provided with a large sheet of paper and some crayons, and they were asked to express their feelings on paper in colors, lines, shapes, and symbols. I paid attention to how each student approached and continued the task as well as to the picture itself. This proved valuable in helping students to reown previously disowned parts of themselves and to identify some who currently might be considered at risk.

The drawing of one student, Jason's closest school friend, seemed very simple and resembled the letters, "JOI." In speaking as though he were each part of his drawing, he described his own feelings of emptiness, loneliness, and confusion, as well as his own suicidal fears:

> This is the part of my brain that says, "Do it."
> This is the part of me that says, "Don't do it."
> I'm a hook with a sharp end. I can hurt you.
> I'm going round and round.
> I'm left hanging. I'm empty inside.
> I'm straight and bright and happy when I don't think about
> Jason.

A portion of our subsequent time was spent on his belief that he must keep himself busy so that he would not think about Jason. His fear was that if he thought about Jason, he might hurt himself. Consequently, this child was expending a tremendous amount of energy in his attempts *not* to acknowledge his feelings and was experiencing a great deal of anxiety. In the group setting, he was able to express his feelings in a safe environment and to receive caring and support from group members.

Subsequent Group

As a result of several students' expressed continuing need, I formed a long-term group and held weekly sessions for the remaining three months of the school year. This group was composed of six girls, three of whom had been in the initial group and wanted to continue. Because some closure had been reached for the other two members of the initial group, I formed another group, which was to meet for 12 weeks. During the first session, Lynne was observed tearing pieces from her notebook as she spoke about her sadness and confusion. In the Gestalt mode of staying with "what is," Lynne was invited to continue to tear her notebook and to see where that might bring her. When asked to give her hand a voice, she said, "I'm tearing up my notebook in little pieces." When asked if there was anyone in her life she would like to tear up, she replied, "Yes. Jason and me."

I directed her to "tear Jason up, tell him how you feel about his leaving you." After she completed her response to Jason, I invited her to become the pieces and give them a voice, at which time she described being "all torn up, broken, nothing but a pile of pieces . . . I should have done something to stop him. I knew. It's my fault. I hate myself."

Lynne seemed to be making progress on undoing her process of retroflecting (turning back onto herself) her anger and destruction when Anna tearfully interrupted, "This is the second time this has happened to me. My brother committed suicide." At this point, the focus of the group's attention turned to Anna.

During Anna's intensive work on her brother's suicide, many of her comments suggested that she believed her peers were laughing at her, thinking she was dumb. So that she could become aware of what was really out there, I invited her to look at each person and to tell me what she observed. She reported seeing each person looking at her and not laughing, but she was still imagining she was dumb.

I told her to "look at each person." At this point, she perceived much genuine warmth from the group members. In addition to the support being given to Anna, each student was now voluntarily holding hands with one or two other group members. The group ended with each girl looking directly at one or more of the other group members and clearly stating what she needed from that other person. Many said, "Don't be my friend and leave me like Jason did."

Many of our subsequent sessions proved to be as intense. During our third session, four of the six members revealed that they had attempted suicide. Two reported at least two prior attempts. The remaining two reported having seriously considered suicide.

Conclusion

I do not, unfortunately, know the actual impact of my work with these students. I do know, however, that I was deeply moved by their capacity for grieving and for caring for each other. Through our work together, I developed a great deal of caring for these young people, whose behavior had previously not drawn me to them.

Several themes emerged from my encounters with Jason's class-mates. They were experiencing the various grief responses and a pro-nounced fear that others would follow Jason's example. Not only were they greatly afraid of being faced with the loss of yet another friend, but many also feared their own suicidal potential. The incidence of previous suicide attempts was alarming. The death of a friend highlighted several other issues as well: poor self-concept, excessive self-demands, fear of loss, grief over previous losses, self-blame, and self-recrimination.

Although this is not a study of the responses of teachers, administra-tors, and counselors in the school, my observation is that they feel unpre-pared to deal effectively with such a tragedy. Perhaps, consequently, they are prone to avoid the issue. In this case, they seemed shocked and almost paralyzed. Most wanted someone else to handle the situation.

Generally, the students who characteristically exhibited such problem behaviors as skipping school and disrupting class were the most verbal participants. These students seemed "stirred up" by Jason's suicide. They were the risk takers again, but this time in a positive and healing way. They were the catalysts who brought their classmates together in more intimate, supportive, and caring ways.

References

Calhoun, L., Selby, J., & Faulstich, M. (1982). The aftermath of child-hood suicide: Influences on the perception of the parent. *Journal of Community Psychology, 10,* 250–254.

Calhoun, L., Selby, J., & Selby, L. (1982). The psychological aftermath of suicide: An analysis of current evidence. *Clinical Psychology Review, 2,* 409–420.

Hill, W. (1984). Intervention and postvention in schools. In H. Seidak, A. Ford, & N. Rushforth (Eds.), *Suicide in young* (pp. 407–415). Littleton, MA: John Wright.

188   THE CHALLENGE OF COUNSELING IN MIDDLE SCHOOLS

Oaklander, V. (1978). *Windows to our children*. Moab, UT: Real People Press.

Phillips, D. (1985). The Western effect: Suicide and other forms of violence are contagious. *The Sciences, 25*, 32–39.

Zinner, E. (1987). Responding to suicide in schools: A case study in loss intervention and group survivorship. *Journal of Counseling and Development, 65*, 499–501.

Chapter 5

The Challenge of Sexual Maturation in Early Adolescence

In writing for *The School Counselor's* special issue on middle school counseling in 1986, Professor Michael Dougherty asked how can we explain the boy "who enters sixth grade looking like a hobbit and leaves it looking like the 'Incredible Hulk'?" or the girl "who enters sixth grade with dreams of womanhood and leaves it as a woman" (p. 167). Physical maturation, and particularly sexual maturation, has significant effects on self-concept and social relationships during the middle school years. Most young adolescents dwell on how to make themselves more attractive and acceptable to their peers. The media finds simple-minded ways to exploit this preoccupation of young people.

One of the many difficult challenges for middle school counselors is to attend to the concerns of adolescents about physical maturation and sexuality. One frustrated counselor recently commented:

> Just when I think I've done all that I can do in preparing students to understand themselves and their changing bodies, a sixth grade girl comes to my office and implores me to help her get an abortion. I'm glad she trusts me enough to come for help, but I don't have any easy answers. All the kids want easy answers. I wish they could talk with their parents as they talk with me. Why are they so afraid of their parents?

The literature on adolescent sexuality is abundant and covers topics such as friendship, sexual identity, and adolescent pregnancy. Chapter 5 presents information to help middle school counselors understand (a) the impact of physical and sexual maturation on students' lives and (b) the implications for middle school counseling programs. In particular, the chapter deals with the difficult issues of contraception and adolescent pregnancy. As Hershel Thornburg notes in the lead article for this chapter, "the behavior of many middle graders is attributable to their identification with stereotypical images or models." Unfortunately, many role models for these youngsters are musicians and sports figures whose physical attractiveness is appealing but whose sexual behavior is hardly exemplary.

Counselors can help young people to think critically about public heroes and to choose role models carefully. In so doing, counselors can help middle school students to understand and live realistically with the complex process of physical maturation and human sexuality.

The Counselor's Impact on Middle-Grade Students

Hershel D. Thornburg

There are many reasons why middle-grade students have emerged as a vital age group in schooling and personal development. The primary focus of this article is on the dominant characteristics of these students and the knowledge base that school counselors must have to deal effectively with them. The behavioral potential of middle graders is emphasized. Understanding of this potential must be reflected in school policies and programs. As middle graders become more complex, so must the skills of the adults who are responsible for educating them. Today's middle graders are total persons engaging in and responding to a total society. It is essential, therefore, that teachers, counselors, and other school personnel prepare themselves more effectively for interactions with these students.

These youngsters acquire considerable intellectual sophistication as they direct their energies toward peer approval, search for autonomy and identity, expend boundless energy, and explore new frontiers. They are both refreshing and fragile; unique, yet bemusing. Educators, however, often do not carefully consider why this is so. A key element in effective middle-grade education is meeting diverse student needs. It would be a mistake to underestimate the complexity of such a task and an equal mistake to perceive the task as impossible. Counselors and others who influence decisions regarding education must accept the challenge to develop effective school environments for today's middle graders.

Developmental Tasks of Middle-Grade Students

One way to understand 9- to 13-year olds is to consider the major skills they should acquire and the tasks they should accomplish within this age range. Such skills and tasks are usually described within three domains of development: physical, intellectual, and social. To apply these developments, it is useful to describe them as developmental tasks, an idea advanced by Havighurst (1952) more than 30 years ago. Developmental tasks can be defined as the skills, knowledge, functions, or attitudes an individual normally acquires during a specific period or age range. My writings (1970a, 1970b, 1979, 1980) have focused specifically on the developmental tasks of middle-grade students. In this article I expand these tasks to 8:

Physical development
- Becoming aware of increased physical changes

Intellectual development
- Organizing knowledge and concepts into problem-solving strategies
- Making the transition from concrete to abstract symbols (new task)

Social development
- Learning new social and sex roles
- Identifying with stereotypical role models
- Developing friendships
- Gaining a sense of independence
- Developing a sense of responsibility

Becoming Aware of Increased Physical Changes

Primarily because of better nutrition, general health care, and prenatal care, the ages of physical change have moved into the preteen years. Characteristic external changes in girls are a gain in weight, an increase in height, breast development, and an increase in hip size and pigmentation of hair (Frisch & Revelle, 1970). Girls begin this growth spurt at around 10, culminating with menarche, usually by the age of 12. The current mean age of menarche is 12.8 years (Hammer & Owens, 1973). The onset of menarche is usually one year earlier in Black girls, although by the age of 15 virtually all girls have experienced it. Menarche should not be confused with the ability to reproduce. Research indicates that the anovulatory period (when eggs are not being released from the ovary) exists in most females for 12 to 18 months following menarche.

Male height, genital growth, and involuntary erections all begin around age 12. Evidence of enlargement of the testes and penis, pubic hair, and an increase in gondotropin by age 13 nearly complete the growth spurt, which begins tapering off by age 14 (Tanner, 1973). The middle-grade boy is not as developed as his female counterpart, and his maturity is not comparable with hers until he is 16. Although it is not clear just how pubertal changes and psychosocial factors are related (Petersen & Taylor, 1980), Adams (1977) has observed that anxiety often accompanies physical growth, particularly when middle graders compare themselves with classmates or the prevailing stereotypes. It is important for these individuals to understand that variance in growth rate is normal and not symptomatic of problems.

Organizing Knowledge and Concepts into Problem-Solving Strategies

During their elementary school years children gradually learn the concept of absoluteness (conservation) and the ability to classify, order, and group objects (concept learning). Middle graders learn that symbols or strategies can be used in various situations and are not limited to a specific context. This ability to generalize is prerequisite to learning strategies for solving problems (Gagne, 1985; Thornburg, 1984). When middle-grade students learn a concept, they create a basis for learning new information and for retrieving relevant information that has been learned. Learning experiences in school can be structured so that there is an easier transition into more sophisticated uses of thought. By Grades 5 and 6, information is ordered, organized, and structured in the mind. By Grades 7 and 8, deductive reasoning and reflective thinking are operating, thus giving greater flexibility to thought.

Making the Transition from Concrete to Abstract Symbols

The process by which thoughts move from concrete to abstract symbols has not been well defined. The ability to make this transition probably begins when middle graders use concrete props for abstract thinking. With use, concrete reference points gradually disappear as an individual's abstract abilities become better defined. Middle-grade students gradually learn symbols (words) that contain abstract components (functions within the mind) rather than concrete ones. As middle graders increase their capacity for abstract thoughts, they tend to abandon the concrete, less flexible, thought patterns for abstract, more flexible reasoning (Thornburg, 1982). For example, concrete thinkers do not demonstrate the ability to see relationships between ideas, whereas abstract thinkers generally do. Concrete thinkers typically function through the literal interpretation of content or classroom materials. By comparison, abstract thinkers are capable of going beyond literal meaning as they both interpret and apply presented information.

The transition from abstract thinking to concrete thinking is believed to occur between the ages of 10 and 12. It is important to understand that these transitional thinkers have predominantly concrete thoughts. During the middle grades they will not become abstract-dominant thinkers except in a few cases.

One major misunderstanding is the belief that middle-grade students should be more abstract, sophisticated thinkers than they are. Research confirms that middle-grade students with predominantly concrete thoughts are often labeled as having learning problems. This is unfortunate because the problem lies more in adults misunderstanding the capacities of middle graders than it does with the learning deficiencies of the students. The problem that students encounter is tied to the transitional nature of cognitive development. Students "turn off" or slow down because they have difficulty coping with the abstract thinking the curriculum demands, yet they come into the classroom primarily with a concrete rather than abstract language system and knowledge base. The problem is not that students are incapable of handling complex thinking processes and cannot be expected to master new subject matter. Instead, students are capable of coping with new, abstract, instructional materials if they are taught the necessary new language and thought processes (Thornburg, Adey, & Finnis, 1985).

Learning New Social and Sex Roles

Society sets patterns of accepted social behaviors. Many traditional roles have given way to more contemporary, alternative roles, particularly for women. As role models become more diverse, middle graders experience more conflict between the traditional roles they are carefully taught and the contemporary roles they observe. Potential conflict areas include greater assertiveness and individuality, greater educational and occupational opportunities, more individual choices and fewer group choices, more open social norms, and changes in family structures.

Archer (1982) and Waterman (1982) found that despite any role conflict or ambiguity, both sexes use the same means in seeking identity. This finding implies that today's middle graders are aware of a more open role system and exercise the opportunity to explore diverse roles void of traditional stigma. Even so, Archer (1985) found that middle-grade girls received little teaching regarding either family roles or career roles. She suggested that the roles of middle-grade girls could be enhanced through more direct discussion of role opportunities and options.

It is clear that educational environments contribute to socialization. Although it is impossible to assess the strength of the impact of an educational environment, it is likely that school configurations specifically designed for 9- to 13-year olds, such as those in middle or junior high schools, will increase earlier socializations. This may be determined partly by the philosophy of the school. If it operates like a mini-high school, then earlier socialization is likely to occur. In contrast, if the school is geared to the physical, educational, and social needs of its students, then early socialization is less likely to be accentuated and contemporary social and sex roles are more likely to be discussed and realized.

Identifying with Stereotypical Role Models

The behavior of many middle graders is attributable to their identification with stereotypical images or models. Middle graders in transition are changing from children into adolescents. Thus, they tend to identify with images of more mature and independent behavior, particularly when displayed by very popular role models such as musicians, artistic performers, and sports figures.

Middle graders are also concerned about their appearances. Clothing and cosmetics merchandizers propagandize a mature, attractive look for children of this age. Research on physical attractiveness indicates that these individuals are very concerned about their appearance. Boys identify strongly with the masculine (mesomorphic) look, which emphasizes their height, shoulder width, and body proportions. Girls are concerned about the shape of their hips, legs, breasts, and waist (Adams, 1977).

The anxieties of these middle graders are accentuated by society's emphasis on early maturation and physical attractiveness (Shea, Crossman, & Adams, 1978). The closer a middle grader's body fits the social stereotype, the greater is his or her reinforcement and the less the anxiety. As adolescents begin to accept themselves for what they are, anxiety about personal appearance is reduced and elements of personal pride begin to appear. The prevalence of athletic events, musical events, beauty contests, award shows, and media productions stressing beauty, manliness, "sexiness," and "withitness" all facilitate middle graders' identity with stereotypes.

Developing Friendships

The curious and exploratory nature of middle graders results in the development of friendships and the formation of peer groups. In Grades 5 and 6, associations are primarily with the same sex; by Grades 7 and 8, heterosexual associations are more common. Knowing one is acceptable to and can accept others is an important accomplishment in human development. At the same time, friendships produce a sense of belonging and a sense of independence from adult monitoring or restrictions. Peer associations are also instrumental in helping middle graders to develop interpersonal skills. Groups share ideas as well as behaviors, solve problems, have good times, and provide a sounding board for each other. Dougherty (1980) suggested that these processes are facilitated if middle graders are taught basic skills in communications and human relations.

Epstein (1983) has noted that persons who become close friends are those who are in close contact with each other. The way in which the school day and students are scheduled will greatly influence the nature of friendships. Epstein has also focused on the importance of status. Status may be defined in terms of what a middle grader has or does. Middle-grade students are most likely to reach out to those of equal or higher status. In such cases, status is defined by various conditions, such as popularity, athletic ability, age, sex, intelligence, or socioeconomic status. Studies on preteen behaviors, including drug use, sexual activities, delinquency, female pregnancy, and runaways, also provides insight into reciprocated friendship behavior.

Gaining a Sense of Independence

As middle graders increase their range of behaviors, they set in motion greater desires for and fulfillment of autonomy or independence. They begin to view themselves as individuals and develop their own role definition independent of adults. Achieving independence has always been difficult for American adolescents; yet, it is this distinction between not being an adult and being one that causes many to become interested in adultlike behaviors.

In the process of normal development, middle graders begin to exercise the right to make choices. As they make these choices, they often have conflicts with parents and other adults (Emde, 1979); Yarrow, 1979). Such conflicts may be generated by the youngster's need to relinquish childhood ties and find satisfying independent behaviors that are not overpowering. Physical maturation causes an individual to want less parental control. Improved social skills learned through peer interaction foster self-reliance and a degree of independence. Although such behavior may indicate independence, it should not be misconstrued by adults as independent behavior that does not need continued guidance and emotional support. Rather, parents and professionals must recognize the middle grader's growing concern with making choices. Suitable experiences that facilitate gradual independence must be provided (Thornburg, 1980, 1982).

Developing a Sense of Responsibility

During the middle grades the dominant influence on a child's behavior shifts from the parents to his or her peers. When this occurs, the likelihood increases that many parental, teacher, or societal standards will be challenged. Preteens will identify discrepancies between adult behavior and their own. They will ask why smoking, for example, is acceptable for an adult but not for them. They are less likely than previous generations to agree with the explanation that it is all right "because parents are older." They will question why teachers favor some students and pick on others. Their friends will be their greatest sympathizers in the process of trying to unscramble these discrepancies. These are some ways in which moral definitions or redefinitions occur.

Many middle schoolers have been reared in a society characterized by individuality. This often is converted into the belief that "no one has the right to tell me what to do." This conviction is often reinforced by older siblings, peers, parents, teachers, and the media, and it raises the question of whether or not an individual exercises personal rights within the context of personal responsibility. In a real sense, adults and society have done children and youth an injustice by failing to teach them the reciprocal relationship between rights and responsibilities. Such learning can occur if students are given increased opportunities to select their own activities and evaluate the outcomes of their behavior. Typically, in classrooms, students respond to activities set up by teachers and evaluated by teachers. Yet, this type of responsibility is not the same as planning, carrying out, and evaluating one's own behavior. Middle graders need the opportunity to do both.

Implications for School Counselors

The basis of one of these eight developmental tasks is related to physical development, the basis of two of them is related to intellectual development, and the basis of five of them is related to social development. In general, schools tend to ignore physical and social development while stimulating intellectual development. In reality, schools should be better balanced, because the developmental needs of middle graders are much broader than academic pursuits. Counselors are more likely than are classroom teachers to interact with students in nonacademic areas. To be effective, counselors must demonstrate this broad knowledge base that middle graders have a need to fulfill during these important developmental years. Below are five capacities counselors should have, although these capacities are not exclusive.

Counselors must have a general information base with respect to the developmental characteristics of middle graders. It is important to understand the capacities of middle graders; the way they develop, learn and behave. It is equally important to understand both the positive and negative sources affecting their social behavior. In essence, counselors must have a general knowledge so they can relate to middle graders on initial contact and begin identifying ways to help them.

Counselors must understand the specific developmental tasks middle graders feel the need for or are expected to achieve. Although the developmental tasks discussed in this article have inherent logic, it is important to understand why each task is set in motion and what factors affecting an individual student either facilitate or inhibit task fulfillment. The behavior of virtually all middle graders can be classified in one of these eight task categories or as an interaction of two or more tasks. Counselors, therefore, must know the categories as well as common behaviors that fall within the categories.

Counselors must be knowledgeable about the specific individual with whom they are interacting. General and specific knowledge bases will prove ineffective in working with a student unless there is a sufficient knowledge base of the student himself or herself. In addition to the general ways these youngsters are described, there are unique or special circumstances affecting most students who seek out a counselor. School performance, family situations, personal feelings and attitudes, and personal behavior are all factors counselors need to know about if they are to be effective with individual students.

Counselors must understand the perspective of the student. Counseling situations are not intended for the counselor to convince the middle grader or for power struggles in which the counselor wins. Students often seek out counselors because of conflicts they encounter with parents, teachers, or friends. Counselors must listen to determine how to best help an individual. The counselor's general and specific knowledge base provides a conceptual framework in which to interpret individual needs from that individual's perspective. Counselors are more likely to help middle graders understand their behavior, broaden their perspective, or accept themselves if they approach the problem from the students' perspective. As a basis of support for students, counselors should provide the direction needed to ease conflict resolution or encourage personal growth as well as to provide a sense of assurance and acceptance.

Counselors should teach skills that encourage decision making. Although the primary role of counselors is not that of teachers, they can be very effective in helping middle graders work through life situations. Counselors can help students bring personal problems into clearer focus and to explore options available to resolve conflict. Counselors can also help students to evaluate whether their solutions are reasonable and how they will convert various options into personal behavior. Counselors do help students understand choice; however, it is critical that they help students decide what choices mean in relation to self and others. Finally, middle graders, like adults, must have some inner feeling that the decision they have made is appropriate and thus self-fulfilling; that is, did the change in behavior solve the problem? Learning these skills will be useful to students well beyond the immediate situations in which such learning occurs.

Summary

In this article I have focused on the developmental and performance capacities of middle graders, approximately ages 9 through 13. Eight tasks were described as unique to this age range. These tasks should be either fulfilled or initiated in the course of normal development. The ability of middle-grade students to cope with these tasks and realize as many as possible should increase their ability to function effectively during adolescence. Middle graders do need support from counselors and teachers because they may frequently be confronted with a task or behavior that they do not know how to resolve. In educational environments, therefore, it is important for adults to better understand the normal development and potential conflict areas of middle graders to effectively assist them in developing and understanding themselves as individuals—cognitively, affectively, and behaviorally.

References

Adams, G. R. (1977). Physical attractiveness research: Toward a developmental social psychology of beauty. *Human Development, 20,* 217–239.

Archer, S. L. (1982). Ego identity status and expressive writing among high school and college students. *Journal of Youth and Adolescence, 8,* 327–342.

Archer, S. L. (1985). Career and/or the family: The identity process for adolescent girls. *Youth and Society, 16,* 289–314.

Dougherty, A. M. (1980). Designing classroom meetings for the middle school child. *School Counselor, 38,* 127–132.

Emde, R. N. (1979). Levels of meaning for infant emotions: A biosocial view. In A. Collins (Ed.), *Minnesota Symposium on Child Psychiatry* (Vol. 13, pp. 129–161). Minneapolis: University of Minnesota Press.

Epstein, J. L. (1983). Examining theories of adolescent friendships. In J. L. Epstein & N. Karweit (Eds.), *Friends in school* (pp. 39–62). New York: Academic Press.

Frisch, R. E., & Revelle, R. (1970). Height and weight at menarche and a hypothesis of critical body weights and adolescent events. *Science, 169,* 397–398.

Gagne, R. M. (1985). *The conditions of learning.* New York: Holt, Rinehart and Winston.

Hammer, S. L., & Owens, J. W. M. (1973). Adolescence. In D. W. Smith & E. L. Bierman (Eds.), *The biologic ages of man* (pp. 139–153). Philadelphia: Saunders.

Havighurst, R. L. (1952). *Developmental tasks and education.* New York: McKay.

Petersen, A. C., & Taylor, B. (1980). The biological approach to adolescence: Biological change and psychological adaptation. In J. Adelson (Ed.), *Handbook of adolescent psychology* (pp. 315–365). New York: Wiley.

Shea, J. A., Crossman, S. M., & Adams, G. R. (1978). Physical attractiveness and personality development. *Journal of Psychology, 99,* 59–62.

Tanner, J. M. (1973). Growing up. *Scientific American, 229,* 35–42.

Thornburg, H. D. (1970a). Adolescence: A reinterpretation. *Adolescence, 5,* 463–484.

Thornburg, H. D. (1970b). Learning and maturation in middle school age youth. *Clearing House, 45,* 150–155.

Thornburg, H. D. (1979). *The bubblegum years: Sticking with kids from 9 to 13.* Tucson: HELP Books.

Thornburg, H. D. (1980). Early adolescents: Their developmental characteristics. *High School Journal, 63,* 215–221.

Thornburg, H. D. (1982). *Development in adolescence* (2nd ed.). Monterey, CA: Brooks/Cole.

Thornburg, H. D. (1984). *Introduction to educational psychology.* St. Paul: West Publishing.

Thornburg, H. D., Adey, K. L., & Finnis, E. (1985, March). *A comparison of gifted and nongifted early adolescents' movement toward abstract thinking.* Paper presented at the annual meeting of the American Educational Research Association, Chicago.

Waterman, A. S. (1982). Identity formation from adolescence to adulthood: An extension of theory and a review of research. *Developmental Psychology, 18,* 341–358.

Yarrow, L. J. (1979). Emotional development. *American Psychologist, 34,* 951–957.

Contraceptive and Sexuality Knowledge Among Inner-City Middle School Students from Minority Groups

Peggy B. Smith
Mariam R. Chacko
Ana Bermudez

Historically, sex education, as an educational concern, can be traced back to the late 1880s. Recently, the sex education movement has been energized by the increasing amount of scientific literature reflecting the urgent need for education to prevent the morbid consequences of acquired immune deficiency syndrome (AIDS). Recent public opinion polls (Sex and Schools, 1986) have indicated that 86% of Americans favor sex education in the schools. This emphasizes that school counselors should focus on the issues of sexuality and contraceptive knowledge among the younger adolescents as they relate to birth control, health promotion, and disease prevention ("Sex and Schools,"). The need for this preventive information has been highlighted recently by the Surgeon General, who suggested that graphic instruction concerning heterosexual and homosexual relationships should commence at the lowest grade possible.

Although AIDS is currently rare in the adolescent population, problems related to adolescent sexual activity, such as sexually transmitted disease and parenthood, are not. Pregnancy rates among adolescents age 12 to 14 continue to be of concern and the prevalence of sexually transmitted diseases, especially chlamydia, is increasing (Mascola, Albritton, Cates, & Reynolds, 1983; Martien & Emans, 1987). The school counselor often must deal with the negative, cumulative effects of sexual behavior, underscoring the importance of the topic. Although initial investigations (Smith, Flaherty, & Webb, 1984; Smith, Nenney, & McGill, 1986) have defined the knowledge and attitude bases of middle and high schools, similar data on the knowledge base of younger adolescents is scarce. This article describes reported sexuality and contraceptive knowledge of inner-city middle school adolescents from minority groups who participated in a free physical examination program. Differences by sex, race, and ethnicity are mentioned. Trends and potential implementation of the findings for the school counselor are highlighted.

Program Description

The free physical examination program provided by the Teen Health Clinic was extended to inner-city middle school campuses in a large public school district in the southwestern United States. The program had several objectives. First, free examinations would promote student participation in sports and extracurricular activities. Second, this was an opportunity to assess students' concepts of sexuality and contraceptive knowledge to determine the need to provide basic sex education. Finally, this was also an opportunity to establish a rapport with students who might need contraceptive services in the future.

During the school year the Teen Health Clinic staff selected five inner-city middle schools. This was based on a request for service by school personnel. School coaches and teachers recruited students and notified parents of their participation in the program. One school requested physicals but chose not to participate in the assessment of knowledge regarding sexuality and contraception. Thus, four schools participated in the assessment. None of the participating schools had a formalized sex education curriculum under way.

Instrument

The instrument used in this survey consisted of open-ended questions eliciting information about the level of sexuality and contraceptive knowledge, source, type and location of sexual knowledge. Examples of questions administered to middle school adolescents are as follows:

1. What does sex mean to you?
2. List five questions you have about sex.
3. Name as many ways as you know of to keep a girl from getting pregnant.
4. Who told you about the things you listed above?
5. How old were you when you learned these things?
6. Where were you when you learned these things?

The questionnaire was administered anonymously to the adolescents while they were waiting for their physical examinations; students were asked to record only ethnicity, sex, and age. The language used was English, written on a sixth-grade level for maximum student response. The credibility level associated with the knowledge source was also ascertained. Responses to questions 1 and 2 were reviewed by the three authors and assigned to one or more of the categories listed in Tables 1 and 2. Chi-square analyses were performed where indicated.

Results

Respondent Population

In four schools approximately 168 adolescents received questionnaires, and 116 students (70%) completed them. The ages of these respondents ranged from 12 to 15 years, the average age being 13. Of the 116 students, 24% were age 12, 44% were age 13, 29% were age 14, and 3% were age 15. Of this group, 60% were girls and 40% were boys. Twenty-seven percent were Hispanic and 73% were Afro-American. Caucasian students did not attend these schools and, therefore, were not involved in the program. Because completion of the questionnaire was voluntary, we did not obtain demographic information for all of the respondents.

Knowledge of Sexuality

Responses to the question "What does sex mean to you?" are listed in Table 1. Sixty-eight percent (79 of 116 students) responded to this question. It was interesting that almost one-third of the respondents stated they "didn't know" what sex meant to them or that sex "doesn't mean a thing." Of the adolescents who stated a recreational point of view ("fun"), 70% were boys.

Responses to "List five questions you have about sex" are shown in Table 2. Forty percent (47 of 116 students) listed one question. Respondents were primarily girls (79%). More than half asked questions related to moral issues. For example, "Is it right to have sex when you love somebody?" and "When are you old enough to be ready for sex?" Moral issues were followed in frequency by pregnancy, the sexual act, and feelings about sex and pregnancy. Examples of the latter were "How does it feel to be pregnant?" and "Will you regret it afterward?"

Table 1
Responses to "What Does Sex Mean to You"

Category	Total N=79	%	Girls n=49	%	Boys n=30	%
"Don't know" or "Doesn't mean a thing"	25	32	18	37	7	23
Romantic	17	21	11	22	6	20
Feelings	12	15	9	18	3	10
Recreational	10	13	3	6	7	23
Anatomic	10	13	6	12	4	13
Unable to categorize	5	6	4	8	11	3

Contraceptive Knowledge by Sex and Race/Ethnicity

Of the 114 adolescents responding to this question and providing necessary demographic information, 81% could name one or more methods of contraception (see Table 3). Girls were more likely than boys to name at least one method, 89% versus 57% ($x^2 = 15.10$, $df = 1$, $p < .05$). Of those

Table 2
Responses to "List 5 Questions You Have About Sex"

Category	Total N=47	%	Girls n=37	%	Boys n=10	%
Moral	28	60	21	57	7	70
Pregnancy	20	42	18	49	2	20
Sexual act	19	40	13	35	6	60
Feelings	16	34	13	35	3	30
Birth control	7	15	6	16	1	10
STD information	4	8	1	3	3	30
Growth and development	2	4	1	3	1	10
Homosexuality	2	4	2	5	0	0
Abortion	2	4	2	5	0	0
Talking to parents	2	4	2	5	0	0
Masturbation	1	2	1	3	0	0

Table 3
Number and Percentage of Students by Race Who Named Contraceptive Methods

	Methods Named			
Race	None		One or More	Total
Black	19	28%	49 72%	68
Hispanic	3	6%	43 93%	46
Total	22	19%	92 81%	114

Note. $x^2 = 10.03$, $df = 1$, $p < .05$.

naming at least one method, girls were more likely than boys to name two or more methods of birth control (69% versus 33%). Of the types of birth control named, condoms were named the most frequently (44%), followed by abstinence (36%), and the pill (8%). Nonprescription birth control methods were also listed by 32%. Other methods were named much less frequently. The method listed most frequently by girls was abstinence and, by boys, condoms.

Hispanics were more likely than were Afro-Americans to name at least one birth control method ($x^2 = 10.03$, $df = 1$, $p < .05$). Hispanic girls had the highest average number of methods named among those naming a method (2.2), followed by Afro-American girls (1.9), Hispanic boys (1.8), then Afro-American boys (1.3).

Knowledge of birth control methods was also measured by the number of questions pertaining to sex. Those who named no method of birth control were more likely to list no questions on sex (86%), compared to those who named at least one method (47%) ($x^2 = 9.703$, $p < .002$).

Sources of Sexual Information by Sex of Respondent

To the question "Who told you about sex?" 30 of the 46 boys and 55 of the 68 girls responded (114 total who indicated their sex). Among the girls, 53% (30 of 68) listed mother, 1% (1 of 68) listed father, and 6% (4 of 68) listed a friend. Among the boys, 17% (8 of 46) listed a friend, 17% (8 of 46) listed mother, and 11% (5 of 46) listed father. Books, school, television, or a doctor were listed as the other sources of information.

Discussion

Sexual concept questions were answered by 57% of the teenagers. Twenty-one percent of boys compared to 54% of girls listed questions about sex. This finding probably illustrates typical, concrete thinking patterns of this age group and is associated with the physiological and developmental differences by sex (Mussen, Conger, & Kagan, 1979).

Differences by sex were also observed in sources of sexual information. Girls proportionately received more information from their mother or both parents compared to boys. The peer group provided sexual information for 17% of the boys but did not function as the primary source. This trend suggests that, at least for the middle school girls in this study, parents are seen as credible and perhaps even approachable in matters of human sexuality. This finding supports school counselors in encouraging parents to continue to initiate dialogue with their adolescents about human sexuality. The sources of information listed by the boys can be interpreted in the following ways. If a general lack of interest is disregarded, the significant influence of the male peer group in setting the sexual frame of reference in early adolescence needs to be considered. Again, this data should encourage parents to discuss sexual matters earlier in their male child's psychosexual development than has perhaps been done previously (Dryfoos, 1985).

Although the questionnaire language was written on a sixth-grade reading level, refusal to complete the first two questions may reflect cognitive ability levels rather than typical adolescent rebellion and noncooperative behavior. Feelings associated with sex may be hard for middle school children to express conceptually, not because the content is proactive and embarrassing but because it is an abstraction that is difficult for this age group to comprehend. This cognitive deficit for this age group still poses a dilemma for the school counselor on how to present important, albeit abstract, information in a health-promoting and timely manner.

Both girls and boys responding to the questionnaire requested more information on the moral aspects of sexual activity and pregnancy. This emphasizes the need for the school counselor to incorporate values into sex education rather than focusing only on growth, development, and the anatomy of the reproductive system. The peak ages at which sexual concepts are learned are between 12 and 13 years of age (Thornburg, 1981), supporting the viewpoint that sex education should be introduced before junior high school.

The responses to questions about contraceptive knowledge from this younger adolescent group reflect several interesting trends. Not surprisingly, condoms were the most prevalent method named by the boys. Surveys of high-school-age adolescents reflect similar trends (Settlage, Baroff, & Cooper, 1973). The familiarity of adolescent boys with this method and its accessibility without requiring a prescription may contribute to this finding. Despite the fact that the condom was listed most frequently, the boys, especially Afro-Americans, seemed to be the least informed about other pregnancy prevention methods. Strategies for rectifying this situation are needed, because it is usually the boy who initiates the sexual encounters in adolescence and early adulthood (Miller, & Simon, 1980).

The responses on contraceptive knowledge by the Hispanics were somewhat surprising. Hispanics were more likely than Afro-Americans to name at least one method, and Hispanic girls had the highest average number of methods named. Considering that this group has high fertility during adolescence (Smith, & Wait, 1986), one may question the reason for lack of translation of knowledge into effective fertility control. Further investigations concerning motivation or cultural factors may provide insight into the reasons it is so difficult for teenagers to implement knowledge into effective practice.

Limited conclusions can be drawn from the investigation, because selection bias may have affected these results. Although parental consent was not reported as a potential deterrent by students or school personnel, the group participation may be affected by self-selecting factors based on the desire for a free school physical examination. In addition, because of the middle school student's limited educational and cognitive background, only the shortest and simplest questionnaire compatible with the desired information was used. Open-ended questions were also used to avoid prompting. In many instances, more lengthy and relevant questions would have produced much more meaningful information. Based on preliminary pilot testing with similar client groups, lengthy inquiries could not be used. Consideration of the length of questions thus limited the scope of the information gleaned and the depth of interpretations of the raw data gathered. In addition, comparisons of our ascertained knowledge base to a middle school with an established sex education program would provide further information.

Unfortunately, no such program in our general region was available for validation. However, information of the type gathered in our survey is important to counselors in school settings because it provides information on sexual practices of the younger adolescent, who is at high risk for pregnancy. Information on beliefs and knowledge about sexuality among middle school students is rare. Such data reveal the formation of sexual attitudes among inner-city teenagers that have an impact on their future sexual relationships.

References

Dryfoos, J. (1985). *Review of programs and services to foster responsible sexual behavior on the part of adolescent boys.* New York: Carnegie Corporation.

Mascola, L., Albritton, W. L., Cates, W., & Reynolds, G. H. (1983). Gonorrhea in American teenagers. *Pediatric Infectious Disease, 2,* 302–303.

Martien, K., & Emans, S. J. (1987). Treatment of common genital infections in adolescents. *Journal of Adolescent Health Care, 8,* 129–136.

Miller, P. Y., & Simon, W. (1980). The development of sexuality in adolescence. In J. Adelson, (Ed.), *Handbook of Adolescent Psychology* (pp. 32–41). New York: Wiley-Interscience.

Mussen, P. H., Conger, J. J., & Kagan, J. (1979). *Child development and personality* (5th ed.). New York: Harper & Row.

Settlage, D. S. F., Baroff, S., & Cooper, D. (1973). Sexual experience of younger teenage girls seeking contraceptives for the first time. *Family Planning Perspectives, 5,* 223–226.

Sex and schools. (1986). *Time, 128,* 54–63.

Smith, P. B., Flaherty, C., & Webb, L. J. (1984). The long-term effects of human sexuality training programs for public school teachers. *Journal of School Health, 54,* 4.

Smith, P. B., Nenney, S. W., & McGill, L. (1986). Health problems and sexual activity of selected inner city, middle school students. *Journal of School Health, 56,* 263–266.

Smith, P. B., & Wait, R. B. (1986). Adolescent fertility and childbearing trends among Hispanics in Texas. *Texas Medicine, 82,* 29–32.

Thornburg, H. D. (1981). Adolescent sources of information on sex. *Journal of School Health, 51,* 274–277.

The Pregnant Adolescent: Counseling Issues in School Settings

Peggy B. Smith

Prevalence statistics on the younger teen indicate that pregnancy in this age group is increasing. In 1961 there were 7,400 births to teenagers under 15 years, and in spite of the liberalized abortion laws the number of births in 1976 to girls under 15 rose to 12,000 (Baldwin, 1979). Because these adolescents are usually still in school when pregnancy occurs, the counselor in elementary and middle schools may be the first professional to provide guidance to the pregnant adolescent (Edwards, Steinman, Arnold, & Hakanson, 1980). The purpose of this paper is to selectively identify and discuss some of the key counseling issues surrounding adolescent pregnancy in the younger teen. They are not all-inclusive, but represent the kinds of problems the counselor must face in resolving the consequences of sexual activity and pregnancy in this younger age group.

Adolescent Sexuality and Cognitive Development

To effectively counsel the adolescent who suspects that she is pregnant, the counselor first needs a basic understanding of the evolving sexual orientation of this group. Contrary to the perceived sexual sophistication of teens, the younger adolescent may be struggling with her sexuality especially as it relates to cognitive and emotional developments. While this psychosexual development is a normal component of adolescent behavior, it exerts a powerful influence on the way younger teens cope with sexual feelings and experiences. For example, the transition from the concrete to the abstract, as described by Piaget, significantly affects the way the adolescent perceives the consequences of her sexual behavior. Associated with these formal operations is the ability to think hypothetically, anticipate future results, and forecast the logical consequences of one's behavior, all prerequisites to contraceptive use. Until such abstractions are mastered, which in some cases may not occur until the adolescent is 13 years of age (Conger, 1973), the relationship of intercourse, ovulation, and pregnancy as well as the need for contraception may not be clear. Not always comprehending the synchronization of the reproductive system, the younger teen is unable to process, serialize, and synthesize contraceptive knowledge. Moreover, relying on concrete examples with concrete conclusions, the teenager's applications of preventive information are limited. Lipsitz (1980) suggests that most young adolescents are unable to think about contingencies, probabilities, or that "it can happen to me." Such cognitive unresponsiveness reflects emotional and intellectual immaturity. This immaturity, however, will not physiologically compensate by a reduction in the ability to conceive. This group of adolescents, once sexually active, is therefore at a serious risk for unintended pregnancy. The counselor thus must first ascertain if adolescents understand the basics of reproduction and if they can comprehend the relationship of intercourse to pregnancy before initiating the counseling process.

For teens whose pregnancies are not confirmed, the role of the counselor is still crucial. The pregnancy scare, while probably not deterring future coitus, will provide the counselor with an opportunity to initiate dialogue concerning contraceptive counseling and pregnancy prevention.

Pregnancy Outcomes

For those teens who are pregnant any counseling encounter will eventually focus on the reality of the conception and on options for dealing with the situation. One of the first steps in resolving a young teen's pregnancy crisis is to convince her that she is actually pregnant. Confusion about basic reproduction may often retard acceptance of this reality. Some teens go so far as to deny that intercourse ever occurred, or that since they don't look pregnant they are not pregnant. The counselor, if aware of the teen's presumptive signs of pregnancy such as amenorrhea, weight gain, or anorexia may have to explain the relationship of these signs to conception. Swift acknowledgment of the inevitable by the teen is crucial. The first trimester is the optimum time to consider all options and to rally the teen's support systems so that preventive contraceptive counseling or the consideration of the alternatives of abortion, adoption or parenthood can be introduced.

These alternatives, however, are fraught with unique dilemmas for both teen and counselor. Since 1973 abortion has legally been available to the adolescent. Although one-third of all legal pregnancy terminations were performed on this age group, the decision to have a procedure by the teen is often difficult. The significant people in her life, which can include her parents and her sexual partner, may be actively attempting to influence her pregnancy-outcome decision. The counselor should be aware that their persuasiveness may be very subtle or very direct. The counselor may have to assume the role of a mediator or actually protect the adolescent from overly coercive parents. In addition to the external pressures, the abortion alternative is time limited. The decision to abort optimally should be made during the first trimester, a time when the younger teen is usually the most confused. The moral aspect of the decision is also important. The counselor should be aware that dialogue with the teen's spiritual leaders as well as her family may be appropriate.

Adoption, seen as a positive solution by some, has become the teen's least chosen alternative. Adolescents potentially interested in this option often succumb to attractions of the single parenthood model set by friends who indicate that they would rather abort than place a child for adoption. The fact that nine out of ten teens nationally will keep their babies and that adoption records are no longer permanently closed diminish this alternative's appeal. Counselors sensitive to the pregnant teen's vulnerability to such influence can perhaps enhance the integrity of the adoption option by initiating intense and continual support early in pregnancy. Aggressive counseling possibly can sustain the original adoption decision to the logical conclusion of termination of parental rights.

Possibly by default, parenthood is the most frequently chosen pregnancy resolution among adolescents. The emotional and educational costs are often great, with only a few adolescents surviving the pressures to enter the middle class mainstream. Key components in this struggle are the ways the family and the father of the baby become involved in the pregnancy process.

The Family in the Counseling Process

Acknowledgement of the family's role in the resolution of the problems associated with younger teen pregnancy is philosophically and pragmatically important. Philosophically, the family as the basic societal unit is given responsibility for the care and nurturance of any young, albeit illegitimate, under its auspices. Its basic resources such as food, shelter, and clothing are usually extended to the single adolescent and her child. Operationally the family also provides a variety of important sexual guidelines that may subtly enhance the possibility that conception will occur. Included in these guidelines are factors such as formal and informal codes of conduct that legislate acceptable social-sexual behavior within the family. Such codes may specify, by design or default, conveyed sexual instructions, dating patterns, curfews, and even sexual practices. The counselor should be aware that some time during the pregnancy such sexual rules need to be reexamined and renegotiated. Otherwise, sexual situations that precipitated the first conception might be maintained, resulting in a second pregnancy. The degree of parental supervision also may enhance the possibility of an unintended pregnancy, especially in light of the fact that the home of the girl or boy is the most frequently cited setting for coitus after school.

As the family is a key factor in the younger teen's coping with pregnancy, the counselor may help to identify concrete ways the family can support the adolescent in this period of crisis. Prior to the actual birth, the family should be encouraged to enroll the adolescent in a prenatal clinic. Entrance into a health care system is accompanied by multiple clerical and administrative problems often exceeding the frustration threshold of the teen. In many cases parental participation is mandatory. Without proof of parental income and a payment deposit, clinic participation is limited. Again, counselors should attempt to involve parents early in the process so that such financial arrangements can be made and medical care provided in the first trimester.

Once the baby is born the family is a key factor in day-care provision. Many adolescents, without the family's help, are unable to secure adequate childcare facilities. Such support services are crucial in the early months of the infant's life; immediate day-care will in many cases allow adolescents to complete an academic year and minimize the risk of permanent school drop out. The counselor should be aware that such services from family members are not without trade-off. Some families, in an effort to help the teen, take all the parental prerogatives. Daily routine and health care needs are determined, in many cases, not by the child's biological mother but by the teen's parents. In extreme cases the child may be temporarily given to other family members in a functional foster care situation. Furstenberg (1978) suggests that such support systems may ultimately trap the young mother in her family unit, limiting her future marital prospects and her ultimate independence.

Involving the Father of the Baby

While the involvement of the family in the counseling process has included both the nuclear and extended definitions, some controversy exists as to whether the putative father should be automatically included in the family counseling. Such involvement appears to subtly influence the couple ultimately to marry. Klerman (1975) found that when teen fathers were substantively involved with the girl during the pregnancy, the pregnancy culminated with a marriage. Studies have also shown (Furstenberg, 1978) that, in general, the problem of adolescent pregnancy is compounded by the contracting of a marriage. The marital bond may subtly discourage academic and vocational effort. Responsibilities of home and husband may preclude educational continuance even when desired. Marriage may also provide an acceptable escape from the unpleasant school or family situation. Research (Smith, Mumford, Goldfarb, & Kaufman, 1975) indicates that the single girl's greater response to education in comparison to her married peer may reflect the lack of negative influences, or a greater motivation and awareness because of her singular need for more education or vocational training. The security of marriage does not seem to promote return to school and may even inspire a decision to stay home at least in the immediate follow-up period studied. In a family planning clinic sample, 70% (51) of the married teenage girls were out of school and remaining at home. The most plausible explanation for the difference is probably the number of living children. Of the married group, 85% (62) had at least one living offspring, while only 33% (138) of the singles had at least one child (Smith, Nenney, Mumford, Kaufman, & Leader, 1979).

The risk of repeat pregnancy is increased among married teens by their mediocre use of family planning services. Counselors should note that married teens, when compared to single teenagers, do not follow up as well on returns for contraceptive refills. In the same survey all patients accepting contraceptive methods are asked to return; yet of 293 scheduled returns, 96% (282) of the patients were single and only 4% (11) were married. The expected ratio of marrieds should have been approximately 15% (41). The lower rate of follow-up compliance for marrieds may be the result of several factors. Lack of child-care alternatives, lack of transportation, desire for additional children, or possibly a general lack of motivation may all minimize the possibility that the married teenager will return for a pill refill.

Recommendations

The convergence of cognitive, physical, and social growth, important developments for this age group, may enhance the girl's susceptibility for unprotected coitus. While counselors who work with adolescents cannot and probably should not try to alter the progression of these milestones, a variety of counseling strategies applicable to both the nonpregnant as well as the pregnant younger teen can possibly mitigate the risks associated with sexual development and maturation during early adolescence.

The first strategy is one of prophylactic education. School policy regarding the inclusion of materials on human sexuality as part of the curriculum should be reexamined. If teens are becoming pregnant in the middle school, then preventive information presented both in group and individual settings should be offered no later than the eighth grade. Education on sexuality "before the fact" can possibly deter initiation of coitus or, if intercourse does occur, encourage use of effective contraception. Such a suggestion is not without problems. Differential cognitive, cultural, and sexual patterns associated with various groups should be considered in curriculum content and emphasis. The politics of sex education in the school is also well known. Infusion or inclusion of such curricula, especially for the very young student, can be controversial. The counseling staff, however, may be able to provide valuable advocacy for provision of such information. Of school personnel, the counselor may be most aware of the sexual conflicts associated with this age group.

A second strategy should focus on selective involvement of the girl's sexual partner. One may want to stress male reproductive health education before conception instead of after. Family planning clinics should foster creative programs to reach this clientele. When pregnancy occurs the teen father should be involved in a counseling process, but his emotional needs possibly should be met in a setting or session independent of the pregnant adolescent and her parents. In the past when the teen boy and girl were perceived as a couple, marriage was expected. Such a psychological pressure when resulting in marriage terminates all the support benefits that may flow from the girl's family membership (Furstenberg, 1978). Subsequent separation or divorce of the girl from the father of the baby usually will not reestablish or reconnect familial ties with her family or origin.

A third strategy should involve the community and develop awareness of the magnitude of the problem. Individual community members or institutional representatives can help develop pregnancy prevention strategies. Community and professional leaders should be carefully educated to avoid using vague but emotionally appealing program descriptions popularized by some in hopes of obtaining support. One should not suggest that such innovations will completely eliminate teen sexuality, venereal disease, and pregnancy. Incorrect emphasis may distort the plight of the younger teenager when remedial or preventive options are considered by community groups. This is especially true when preventive alternatives are considered. Nonpregnant teens, not to mention the male sexual partners, may not receive accurate information or services that could prevent unintended pregnancy.

Once aware of the problem the community can identify alternatives compatible with local mores and standards. These can run the gamut of alternatives, from parenting classes to comprehensive family-planning services. When generated from local concerned citizens, these measures will pay dividends. Since their impetus is community leadership, they enhance acceptability, and maximize the possibility of continuation. Local involvement may also provide trained professionals who spontaneously involve themselves in the community effort at little or no cost. Conversely, if activities are orchestrated in a professional way, previously pregnant teens may voluntarily come forward and serve as peer counselors to warn their nonpregnant contemporaries of the consequences of unintended pregnancy.

Unfortunately a group of these younger teens, as the statistics reflect, will conceive; pregnancy prevention strategies become no longer appropriate and another strategy of maximizing prenatal outcome becomes the approach. Regardless of whether medical risks are associated with age instead of timely prenatal care, early entrance and continued maintenance in a health care system could address both factors. Several components exist in the maximization strategy. The first step in such a program would be to reach adolescents in the first trimester who are possibly pregnant. Information on presumptive behavior, in addition to physical signs, could provide counselors a potent diagnostic tool to work with teens. Such a tool would allow more options for young teens; however, operationalizing such a suggestion may require a redefinition to carefully balance the health benefits against the possible intrusion in the minor's right of privacy.

References

Baldwin, W. (October, 1979). *Adolescent pregnancy: A national problem.* Paper presented at the Johns Hopkins conference on adolescent pregnancy, Baltimore.

Conger, J. (1973). *Adolescence and youth.* New York: Harper & Row.

Edwards, L. E., Steinman, M. E., Arnold, K. A., & Hakanson, E. Y. (1980). Adolescent pregnancy prevention services in high school clinics. *Family Planning Perspectives, 12,* 6–14.

Furstenberg, F. F., Jr. (August, 1978). *Burdens and benefits: The impact of early child-bearing on the family.* Paper commissioned by the Family Impact Seminar for its study "Teenage pregnancy and family impact: New perspectives on policy," Washington, DC.

Klerman, L. V. (1975). Adolescent pregnancy: The need for new policies and new programs. *Journal of School Health, 45,* 263–267.

Lipsitz, J. L. (1980). Adolescent psycho-sexual development. In P. B. Smith, & D. M. Mumford (Eds.), *Adolescent pregnancy perspectives for the health professional.* Boston: G. K. Hall.

Smith, P. B., Nenney, S. W., Mumford, D. M., Kaufman, R. H., & Leader, A. J. (1979). *Selected family planning and general health profiles in a teen health clinic.* Unpublished manuscript. (Available from Peggy B. Smith, OB/GYN Department, Baylor College of Medicine, Houston, TX 77030.

Smith, P. B., Mumford, D. M., Goldfarb, J. L., & Kaufman, R. (1975). Selected aspects of adolescent postpartum behavior. *Journal of Reproductive Medicine, 14,* 159–165.

Pregnancy Counseling for Teenagers

John Eddy
Ernest H. McCray
David Stilson
Nancy DeNardo

Foster and Miller (1980) stated, "few authors have discussed the role of counselor support during adolescent pregnancy…" (p. 236). Fyfe (1980) wrote, "Counselors in both school and agency settings are repeatedly involved in counseling situations that include sex-related problems" (p. 147). This article provides an approach to counseling the pregnant adolescent using a step-by-step method. This system uses a structured interview providing both the client and the school counselor with a positive experience.

The Problem

According to the 1979 report of the Office of Adolescent Pregnancy in Washington, D.C., over one million girls become pregnant annually. Of this number, approximately 600,000 have their babies, 300,000 choose abortions, and 100,000 have miscarriages or give up their infants for adoption (Poveromo, 1981).

Increases in sexual activity among teenage girls in America and exaggerated fears over usage of birth control pills have given rise to teenage pregnancies (Long, 1980). Moreover, results of a survey of 1,717 girls, 15–19 years old, showed an increase in sexual activity from 30% in 1971 to 49.9% in 1979. Actual pregnancies from that same group increased from 28.1% in 1971 to 32.5% in 1979. In addition, 55.5% of the 17-year-old males, 66% of the 18-year-old males, and 77.5% of the 19-year-old males had engaged in sexual intercourse (Kantner & Zelnick, 1979).

As Quinby (1980) pointed out, 80% of all first teenage pregnancies are conceived out of wedlock. Even a larger increase in teenage pregnancies would occur if family planning programs were not available.

Another factor influencing the sexual activity of youth is the change in family structure in America (Lifton, Tavantzis, & Mooney, 1979).

Projections suggest that soon 45% of all children in the United States will be in single-parent families. The rapid geographic mobility of our society removes people from familiar settings and community supports. Today children and adults struggle as they seek support and help in facing life crisis. (p. 161)

Although uncommon in the past, broken households are estimated to be one out of seven children raised by a single parent and in cities up to one in four (Toffler & Toffler, 1981).

Surveys indicate that religious groups (Hopkins, 1980) and parents (Foster & Miller, 1980) are not providing youth with adequate information on teenage pregnancy. Attitudes may be changing, however, among many ministers. "Today an effective and competent minister must be at least conversant in psychotherapy, theological study, and counseling" (Faulkner, 1982, p. 22).

In addition to the lack of information provided to the teenager, "family life education, sex education, and contraceptive techniques are not permitted to be taught in some schools" (Foster & Miller, 1980, p. 236). The school counselor needs a systematic approach to deal with youths who are facing the difficulties of pregnancy. There are many variables involved in counseling any client, but the following suggestions might be helpful.

Pregnancy Counseling for the Individual

Level 1: Introduction and Rapport Development

The objective in level 1 is that the counselor, through provision of a caring atmosphere for the client's present needs, will enable the client to more easily express her problem.

CLIENT: Mrs. Brown, I've got to talk to you.

COUNSELOR: Okay, Jackie, I appreciate your taking time to come in. I sense a definite urgency in your voice.

The counselor should speak slowly if he or she notices that the client is particularly nervous and upset. Speaking slowly tends to slow down thought processes so that the client can think more clearly. The counselor should also be aware of his or her own body language, eye contact, etc., and give full attention to the client, including her physical comfort. By attending to such details, a counselor is building a relationship and establishing a level of comfort from the start.

Level 2: Legality and Confidentiality

Level 2's objective is that the counselor, through inspection of existing laws and policies, will provide the client with guidelines as to the possible limitations of confidentiality in this case.

CLIENT: I've got something very scary I need to tell someone, but I don't want my parents to know.

COUNSELOR THINKS: (This could be a serious problem dealing with pregnancy or suicide. What are my legal rights and responsibilities in dealing with this case: Whom do I have to report?)

COUNSELOR RESPONDS: Jackie, I see something is really bothering you, and I appreciate the trust and honesty you have shown in coming to me with your problem. Now, I want to be completely honest with you, I want to help you, but if this involves others...? (Time is needed here to think about it.) Do I have your permission to see your parents, if absolutely necessary?

Level 3: Affective Empathy

The objective in level 3 is that the counselor, through reflection of the client's affect, will provide the client with an empathic support system.

CLIENT: Well, uh (sobbing now), I don't know who to turn to. (silence) I'm so nervous and afraid.

COUNSELOR THINKS: (This could be a good time to respond to her affect and supply empathic support.)

COUNSELOR RESPONDS: I want to be your friend and try to help. Let's work together on this. Okay?

Level 4: Directive Versus Nondirective Approach

Level 4's objective is that the counselor will decide how directive or nondirective to become with this client, by observing the client's body language, voice level, and other factors.

CLIENT: Well, I'm pregnant! I feel so confused! My parents will just die! Please, tell me what to do!

COUNSELOR THINKS: (This could require more affective responses that will influence my decision as to how directive or nondirective to be. Also, will my personal values become a problem in providing the student with all possible options? If I cannot consider abortion as an option, for example, perhaps the client needs to be referred to someone else.)

COUNSELOR RESPONDS: You feel confused over what has happened, Jackie, and you'd like some advice. I understand what you must be going through now, and we can explore some alternatives together. (At this point, it could be important to determine how she has verified the pregnancy. Many young girls panic at a missed period and assume pregnancy.)

Level 5: Background Information

The objective in level 5 is that the counselor, through personalizing the choices with the client, will enable the client to deal with the problem from her present level of possibility. At this point, the counselor could ask the client how she sees the problem and what alternatives seem realistic to her. Or the counselor can begin gathering background data that will be important later.

Level 6: Alternatives

Level 6's objective is that the counselor, through provision of a wide variety of alternatives, will thoroughly explore with the client as many solutions as possible. The counselor would then obtain or suggest certain relevant factors, such as those listed in Table 1.

Table 1
Relevant Factors and Key Thoughts

Factors	Key Thoughts
A. Personal Choice	1. Does she *want* the baby?
	2. Does her partner want the child?
B. Religious Influence	1. What is the significance of what she has done versus the church's doctrine?
	2. Does her church allow abortion?
	3. If the client has no religious affiliation, does she want referral to a clergyperson to discuss her alternatives?
C. Present Family	1. Can she stay at home during pregnancy?
	2. Does she have other relatives to whom she can turn?
	3. Would she rather live elsewhere during this time?
	4. Would the partner or partner's family be of assistance?
D. Future Family	1. Is marriage a possibility?
	2. Where would they live?
E. Financial Possibility	1. Do they have the money to have the baby?
	2. Could they support the baby?
F. Referral Sources	1. Could such agencies as Planned Parenthood or a home for unwed mothers be of assistance?
	2. Is adoption possible?
	3. Is other individual counseling necessary? If so, where?
G. Career Options	1. What about short-range goals, such as completion of the school year and obtaining a diploma?
	2. What future limitations are placed on long-range goals—i.e., possible loss of future educational or career alternatives?
H. Informational Services	
1. Medical Services	1. What hospitals, clinics, and specialized physicians are available in the area?
2. Parenting Skills	2. What childbirth, civic, and single-parent instructional groups are locally available? Could role-playing parenting skills be helpful?
3. Child Care Services	3. Is a directory of child care services available in the community?
I. Follow-up	1. The counselor and client together can look into these and other resources for help.
	2. Further counseling sessions may be scheduled to encourage and guide the client.

A Model for Counselors

The school counselor is often in a strategic position to offer adolescents guidance and counseling in coping with pregnancy. Providing teenagers with competent, concise, and candid information is a valuable service by the school counselor for both adolescents and their parents or guardians. In this article, ideas were outlined to help the school counselor deal with the pregnant adolescent client. Therefore, the school counselor who uses this model has a step-by-step procedure that school counselors have been asking for in their counseling educational training (Eddy, 1981).

References

Eddy, J. (1981). *Survey of school counselors on their training needs.* Unpublished study, North Texas State University, Denton.

Faulkner, B. (1982). A theology of personal growth for support groups. *The Quarterly Review: A Survey of Southern Baptist Progress, 42,* 20–25.

Foster, C. D., & Miller, G. M. (1980). Adolescent pregnancy: A challenge for counselors. *The Personnel and Guidance Journal, 59,* 236–240.

Fyfe, B. (1980). Counseling and human sexuality: A training model. *The Personnel and Guidance Journal, 59,* 147–150.

Hopkins, J. (1980). Teen survey has surprise. *The United Methodist Reporter, 8*(46), 3.

Kantner, J. & Zelnick, M. (1979). *Teenage pregnancies.* Unpublished study, Johns Hopkins University, Baltimore.

Lifton, W. M., Tavantzis, T. N., & Mooney, W. T. (1979). The disappearing family: The role of counselors in creating surrogate families. *The Personnel and Guidance Journal, 58,* 161–165.

Long, M. (October 19, 1980). The crisis in our schools. *Family Weekly,* 4–6.

Poveromo, T. (1981). I never thought it could happen to me: The stories behind the teenage pregnancy statistics. *Sourcebook,* 22–25.

Quinby, B. (December 7, 1980). Teenage mothers: When children become parents. *Family Weekly,* 20.

Toffler, A., & Toffler, H. (March 22, 1981). The changing American family: Welcome to the "Electronic Cottage." *Family Weekly,* 10–13.

Chapter 6

The Challenge of Academic Achievement in Early Adolescence

Americans are becoming increasingly aware of the need for schools to promote academic excellence. Individuals in the business community and elsewhere complain that young people do not have the basic academic skills necessary for economic success in a competitive world. Governmental and private commissions have noted the high dropout rate in America's schools and the generally poor record of public schools in promoting excellence. Politicians and other public figures point to Japan and some European countries as having a monopoly on excellence in education. Although many of these claims are exaggerated, educators in the United States must account for the failure of schools to motivate young people to stay in school and to strive for high levels of academic achievement.

The main issue raised in Chapter 6 is how middle school counselors can contribute to schools' efforts at improving academic achievement among young teenagers. These days middle schoolers often have considerable freedom. Many are latchkey children who may choose what to do when they arrive home from a day at school. More often than not they choose leisure, neglecting their academic responsibilities. This chapter presents classroom guidance strategies for middle school counselors to use in helping youngsters develop a reasonable "work ethic." These classroom programs cover such topics as the following:

- Helping students feel comfortable in the classroom
- Teaching students to listen carefully to classroom instruction
- Suggesting appropriate ways for students to cooperate with teachers
- Identifying and practicing effective time management skills
- Developing effective ways to study academic material
- Helping students view themselves as capable learners
- Affording students opportunities to consider the benefits of hard work
- Identifying public figures who model beneficial work habits

Middle school counselors can play an important role in helping young people see themselves as capable students who have the potential to realize academic success. As Thelma Blumberg's article in Chapter 6 suggests, counselors often take the lead in "transforming low achieving and disruptive adolescents into model students" and thus play a significant part in the academic mission of middle schools.

Succeeding in Middle School: A Multimodal Approach

Edwin R. Gerler, Jr.
Nancy Shannon Drew
Phyllis Mohr

Does counseling help students learn the basic school subjects? Can counseling improve students' attitude toward school and classroom behavior? Research on school counseling programs over the last two decades has shown that counselors can affect the learning climate in schools through behavior modification (Thomas, 1974), affective education (Wirth, 1977), interpersonal communication training (Asbury, 1984), and imagery/relaxation training methods (Danielson, 1984; Omizo, 1981). Gerler's (1985) review of elementary school counseling research from 1974-1984 provided conclusive evidence that counselors can make a difference in children's grades, classroom behavior, attitude toward school, and self-esteem. Similarly, St. Clair's (1989) review of middle school counseling research showed that counselors can improve classroom behavior, reduce students' anxiety, and improve self-concept. St. Clair noted, however, that published studies of middle school counseling constitute only a small part of counseling literature. Much remains to be done in terms of examining the effects of counseling programs on the learning climate in middle schools.

The Multimodal Model and Learning

Lazarus (1985) has argued persuasively that cognition and learning are parts of a psychological whole in human functioning. He delineates the domains in human psychological makeup with the convenient acronym, "BASIC I.D," which stands for Behavior, Affect, Sensation, Imagery, Cognition, Interpersonal Relations, and Diet/Physiology. Lazarus and proponents of the multimodal counseling model believe that cognition and learning are affected by what happens in the other domains so that

students who have behavior problems, emotional disturbances, interpersonal difficulties, or any number of other psychological difficulties
are likely to experience learning problems. Further, proponents (Gerler,
1982, 1987; Keat, 1979) of this viewpoint have suggested that to promote cognitive development and success in learning, teachers and counselors should collaborate to provide students with classroom experiences
that stimulate growth in a variety of domains.

Research and various case studies have shown the multimodal
approach to influence variables important to children's learning. Case
studies, for example, have demonstrated the positive effects of multimodal programs on children's interpersonal skills and emotional growth
(Keat, 1985), on children's self-concept (Durbin, 1982), and on children's school work (Starr & Raykovitz, 1982). Another case study (Keat,
Metzgar, Raykovitz, & McDonald, 1985) showed that a multimodal
counseling group improved the school attendance of five third-grade
boys. Studies of multimodal approaches to group guidance and
counseling in elementary schools have yielded positive results in such
areas as school attendance (Gerler, 1980), classroom behavior
(Anderson, Kinney, & Gerler, 1984), achievement in mathematics and
language arts (Gerler, Kinney, & Anderson, 1985), and reducing
procrastination (Morse, 1987).

Although various studies have tested multimodal approaches with
children in elementary school settings, research on the effects of multimodal programs with young adolescents in middle schools has been
limited. The purpose of this study was to examine the effects of the
multimodal program, "Succeeding in School," with potential dropouts in
grades 6-8. Previous research on "Succeeding in School" (Gerler &
Anderson, 1986) with 900 fourth and fifth graders across North Carolina
showed the program to have positive effects on attitude toward school,
classroom behavior, and language arts grades.

Method

Participants

This study involved 98 students in grades 6-8 from five middle schools
in an urban North Carolina school district. The participants were from
varying economic, social, and cultural environments and all were
identified as potential dropouts by the school system. Counselors at the

five middle schools volunteered to conduct classroom guidance sessions for the study.

Procedure

The middle school counselors who volunteered to participate received packets of study materials that included (a) directions for implementing the study, (b) a ten-session, classroom guidance unit entitled "Succeeding in School," (c) instruments to measure the effects of the unit and directions for scoring the instruments, and (d) forms for recording the data collected. The counselors also participated in an orientation session prior to implementing the program. Parent permission was required of all students involved in the program. (A 20-page packet of materials for conducting this study is available for elementary and middle school counselors who are interested in implementing and evaluating this program in their own schools. Persons interested in obtaining a copy of this packet should write to: Edwin R. Gerler, Jr., Department of Counselor Education, North Carolina State University, Raleigh, North Carolina 27695-7801.)

Counselors' directions for implementing the study. Counselors received careful written instructions for implementing the classroom guidance study in their schools. The instructions identified the purpose of the study and outlined specific steps for counselors to follow in carrying out the study. These steps directed counselors (a) to explain to school principals the purpose of the study and to assure principals that all data collected would be kept confidential and that no student would be identified individually to anyone outside the school, (b) to discuss the nature of the study with teachers whose pupils were participating and then to assign students randomly to treatment and control groups, (c) to conduct the classroom guidance unit "Succeeding in School" once per week for ten weeks with the treatment group participants [control group members received the same unit after the study was completed], (d) to administer an *Attitude toward School* (Miller, 1973) instrument to each student during the week before and the week after the classroom guidance unit was presented, and (e) to have teachers complete an *Elementary Guidance Behavior Rating Scale* (Anderson, Kinney, & Gerler, 1984; Gerler, Kinney, & Anderson, 1985) for each student and record students' conduct and subject matter grades immediately before and after the guidance unit.

The classroom guidance unit. The classroom guidance unit, "Succeeding in School," which counselors conducted with the treatment group children involved the following ten 50-minute sessions (Gerler, 1987):

SESSION 1: SUCCESSFUL PEOPLE

A. Discuss reasons for the unit and ground rules for discussion.
B. Place the names of several successful people on the chalkboard (Sally Ride, astronaut; Michael Jackson, singer; Jesse Jackson, politician) and have the students discuss what these successful persons have in common. Focus the discussion on success and what it takes to be successful.
C. Have students add names to the list of successful people and continue to discuss ingredients of success.
D. Have students discuss times they have worked hard at school and experienced success.
E. Ask students to consider what successes they expect to experience in the future.

SESSION 2: BEING COMFORTABLE IN SCHOOL

A. Review highlights of the first session.
B. Introduce the topic of relaxation. Discuss why and how different people relax.
C. Discuss several methods of relaxation and have the students practice some of these methods.
D. Discuss times that the students felt relaxed at school. (Differentiate between feeling relaxed and being excited or having fun.)

SESSION 3: BEING RESPONSIBLE IN SCHOOL

A. Review the session on relaxation.
B. Discuss how the students can sometimes learn the meaning of responsibility from reading stories about responsible people.
C. Suggest some stories or books the students might read.
D. Define responsibility in terms of self and others.
E. Discuss times that the students behaved responsibly at school.

SESSION 4: LISTENING IN SCHOOL

A. Review the meaning of responsibility and ask students to share examples of their responsible behavior since the previous session.

B. Ask students to close their eyes and listen to the sounds in the room.
C. Have students discuss the experience and the importance of careful listening at school and elsewhere.
D. Define a good listener as someone who pays attention, knows what is said, and does not interrupt or distract.
E. Conduct some listening roleplay experiences.
F. Discuss times that students listened in school with good results.

SESSION 5: ASKING FOR HELP IN SCHOOL

A. Review listening skills.
B. Conduct the activities to help students practice the skills of listening and asking questions.
C. Discuss times that the students have had to ask questions in school and have received help.

SESSION 6: HOW TO IMPROVE AT SCHOOL

A. Review the skills of listening and asking questions.
B. Have students discuss how these skills might help to improve their school work.
C. Ask students to identify a subject they would like to improve in and to discuss how they might work toward the improvement.
D. Have individuals identify improvements they have already made in their school work.

SESSION 7: COOPERATING WITH PEERS AT SCHOOL

A. Review student reactions to the previous session.
B. Write the word "cooperation" on the chalkboard. Have students suggest words using each letter of "cooperation" to reflect the spirit of cooperation (e.g., caring, others, etc.).
C. Conduct roleplay activities that help students practice cooperation.
D. Discuss times that students have cooperated with each other at school.

SESSION 8: COOPERATING WITH TEACHERS

A. Review the session on cooperating with peers.
B. Have students complete the following sentences: "If I were teacher for a day, I'd..." "I wish my teachers would..." "I would like to talk with a teacher about..."

C. Conduct a "Dear Abby" activity. Hand out blank cards and have students finish the statement: "I would like to get along better with my teacher, but my problem is…"
D. Have students discuss ways they have cooperated with their teachers.

SESSION 9: THE BRIGHT SIDE OF SCHOOL

A. Review the discussion about cooperating with teachers.
B. Have students identify some things about school they dislike and then consider what might be positive about those things.
C. Have students describe some positive happenings at school.

SESSION 10: THE BRIGHT SIDE OF ME

A. Review the highlights of the previous nine sessions.
B. Have students describe what they learned about themselves and their strengths during the sessions.
C. Give students the opportunity to receive positive feedback from one another.

Instrumentation and data collection. Counselors used the following five measures to assess students' progress resulting from participation in the classroom guidance unit:

1. *Ratings of student behavior.* Teachers completed the *Elementary Guidance Behavior Rating Scale (EGBRS)* for each pupil in the treatment and control groups during the week before and the week after counselors led the classroom guidance unit. The *EGBRS*, which was designed by a team of counselors, counselor educators, and education consultants and used in two previous elementary school guidance studies (Anderson, Kinney, & Gerler, 1984; Gerler, Kinney, & Anderson, 1985), consists of 20 items in which teachers rate negative classroom behaviors on a Likert scale ranging from "behavior observed constantly"=5 to "behavior observed never"=1. The highest total score possible on the scale is 100 and the lowest possible is 20, with lower scores indicating preferred classroom behavior. Items from the *EGBRS* include "How often does the student interfere with the activities of others, fail to give attention to the task at hand, or use available time unwisely?" No data on reliability or validity are available on this instrument.

2. *Students' conduct ratings.* Teachers who volunteered their students to participate in the study recorded classroom conduct ratings for treatment and control group members before and after the classroom

guidance unit. Conduct ratings were based on a 10-point scale with 1 being the highest rating and 10 the lowest.

3. *Students' attitude toward school.* Participants in the treatment and control groups completed a modified version of the *Attitude toward School* instrument (Miller, 1973) during the week before and the week after the guidance unit. This instrument has been used by the Minnesota Department of Education to assess the effects of psychological education activities. The instrument consists of 25 multiple-choice sentence completion items which assess students' attitudes toward such matters as teaching, subject matter, and homework. Each item offers four choices to students with the first choice indicating the most negative attitude toward school through the fourth choice indicating the most positive attitude. The highest total score possible on the scale is 100 and the lowest possible is 25, with higher scores indicating more positive attitudes toward school. No data on reliability or validity are available on this instrument.

4. *Students' grades.* Teachers who volunteered their students to participate in the study recorded grades for treatment and control group members before and after the classroom guidance unit. The grades were based on a 12-point scale with A (or A+) = 12 through F = 1. The pretreatment grades were regular classroom grades averaged from the grading period immediately prior to the guidance unit. The post-treatment grades were regular classroom grades averaged from the grading period during which the guidance unit was implemented.

Results

No significant changes were observed on any of the dependent measures with the exception of the *Attitude toward School* instrument. Table 1 shows the pre/post means and standard deviations of participants' scores on the *Attitude toward School* instrument. All groups showed improved scores on the instrument, with the treatment group showing a mean increase of 2.19 and the control a mean increase of 1.21. The treatment groups' improvement was significant, $t = 1.981$, $p < .05$. This improvement seems to have been largely accounted for by the increased scores among females in the treatment group. Females in the treatment group showed a mean increase on the instrument of 3.36, a significant gain, $t = 2.758$, $p < .01$. Male participants in the treatment group showed a gain of only 1.56 on the measure.

Table 1
Means and Standard Deviations on Pre/Post-Scores for
Attitude Toward School Measure

Groups	Pre		Post	
	M	*SD*	*M*	*SD*
All Participants:				
Treatment (*n* = 49)	65.55	10.42	67.74	10.28
Control (*n* = 49)	66.69	10.59	67.90	11.08
Female Participants:				
Treatment (*n* = 17)	65.88	11.15	69.24	9.90
Control (*n* = 17)	65.65	9.94	68.71	12.23
Male Participants:				
Treatment (*n* = 32)	65.38	10.19	66.94	10.55
Control (*n* = 32)	67.25	11.03	67.47	10.60

Note. School attitude scores ranged from 25 to 100 with higher scores indicating positive attitudes toward school.

Discussion

The "Succeeding in School" program seemed to have a positive influence on middle school students' attitudes toward school. This finding is consistent with results of an earlier study (Gerler & Anderson, 1986) in North Carolina which showed the program improving the school attitudes of children in grades four and five. The finding is also consistent with reports of the program's effects on elementary school children in Florida's Dade County Public Schools (Ruben, 1989). The implications of these results are important because truancy and dropping out of school appear to be rooted in the upper elementary and middle school years. A previous longitudinal study (Gerler, 1980) showed, in fact, that guidance strategies of this kind have positive effects on school attendance. Thus, counselors and teachers who implement such programs in their classrooms may contribute to dropout prevention efforts of school systems.

Interestingly, the middle school girls participating in the "Succeeding in School" program seemed to improve their attitudes toward school more than did the boys. This finding raises questions about the content and implementation of the program and other similar classroom guidance strategies: How can we tailor these programs to meet the developmental needs of middle school boys? What aspects of the content or implementation of the programs are better suited to girls than boys? A component that could have been included in this study and probably should be included in future studies of this kind is a pre-, post-measure of psycho/social development. Interestingly, a recent study of moral reasoning (Mohr, Sprinthall, & Gerler, 1987) indicated that girls in early adolescence reasoned at higher developmental levels than boys when confronted with social dilemmas related to drug use. These findings suggest that psychological education programs and classroom guidance strategies need to pay special attention to apparent developmental differences between boys and girls in early adolescence.

The outcomes of this study must be viewed cautiously. To begin with, since the *Attitude toward School* measure has undetermined reliability and validity, the scores collected from the instrument cannot be viewed with complete confidence. Some caution is also necessary regarding the assignment of students to the treatment and control groups. Because of practical considerations, counselors could not always randomly assign individual students to the treatment and control groups. Analysis of pretest data, however, showed no significant differences between the groups, thus providing reasonable assurance that random assignment was effective.

Another limitation of this study was the lack of a placebo group. Critelli and Neumann (1984) have argued persuasively in favor of using placebos in studies of psychological interventions. The lack of a placebo creates the possibility that other factors, including the novelty of the experience, or perhaps the intensity of it, caused the observed changes. Virtually all the students involved in the study, however, had experienced classroom guidance in elementary school. It seems likely, therefore, that the content of the guidance sessions rather than the novelty of the experience contributed to the treatment group's progress on the *Attitude toward School* measure.

Conclusion

The "Succeeding in School" program has been shown to have important effects on the educational process in elementary and middle schools. The present study adds some additional information about the influence of the program on middle school students. Many other questions about the program need to be studied, in particular, how the effects of the program differ between boys and girls. Additional research with "Succeeding in School" is currently being completed in several North Carolina school systems and should help to answer some of these questions.

References

Anderson, R. F., Kinney, J., & Gerler, E. R. (1984). The effects of divorce groups on children's classroom behavior and attitude toward divorce. *Elementary School Guidance and Counseling, 19*, 70–76.

Asbury, F. R. (1984). The empathy treatment. *Elementary School Guidance and Counseling, 18*, 181–187.

Critelli, J. W., & Neumann, K. F. (1984). The placebo: Conceptual analysis of a construct in transition. *American Psychologist, 39*, 32–39.

Danielson, H. A. (1984). The quieting reflex and success imagery. *Elementary School Guidance and Counseling, 19*, 152–155.

Durbin, D. M. (1982). Multimodal group sessions to enhance self-concept. *Elementary School Guidance and Counseling, 16*, 288–295.

Gerler, E. R. (1980). A longitudinal study of multimodal approaches to small group psychological education. *School Counselor, 27*, 184–190.

Gerler, E. R. (1982). *Counseling the young learner.* Englewood Cliffs, NJ: Prentice-Hall.

Gerler, E. R. (1985). Elementary school counseling research and the classroom learning environment. *Elementary School Guidance and Counseling, 20*, 39–48.

Gerler, E. R. (1987). Classroom guidance for success in overseas schools. *International Quarterly, 5*, 18–22.

Gerler, E. R., & Anderson, R. F. (1986). The effects of classroom guidance on children's success in school. *Journal of Counseling and Development, 65*, 78–81.

Gerler, E. R., Kinney, J., & Anderson, R. F. (1985). The effects of counseling on classroom performance. *Journal of Humanistic Education and Development, 23,* 155–165.

Keat, D. B. (1979). *Multimodal Therapy with children.* New York: Pergamon.

Keat, D. B. (1985). Child-adolescent multimodal therapy: Bud the boss. *Journal of Humanistic Education and Development, 23,* 183–192.

Keat, D. B., Metzgar, K. L., Raykovitz, D., & McDonald, J. (1985). Multimodal counseling: Motivating children to attend school through friendship groups. *Journal of Humanistic Education and Development, 23,* 166–175.

Lazarus, A. A. (1985). *Casebook of multimodal therapy.* New York: Guilford Press.

Miller, G. D. (1973). *Additional studies in elementary school guidance: Psychological education activities evaluated.* St. Paul: Minnesota Department of Education.

Mohr, P. H., Sprinthall, N. A., & Gerler, E. R. (1987). Moral reasoning in early adolescence: Implications for drug abuse prevention. *School Counselor, 35,* 120–127.

Morse, L. A. (1987). Working with young procrastinators: Elementary school students who do not complete school assignments. *Elementary School Guidance and Counseling, 21,* 221–228.

Omizo, M. M. (1981). Relaxation training and biofeedback with hyperactive elementary school children. *Elementary School Guidance and Counseling, 15,* 329-332.

Ruben, A. M. (1989). Preventing school dropouts through classroom guidance. *Elementary School Guidance and Counseling, 24,* 21–29.

Starr, J. & Raykovitz, J. (1982). A multimodal approach to interviewing children. *Elementary School Guidance and Counseling, 16,* 267–277.

St. Clair, K. L. (1989). Middle school counseling research: A resource for school counselors. *Elementary School Guidance and Counseling, 23,* 219–226.

Thomas, G. M. (1974). Using videotaped modeling to increase attending behaviors. *Elementary School Guidance and Counseling, 9,* 35–40.

Wirth, S. (1977). Effects of a multifaceted reading program on self-concept. *Elementary School Guidance and Counseling, 12,* 33–40.

Effects of a Classroom Guidance Unit on Sixth Graders' Examination Performance

Natalie Susan Wilson

Helping low-achieving and underachieving students to improve their academic performance is one of the greatest challenges now facing counselors and other educators. During the past 25 years, many counseling approaches have been used in an attempt to assist these students, including group counseling (Altmann, Conklin, & Hughes, 1972; Benson & Blocher, 1967; Finney & Van Dalsem, 1969), individual counseling (McCowan, 1968; Schmieding, 1966), alternate group and individual counseling (Mezzano, 1968), peer counseling (Vriend, 1969), and behavioral strategies (Andrews, 1971; Ladouceur & Armstrong, 1983).

Although no single method has consistently produced positive results, a recent review (Wilson, 1986a) of studies evaluating counselor interventions with low-achieving and underachieving elementary, middle, and high school pupils found that characteristics of successful treatment programs included (a) counseling with study skills instruction, (b) leader-structured rather than client- or group-structured approaches, and (c) group rather than individual counseling. The review also revealed that, among programs providing study skill training, most offered such instruction through individual or small-group counseling formats. Recently, interest has been increasing in the use of classroom-based study skills units that allow counselors to work with more students than can be served by traditional one-to-one or small-group approaches. Although descriptions of classroom guidance programs focusing on study skills and habits are now appearing in the literature (Beale, 1981; Castagna & Codd, 1984; Maher & Thompson, 1980), the impact of these programs on academic performance is unclear because very few have been evaluated with experimental designs or any other method of assessment.

Students making the transition from elementary to middle school may need special assistance in developing appropriate study and test-taking skills, habits, and attitudes. In middle school, pupils typically encounter for the first time examinations covering the work of a semester or a full year. Faced with this new academic requirement, they may become anxious, study ineffectively, and perform far below their ability (Wilson, 1986b). Low-achieving students, who already are struggling to cope with the greater demands of the middle school curriculum, are especially at risk of acquiring poor examination-related habits and attitudes that may handicap them throughout their educational careers.

In this study I evaluated the effectiveness of a guidance unit offered on four consecutive days and intended to help classroom-sized groups of low-achieving middle school students to prepare for final examinations. I designed the unit to include the dimensions of successful treatment programs described above: (a) a combination of study skills training and counseling support, (b) a structured or leader-directed format, and (c) a group setting. Because researchers had suggested in previous investigations that peer group influence can be a powerful tool in positively affecting achievement (Anderson, 1976; Vriend, 1969), a group-centered rather than a lecture approach was used in the classroom to achieve maximum peer interaction.

The purpose of the investigation was to address the following questions:

1. Would students who participated in the guidance unit make significantly higher grades on their final examinations than would students in a control group who did not participate in the unit?
2. Would students participating in the unit fail significantly fewer examinations than would students in the control group?

Method

Participants

The participants were sixth-grade students at the only middle school in a rural Virginia county, which has a total enrollment of about 3,000. Students with one or more failures in their five academic subjects (English, reading, mathematics, science, and social studies) at the end of the fourth of six marking periods were included in the study. Failure was defined, according to the school district's policy, as grade below 74.5%. Students enrolled in special education programs, including classes for the mentally retarded and learning disabled, were excluded from consideration. The school reflected a mixed ethnic composition (65% White and 35% Black), with the largest proportion of students from families of middle socioeconomic status.

Counselor

The middle school counselor conducted the four-day unit. Her orientation program consisted of two sessions with me, in which I gave her an overview of the study, a detailed guide to conducting the activities, and all student handouts. The orientation also included an observation component, in which the counselor observed me conducting the third session of the unit with a sixth-grade class used as the pilot group. The counselor had a master's degree in education, had completed a one-semester practicum at the middle school level, and was certified as a secondary school counselor. Her experience included a one-year, half-time position as a counselor for Grades 7 and 8 and several years of teaching at the secondary level. The middle school position was her first full-time job as a counselor.

Treatment Materials

The unit consisted of four 50-minute sessions of activities that I developed to assist students in exploring study skills, habits, and attitudes related to preparing for and taking examinations. Two weeks before the study began, I conducted a field test of the unit in the same middle school in a sixth-grade art class. I selected this class from among the nonacademic exploration classes because it included a high proportion of students (8 out of 24) with one or more failures. As a result of feedback from the pilot group, I revised portions of several activities for the final experiment. Students participating in the field test were not considered in selecting participants for the study.

The unit capitalized on adolescents' involvement and interest in peer relationships by using a small-group rather than a lecture approach, in which students worked together in groups of five or six to explore problems and solutions related to taking examinations. The sessions followed a four-part process: (a) identification of problems in preparing for and taking examinations, (b) assessment of examination-related habits and attitudes, (c) exploration of causes of examination problems and development of possible solutions, (d) application of knowledge and concepts acquired in the unit to typical examination problems. Activities included small-group discussions, completion of a checklist and profile of study and test-taking habits, and group problem-solving exercises. A counselor's guide to the unit contained objectives for each session and step-by-step instructions for conducting the activities. A summary of the four sessions is provided below. The unit is presented in its entirety in Wilson (1986b).

First session. The counselor began by explaining that she would be working with students for the next four days to help them do their best on the upcoming examinations. After reviewing the purposes of tests and examinations, the counselor listed on the board four areas relating to test preparation: (a) study habits at school, (b) study habits at home, (c) test-taking habits, and (d) study and test-taking attitudes. Students then formed small groups, selected a recorder to take notes on their discussion, and, using the four areas as a guide, identified problems they encountered in preparing for and taking tests and examinations. Such problems included difficulty in organizing study material, conflicting demands on after-school time, postponing study until the night before a test, difficulty in concentrating during tests, and failure to proofread tests. After recorders presented their groups' responses orally, the counselor led a class discussion focusing on the most frequently cited problems. The counselor collected the recorders' papers for use in the third session.

Second Session. Each student received a multiple-choice *Checklist of Study and Test-Taking Habits* developed for the unit. The checklist was designed to promote self-examination of students' present study and test-taking habits and attitudes and consisted of 28 multiple-choice items assessing the four areas identified in the previous session. The counselor guided the students through the checklist as a class, with volunteers reading the questions aloud. Students then took turns guessing which answers were most appropriate, awarded themselves 0, 1, or 2 points for their own responses according to the counselor's instructions, and discussed the choices. The counselor collected the checklists for use in the next session.

Third Session. The counselor returned the checklists and helped the students plot their scores in each of the four areas on a *Study and Test-Taking Profile* created for the unit. This profile is a chart on which students can graph their scores in each of the four areas assessed in the *Checklist of Study and Test-Taking Habits*; study habits at school, study habits at home, test-taking habits, and study and test-taking attitudes. Scores range from a low of 0 to a high of 14 for each area. A shaded strip across the center of the graph allows students to see where average scores will fall for each area.

After separating into their original groups from the first session, the students used the recorders' papers from the first day and their own profiles to review and expand the list of examination problems they had developed during the first session. Each group then discussed possible causes of these problems and suggested ways to solve them. The recorders presented the results of group discussions to the entire class as they did in the first session.

Fourth Session. After the class had formed the same groups as before, each group received one of five Exam Emergency handouts, vignettes depicting problems typically encountered by middle school students in preparing for and taking examinations. For example, the "Football Fred" vignette described a student who has trouble finding time for both football practice and his school work. Groups discussed the possible causes of and solutions to their examination emergencies, and recorders presented the vignettes and the results of group discussions to the class. The counselor concluded the unit by helping students summarize what they had learned and develop goals for improving their own examination performance. Some of the more common goals included organizing a regular study time and sticking to it; bringing home all necessary study materials, such as textbooks and notebooks; reviewing old texts and quizzes before examinations; and studying well in advance of examinations rather than the night before.

Procedure

The school's printout of student grades was first examined to determine how many sixth graders had at least one failure at the end of the fourth marking period. The 52 identified students were randomly assigned to one of two groups, and the two groups were then randomly assigned to either the experimental or the control condition by flipping a coin.

The experimental students participated in the guidance unit with the middle school counselor during their sixth or seventh period, when they ordinarily would have their nonacademic exploration class (music, art, band, or library skills). The unit was presented for four consecutive days two weeks before final examinations. I did not tell exploration class teachers whether the experimental students were in the treatment or control group, but it was necessary to give the teachers these students' names so they could be excused from the exploration class. On the four days of the unit, the experimental students reported directly to a designated sixth-grade classroom that was available for both periods. Students in the control group received no additional guidance services and remained in their exploration classes.

At the end of the unit, the counselor prepared a summary of the sessions for use in evaluating treatment fidelity, the degree to which the unit had been delivered according to my specifications. The counselor's summary and posttreatment conferences with me revealed that, with the sixth-period group, she had conducted the unit according to the guide. In the seventh period group, however, the counselor had presented the Exam Emergency vignettes on the fourth day of the unit as an individual activity rather than as a small-group activity in an effort to keep students on task.

Because of the brevity of the unit, students missing one or more sessions were excluded from the final analysis. This resulted in five participants being dropped from the study—two in the sixth-period group and three in the seventh-period group—leaving 24 experimental students and 23 control students for the final analysis. To determine whether loss of participants had resulted in nonequivalent groups, students' grade quotients and pretreatment failure rates were compared using t tests. The results indicated that, although the mean grade quotient of the experimental group was slightly higher and the pretreatment failure rate somewhat lower than the quotient and rate of the control group, the differences were not statistically significant (see Table 1). Moreover, the statistical analysis was designed to adjust for these differences.

Instruments

For analysis, the scores of the experimental students in the two periods were pooled, as were the scores of the two groups of control students. For each student involved in the study, a final examination mean was calculated from examination grades in the five academic subjects. Grades were analyzed in their original values on a 0-100 scale with grades below 74.5 designated as failing. A mean final examination score was calculated for the treatment group and for the control group. The

Table 1
T-Tests for Initial Differences Between Groups

Variable	n	M	SD	t	df	p
Grade quotient						
Experimental	24	96.25	13.37			
				-1.31	45	.196
Control	23	91.61	10.66			
Pre-treatment failure rate						
Experimental	24	2.00	1.14			
				0.51	45	.612
Control	23	2.17	1.19			

number of examinations failed was also determined for each student and a mean was calculated for each group.

Results

A one-way analysis of covariance (ANCOVA) was used to analyze the data collected, with treatment or participation in the guidance unit serving as the independent variable. Pretreatment failure rate was employed as a covariate to control statistically for any potential pretreatment differences that could confound posttreatment differences between the groups. A level of significance of .05 was used in evaluating the results. Results of the ANCOVA revealed that there was a main effect for treatment on examination average (see Table 2).

Students in the treatment group ($M = 73.96$) scored significantly higher on examination average than students in the control group: $M = 68.62$, $F(1.44) = 4.33$, $p < .05$. There was no significant difference in examination failure rate between experimental students ($M=2.25$ and control students ($M = 2.65$), $F(1.44) = 1.19$, $p > .05$). Table 3 presents unadjusted means for examination average and examination failure rate for each group, as well as posttreatment means and differences adjusted for the effects of the covariate.

Table 2
Analysis of Covariance for Exam Average and Exam Failure Rate Using Pretreatment Failure Rate as a Covariate

Source of Variation	df	MS	F	p
Exam average				
Covariate				
Pretreatment failure rate	1	1542.13	20.02	.000
Treatment				
Guidance unit	1	333.64	4.33	.430
Exam failure rate				
Covariate				
Pretreatment failure rate	1	16.93	10.97	.002
Treatment				
Guidance unit	1	1.83	1.19	.282

Table 3
Descriptive Statistics for Effects of the Guidance Unit on Exam Average and Exam Failure Rate

| | Unadjusted | | Adjusted | Adjusted |
Item and Group	M	SD	M	Differences
Exam average				
Experimental	74.39	6.09	73.96	
				5.34*
Control	68.17	13.62	68.62	
Exam failure rate				
Experimental	2.21	1.29	2.25	
				-0.40
Control	2.70	1.46	2.65	

*Significant at the p < .05 level.

After the differences were adjusted for examination average, the experimental students scored 5.34 points higher than the control students, a difference that is significant at the $p < .05$ level. The adjusted difference between groups for examination failure rate was only $-.40(p > .05)$. The finding of no significant difference between groups for examination failure rate may have been partly due to the coarseness of the measure. Nevertheless, the effect was in the predicted direction, with the experimental group failing fewer examinations than did the control group.

Discussion

The findings indicated that students who participated in the unit attained significantly higher examination averages than did students in the control group. Some cautionary notes are needed, however. First, variability in the control students' examination grades was greater than in the grades made by the experimental students (see Table 3). Two of the control students each had a grade of zero on one examination and one had zeros on two examinations, because of their failure to attend examination sessions for certain courses and subsequent failure to attend examination makeups. Some of the experimental students had extremely low grades on their examinations, but none had a zero on any examination. The three control students' scores were included in the analysis, just as the middle school included them in calculating those students' final examination averages and yearly cumulative averages. Although the control students' zeros certainly contributed to the difference between the experimental and control groups, deleting their scores from the analysis would have had the effect of ignoring the practical considerations operating in a public school setting and removing the lowest performing participants from the study, thus biasing the results in a negative direction.

Second, the possibility of a Hawthorne effect (Roethlisberger & Dickson, 1939) cannot be discounted in evaluating the results. Although the original research design called for the counselor to conduct guidance activities unrelated to study and test-taking skills and attitudes for an equal amount of time with the control students in the week after the experiment, this procedure would have interfered with her preregistration activities with seventh graders and disrupted exploration classes for two consecutive weeks instead of one week. Consequently, the plan was modified, and the control students received no special activity to control for the attention factor potentially present in a novel intervention. Like all sixth graders in the middle school, however, the control students had participated in several classroom guidance sessions regularly conducted by the counselor during the year as part of the developmental guidance program.

Given these limitations, this study provides additional evidence that treatment programs combining study skills instruction with counseling in a structured group setting can have positive effects on the academic performance of low-achieving and underachieving students. Because the treatment consisted of several different elements, such as study skills training, counseling support, small-group format, and classroom setting, precisely which components contributed to achieving these results is not clear. Nevertheless, the superior examination performance by the students in the experimental group lends support to the use of brief classroom guidance programs by school counselors. Because many treatment programs of much greater duration fail to obtain positive results (Wilson, 1986a), the effectiveness of a four-day intervention merits continued investigation.

The study suggests several directions for further research on this type of counseling intervention. First, subsequent investigations should involve more counselors. Although the unit was highly structured and the counselor was given detailed directions for conducting all activities, the possibility of confounding counselor characteristics with treatment outcomes could not be avoided because the middle school had only one counselor. Second, including more students in treatment groups would provide a more precise test of the efficacy of classroom-based interventions. Loss of participants resulted in treatment groups of only 15 and 14 students, larger than the average group counseling size but smaller than the typical class size. Finally, a variation of the experimental design could be used, in which the unit's effectiveness with a sample of individual students or several small groups of students is contrasted with the efficacy of the same unit with one or more classroom-sized groups. Such a design would permit a systematic comparison of a classroom guidance intervention with traditional strategies for working with low achievers and underachievers.

References

Altmann, H. A., Conklin, R. C., & Hughes, D. C. (1972). Group counseling of underachievers. *Canadian Counsellor, 6,* 112–115.

Anderson, R. (1976). Peer facilitation: History and issues. *Elementary School Guidance & Counseling, 11,* 16–25.

Andrews, W. R. (1971). Behavioral and client-centered counseling of high school underachievers. *Journal of Counseling Psychology, 18,* 93–96.

Beale, A. V. (1981). Developmental guidance: The counselor in the classroom. *NASSP Bulletin, 65,* 51–59.

Benson, R. L., & Blocher, D. H. (1967). Evaluation of developmental counseling with groups of low achievers in a high school setting. *School Counselor, 15,* 215–220.

Castagna, S. A., & Codd, J. M. (1984). High school study skills: Reasons and techniques for counseling involvement. *School Counselor, 32,* 37–42.

Finney, B. C., & Van Dalsem, E. (1969). Group counseling for gifted underachieving high school students. *Journal of Counseling Psychology, 16,* 87–94.

Ladouceur, R., & Armstrong, J. (1983). Evaluation of a behavioral program for improvement of grades among high school students. *Journal of Counseling Psychology, 30,* 100–103.

Maher, M. F., & Thompson, M. K. (1980). The developmental guidance workshop: Outreach in action. *School Counselor, 28,* 39–49.

McCowan, R. J. (1968). The effect of "brief contact" interviews with low-ability, low-achieving students. *School Counselor, 15,* 386–389.

Mezzano, J. (1968). Group counseling with low-motivated male high school students—Comparative effects of two uses of counselor time. *Journal of Educational Research, 61,* 222–224.

Roethlisberger, F. J., & Dickson, W. J. (1939). *Management and the worker.* Cambridge, MA: Harvard University Press.

Schmieding, O. A. (1986). Efficacy of counseling and guidance procedures with failing junior high school students. *School Counselor, 14,* 74–80.

Vriend, T. (1969). High-performing inner-city adolescents assist low-performing peers in counseling groups. *Personnel and Guidance Journal, 47,* 897–904.

Wilson, N. S. (1986a). Counselor interventions with low-achieving and underachieving elementary, middle, and high school students: A review of the literature. *Journal of Counseling and Development, 64,* 628–634.

Wilson, N. S. (1986b). Preparing for examinations: A classroom guidance unit. *School Counselor, 33,* 297–305.

Transforming Low Achieving and Disruptive Adolescents into Model Students

Thelma L. Blumberg

The growing problem of discipline from mild behavioral disruptions to criminal activity, confronts the junior high school counselor daily. The topic has been reviewed by many researchers in terms of both etiology and treatment (Birman & Natriello, 1978; Doyle, 1978; Feldhusen, 1978; Litt, 1978; Quay, 1978). Doyle (1978), for example, has discussed the question of whether students today behave worse than they did in the past. He concluded that problems caused by disruptive behavior in the classroom were less serious at the turn of the century than they are now because disruptive students could be removed from school or did not attend at all. The same year, Feldhusen (1978) outlined four broad reasons for current school problems: (a) psychological and sociological variables, (b) television, (c) political and social influences, and (d) the school itself.

Intervention: An Overview

Regardless of the reason, those who have reviewed current research on behavior management do agree that the use of behavior management through social and material reinforcement systems can be highly effective and rewarding (Feldhusen, 1978; Jenson, 1978). Harris (1972) and Ulrich, Stachnik, and Mabry (1974) have reviewed numerous studies that demonstrate the successful use of behavior management strategies for adolescents in school. Social and material reinforcement in the schools using such systems as token economies, contingency contracting, and group contingencies have been described by Blackman and Silberman (1975), Buckley and Walker (1973), Harris (1972), Homme (1977), Patterson (1977), and Zifferblatt (1970).

Intervention: On the Scene

Important questions face the school counselor. How can these tried and proven techniques be sandwiched into busy schedules: Is it possible to serve many children on an individual basis? How can a counselor learn what a student is doing on a daily basis in all classes when the child moves from one classroom teacher to another? An exciting and flexible tool that helps counselors respond to these needs has been designed. It is a Daily Progress Report (DPR), an ordinary, simple device that resembles the conduct slip sometimes used by school counselors and administrators (see Figure 1). The results of using it have been so dramatic and rewarding that it is believed to be adaptable for use in a variety of institutions by almost anyone whose service is related to the field of mental health.

Daily Progress Report: Description

The DPR has a space for teachers to enter a grade of "poor, fair, good, or excellent" for behaviors that are selected as basic. Those that can be chosen are "on time for class, brought materials, previous home assignment completed, drill, completed classwork, and conduct and cooperation." There is also space for teachers to add special remarks and for parents to sign and write comments.

Case Study: Billy

The story of Billy demonstrates the power of the DPR to reverse the disruptive behavior pattern of a junior high school student who had been experiencing serious behavior problems since kindergarten. Although the DPR works even on a short-term basis, Billy, a seventh grader, carried one for an entire semester. When first referred, his behavior was so disruptive that his teachers were certain he was seriously emotionally disturbed. A review of Billy's earlier evaluations, however, suggested that he was a learning-disabled child. Because his behavior had prompted nothing but scolding and punishment all of his life. Billy genuinely believed he could never behave appropriately in school.

DAILY PROGRESS REPORT

Student's Name _____ Grade _____ Date _____

To Teacher: Please evaluate this student in the areas stated during your class.
Use appropriate words such as
POOR — FAIR — GOOD — EXCELLENT

To the Student: This form is to be presented to each teacher at the beginning of the class and picked up at the end of the class. The completed form is to be returned to:

	Teacher's Signature	On Time For Class	Brought Materials	Previous Home Assign Completed	Drill	Completed Classwork	Conduct cooperation	Comments
1								
2								
3								
4	LUNCH							
5								
6								
7								

Parent Signature: _____

Comments: _____
_____
_____

Figure 1
Daily Progress Report

Background and Description

Billy had recently returned to his mother's home after spending most of his years in foster care. By the age of eight, he had already lived in four different homes. He was a blond, blue-eyed child, short for his 13 years, and thin. Although he had average to high average intellectual potential, he was a low achiever, and he was on medication for hyperactivity. His spelling ability, his weakest area, was five years below that expected of someone his age.

Billy's Specific Problems

When I first met Billy in February, he had already failed all subjects for the first semester and had received all "Us" in conduct on his report cards. Classroom behaviors included constantly taking and interrupting the teachers, daily altercations with peers, and scratching his arms and face until they bled. Billy's mother was so discouraged with his frequent disciplinary removals from school that she spoke of returning him to foster care.

Techniques Used

1. Billy was seen each day before school, very briefly, at which time each favorable item on the DPR was reviewed orally, and he was praised enthusiastically.

2. When Billy made even small changes in behavior in the beginning, material rewards were used to motivate him. Based on how many good ratings he earned each week, he could choose from various pens, pencils, erasers, and other school supplies.

3. As Billy's behavior improved, the use of these items was phased out. For larger blocks of good behavior he could earn such rewards as being escorted to the teachers and administrators of his choice to share his improved DPRs with them, choosing from a variety of used American Automobile Association city and state maps that he treasured highly, and choosing from various good behavior certificates to take home.

4. Conferences were held with Billy's cluster teachers. They were asked to verbalize their good comments to Billy as they wrote them on the DPR.

5. While seeing Billy daily, I found it required little additional effort on my part to offer him structure for learning to spell, which was his greatest weakness. Also, he enjoyed bringing in pictures he had drawn to be hung on my office walls.

6. Conferences were held with Billy's mother, and she too was urged to praise him for his good efforts with DPR.

The following results in Billy's progress were realized by June when (a) he received all passing grades on his report card and "satisfactory" for conduct from all of his teachers, (b) the destructive scratching of his face and arms was eliminated completely, and (c) his mother reported she was much better able to manage him at home.

Beneficial Side-Effects

Billy's progress provided poignantly touching experiences for me. One day I had a backup of students waiting in my office; consequently, in my haste, I skipped something important on Billy's DPR; "Excellent +++" had been marked in the column for conduct. When he brought this to my attention, I was struck with its importance to him; I realized the extreme significance of the smallest success in a young life so lacking in any success until then.

On another occasion, I suggested to Billy's mother that she let him know she was pleased with his changing behavior. When he came in the next day, I could tell by his satisfied expression that he had something very special to tell me. I was stunned when he described in dramatic detail the simple fact that his mother hugged him. Best of all, I have my own permanent written records documenting the change in his teachers' comments, which have evolved from remarks such as "does obscene things" and "had to be restrained" to "conduct is excellent."

Directions for Daily Progress Report

Only important highlights of how to maintain a daily progress report are outlined here, because space does not permit in-depth explanations.

1. *Gather background information.* Examine cumulative, confidential, and even elementary records for strengths and weaknesses.

2. *Establish rapport.* Use any strengths, hobbies, interests, or talents uncovered in the records that you can sincerely praise to build confidence and self-esteem.

3. *Determine reinforcement.* Make a judgment about which reinforcement to use to stimulate good DPR ratings. For some students a mere pat on the back is sufficient; however, others need material motivators just to get started. There is an opportunity to be innovative in determining what reinforcement to use by searching for desirable prizes that cost little or nothing.

4. *Build enthusiasm.* Getting a student to carry a DPR is a delicate matter. Examples of questions to ask include:

- Is there anything you would change in school?
- How can I help you in school?
- Do you sometimes do good things in school that nobody notices?

Students' responses to these questions will inevitably provide openings for the following statements, which must always be presented enthusiastically: "I have a great way to show everyone the good things you do," and "When you show me your DPR, I am going to be looking only for the good things and I will ignore the bad things.

Quite often, in the beginning, the students will show the counselor the DPR and complain about their own behavior. The counselor is then placed in the position of reassuring the student that it really is not so bad and that there is a chance to improve the following day. The emphasis placed on the "good things" is a crucial strength of the entire procedure.

5. *See the student daily.* Take time to read aloud with the student all the positive or improved teachers' ratings and comments on the DPR. When the comments are good, the opportunity is there to discuss why the ratings are improved and to praise the behavior, thus strengthening it. The visit with the student can be very brief, before school, after school, or during lunch.

6. *Involve teachers, administrators, and parents.* Meet with teachers to explain the counseling process. Suggest that they verbalize good comments in addition to writing them. Praise them for their efforts, thus reinforcing their cooperation. Ask administrators or lunchroom monitors to sign the DPR during lunch period also. This completes the picture of the student's entire day. When possible, encourage the parent to reinforce at home the student's good behavior in school.

Implications for Counselors

1. The DPR provides an accurate, complete, immediate picture of a student's daily activities.
2. The DPR can be adapted to an infinite variety of situations and serves as a ready-made contract either for a few days or for an entire semester.
3. Use of the DPR requires a minimum amount of time and can provide maximum individual therapeutic service to a large number of students.
4. The environment is changed so that the students and administrator may view each other positively rather than as criminal and policeman.
5. The counselor plays an exciting role as intermediary for better family relationships.
6. A collection of DPRs may be used as a research tool for preparing scholarly works.
7. It is possible for the counselor to enjoy instant gratification by reading teachers' comments and observing the student's euphoria.

As students progress using the DPR the counseling process poses challenges worthy of further exploration. Student dependency on the therapist and administrative inflexibility sometimes become issues. Needs arise for teaching children who have made great strides to deal with setbacks and, better still, to internalize their new positive behaviors. In view of the drama taking place, some of these are stimulating issues.

Conclusion

Close examination of disruptive students reveals much frustration at being trapped into hopeless roles with few exits. It becomes the responsibility of the school to use tools such as the DPR to persuade these youngsters that acceptable conduct need not be an impossible dream. Inevitably, when behavior improves, so does self-esteem and achievement.

References

Birman, B. F., & Natriello, G. (1978). Perspectives on absenteeism in high school. *Journal of Research and Development in Education, 2,* 29–38.

Blackman, G. J., & Silberman, A. (1975). *Modification of child and adolescent behavior.* Belmont, CA: Wadsworth.

Buckley, N. K. & Walker, H. M. (1973). *Modifying classroom behavior.* Champaign, IL: Research Press.

Doyle, W. (1978). Are students behaving worse than they used to behave? *Journal of Research and Development in Education, 2,* 3–16.

Feldhusen, J. F. (1978). Behavior problems in secondary schools. *Journal of Research and Development in Education, 11,* 17–28.

Harris, M. B. (1972). *Classroom uses of behavior modification.* Columbus, OH: Merrill.

Homme, L. (1977). *How to use contingency contracting in the classroom.* Champaign, IL: Research Press.

Jenson, W. R. (1978). Behavior modification in secondary schools: A review. *Journal of Research and Development in Education, 11,* 53–63.

Litt, I. (1978). The role of the pediatrician in management of secondary school behavior problems. *Journal of Research and Development in Education, 11,* 92–100.

Patterson, G. R. (1977). *Living with children.* Champaign, IL: Research Press.

Quay, H.C. (1978). Behavior disorders in the classroom. *Journal of Research and Development in Education, 11,* 8–17.

Ulrich, R., Stachnik, T., & Mabry, J. (1974). *Control of human behavior.* Glenview, IL: Scott, Foresman.

Zifferblatt, S. M. (1970). *Improving study and homework behaviors.* Champaign, IL: Research Press.

Conflict Resolution and Interpersonal Skill Building Through the Use of Cooperative Learning

Amalya Nattiv
Gary F. Render
David Lemire
Kristin E. Render

As counselors and educators, many of us are concerned about a lack of classroom harmony and inadequate interaction and conflict resolution skills among our students. These are issues about which we complain, along with worrying about how to teach all the required content and still do the hundreds of other things that educators are expected to accomplish. Unfortunately, many of us salve our consciences by feeling badly and stop there, blaming our lack of action on being overworked.

The Need for Integration Skills and Conflict Resolution Development

Johnson and Johnson (1975) reviewed the literature on the inability of students to work together and revealed some startling findings:

1. The tendency for children to compete in conflict-of-interest situations often interferes with their capacity for adaptive cooperative problem solving.
2. American (United States) students so seldom cooperate spontaneously on experimental tasks that it seems that the environment is barren of experiences that would sensitize them to the possibilities of cooperation.
3. Not only do American (United States) children engage in irrational and self-defeating competition, but the American (United States) children (in comparison with children from other countries) are willing to reduce their own rewards to reduce the rewards of a peer.
4. The socialization of American (United States) children in competitive attitudes and orientations is so pervasive that students

often believe that helping a person in distress is inappropriate and is disapproved of by others.

These findings are not limited to school-age individuals. The negative effects of competition are widespread in the adult world of work. The business world has focused on the widespread lack of interpersonal communication skills, which are among the problems facing American (United States) employers today. With 70% to 80% of jobs today requiring a complex coordination of effort and ideas (Graves & Graves, 1985), it is imperative that we integrate effective communication skills and conflict resolution into the curriculum of American (United States) schools.

Beyond the reasons of economic health and preservation of a way of life, the hope for world peace is in the hands of the younger generation: World Peace begins at a personal level. Peace begins in the hearts and minds of individuals as they interact in families and classrooms. Unless we equip our students with the specific skills needed to develop effective ways of interacting, peaceful coexistence will remain a dream.

Educator Frustration

One of the greatest frustrations faced by well-meaning educators and counselors is that they do not know how to teach cooperative skills, except by making these skills the content of a unit of study. Such an approach takes valuable time away from other content areas that educators feel pressured to address. Many educators feel vulnerable to the criticism that teaching conflict resolution and addressing interpersonal skills fall into the category of the social curriculum and are, therefore, not legitimate content areas for schools, which should focus only on academics. Because affective goals are included under the scope and sequence for democracy and citizenship for most school districts, and because the learning process is an integrated one that does not artificially separate cognitive and affective components, interpersonal skill development is a valid component of instruction. Nevertheless, the time factor discourages some educators. Even the opportunity to involve school counselors in affective skill development is lost because the average secondary school "counselor" is often involved in noncounseling tasks. A second drawback is that spending one to three weeks on a unit without follow-up practice or reinforcement may not be an effective way to teach complex skills. Much practice in communication and cooperative skills is necessary to achieve mastery.

A Solution

There is a way of teaching important cooperative and communication skills that does not detract from other content areas and can be practiced and reinforced throughout the year. By using a cooperative learning instructional strategy, students can engage in learning all sorts of content through a process that helps students develop communication abilities. The skills on which the educator wants to focus become not only the "what" of instruction but also the "how" of learning. Before explaining how this method of teaching works, we need to examine some of the specific skills involved in learning to resolve conflicts.

Skills Prerequisite to Conflict Resolution

First of all, conflict resolution is a complex skill built upon practice and mastery of simpler communication skills. The ability to interact requires awareness of others, awareness of the distinction between self and others, a desire to connect with others, the ability to lower negative psychological defenses when they get in the way, skill in listening and hearing, awareness of one's feelings and thoughts, and the ability to respond to the feelings and thoughts of others. This partial list represents a set of assumptions that we take for granted that children have learned by the time they arrive at school; these assumptions are unwarranted.

Task and Social Emotional Skills

Cooperative learning focuses on group interaction skills that are often divided into task skills and social/emotional (maintenance) skills in the literature (Schmuck & Schmuck, 1983). Skills that focus on the task at hand include the following: listening to ideas of others, contributing ideas, paraphrasing, checking for understanding, clarifying, summarizing, staying on the subject, distributing the task according to the amount of time available, gathering data, analyzing data, and arranging data in a presentable form.

Maintenance skills have to do with the affective tone of the group. Maintenance skills overlap with task skills, but the purpose of these skills is to help the group maintain favorable interpersonal interactions and cohesion. Positive maintenance procedures can assist with effective task accomplishment. Maintenance skills include the following: reflective listening, encouragement, praise, gatekeeping (making sure that everyone has a chance to participate), guarding against dominance by one or two members, compromising, harmonizing, appropriate joking to alleviate tension, and expressing feelings.

Dishon and O'Leary (1984, p. 57) have categorized classroom task and maintenance skills in the following way:

Task Skills	Maintenance Skills
Check others' understanding of the work	Encourage
	Use names
Contribute ideas	Encourage others to talk
Stay on task	Respond to ideas
Get group back to work	Use eye contact
Paraphrase	Show appreciation
Ask questions	Share feelings
Follow directions	Disagree in an agreeable way
Stay in own space	Keep things calm

Interaction Orientation

Another way of conceptualizing interaction skill development focuses not so much on the specific behaviors as on the desired value orientations. For instance, democratic participation, appreciation of diversity, reciprocal respect, and Dewey's scientific method can be considered components of the conflict resolution process. Many activities that develop these orientations have been developed for use in schools. These cooperative activities, in turn, help individuals develop the specific behaviors described earlier, which are prerequisite skills to conflict resolution.

How Cooperative Learning Encourages Interactive Skills

Cooperative learning strategies help students develop specific skills as well as value orientations through activities that progress from the simple to the sophisticated. Conflict resolution is one of the more sophisticated activities toward which students work. Although a more detailed description of cooperative learning is available (Nattiv, 1988), the key components relevant to the skill-building process are excerpted here. Cooperative learning includes several instructional strategies in which students are grouped in teams in which they work together toward a common goal. Cooperative learning strategies are appropriate for teaching all age groups, content areas, and cognitive levels. A typical learning cycle might follow the following pattern:

> The teacher or counselor introduces the unit, as might be done in a traditional classroom, including motivating material and, perhaps, some direct instruction. Then teams work together on learning the content. This task could be accomplished through such diverse methods as: (1) peer tutoring with flash cards, (2) role differentiation (which involves each person in the group becoming an expert on a part of the material and then teaching the rest of the group), (3) worksheets, or (4) the creation of a group project in which each student contributes a component. Team members make sure that everyone in the group understands all of the material. Then students are individually assessed through quizzes, completion of individual materials, or other means. Last, teams receive recognition for their effort. This learning cycle typically takes a week and can be repeated weekly in a four-week unit.

Each cooperative learning team is ideally heterogeneous in the sense that the team reflects a microcosm of the diversity of the class as a whole along the dimensions of academic achievement, ethnicity, and sex. For instance, a high-achiever, a low-achiever, and two middle-achievers on each team of four students would provide academic heterogeneity. The ratio of boys and girls as well as different ethnic backgrounds should also be reflected on each team. Heterogeneity on these three dimensions has been instrumental in increasing achievement and breaking down ethnic barriers or stereotypes.

Each student on a cooperative learning team is responsible for doing his or her share of the work and is held accountable through some form of evaluation, such as a worksheet, oral report, quiz, presentation, or teacher observation. Generally, teams are rewarded based upon the contributions of each member. Thus, there is a great deal of attention by team members to make sure that all teammates have an understanding of the content and skills necessary to complete the work successfully. Ensuring accountability is a safeguard to make certain that no individual is rewarded on the merit of the group's work without contributing his or her fair share of effort.

Students in both cooperative learning groups share a common feeling: They feel like a team. As experienced by the authors, students have frequently reported an increased feeling of mutual concern and liking for others; they want to help each other; they want the team to succeed. Such outcomes are fundamental to the success of the cooperative learning method. Such outcomes are a result, in large part, of the emphasis placed on the initial teambuilding efforts in which students first learn how to help each other work together toward the common goal of learning more successfully.

Teambuilding

Team identity building is practiced when teams first form. Students get to know each other better and learn some essential skills of group work. Activities for getting to know teammates can begin with low-risk exercises and, as trust builds, activities can become more personal. First, teams engage in exercises in which they learn more about each other. Members play name games or interview each other on a selected topic. Then the group decides on a team name by reaching consensus. Many cooperative learning activities encourage differences of opinion. But in this initial phase, learning the skill of reaching a consensus is valuable. Team members feel much more a part of their team if they all agree on the name of the team. Students practice the three rules of coming to consensus: (a) each member has a say, (b) no decision is reached unless all members consent, and (c) no one is to consent if one has a serious objection (Kagan, 1988).

Deciding on a team name by consensus or creating a team banner, logo, mural, or cheer add to the feeling of group cohesion. The mural or logo is often displayed in each group's area so teams can be identified more easily. In addition to the finished product, these activities are also used to demonstrate the process of group decision making, which includes participation, consensus, and respect for others. Additional types of teambuilding activities include the following: learning to respect individual differences, experiencing mutual support, discovering improvement in team performance that comes with practice, and finding out that four heads are better than one. Exercises in valuing individual differences demonstrate that it is acceptable to have different viewpoints. Everyone has a right to an opinion or perspective. In fact, diversity can enrich the group. Additional games and activities can further reinforce group cohesion. Usually this initial teambuilding process can be conducted in less than an hour.

Ongoing Skill Building

Initial teambuilding sets the stage for developing further interaction skills through ongoing skill building. Educators or counselors usually introduce cooperative learning by beginning with simple strategies, such as *Student Teams Achievement Divisions* (STAD) (Slavin, 1980), in which all students work together to master basic factual material, tutor each other, cooperate within their group, and compete against other groups. At this initial level, the teacher may notice a lack of ability in some skills, such as maintaining eye contact or knowing the difference between giving help to a teammate and just giving the answer.

One positive aspect of ongoing skill building is that it can be practiced while students are focusing on academic content. Additional time is often not necessary. We suggest that teachers or counselors select one skill to work on at a time. For instance, if the deficient skill is "giving supportive encouragement," the teacher or counselor can perform pretests by tallying the number of positive remarks that are heard in five minutes of walking around the room listening to groups. The educator can tell the students that encouragement is an area in which the class can improve and that this skill will be the focus for the next week while students are engaged in learning academic content. The counselor or teacher can then explain the rationale for developing this skill.

The next day another five-minute tally can be made of the frequency of the desired behavior. The tally can be done either by the teacher, the counselor, or a student. A third tally can be made later in the week. It is not recommended that teams compete to see who can get the most tallies. Rather, a class tally indicating progress of the whole group reinforces the message that cooperation is a joint effort. Having special attention focused on improving one behavior at a time, students' awareness of that behavior can be increased. By engaging in the behavior and focusing on practicing that behavior, students or teachers can improve that behavior.

As students become comfortable with the simpler cooperative learning techniques, they can be introduced to more complex methods in which individual tasks and separate roles are assigned to each team member and in which competition between teams is discontinued. Such methods as Jigsaw (Aronson, 1978), and project methods like Co-op Co-op (Kagan, 1988) and Group Investigation (Sharan & Sharan, 1976) are examples of more complex cooperative methods. At higher levels, encouraging different opinions and multiple points of view are often part of the methods, so conflict resolution becomes an essential skill. The earlier skills that students have developed, such as listening to others and valuing others' contributions, are useful for resolving conflicts.

Kagan (1988, p. 109) has emphasized the multiple approaches to conflict resolution between two members of a group. Kagan has used a poster that displays eight strategies and has recommended direct instruction, role-playing, and processing of the consequences. Kagan's approaches to conflict resolution are the following:

1. Sharing: We can both do it.
2. Taking turns: We can do it your way this time and my way the next.
3. Compromising: Give up some and get some.
4. Chance: Flip a coin or toss dice.
5. Outside help: Let's ask a teammate, classmate, teacher, or counselor.
6. Postpone: Later—when we cool down, we can deal with this.
7. Avoid: Agree to disagree—with respect.
8. Humor: Express, but not at the expense of another person.

Another approach is to make conflict resolution the focus of the content as well as the process of a lesson. The teacher creates a structured conflict or dilemma, gives students the opportunity to interact, and includes the most essential component of learning from the experience—time to talk about the experience and consider it afterwards. Kagan adapted a scenario called "Truck Driver" from Thayer (Kagan, 1988), which is an appropriate example. Scenarios involving conflict can also easily be chosen from relevant content that is part of the curriculum. Team members can choose to defend opposite sides in a debate. Teams can be asked to rank-order items on a list according to their importance and give a set of criteria. Any content involving attitudes and values (i.e., politics or religion) can become fertile ground for conflict resolution skill development. The key to successful conflict resolution is to build upon previously developed skills and to allow processing time after the experience. Some of the prerequisite skills include the following:

1. Sharing
2. Appreciating or showing appreciation
3. Letting everyone have a say
4. Valuing diversity
5. Contributing, giving ideas

6. Checking for understanding
7. Checking for consensus or lack of consensus
8. Disagreeing politely
9. Paraphrasing

The greatest advantage of using cooperative learning for improving students' interpersonal skills and the consequent positive classroom atmosphere is that cooperative learning is a process that offers opportunity for practice. Opportunity for practice occurs even when no time is devoted to dealing with the skills as the content focus of a lesson. Many educators and counselors believe that interpersonal skill development is important in its own right and deserves special attention. Interpersonal skill development arranged in a cooperative learning classroom or school is highly effective.

References

Aronson, E. (1978). *The jigsaw classroom.* Beverly Hills: Sage.

Dishon, D., & O'Leary, P. (1984). *A guidebook for cooperative learning: A technique for creating more effective schools.* Holmes Beach, FL: Learning Publications.

Graves, N. B, & Graves, T. D. (1985). Creating a cooperative learning environment: An ecological approach. In R. Slavin, S. Sharan, S. Kagan, R. Hertz-Lararowitz, C. Webb, & R. Schmuck (Eds.), *Learning to be cooperative: Cooperating to learn* (pp. 403–436). New York: Plenum Press.

Johnson, D. W., & Johnson, R. T. (1975). *Learning together and alone: Cooperation, competition, and individualization.* Englewood Cliffs, NJ: Prentice-Hall.

Kagan, S. (1988). Cooperative learning resources for teachers. Riverside, CA: Reprographics, University of California, Riverside.

Nattiv, A. (1988). Cooperative learning: An overview. *Journal of Humanistic Education, 12,* 2–7.

Schmuck, R. A., & Schmuck, P. A. (1983). *Group processes in the classroom.* Dubuque, IA: Brown.

Sharan, S., & Sharan, Y. (1976). *Small-group teaching.* Englewood Cliffs, NJ: Educational Technology Publications.

Slavin, R. (1980). *Using student team learning.* Baltimore: Johns Hopkins University Center for Social Organization of Schools.

Chapter 7

The Challenge of Career Exploration in Early Adolescence

In search for identity, young adolescents struggle not only with the question of "Who am I?" but also with the question "Who will I become?" The latter question is often answered in terms of future occupation. Adolescents face an ever-changing world of work, a fact that is often neglected by overburdened middle school counselors. The economic, political, and social change that have brought women and minorities into the work force in large numbers have altered how youngsters must be prepared to enter the world of work. Chapter 7 discusses issues related to career development in early adolescence and offers suggestions to help middle school counselors promote students' career exploration. The chapter offers four articles that explore varying aspects of the world of work.

The first article, "What Can School Do for Me?': A Guidance Play," presents a creative approach to career education for middle schoolers. The author notes that the play is "an entertaining and effective way of helping students appreciate the relationship between their present work in school and their future work in the world of careers."

The second article, "Career Exploration for Middle School Youth: A University-School Cooperative," suggests the value of institutional cooperation in career education. This program involved students, parents, teachers, and university personnel in a broad-spectrum approach to career exploration. Through this project, students "developed self-knowledge, the ability to work together cooperatively on projects, and the skill of communicating more effectively" each of which is a key to career success.

The third article, "Teaching Job Search Skills to Eighth-Grade Students: A Preview of the World of Work," describes eight lessons to help youngsters develop needed skills for finding work. These skills included how to write a resume, how to fill out a job application, and how to interview effectively for a job.

The final article, "Career Education for Students with Disabilities," recommends innovative approaches for working with students who have special needs. The authors address the following important issue: Are we really going to "give all students, including those with disabilities, the opportunity to become competent and productive adults after they leave school?" This last article underscores the main point of Chapter 7, namely, that educators must break away from traditional practices so that comprehensive career education programs can become an integral part of middle schools.

"What Can School Do for Me":
A Guidance Play

Natalie Susan Wilson

Assisting students in understanding the relevance of school to their future in the world of work can be a difficult task for counselors. Pupils frequently complain that much of their academic work is boring, while counselors find that simply encouraging students to do their assignments and reminding them of the value of an education are not enough to motivate them. The play, "What Can School Do for Me?," uses an entertaining format to help students recognize the importance of school to their own occupational goals. The play was developed as part of the activities celebrating National Career Guidance Week at King George Middle School in King George, Virginia.

First presented in the fall of 1981, "What Can School Do for Me?" is a fantasy in which a middle school student and a superhero companion take a tour of the world of careers. The cast consists of twelve characters, several of which can be played by a single actor. Since most of the parts are short, relatively few rehearsals are required. Costumes are minimal, and all props are readily available within the school or may be borrowed from the actors themselves. Moreover, a stage is not even necessary, merely an open area with a screen placed at one side for entrances and exits. The play lasts approximately fifteen minutes, including scene changes.

The Script of "What Can School Do for Me?"

Characters:

First painter	Second child
Second painter	Wonderworker
First student	Mechanic
Second student	Car
Teacher	Medical laboratory technician
First child	Football player

(Three chairs, two desks, and a small bench are at the back of the stage, and a music stand or easel is near the front on the right-hand side. Two actors wearing overalls and painters' caps enter. Each carries a paint bucket and a large rectangular posterboard sign. They pause in the center of the stage and put down the buckets and signs.)

FIRST PAINTER: We're sign painters. Our signs help people find what they're looking for.

SECOND PAINTER: We're here today to show you how what you learn in school can help guide you toward your goals in the world of careers.

FIRST PAINTER: Our play is called, "What Can School Do for Me?" *(They display a sign with the title on it.)* Actors in the play are... *(They flip the sign over to show the names of the actors, while the first painter names them, and then place the sign on the music stand.)*

SECOND PAINTER: We'll be introducing each act and scene for you like this.

SIGN PAINTERS *(in unison, displaying second sign that reads "ACT I")*: Act I! *(They flip the sign over to read "SCENE I.")* Scene I! *(They place the sign on the stand and bring up the desks and chairs from the back of the stage. They place one desk with two chairs on either side near the front, place the other desk and chair slightly farther back, and exit).*

Act I, Scene I

(Three actors enter, two dressed as students and one as a teacher. The students carry folders and pencils, and the teacher carries a large stack of dittos and a pen. The students sit facing each other at the front desk and work in their folders, while the teacher sits correcting papers at the back desk.)

FIRST PAINTER *(to the second student)*: Work, work, work! All we ever do in school is work! What do we have to do this stuff for, anyway?

SECOND PAINTER: A lot of my work doesn't make any sense to me, either. I want to be an automobile mechanic when I get out of school, and I'm not going to have to know any of this!

FIRST PAINTER: If I see one more ditto today, I'll scream.

TEACHER *(going over to students and placing the entire stack of dittos on the desk)*: Now, class, for tomorrow, do pages 1 through 20 of these worksheets.

FIRST PAINTER: Aagh! *(All exit.)*

SIGN PAINTERS *(displaying sign)*: Scene II! *(They place the sign on the stand, put all the furniture at the back of the stage except for one desk and chair, which they leave at the front, and exit.)*

Act I, Scene II

(The first student from Scene I enters, carrying a folder and a pencil. The student sits at the desk and begins working.)

FIRST STUDENT *(throwing down pencil and giving sigh of disgust)*: Work at school, work at home! I don't see the point of any of this homework! It's not going to help me get the kind of job I want. I'm never going to get all of these spelling definitions finished. *(The student wearily picks up the pencil and continues working. Two actors dressed as young children run in. One is in hot pursuit of the other, who clutches a comic book. Throughout their dialogue, they continue to run around the stage.)*

FIRST CHILD: Gimme my superheros comic book!

SECOND CHILD: I just want to look at it for a minute!

FIRST CHILD: You can't! It's mine! Give it here!

SECOND CHILD: Aw, come on!

FIRST CHILD: Give it back right now, or I'll tell!

FIRST STUDENT: I can't stand it! *(He or she yells toward offstage.)* Mom! Get these kids out of here so I can do my homework! *(The children run off.)* Maybe if I put my head down and take a break for a few minutes, I'll feel more like finishing my work, I'm so tired… *(The student yawns and goes to sleep. The sound of eerie music is heard offstage. Note: music may be supplied by an actor who can play an instrument such as the clarinet or by having all of the offstage actors say "Oo!" simultaneously. An actor dressed in a jogging suit and a flaring cape runs in and stands triumphantly in the center of the stage).*

WONDERWORKER: Ta-Da!

FIRST STUDENT *(lifting head and wiping eyes)*: Hey, who are you?

WONDERWORKER: I'm Wonderworker! I'm here to take you on a flying tour of the wonderful world of work! We're going to look at workers in different careers and find out what school did for them.

FIRST STUDENT *(sarcastically)*: How did I get so lucky?

WONDERWORKER *(shrugging shoulders)*: Don't ask me, kid. I don't book the tours. I just guide them. Are you ready?

WONDERWORKER: I'm not really sure. I'm sort of new at this flying business. Hang on to my cape, and we'll take off.

FIRST STUDENT *(grabbing cape and shutting eyes)*: Don't go too fast. I'm afraid of heights.

WONDERWORKER *(adjusting cape)*: Don't bend the threads, kid. These outfits don't grow on trees, you know. Here we go! *(Wonderworker leads the student in a mad dash around the stage, with periodic leaps into the air.)* Up, up, and away! Up, up, and away! *(they pause, panting.)*

FIRST STUDENT: We don't seem to be getting anywhere.

WONDERWORKER *(clutching chest and breathing hard)*: Sometimes it takes a while to work up steam. *(They begin running again.)* Up, up, and away! Up, up, and away! *(They race offstage.)*

(The sign painters enter, carrying a sign that reads "ACT II.")

SIGN PAINTERS *(displaying sign)*: Act II! *(They reverse the sign to read "SCENE I,")* Scene I! *(They place the sign on the stand, put the desk and chair at the back of the stage, and exit.)*

Act II, Scene I

(An actor wearing a posterboard "sandwich" sign depicting the front and rear views of an automobile enters. The car walks around the stage and makes engine noises before stopping at the front. The car is followed by an actor dressed as an automobile mechanic in overalls and cap and carrying a car manual and a "creeper"—a flat board with wheels on which a mechanic reclines to perform work underneath a car. The mechanic lies down on the creeper and begins working on the car's "leg" with a wrench while consulting the manual.)

CAR *(as mechanic turns wrench)*: VROOM, VROOM! *(Wonderworker and first student race in.)*

FIRST STUDENT: Are you an automobile mechanic?

MECHANIC: No, smart guy! I'm a blacksmith, and this is my horse.

CAR *(as mechanic twists wrench on leg)*: Hey, watch the paint job?

WONDERWORKER: Could you please tell us what school did for you on the job?

MECHANIC *(getting up and wiping brow)*: Well, just between you and me, I wasn't all that crazy about school when I was a kid. But I use the skills I learned every day on the job. I need to use math to make out the bills, order parts and keep track of costs. And if I couldn't read this manual, I couldn't fix the car.

FIRST STUDENT: And school helped with that?

MECHANIC: Sure! Besides, working in school with my teachers and the other students was a good way to practice getting along with people. I have to be able to talk to my boss and the people who bring in their cars to be repaired. When some customer gets all steamed up because a car isn't ready, I need to use all the listening and communication skills I learned in school.

WONDERWORKER: Thanks a lot. We're got to go now. Hang on, kid.

FIRST STUDENT *(grabbing cape)*: Not so fast this time, okay? I think I left my stomach somewhere over Cleveland.

WONDERWORKER: Up, up, and away! *(They race off, and others exit.)*

(The sign painters enter with a sign reading "Scene II.")

SIGN PAINTERS *(displaying sign)*: Scene II! *(They place the sign on the stand, bring up a desk and chair to the front, and exit.)*

Act II, Scene II

(An actor enters, dressed in a white laboratory coat and carrying a microscope, a lancet, a pad of paper, and a pen. The laboratory technician sits at the desk and makes notes while looking into the microscope. Wonderworker and the student race in.)

WONDERWORKER: Let's ask this medical laboratory technician how school was useful for this job. How did school help you with your career?

LAB TECHNICIAN: When I was in school, I was always more interested in science than any of my other subjects. Sometimes I had trouble seeing the importance of some of the work I had to do.

FIRST STUDENT: That's just how I feel! I'd much rather do math problems than spelling definitions!

LAB TECHNICIAN: But once I got this job, I found out that being part of being successful in a career is trying to do your best on all of your tasks. Sure, I like some of the things I do better than others. Filling out lab forms isn't as much fun as analyzing blood samples. But if I don't do it right, the doctor could make a wrong diagnosis.

FIRST STUDENT: I guess I never thought of it like that.

LAB TECHNICIAN *(to Wonderworker)*: Say, I bet your blood would be really interesting to look at! How about if I take a little sample? *(He or she holds up lancet.)*

WONDERWORKER *(recoiling)*: Uh, I don't think so. I'm not crazy about the sight of blood—especially when it's mine! We have to be going now, anyway. Come on, kid. Let's go visit another worker. Up, up, and away! *(They run off, followed by the lab technician.)*

(The sign painters enter, carrying a sign reading "SCENE III.")

SIGN PAINTERS *(displaying sign)*: Scene III! *(They place the sign on the stand, return the desk, chair, and lab materials to the back, and bring up the bench. They exit).*

Act II, Scene III

(An actor enters, dressed in a football uniform and carrying a football helmet. A towel is slung over one shoulder. The football player sits down wearily on the bench and wipes off perspiration with the towel. Wonderworker and the student rush in).

FIRST STUDENT: Wow! A professional football player! I bet you didn't learn your career in school!

PLAYER: Where do you think I got started in football? I played varsity in high school and then went to college on a football scholarship.

FIRST STUDENT: But you don't need to know grammar or geography to be a football player, right?

PLAYER: Don't knock what you learn in school, kid. I won't be playing football forever, you know. The average player in the NFL only lasts for about four years. In a short occupation like this one, I have to be especially concerned about career planning. I'll be needing all the skills I learned in school to begin a whole new career in just a few years—or even earlier, if my passes keep getting intercepted like they are today!

WONDERWORKER: Don't forget, school can teach planning and organizational skills as well as academic skills. Planning long-term projects and keeping track of materials and assignments can get you ready to use these skills when they really count—in the world of work!

PLAYER: That's right! And learning to work with your teachers and fellow students can help prepare you to deal with a coach and teammates. That's really being on the ball!

WONDERWORKER: Thanks for talking to us, and good luck in the second half. Come on, kid. It's time to take you back. Up, up, and away! *(He or she prepares to take off.)*

FIRST STUDENT *(grabbing cape and stopping Wonderworker momentarily)*: Do you always have to say that?

WONDERWORKER: I need all the help I can get. Here we go! Up, Up, and away! *(They race off, followed by the football player.)*

(The sign painters enter with a sign reading "SCENE IV.")

SIGN PAINTERS *(displaying sign)*: Scene IV!! *(They place the sign on the stand, return the bench to the back, and set up a desk and chair at the front. They take a book, a folder, and a pencil out of the desk, lay them on top, and exit.)*

Act II, Scene IV

(Wonderworker and the student run in.)

WONDERWORKER: Well, what do you think about school now?

FIRST STUDENT: You know, Wonderworker, I guess school prepares you for having a job in all kinds of ways. Not only do the skills you learn help you get and keep a job, but learning to get along with teachers and classmates helps you work with others in your career.

WONDERWORKER: And remember, learning how to plan and be organized at school are also important skills you can develop and practice for later use on the job. Being a student is really a lot like being a worker.

FIRST STUDENT *(wryly)*: Except you don't get paid for going to school!

WONDERWORKER: That's true. And you don't get paid for going to school!

WONDERWORKER: That's true. And you don't get fired if you make a mistake!

FIRST STUDENT: I really appreciate the tour and advice, Wonderworker. *(He or she sits down at desk and picks up book.)* Say, before you go, what do you know about algebra?

WONDERWORKER *(edging away)*: Algebra? Uh, wouldn't you rather see me fly faster than a speeding bullet? Don't forget our trip. Up, up, and away! *(He or she races off.)*

FIRST STUDENT: Goodbye, Wonderworker! *(yawning)* Gosh, I'm tired after all that traveling. *(He or she puts head down and sleeps.)*

(The sign painters enter, carrying a sign that reads "ACT III.")

SIGN PAINTERS *(displaying sign)*: Act III! *(they flip the sign over to read "SCENE I.")* Scene I! *(They place the sign on the stand and exit.)*

Act III, Scene I

FIRST STUDENT *(lifting up head and stretching)*: Where are you, Wonderworker? Gone, I guess. What a trip! I'd better get going on this homework. *(The student begins working. The children rush in.)*

SECOND CHILD *(clutching a comic book)*: I told you I'd give it back when I finished reading it!

FIRST CHILD: You better give me that comic book right now! *(They continue to yell at each other and run around the stage.)*

FIRST STUDENT *(shaking head wearily)*: It seems like I've never been away. *(He or she yells toward offstage.)* Mom! Mom! *(He or she chases children around the stage and off.)*

(The sign painters enter, carrying a sign that reads "THE END.")

SIGN PAINTERS *(displaying sign)*: The end! *(They place the sign on the stand and exit.)*

Follow-up Activities

After the play was presented, a series of follow-up activities were conducted in the group guidance classes, which are a regular part of the sixth grade schedule at King George Middle School. Students discussed their reactions to the play and were assisted in relating their academic work to tentative career goals. The relevance of various school subjects to the job-seeking process was reviewed, such as the use of reading, grammar, and communication skills in completing job applications and participating in interviews.

To encourage individual career exploration, sessions were also conducted to orient students to the occupational resources in the guidance office, including an introduction to the *Guidance Information System* computer program, which contains information on a wide variety of educational and career alternatives. Several teachers invited the counselor to meet with their classes in additional sessions to assist pupils in using the *Guidance Information System* to explore careers of their choice. Finally, all sixth grade sections participated in a series of classroom plays focusing on attitudes toward school and work. Students formed groups, selected from a number of open-ended situations, and worked for several weeks writing, rehearsing, and performing the plays.

"What Can School Do for Me?" has been enthusiastically received by middle school students and teachers. Reactions have been so favorable that the play is being made a permanent part of *National Career Guidance Week* activities and will be presented to the new sixth grade class each fall. The addition of an evening performance is also being considered so that parents and members of the community may attend. "What Can School Do for Me?" has been an entertaining and effective way of helping students appreciate the relationship between their present work in school and their future work in the world of careers.

Career Exploration for Middle School Youth: A University-School Cooperative

Natalie Rubinton

Career guidance for children in middle and junior high schools should be a joint effort of the schools, the community, and the family. Such a comprehensive approach to career education formed the basis for the federally funded project, *Career Exploration for Youth* (CEY). Developed and implemented by career educators for Kingsborough Community College of the City University of New York and Community School District #22, both in Brooklyn, New York, this project served more than 1,200 participants, including children in both public and parochial middle and junior high schools and their teachers, counselors, administrators, and parents. From the inception of the program in November 1981 to its conclusion in July 1982, a high level of participation was maintained, serving an average of 550 people each week.

The program contained four components, which were financially supported by the federal grant and thus were offered free to all participants. The program was developed with the clear understanding that the middle and junior high school years (approximately ages 9 through 13) are crucial years for students to be involved in career education. Super (1957) described this age period as one in which students learn about their likes, dislikes, values, and abilities and how these attributes are related to careers. This learning needs to take place experientially. Thus, a series of "hands-on" career courses were presented to the students as the first of four program components.

Facilitating career maturity in this age group requires the significant input of parents familiar with career development and the world of work (Evans, Hoyt, & Mangum, 1973). Thus, a career decision-making course for parents was included as the second component. Infusion of career development concepts into the regular curriculum in each grade is a recommended goal of any ongoing career education program (Quarles, 1981). Thus, a course was offered to teachers and other classroom and school personnel as the third component. The goals were to teach basic knowledge, understanding, and methods of teaching career education as an integral part of the school curriculum. Finally, the children who participated in the project were offered a recreation component to complement their career education courses.

The project used the college facilities on Saturdays from 8:30 A.M. to 4:30 P.M. in a series of four-week cycles. The class sessions were scheduled in two-hour blocks of time with a short break between classes. The equipment and mannequins in the nursing laboratories were available for the unit on health careers. The gymnasium was used for all the recreational activities. The theater and radio station were used for the units on media and communications. The books, filmstrips, career games, computer-assisted guidance system, and related career materials from the Career Resource Center were used by children, parents, and teachers. The Media Center was used to show films to all participants. The library was available for research and recreational reading.

Childrens' Program

The activities of the childrens' component of CEY included:

- Examination of myths about careers
- Examination of biases against and for careers familiar to the children
- Motivation to explore unfamiliar and nontraditional careers
- Generation of career-related options in cluster areas of interest to children
- Provision of direct participation in career experiences
- Introduction of role models
- Relating of careers to the values of the children

The children's workshops were all activity oriented and designed to enhance exploration of the following career clusters: business and office ("The Business of Sports"), marketing and distribution ("Getting the Business"), communications and media ("Things That Go Bleep" and "On Stage"), and public service ("At Your Service" and "Health and Hospitals"). Each of the cycles provided at least one class in each career cluster. The number of children in any one class was limited to 15 to facilitate the experiential nature of the program. Extra sections were added to accommodate high interest in a particular cluster.

The recreation program, coordinated by the Kingsborough Community College Physical Education Department, allowed youngsters to select supervised instruction from the offerings in tennis, floor hockey, swimming, basketball, aerobic dance, tumbling, organized games, and creative crafts. The recreation aspect of the program was extremely important in motivating youngsters to commit their Saturdays to an educational experience. There was a good balance of skill building and play in all of the recreation areas. Those children interested in sports, for example, were able to register for a career course titled "The Business of Sports," participate in skills training, and play tennis. Others could register for "Things That Go Bleep," a unit about careers in the technologies and media, as well as swimming instruction.

Children were recruited from their own classrooms with printed literature and brochures describing the project. Before each cycle of classes, children attended a registration conference at the college, where they were able to select the career cluster and recreation component related to their area of interest.

A total of 461 children registered for the career courses and recreation component; they represented the ethnic, cultural, and socioeconomic diversity of the district. The majority of these children participated in all four cycles.

Most children were in the fifth and sixth grades; 56% of the registrants were girls and 44% were boys. Participants came from 62 different elementary, intermediate, and junior high schools, seven of which were nonpublic.

Instructors were recruited form Kingsborough Community College, from junior high schools and high schools within and outside the district, and from business and industry. People who enjoyed working with children in an informal, nontraditional manner and who knew their particular field or skill well met the major criteria for selection as instructors. The program was coordinated through the director of counseling, and there was one over-all administrator and one director for each of the four components.

Parent's Program

The parents of the children enrolled in the CEY program were registered in a course in career decision making and participated in a variety of workshops on career development. The course, coordinated by the Department of Student Development, was modeled on an existing college course and adapted to the special needs of the parents. Parents also could choose to attend additional one-session career-related workshops during the same time period.

The course gave parents an opportunity to explore careers in relation to their interests, aptitudes, abilities, values, and life experiences. The methods of instruction included group discussion, lectures, guest speakers, exercises in self-exploration, administration of an interest inventory, a research project, and visits to work sites.

The principal objective for the course was to develop an increased awareness of the process of career decision making and an acquaintance with the facilitation of this process in youngsters. Some of the topics included individual goal setting; self-assessment; the relationship of abilities, interests, and values to career choice, the current and projected job market, and the decision-making process. The workshops, designed with the same objectives, dealt with resume writing, job search and job interview techniques, time management, and occupational information in the career areas of business, health, communications, and computers. A total of 89 parents registered for the course, and 309 parents participated in the workshops. The instructors were recruited primarily from the college's Department of Student Development, with additional consultation provided by people in business and industry and from several academic departments at the college.

School Personnel Program

The third component was a course titled "Education 82: Theories and Techniques of Career Exploration," which enrolled 245 school personnel from District #22. Participants included teachers, counselors, paraprofessionals, teacher aides, school secretaries, and administrators. The activities of this course consisted of:

- Provision of basic knowledge, understanding, and methods of teaching career education.
- Assistance in the integration or infusion of career education into the existing school curriculum.
- Implementation of ideas, goals, and methods of career education in teachers' classrooms or school settings.

Participants were given an additional incentive to take the course when the New York City Board of Education formally approved it as satisfying the requirements for various salary increments and differentials.

Instructors encouraged the review of career exploration materials relevant to the developmental stages experienced by elementary and junior high students. Special field visits to comprehensive work settings such as hospitals and museums and various consultants from business, industry, and academia were used to acquaint the school personnel with career education networks and resources throughout the city. A final group project required all students to design and reproduce a career resource manual and to develop lesson plans for elementary and junior high schools, incorporating career education into the regular curriculum.

Evaluation

An extensive evaluation of this program was undertaken. *The Career Awareness Inventory, Elementary Level* (Fadale, 1975), was used to assess changes in vocational maturity and knowledge of careers. Pretesting and posttesting were conducted with a sample of 323 children in all the classes involved in the project. The mean scores increased from the pretest to the posttest for the majority of the project students, suggesting a general increase in vocational maturity and knowledge of careers. Session and program evaluations were requested of all children, parents, and teachers in the project. The results suggest that both intended and unintended outcomes were achieved.

As part of the overall evaluation of the program, children were asked to agree or disagree with a number of statements about the class activities. Of the 323 children, 90% indicated that they liked going to classes at a college, 85% indicated that one of the things they liked most was using equipment and facilities, 86% indicated that it was fun to work with other children on a project, and 76% indicated that they liked the special guests and consultants.

Several types of activities for the children were particularly successful: (a) activities that enabled children not only to see but also to use equipment, (b) those activities that gave children an opportunity to introduce their own experiences and concerns, and (c) activities that stressed self-expression and cooperation among participants.

Many of the classroom teachers devised activities that required children to be creative and to express their own thoughts and feelings. Thus, one teacher had children produce a sound and slide show, another had them develop a collage, and still another directed them to create a dance depicting the world of work in an urban community. The action and self-expression involved in producing a dance were viewed as ideal for helping children not only to understand the public service career cluster but also to develop an appreciation of public service workers.

The intended outcome of increasing children's knowledge of career clusters and occupations was achieved for some, although not all, program participants. Some teachers observed that the children developed self-knowledge, the ability to work together cooperatively on projects, and the skill of communicating more effectively. These outcomes seem to be critical to childrens' career success.

The unintended outcome of doing something fun and constructive with other children was important both to the parents of the participants and to the children themselves. This outcome demonstrates the need for more publicly supported, organized activities for children in this age group.

Increasing parental awareness of the decision-making process was validated by parents' ratings of each individual session of the course for parents. The relative importance of learning in the four areas of goal setting, self-assessment, knowledge of reality factors, and exploration of the current and future job market were assessed through questionnaires in which the parents rated the degree of helpfulness of each session. In general, all of these topics were helpful, with self-assessment and the exploration of reality factors considered slightly more valuable than the others. Asked to describe the most important outcome, one of the instructors cited parents' increased ability to think of themselves as individuals who had the power to change their lives and their greater appreciation of their children's individuality in developing career plans.

Participants in the Career Course for School Personnel responded to a four-page evaluation questionnaire. They indicated confidence about applying their new skills in infusing career education into the curriculum at their schools. Responses to the questionnaire demonstrated that the teachers believed they had gained in a variety of ways: They shared feelings and attitudes about work and career choices; they shared strategies and techniques for lesson development and implementation; they learned about specific resources and materials they could use with their grade levels; and they learned about specific careers and career clusters. Most school personnel valued the field trips as an opportunity to learn about careers and job clusters with which they were unfamiliar. They cited as most valuable those field-trips organized to allow them "behind the scenes" to see not just the public side but also the hidden side of an industry such as the printing business.

As a spinoff of this project, a Career Resource Center has been established at Kingsborough Community College. It is available to all school personnel, both on and off campus, and includes career exploration material such as film strips, career kits, audio and video cassettes, a mini-computer with disks on career exploration, books, and pamphlets. The Career Resource Manual and the booklet of sample lesson plans, cooperatively produced by the District #22 Staff, was distributed throughout the district. The Education 82 course developed under the grant has been incorporated into the education course offerings available at the college.

Considering the previous lack of a systematic career guidance system for the children, parents, and teachers in the middle and junior high schools in Community District #22, the results of this program are encouraging, Children not only found the experience fun and constructive, but they significantly increased their career awareness and knowledge. Self-understanding and communication skills were also enhanced. Those career activities that were considered experiential were valued highly by the children. Self-knowledge and an increased awareness of the career decision-making process were the most valuable outcomes of the course for parents. The school personnel, in assessing the helpfulness of the CEY project, cited increased confidence in their ability to incorporate career education into their curricula.

The best tributes to the success of this project are continuing inquiries from interested parents and teachers about the availability of the program for the 1982-84 academic years. The response to CEY by the community was overwhelmingly enthusiastic, indicating that this comprehensive approach to career education fills a genuine need. It is hoped that other colleges and community school districts will use this project as a model and view it as an example of a community college truly serving the needs of its "community."

References

Evans, R., Hoyt, K., & Mangum, G. (1973). *Career education in the middle/junior high school.* Salt Lake City: Olympus.

Fadale, L. M.. (1975). *Manual for the Career Awareness Inventory (Elementary Level).* Bensenville, IL: Scholastic Testing Service.

Quarles, G. (1981). *Implementing career education: A staff development instructional guide.* New York: New York City Public Schools.

Super, D. E. (1957). *The psychology of careers.* New York: Harper & Row.

Teaching Job Search Skills to Eighth-Grade Students: A Preview of the World of Work

Shelda Bachin Sandler

To what extent can eighth graders profit from a unit of job search skills as taught by the school counselor in scheduled developmental guidance classes? Or, to restate the question, how much learning actually takes place in the classroom when that learning directly affects an individual's future in the world of work? This is the premise with which I began this mini-study.

As the school counselor, I meet with each middle school class (Grades 6–8) for one period per week for developmental guidance. The topics, according to the curriculum guide, include units such as study skills, interpersonal relationships, drugs, communication skills, and careers, to name just a few.

This study was conducted with 52 eighth-grade boys and girls. Many of the students in this district enter the world of work immediately after graduation from high school; some, like so many of their counterparts of the '80s, maintain a part-time job while still attending high school. In addition, several of the eighth graders shared with me their desire to work during the summer vacation.

With this in mind, it seemed to me that job search skills would rank high in interest level. The method I used to teach was a combination of lecture, discussion, question and answer, audio-visual aids (overhead projection, videotape, and chalkboard), and handouts. The object was to vary the teaching method enough to maintain interest while teaching the basic elements of the job search. Many of these students had previously indicated that they were currently searching for summer or part-time jobs.

Lesson 1. This was basically a motivating lesson. It consisted of a pretest (see Appendix A), an overview of the unit, and a multiple-choice game based on job titles from the *Dictionary of Occupational Titles* (U.S. Department of Labor, 1977). Interest, as expected, was greatest during the game. The game was included as the motivator to introduce the unit.

Lesson 2. This consisted of an explanation and examples of resumes. Students were shown two resume styles, and discussion followed about what information is necessary to put on a resume and what information is not. A resume-writing workshop was not scheduled because eighth graders typically have few functional skills or work-related experiences. Therefore, this lesson included only a discussion about resumes. Samples of various resume styles were shown using overhead projection or handouts.

Lesson 3. This involved a discussion of the importance and uses of cover letters and follow-up, or thank-you, letters. The students were shown what information is included in these types of correspondence, again, by use of lecture, overhead projection, and handouts.

Lesson 4. This session focused on the most effective way to fill out a job application. Each of the students was given a blank job application, and after a detailed explanation of the do's and don'ts of answering the questions, they were given class time to complete the application under the direction of the counselor.

Lessons 5 and 6. This was the beginning of a segment about interviewing behaviors, both positive and negative. The counselor explained that positive behaviors are those that lead to a job offer and negative behaviors are those that have a tendency to eliminate ("deselect") the applicant. The students and counselor also discussed what the interviewer looks for during the interview and typical interview questions and answers were role-played. At the conclusion of Lesson 6, a volunteer from the class was chosen to be interviewed on videotape during a "mock" job interview. The students selected a "job" from a list of jobs similar to those that might be found in the classified section in the newspaper. This particular list of jobs, however, was written by the counselor and aimed at the skills and availability of an eighth-grade student. A day and time were determined for the interview; and with the counselor role-playing the part of the interviewer, each student volunteer was interviewed and videotaped in a one-on-one setting.

Lesson 7. This took place immediately after the videotaped interview. During this class period, the videotape was shown to the class and the "applicant" was critiqued, first for strengths that might lead to a job offer and then for areas that might be improved. At no time were judgmental terms such as "good" or "bad" used. In addition, the student volunteers were given a great deal of positive reinforcement from the counselor for taking the risk of being interviewed and then having the interview critiqued by their peers. In addition to verbalizing the critique, the student observers were required to put their observations into writing using the *Interview Observation Checklist* (see Appendix B). These checklists were then given to the student "applicant" at the end of the class period.

Lesson 8. The final lesson was devoted to any unfinished business, unanswered questions, how to read abbreviations in classified ads ("want" ads), use of references, and a short explanation of networking and employment agencies. The culminating activity involved the posttest (see Appendix A) and a brief evaluation of the unit (see Appendix C).

Conclusion

Based on the sample of 52 students, as represented by two schools in the same school district, it seems evident that eighth-grade students can, indeed, benefit from a unit that teaches job search skills. As indicated by results of the posttest, the average score was increased by 24.7 points. Only three students scored lower on the posttest than they did on the pretest. The mean rose from 26.3 (pretest) to 50.0 (posttest), and the median went from 30.0 to 50.0. The mode jumped 25 points, from 30.0 (pretest) to 55.0 (posttest). The scores on the pretest ranged from 0-55; however, the scores on the posttest ranged from 10-85. the standard deviation was 11.19 (pretest), 14.4 (posttest), and the coefficient of correlation was 0.37.

As I expected from my personal experience as a teacher and a counselor, the favorite part of this unit was the mock videotaped interview. In addition, the students have indicated that they believe the typical interview questions and answers will be the most helpful to them when they actually begin their job search. Almost half of the students responded that they plan to use all of the techniques presented during their own search, and about 40% indicated that they would emphasize all of these techniques if they were helping a friend during his or her job search (see Appendix C).

According to the survey, the least enjoyable part of the unit was resume writing, perhaps because these students are too young to have work-related information to include in a resume; therefore, they could not participate in a resume-writing workshop, an activity that certainly would have added more interest to the lesson.

In conclusion, it is evident that learning did take place over the eight-week period. Furthermore, it would be interesting to follow these same students throughout their high school and college years to monitor their success, whether it be for a full-time permanent job after graduation or for a part-time job while they are still in school.

References

Bolles, R. N. (1987a). *What color is your parachute?* Berkeley, CA: Ten Speed Press.

Bolles, R. N. (1987b). *The quick job hunting map.* Berkeley, CA: Ten Speed Press.

Jackson, T. (1983). *Guerrilla tactics in the job market.* New York: Bantam.

Jackson, T. (1985). *The perfect resume.* New York: Doubleday.

U.S. Department of Labor. (1977). *Dictionary of occupational titles.* (4th ed). Washington, DC: U.S. Government Printing Office.

Appendix A

Pretest and Posttest

1. A brief outline of a person's educational history and work experience is a(n) _____.

2. Another name for a Letter of Application is a(n) _____ _____.

3. After a job interview, an individual should send a(n) _____ _____ to the interviewer.

4. On a job application, how should a person answer questions that do not apply to him or her? _____

5. At what time should an applicant arrive for a job interview, assuming he or she has a 10:30 appointment?_____

6. If an interviewer asks about your strengths, how many will you list? _____

7. If an interviewer asks about weaknesses, how many will you list and how will you present your weaknesses?

_____

8. How many blank spaces (unanswered questions is it permissible to have on a job application? _____

9. Name three articles of clothing a person should never wear to a job interview.

    _____

10. _____

11. _____

12. The interviewer offers you a doughnut at the beginning of your job interview. What do you do?

    _____

13. At what point during the job search do you inquire about salary?

    _____

14. Name two resume styles.

    _____

15. _____

16. In what kind of order does a resume list work experience and educational history? _____

17. What information is never included in a resume?

    _____

18. What color(s) of paper is(are) acceptable for a resume?

    _____

19. What does a person do first when meeting the job interviewer?

    _____

20. What percentage of available jobs appear in the Classified Ads section of the newspaper? _____

Appendix B
Interview Observation Checklist

Please Rank Each Question From 1-4:

1. not at all
2. rarely
3. sometimes
4. frequently

Did the interviewee:

1. Introduce himself or herself to the interviewer?
2. Shake hands with the interviewer at the beginning and at the end of the interview?

    3. Maintain a relaxed posture?
    4. Speak clearly?
    5. Look directly at the interviewer?
    6. Show confidence in himself or herself?
    7. Show enthusiasm?
    8. Answer the questions directly?
    9. Express himself or herself clearly?
  10. Ask appropriate job-related questions?

(For additional comments, use reverse side of paper if necessary.)

Appendix C

Job Search Evaluation

1. Which part of the job search unit do you think will be most helpful
    to you in finding a job? Circle one.

    Resumes
    Cover letters
    Applications
    Follow-up letters
    Interview behaviors and questions
    Videotaped interview
    Other (be specific) _____

2. On the whole, how useful will this unit be to you in finding a job?
    Circle one.

    Very useful
    Somewhat useful
    Not useful at all

3. Which part of this unit did you enjoy the most? Circle one.

    Resumes
    Cover letters
    Applications
    Follow-up letters
    Interview behaviors and questions
    Videotaped interview
    Other (be specific) _____

4. Which part of the unit did you like the least? Circle one.

   Resumes
   Cover letters
   Applications
   Follow-up letters
   Interview behaviors and questions
   Videotaped interview
   Other (be specific) _____

5. If you were to help your best friend in his or her job search, which part of the unit would you emphasize? Circle one.

   Resumes
   Cover letters
   Applications
   Follow-up letters
   Interview behaviors and questions
   Videotaped interview
   Other (be specific) _____
   All of the above
   None of the above

6. What part of the unit are you most likely to use in your own job search? Circle one.

   Resumes
   Cover letters
   Applications
   Follow-up letters
   Interview behaviors and questions
   Videotaped interview
   Other (be specific) _____

Career Education for Students with Disabilities

Donn E. Brolin
Norman C. Gysbers

In our previous article on the subject (Brolin & Gysbers, 1979) ten years ago, we described as marginal the assimilation of most students with disabilities into the mainstream of society. Although experts believed that most students with disabilities had the potential to become productive and independent citizens, the results from educational and rehabilitation efforts were basically ineffective in preparing many of them for life after school. Societal ignorance and stereotypes about students with disabilities were also identified as serious deterrents to their successful career development and employment. What has happened in the past ten years? What is the status of former students with disabilities? Is it any better than what was achieved in the 1970s, when many promises and mandates were promulgated by federal and state agencies?

In this article we review some of the major developments in the past ten years involved with improving the preparation of students with disabilities for life after school. We will also describe the Life-Centered Career Education (LCCE) approach for these students, identify some programs that are using the LCCE Curriculum to better help students become more productive and functional, and then present a challenge to counselors concerning how they can, using a systematic guidance approach, help students to become more competent individuals. We conclude the article with what we consider to be the unfinished agenda—an agenda that needs to be addressed in the future if we are to truly meet the needs of students with disabilities.

Developments in the 1980s

Several developments occurred in the 1980s to reflect a continuing concern for the welfare of students with disabilities. One example of a development is semantics. Today, terminology describing students with disabilities has changed from the handicapped, mentally retarded, or handicapped people, to a more humanistic and less dehumanizing term reflecting that they are students first and that they have a disability second. Thus, the term handicap, which we used in our article's title in 1979, has been changed to disabilities.

In addition, as career education terminology subsided in the 1980s, a new term that closely resembled the career education concept was introduced. The term was introduced by Madeleine Will, Assistant Secretary of the U.S. Office of Special Education and Rehabilitative Services (OSERS). It was called "transition," which she defined as "...an outcome-oriented process encompassing a broad array of services and experiences that lead to employment" (Will, 1984, p. 2). The transition period included high school, graduation, postsecondary education or adult services, and the initial years of employment. The transition concept, like career education, requires interdisciplinary cooperation in the schools and with community service agencies and employers, as well as meaningful parent involvement. As pointed out by Chadsey-Rusch, Rusch, and Phelps (1989), collaboration is essential to a successful transition-oriented program so students receive planned, appropriate, and nonduplicated services.

Need for Transitional Services

It is apparent from the literature that the transition of students with disabilities from school to work is not better today than it was in previous decades. Studies of former students with disabilities (Hasazi, Gordon, & Roe, 1985; Mithaug, Horiuchi, & Fanning, 1985; Edgar, 1985) clearly reveal that the majority of them have extreme difficulties finding and securing adequate employment and becoming independent. Furthermore, a Louis Harris and Associates (1986) telephone survey with a cross section of 1,000 people with disabilities age 16 and over found two-thirds not working, and most of those who did work were working only part-time. The evidence is clear that the vast majority of students with disabilities never attain a satisfactory level of career development consistent with their capabilities. This unfortunate outcome occurs despite the frequent proclamation that one of the most fundamental tenets of education is to develop to the maximum degree possible the abilities of all its students, so they can become employed, develop personal and social skills, and function as independent citizens.

Legislation

During the 1980s, federal and state legislation was passed to promote and enhance the career development of students with disabilities. Section 626 of the *1983 Amendments to the Education of the Handicapped Act of 1975* addresses the educational and employment transition difficulties of these students. This legislation authorized $6.6 million in grants and contracts to be spent annually by OSERS to improve and strengthen education, training, and related services. During 1984-1988, 180 model demonstration projects were developed and implemented in a wide variety of educational settings to facilitate the transition of youth and adults with disabilities into the work force (Dowling & Hartwell, 1988).

Another important legislative effort was the *Carl D. Perkins Vocational Education Act of 1984*, which provides funds to implement many career development services for students with vocational educa-tion opportunities provided to students and parents no later than ninth grade, guidance and counseling services by trained counselors, assess-ment of abilities, interests, and needs, and inclusion of vocational services as a component of the student's IEP. The Act is designed to pro-vide support to students, including those with disabilities, in vocational programs to enhance their independent functioning.

Other legislation passed in the 1980s to further enhance the career development of persons with disabilities included the *Rehabilitation Act Amendments of 1986, Job Training Partnership Act of 1982,* and the *Developmental Disabilities Act Amendments of 1984*. Each of these Acts requires interagency cooperation and a greater emphasis on providing these individuals with vocational training, employment, and independent living services. Supported employment was introduced in rehabilitation and developmental disabilities legislation as both a service and an employment outcome for people with severe disabilities who required ongoing support in order to maintain competitive employment. Thus students who previously had no options other than sheltered employment or day-activities programs now have a variety of employment possibili-ties, which can be further enhanced through career education.

Federal and State Agency Efforts

The transition movement has brought together a variety of educational and state agencies to interface with advocate groups, parents, and students with disabilities so that better ways to coordinate and plan services can be devised. One example is the efforts of the Special Education Regional Resource Centers who sponsored, with the Rehabilitation Services Administration, a series of major conferences bringing together representatives from all possible professional agencies, schools, and advocate groups to work and plan services (Brolin & Schatzman, 1989). Interagency agreements to increase transition and coordination were developed between state rehabilitation agencies, developmental disabilities, and schools, so more substantial efforts could be provided for the students. In many respects these efforts were a rekindling of much of what had occurred in the 1970s but was never adequately carried through (Szymanski, King, Parker, & Jenkins, 1989).

Professional Organizations

The major professional educational groups that continue to promote the career development of students with disabilities are the Division on Career Development (DCD) of The Council for Exceptional Children, the Special Needs Division of the American Vocational Association, and The National Association of Vocational Education Special Needs Personnel (NAVESNP), which is affiliated with the American Vocational Association and the American Rehabilitation Counseling Association (ARCA) of the American Association for Counseling and Development. These groups conduct state, regional, and national conferences on career development, publish journals and other important documents, lobby for and promote important career development legislation, promote research activities, and offer inservice and preservice opportunities. Recently, the Division on Career Development prepared a position paper on special education's responsibility to adults with disabilities, which has become a policy statement for the entire organization of The Council for Exceptional Children (CEC).

A Functional Skills Approach

Many leaders concerned about the education of students recognize the importance of and the need for career development programs and services. Unfortunately, these programs and services are still not major priorities in most schools. If employment and living successfully in the community are major educational goals for students with disabilities, we must offer a curriculum that will lead to these accomplishments (Kokaska & Brolin, 1985). Otherwise, as Edgar (1987) has found, more than 30% will continue to drop out of secondary programs and only 15% will secure jobs with a salary above the minimum wage. We endorse Edgar and others who believe a major change in secondary programs for students with disabilities is urgently needed and that there be, once and for all, a shift in focus of secondary curriculum to a more functional approach that will give these students the competencies they need to survive in today's society.

The *Life-Centered Career Education Curriculum* (Brolin, 1978, 1983, 1989) is a career development functional approach that has been implemented in many school districts across the country. The *LCCE Curriculum*, available since 1978, focuses on 22 major competencies that students need to succeed in daily living, personal-social, and occupational areas after they leave school (Table 1). The 22 *LCCE* competencies further subdivide into 97 (previously 102) subcompetencies that relate to one or more of four important career roles that constitute a total worker. These four career roles consist of the work of an employee, the work that is done in the home, volunteer work, and productive avocational activities. *LCCE* is designed to facilitate the student's individual growth and development for all the major roles, settings, and events that constitute a person's total life career development. It is a K through grade 12+ approach built on the four stages of career awareness, exploration, preparation, and assimilation and requires a close and meaningful partnership between educators, the family, and community agencies, employers, and other resources. Hoyt and Shylo (1987) reported *LCCE* to be an effective curriculum that combines important daily living skills instruction with an employability skills focus.

Currently, the senior author and his associates are conducting a U.S. Department of Education-sponsored *LCCE/Employability Enhancement Project* in cooperation with the University of Arkansas Research and Training Center in Vocational Rehabilitation. The project involves comprehensive implementation procedures and validation of newly developed career assessment and instructional materials in several school districts throughout the country. The project is designed to demonstrate that students provided with the *LCCE* approach will gain much greater career and life skills competence and have a significantly better post-school adjustment than those who receive more conventional academic education.

Table 1
Life-Centered Career Education (LCCE) Curriculum

Curriculum Areas	Competency
Daily living skills	1. Managing personal finances
	2. Selecting & managing a household
	3. Caring for personal needs
	4. Raising children & meeting marriage responsibilities
	5. Buying, preparing, & consuming food
	6. Buying & caring for clothing
	7. Exhibiting responsible citizenship
	8. Utilizing recreational facilities and engaging in leisure
	9. Getting around the community
Personal-social skills	10. Achieving self-awareness
	11. Acquiring self-confidence
	12. Achieving socially responsible behavior
	13. Maintaining good interpersonal skills
	14. Achieving independence
	15. Making adequate decisions
	16. Communicating with others
Occupational guidance & preparation	17. Knowing & exploring occupational possibilities
	18. Selecting & planning occupational choices
	19. Exhibiting appropriate work habits & behavior
	20. Seeking, securing, & maintaining employment
	21. Exhibiting sufficient physical-manual skills
	22. Obtaining a specific occupational skill

Some Sample Programs

The *Life-Centered Career Education Curriculum* has been widely adopted in many school districts across the United States and foreign countries since its first publication by The Council for Exceptional Children (CEC) in 1978. The third edition of the curriculum guide was published by CEC in 1989, along with several companion products, that is, a *Trainer/Implementation Manual*, two *Activity Books*, and an *LCCE*

Inventory to assess student competency levels. Some examples of the school districts that exemplify comprehensive adoption of the *LCCE Curriculum* are:

1. Marshall (Missouri) Public Schools (Kim Ratcliffe, Director of Special Services) have used *LCCE* to become the framework for their major goal of preparing their students for life. The *LCCE* competencies are infused into the K through 12 curriculum and include community awareness, increased parent participation, advisory committees, and a staff inservice. As classroom lessons are developed around actual work needs, academic, occupational, and personal-social competencies take on a new meaning and give students a humanistic concept of work involving home, community, and school relationships.

2. Moberly (Missouri) Public Schools (George Wilson, Director of Special Education) have used *LCCE* subcompetencies to translate into locally-stated goals and objectives, meet them with specified activities, materials, resources, and evaluation techniques. Their work is stored in the computer and disseminated to each special education teacher in looseleaf binders so that the material can be kept current.

3. District #742 Community Schools in St. Cloud (Minnesota) (Thomas Prescott, Coordinator of Secondary Special Education) have combined locally defined basic skills and *LCCE* competencies to develop specific courses that include the *LCCE Curriculum*. *LCCE* is used to provide a structure for writing clear program goals and knowing how each of the classes, activities, services, and roles contribute toward those goals. IEP goals focus on *LCCE* competencies, which has led to a great networking benefit between schools using the *LCCE* program.

Space prohibits describing other programs, although such school districts as Minneapolis, St. Paul, Brainerd (Minnesota), Jackson (Michigan), Shawano (Wisconsin), Aurora (Colorado), Richmond (California), Joplin (Missouri), Bolivar (Missouri), and Osceola (Arizona) are other good examples.

The Challenge for School Counselors

The challenge for school counselors to respond to the career development needs of students with disabilities is as great today as it was in 1979—perhaps even greater! Today, however, because of changes in how guidance is being conceptualized and practiced in the schools, the opportunity for school counselors to meet this challenge has increased substantially. Why? Because guidance in the schools is increasingly being conceptualized and practiced as a comprehensive competency-based program.

Gysbers and Henderson (1988) described one model of a comprehensive program as having four program components. These components are guidance curriculum, individual planning, responsive services, and system support. The model is competency-based (student competencies) with identified percentages of counselor time devoted to carrying out guidance activities in each component.

This model, and others like it that have similar components, is ready-made to incorporate selected competencies from the *LCCE* list of 22 competencies. Competencies 10 through 15, and 17, 18, and 20, for example, are particularly appropriate for inclusion in the guidance curriculum. Since most programs that have a curriculum component already have competencies identified, it is recommended that they be reviewed in light of the *LCCE* competencies. Are there gaps? What modifications may be required to serve students with disabilities?

Once this process is complete, the next step is to review the sequence of the competencies—which ones are to be accomplished by which grade level or grade level grouping. If a sequence had not been established already in the program, the sequence of awareness, exploration, and preparation might be considered.

Career Awareness

This phase is particularly important during the elementary years, although it continues throughout the life span. During this phase, guidance activities, delivered through the guidance curriculum, focus on helping students with disabilities begin to learn about their feelings, values, and potential. The focus also is on helping these students develop feelings of self-worth and confidence, to become aware of socially desirable behaviors, and to become aware of the need to develop communication skills to relate to others.

In the case of the occupational competencies, the focus is on developing positive attitudes about work, to begin to see themselves as potential workers, and to become aware of different kinds of jobs and job responsibilities. In addition, the focus is on the development of a work personality and to become aware of the kinds of work habits and behaviors required to be successful.

Counselors can help teachers to identify the emerging interests and needs of their students and the special aptitude and abilities that each seem to possess. A variety of career awareness activities, involving parents and community resource people, should include speakers, media, field trips, home assignments, career games, role playing, puppetry, cooperative learning, and simulated business activities. Motivating and realistic learning experiences can increase academic learning as well as promote career development.

Career Exploration

Exploration is emphasized during the middle school-junior high school years. Here guidance activities assist students with disabilities to carefully explore their abilities and needs, the requirements of the labor market, and unpaid work roles and avocational/leisure activities through tryout experiences. In the personal-social area of the *LCCE*, for example, guidance activities focus on exploring abilities, needs, and interests. In the occupational area, guidance activities emphasize exploration of occupational clusters through hands-on experiences, both in and out of school. Work samples, simulated job tasks, and community jobs can be used in the development of work habits and behaviors required for future employment. In addition, such activities provide students with necessary experiential referents to enable participation in career decision making. Career and vocational assessment are important to conduct with each experience so that students can examine interests and aptitudes. Also important to emphasize at this stage is exploring the unpaid work roles of homemaker, family member, volunteer, and a person who engages in productive avocational/leisure activities.

Preparation

Although preparation begins in early childhood and continues through-out life, special attention is required during the latter part of middle school-junior high school and during high school. Guidance activities through the curriculum component as well as other components of the program emphasize the development and clarification of personal-social and occupational competencies. Specific interests, aptitudes, and skills are further clarified and life-styles more clearly delineated. In the occupational area, career choices, although still tentative, are more specially related to vocational and academic instruction. Students with disabilities will need additional help during this phase to select from the variety of courses and experiences available. Preparation for most students with disabilities requires a substantial experiential component. Comprehensive vocational evaluation (vocational tests, work/job samples, situation assessment, job tryouts) also is important in examining the realism of their choices and their education and training needs. Many students with disabilities may require more than the traditional amount of time to prepare for an occupation and for work in the other three work-role areas. Finally, most students with disabilities have life-long learning needs. These needs should be taken into account with placement, follow-up, and other supportive guidance activities.

Counselor Competencies

To carry out guidance activities during the various phases of the guidance curriculum requires counselors who can accomplish the following activities:

1. conduct or arrange for career assessment for students with disabilities
2. develop and use community resources, particularly for referral purposes
3. become an advocate for students with disabilities
4. contribute to the development and monitoring of individual learning programs in cooperation with other educators and parents
5. consult with parents concerning the career development of their children
6. consult with other educators concerning the development of self-awareness and decision making competencies in students with disabilities
7. work with students with disabilities in the selection of training opportunities and the selection of job possibilities
8. counsel students with disabilities

Comprehensive guidance program models, such as the one described by Gysbers and Henderson (1988), offer a structure to organize, implement, and manage the schools' guidance activities and services. Through this model's guidance curriculum, individual planning, responsive services, and system support program components, school counselors can work directly and effectively with all students including those with disabilities. In addition, they can work directly and effectively with teachers, parents, administrators, and members of the community to accomplish the goals of the program.

The Unfinished Agenda: Challenge for the 1990s

Over the past 20 years, the need to provide better educational and rehabilitation services to students with disabilities has been widely recognized throughout this country. Legislation has been passed resulting in money to develop programs, conduct research, hire additional personnel, and offer more services in schools and adult service agencies. But it appears from our experience and the data presented in the literature that students with disabilities are not attaining greater vocational and independent living success than they did in previous years.

The agenda is unfinished. What do we need to do to finish the agenda? In our opinion, some of the major challenges that need attention to better meet the needs of students with disabilities are the following:

One challenge is the double-edged sword that exists in our educational programs. On the one hand, educators promote the concept of career and life skills training for these individuals and, on the other hand, they increase academic requirements and proficiency tests for graduation. Thus, academic training becomes the predominant thrust in the education of all students. The result, as McBride and Forgone (1985) found, is less time available for career and vocational education (only 7 of 593 short-term instructional objectives for 90 Florida junior high school students with disabilities were career and vocational).

Another challenge is for professionals to break out of their traditional disciplines and approaches. Why do many professionals continue to have stereotypes and negative attitudes toward these individuals? Students with disabilities are not a monolithic group! They vary considerably in ability levels, and most can benefit from regular class placement like everyone else. Some have special needs that require modification or individual attention. Professionals need to view these students in this perspective rather than in a stereotypic and limiting manner. An accepting learning environment must be provided so these students can also benefit from our educational system.

Too many schools depend on other agencies to provide for the career development needs of students with disabilities. But in reality most do not have the time, staff, or money to provide quality services. Perhaps school-based rehabilitation counselors, as suggested by Szymanski et al. (1989), are one solution to providing some of the students with a specialized transition service if they need it.

Schools must become more flexible and willing to change their programs to meet the real needs of their students. Although schools may also cite money, time, resources, and personnel shortages as barriers to change, the real culprit is the unwillingness of many educators to change. This includes institutions of higher education and their administration and teacher and counselor education programs. As Knowlton and Clark (1987) indicated, until educators come to grips with how to effect systemwide change, the struggle will go on as before.

Are we really going to finish the agenda and give all students, including those with disabilities, the opportunity to become competent and productive adults after they leave school? If so, we strongly must break away from traditional practices so that comprehensive career education and guidance programs are truly implanted in our nation's schools. As stated in our previous article, we must think with both our hearts and our heads and provide an atmosphere that will help all individuals learn more about themselves and prepare them for the many options that await them if we do the job right.

References

Brolin, D. E., & Schatzman, B. (1989). Lifelong career development. In D. E. Berkell & J. M. Brown (Eds.), *Transition from school to work for persons with disabilities* (pp. 22-41). New York: Longman.

Brolin, D. E. (1978, 1983, 1989). *Life-centered career education: A competency-based approach*. Reston, VA: The Council for Exceptional Children.

Brolin, D. E., & Gysbers, N. C. (1979). Career education for persons with handicaps. *The Personnel and Guidance Journal, 57*, 258-262.

Chadsey-Rusch, J., Rusch, F. R., & Phelps, L. A. (1989). Analysis and synthesis of transition issues. In D. E. Berkell & J. M. Brown (Eds.), *Transition from school to work for persons with disabilities* (pp. 227-241). New York: Longman.

Dowling, J., & Hartwell, C. (1987). *Compendium of project profiles.* Champaign: University of Illinois, Transition Institute at Illinois.

Edgar, E. (1985). How do special education students fare after they leave school? A response to "Factors associated with the employment status of handicapped youth exiting high school from 1979 to 1983." *Exceptional Children, 51,* 470–473.

Edgar, E. (1987). Secondary programs in special education: Are many of them justifiable? *Exceptional Children, 53,* 555–561.

Gysbers, N. C., & Henderson, P. (1988). *Developing and managing your school guidance program.* Alexandria, VA: American Association for Counseling and Development.

Louis Harris and Associates, Inc. (1986). *The ICD Survey of disabled Americans: Bringing disabled Americans into the mainstream.* New York: International Center for the Disabled.

Hasazi, S. B., Gordon, L. R., & Roe, C. A. (1985). Factors associated with the employment status of handicapped youth exiting from high school from 1979 to 1983. *Exceptional Children, 51,* 444–469.

Hoyt, K. B., & Shylo, K. R. (1987). *Career education in transition: Trends and implications for the future.* Columbus: ERIC Clearinghouse on Adult, Career, and Vocational Education, The Ohio State University.

Kokaska, C. J., & Brolin, D. E. (1985). *Career education for handicapped individuals* (2nd ed.). Columbus, OH: Merrill.

Knowlton, H. E., & Clark, G. M. (1987). Transition issues for the 1990s. *Exceptional Children, 53*(6), 562–563.

McBride, J. W., & Forgone, C. (1985). Emphasis of instruction provided LD, EH, and EMR students in categorical and cross-categorical resource programs. *Journal of Research and Development in Education, 18,* 50–54.

Mithaug, D., Horiuchi, C., & Fanning, P. (1985). A report on the Colorado statewide follow-up survey of special education students. *Exceptional Children, 51,* 397–404.

Szymanski, E. M., & King, J. (1989). Rehabilitation counseling in transition planning and preparation. *Career Development for Exceptional Individuals, 12*(1), 3-10.

Szymanski, E. M., King, J., Parker, R. M., & Jenkins, W. M. (1989). The state-federal rehabilitation program: Overview and interface with special education. *Exceptional Children, 56,* 70–77.

Will, M. (1984). *OSERS programming for the transition of youth with disabilities: Bridges from school to working life.* Washington, DC:

Office of Special Education and Rehabilitative Services, U.S. Department of Education.

Chapter 8

The Challenge of Organizing a Middle School Counseling Program

In his thought provoking article, "The Relevant Counselor," published in *The School Counselor* in 1986, Edwin Herr concluded:

> ...because there are so many needs for counselors' skills and so many different ways in which school counselors have demonstrated their effectiveness in schools across the country, the problem is how to avoid holding them responsible for so many diverse expectations in any given setting that their effectiveness is diluted. (p. 13)

The challenge for middle school counselors is to develop focused programs that meet specific developmental needs of young adolescents. Much like the students they serve, middle school counselors must develop their own professional identities which are expressed in well defined and accountable school guidance programs. This chapter discusses issues related to counseling program development in middle schools and suggests ways to create and manage counseling programs that help youngsters in the difficult transition from childhood in elementary school to adolescence in high school.

This chapter concludes with a provocative article by Sidney Simon which lists "tongue-in-cheek" reasons for eliminating school counseling programs:

1. "The American family has never been stronger."
2. "...alcohol and drug use among students is at an all-time low."
3. There are no reliable statistics showing that students "are committing suicide or have suicidal tendencies."
4. No student comes to school as "a victim of child sexual abuse anymore."
5. "Without the problems generated by peer group pressure, who needs to pay the salaries of counselors?"
6. "Boys and girls today do not even seem to be curious about sexuality, and with this curiosity gone, none of the girls get pregnant."
7. "Because there are no more alcoholics, there cannot be any children of alcoholics in the schools...."
8. "Children no longer drop out of school."
9. "There are no children with weight problems."
10. "All of the adults who serve children work together cooperatively."

Simon's article is a fitting conclusion to a book intended to help middle school counselors recognize why their services are essential to adolescents trying to answer the question, "Who am I?"

The Counselor and Modern Middle-Level Schools: New Roles in New Schools

Paul S. George

When I was a boy, living in a small mining town outside Pittsburgh, Pennsylvania, my parents, aunts, uncles, and other members of my family and my community were proud of the schools. They were convinced that America had won the war, not because of the bomb, but because of the steel that came from the mills and the students that came from our schools. It was a time of great confidence and affirmation. America was on top of the world. Then, on October 4, 1957, during my junior year in high school, the world's first satellite (Sputnik) shot into orbit and a hundred years of American confidence were destroyed. It has been getting worse every year since then. Today, American citizens are convinced that, whether it is steel or students, tractors or testing, the product just is not as good as it used to be.

The current criticism of education reached its zenith in 1983, with publication of the federal government's *A Nation of Risk* (U.S. Department of Education, 1983), in which American educators were accused of being so incompetent and worthless that their actions came close to being treasonous. In less than half a century, a complete reversal had occurred in American public opinion: Schools, teachers, and even counselors had gone from being viewed as the most effective group of educators in the world to being viewed as treasonous and incompetent.

In response to this caustic criticism, educators have mounted incredible efforts to improve the schools or to demonstrate that public schools are far better than the citizenry has been led to believe. Foremost among these efforts has been the last decade of research in an area that has come to be known as "educational effectiveness." Following a strategy similar to research in business and industry, educational researchers have been searching for the "keys to school productivity and success (cf. Ouchi, 1981; Pascale & Athos, 1981; Peters & Waterman, 1982). Fortunately, they seem to have discovered some very important, critical factors in school success. Today, the results of this research are being read eagerly by public school educators everywhere; hundreds, if not thousands, of school districts are implementing school effectiveness programs based on the research (George, 1983a).

The school effectiveness movement may be one of the most important thrusts in the closing decades of 20th-century education, and it has tremendous implications for the work of school counselors at all levels, especially in middle schools and junior high schools. In this article I explore the results of effectiveness research in corporate and school settings and suggest new roles for school counselors that are congruent with the recent findings.

Much of the related research, in both corporate and academic spheres, is of the kind known as "outlier" studies. That is, if one wants to know what makes a successful corporation, then one ought to examine closely those corporations that have been dramatically successful, those that lie outside the common group. Researchers in the corporate sphere have successfully identified a number of characteristics of exceptionally productive companies, common traits that exist despite the size, location, or product of those firms.

Among the most important common elements of such corporations, sometimes referred to as "Type Z" firms, are:

Long term employment. Employees of the most profitable companies often spend their lives working for only one or two different employers. Executives in these industrial groups tend to start at the bottom of a company and work their way up in the same company.

Stable, supportive, social situations. A strong brand of egalitarianism complements the sense of community felt within the company. Regardless of the size of the firm, employees often spend much of their personal family lives associated with the families of other company employees.

Holistic view of persons. Management tends to think of the employees of the company as "associates" rather than as common workers. The individual employee is given attention in ways unmatched in other corporations. For example, Type Z companies tend to have fringe benefit programs in areas such as health, leisure time, and education that far outdistance those in competing companies.

Individual responsibility plus teamwork. Highly productive American corporations allow for plenty of individual effort and reward, and they also organize in ways that demand teamwork on common projects that go beyond each individual's specialty.

Participatory decision making. Each individual has a voice, at the appropriate level, in the decisions affecting his or her life in the company.

Development of interpersonal communication skills. Because people in these companies spend their lives together working closely on common projects, they must learn to communicate and cooperate effectively. Corporations that break profit and production barriers invest thousands of dollars on training to help employees develop their interpersonal skills.

Common goals. Perhaps the most significant characteristic of these highly profitable companies is that the employees share a concept of the purpose of the company in the corporate world and in American society. These firms tend to value service, quality, and people above the concern for profit that seems to be the sole motivating force in less successful corporations.

Strong leadership. Leaders who believe in the company, love the product and the employees, and can manage and motivate groups of people are always present at the forefront of the most productive corporations.

Researchers in the area of school effectiveness have also been able to identify a number of common characteristics of successful schools, regardless of where the schools are located, the size of the schools, or the socioeconomic backgrounds of the students. The late Ronald Edmonds (1979), one of education's first proponents of the effectiveness concept, stated that directly as a result of this research, "We can, when-ever and wherever we choose, successfully teach all children whose schooling is of interest and we already know more than we need to know to do so" (p. 15). Edmonds and other researchers developed lists of the characteristics of those schools that have demonstrated that they are more productive, academically, than predictions made for them based on the characteristics of the homes from which their students came. Schools that make a significant difference in the academic lives of the students have:

- A safe and orderly environment
- A clearly articulated sense of mission
- A climate of high expectations for student learning
- Strong instructional leadership
- Frequent monitoring of student progress

- Effective instruction
- Good home and school support systems

A more detailed description of the characteristics of effective schools and highly productive corporations (George, 1983a) reveals that successful institutions have much in common. Productivity and success seem to emerge from common themes, regardless of the type of institution. One of the most striking similarities is the common emphasis on the persons involved in the process. The leaders of highly successful institutions, whether involved with steel or students, recognize the worth and dignity of the human beings who are at the heart of the process. Productive corporations and successful schools both recognize and deal with the wholeness of the persons who are so important to the mission of the institutions.

For school counselors, the implications of this common focus are almost infinite. In the business world, for example, large companies devote significant resources to what once was called personnel and is now more often referred to as human resource development. Huge sums are funnelled into the effort to improve productivity by developing employees as workers and as persons. On the other hand, school systems have a reputation for giving lip service to human resource development but supplying few resources for the effort. As a result, in many schools the school counselor may be the only person who recognizes the need to focus on the students' personal development as well as on their academic achievements.

Characteristics of Successful Schools

School counselors need to be aware of some important shifts that have been occurring in the affective emphasis of American middle schools. For most of the last 20 years educators in many middle schools have focused on the uniqueness of each learner by developing programs that stress individualization (George, 1983b). More recently, these same educators have begun to recognize that middle graders have another great need, in the affective area: They need to learn how to become effective group members (Lipsitz, 1984).

Successful schools for middle graders—those that meet important criteria in both the academic and affective development of these students—have begun to work toward meeting the dual affective needs of these students: the need to discover their unique individuality and the need to embrace and become effective members of small and large groups for the rest of their lives (Lipsitz, 1984). Counselors who care about the work in schools for middle graders must respond to and facilitate the accomplishment of these goals. The results of effective-need research in the corporate and educational spheres indicate that effective schools for middle graders need to incorporate the following five fundamental principles in their programs.

Common Mission

Schools that are successful in offering balanced programs that meet both the academic and affective needs of middle graders tend to be very similar to each other. These schools may be different sizes, in different locations, and have different names, but their programs and organization are often dramatically similar. Such schools have educators who share a common sense of mission about the importance of education for middle graders and the special nature of children at that age.

Program Alignment

Effective middle schools offer programs that are congruent with this vital philosophical commitment. If the philosophy of the school stresses the need for mastery of the basic skills, then the program offers sufficient means for the goal to be accomplished. If the philosophy of the school stresses the importance of improving the self-esteem of middle graders, then the school takes a proactive stance in designing opportunities for this to happen. If the mission of the school includes the need for exploration in the curriculum, then the program schedule makes such options easy to exercise. The school's program becomes a concrete expression of the staff's philosophy.

Inspired Instruction

Educators in schools that offer inspired instruction are able to identify and employ teachers and others who agree with the school's mission and are capable of implementing the program in their classrooms and elsewhere. Inspired instruction is manifested in ways that result in students learning what the school and the community have decided they should learn. Members of the school's staff begin with the confidence that they can be successful, even with the most difficult and challenging students in the school. They believe their goals are extremely important and work diligently to accomplish them.

Group Involvement

Successful programs are organized in ways that result in almost every student and staff member believing that they are important members of very important groups. Large schools are organized so that students are provided with the opportunity to belong to small groups within the larger school. Vital subgroups are created in which an "ethos of caring" emerges. Students come to view themselves as members of the same team as the teachers; rather than being on opposing sides, they are together, pursuing the same purposes. Teams, advisory groups, schools-within-the school, and other similar arrangements unite teachers and students in ways, and for longer periods of time, so that a genuine sense of community begins to develop.

Spirited Leadership

The final ingredient for successful middle schools is spirited leadership. Winning schools, like highly productive corporations, are led by administrators, counselors, and teachers who have decided that the school is the best avenue they have for making a difference in the world. These leaders have a vision of what makes schools successful and they are capable of inspiring other members of the staff to move toward the same goals. They are people who love schools for middle graders and the students in those schools. Such educators enjoy being close to the action, and their involvement demonstrates both their commitment and skill. They are instructional leaders who are respected by other staff members for what they can do as well as what they say. Lastly, spirited leaders have the capacity to manage groups of professionals in ways that move the school toward realizing the mission on which they have all focused.

The education of middle graders in American schools has entered a new phase. A great deal more is now known about how to accomplish the goals of the school, and educators have come to understand how much more important, and how complex, is the affective component of this educational process. What roles will effective school counselors perform in these effective schools for middle graders? How can counselors help the staff and the students move toward the realization of the goals they all embrace? Will school counselors be important people in such schools?

New Roles for the Counselor

Even though educators have isolated the characteristics of successful schools for middle graders and have arrived at a new professional consensus about the important role of the affective component in such schools, there is much more to the success of such schools. Educators have also discovered that creating new schools that manifest the characteristics of highly productive institutions is not automatic, nor is it easy. Effective schools do not just appear magically, like Athena from the forehead of Zeus. It is much easier to find such schools than it is to create them by transforming unproductive schools into successful ones.

Although educators are not able to state, conclusively, which ingredients are the most important to school success and which must precede the emergence of the others, most educators seem to believe that the leadership factor is the crucial characteristic that stimulates the growth of the others. I contend that most schools have not moved swiftly and naturally to a place where they can demonstrate increased success partly because school counselors have not played an important schoolwide role in this area. Unfortunately, many current school administrators (principals and assistant principals) are too often not naturally inclined to value or even recognize the necessary ingredients for success when those ingredients are not part of the budget or schedule. In all fairness, it is also likely that today's school administrators are so harried that they do not often have nor realize the need to take the time to implement success-oriented innovations. School administrators are not always affectively oriented people.

There is, then, in many schools that are less successful than they might be a vacuum of leadership skills and attitudes. School administrators do not naturally recognize the required ingredients, and school counselors have been so busy with other legitimate activities that they, too, are often uninvolved. It is also possible that school counselors have not viewed themselves as legitimately involved in school reorganization and revitalization. Many counselors have recognized the typical school for what it too often is—an affective desert—and have retreated to their counseling spaces where they have attempted to create an affective oasis, one spot in the school where students can come for affective refreshment.

Unfortunately, in most schools the ratio of counselors to students often results in a situation in which only a few students—those dying from affective thirst—find their way to the oasis and the growth and renewal it can provide. Hundreds, sometimes even thousands, of other students pass in and out of the school without ever having had contact with the counselor. Although these students might not have been in crises, their school lives may have been significantly less meaningful than they might have been had they had the opportunity for contact with a counselor.

School counselors must assume a new set of schoolwide roles. These roles should fit the need for what might be called an "educational ombudsman"; that is, one person in the school who assumes the responsibility for ensuring that fundamental program components are implemented successfully. For schools to become more effective they must become more affective, and the school counselor is the person most likely to be successful in stimulating schools to move in this direction. Some might argue that, considering the current status of counseling in the schools, it would be impossible for counselors to find the time and energy to accept and act in these new roles. I believe that when the critical nature of the school counselor's role in school improvement becomes apparent, counselors will find a way. And, when others in the school and the community observe the results of these new activities, counselors will be viewed as far more essential to school success than they are often perceived to be.

What are the new schoolwide roles that only counselors can do well? What does an educational ombudsman look like and act like? What will the school's official affective advocates be doing in the next few years if they accept the burden of schoolwide improvement? Counselors must, of course, think of themselves and their roles in significantly different ways. In the age of "high tech," as schools move more closely to becoming supervised correspondence courses and as students now interact with computers instead of mimeographs, counselors must become the skilled technicians of the "high touch" (Naisbitt, 1982) response. How can this be accomplished?

Nurturing the School Mission

First, the school counselor in today's successful schools for middle graders must participate more vigorously in forming a new vision of what those schools can and should accomplish. No one else in the school is more attuned to those needs of middle graders that require a more potent response from the school. No one is more child centered. No one is better able to point out that these students are much more than cognitive beings and that there is no inherent conflict between the need to raise test scores and the need to attend to the affective side of students' lives. And no one else is likely to have the skills of group facilitation and organizational development that will enable the school staff to move together to a new sense of mission. If not the counselor, then who?

Guiding Program Alignment with the Mission

In most middle schools today, there are few staff members who are charged with what are sometimes referred to as "oversight" responsibilities. It is rare to find a school in which a staff member is identified with the task of seeking balance in the school's curriculum. Consequently, many schools for middle graders are characterized by an imbalance in the curriculum that often excludes, or at least downplays, the importance of anything that is not being measured on achievement tests. The school counselor, whose only vested interest in the affective domain (which few others claim), may be uniquely able to fulfill a role in curriculum coordination from which others shrink.

Facilitating Inspired Instruction

Middle-level schools are in dire need of staff members who are familiar with the research on teacher effectiveness and who can interpret this research to help teachers realize that there is more to good teaching than what has come to be called "direct instruction." The teaching staff also needs to be encouraged to improve by a colleague who has the values, insights, and skills that permit the teachers to identify and build on their own strengths. The counselor is one of the few people in the school who are trained to observe human behavior closely and to provide feedback carefully, so that such information can become growth producing rather than intimidating and discouraging. Although it may be true that counselors rarely see this role as a part of their professional responsibilities, it is also true that there is virtually no one else in the school who values the professional growth of the staff members enough to make it a high priority.

Guaranteeing Group Involvement

Who, more than the school counselor, understands the deep human need to be an important part of an important group? Probably many, if not most, of the serious problems counselors deal with at the middle and junior high school level are directly related to students' failure to adapt themselves in ways that permit them to enjoy valid group membership. This is the new role that counselors will find most familiar and most comfortable.

One of the most important programs in the long history of the junior high school-middle school movement has been the teacher-based guidance effort often called the advisor-advisee program. It is both the most popular component of the curriculum of middle-level schools and the most disliked. Ironically, it is sometimes the most valuable use of the school day and at other times a nearly complete waste of everyone's time. It is often the program most attractive to some parents and the most offensive to others. Many of the difficulties advisory programs encounter could be eliminated if school counselors believed that the success of the programs was a very important part of their primary responsibilities in the school.

When teachers resist advisory programs, it is almost always because they do not understand the actual purpose of such efforts. When students dislike the programs, it is almost always because the teachers do not have the interest or skill to conduct the programs successfully. When parents question the programs, it is almost always because they have not been explained clearly to them. In all of these cases, it is the counselor who is likely to be the single, most important resource in the school.

The counselor can help the staff develop a firm rationale for the advisory program and can acquaint new faculty members with the goals of the program on an annual basis because it is the counselor who has the knowledge of resources that teachers can use in their classroom advisory efforts. The counselor is most able to evaluate the success or failure of individual faculty member's efforts to implement the program as well as to evaluate the program on a schoolwide basis. If the counselor does not do all these things, there will be no teacher-based advisory programs for a long time.

There is a growing national consensus that, in addition to advisory programs, interdisciplinary team organization is also a central component of modern middle-level schools. There are few advocates for having teachers organized according to their disciplines at the middle level. Instead, more and more middle schools and junior high schools are adopting the pattern of interdisciplinary groups, teams, families, or houses, in which teachers share the same students, the same part of the building, and the same schedule, rather than the same subject. Life on interdisciplinary teams is complex and varied, occurring in a number of distinct phases (George, 1982), with special roles for the school counselor to play in each of those areas.

The first phase of team life is the organizational process. Because members of the counseling staff often are most active in scheduling students, they can get the teams off to the right start by scheduling them so that there is a "good" fit between the teachers and the students they teach. That is, it is critical that the teams be arranged so that a group of two to five teachers, in one part of the building, have all the same students in common. This relatively simple act will permit teachers to improve the school experience in a number of ways.

Teachers who share the same students can develop a common program that is considerably more powerful than can one teacher working alone. Common rules on the team, for example, are applied with greater ease because each teacher is being assisted by a number of others who are committed to the same rules for the same students. The counselor can be helpful by working with the teachers to establish reasonable rules with rational consequences that middle graders will perceive as fair. Common headings for written work and homework regulations, along with common notebook formats and other such routine necessities, will make life simpler for students and more rational for the teachers.

For teachers, the most important benefit from being organized into teams is probably that they make parent conferences more pleasant and productive. In many middle-level schools, where teachers face parents alone and are uninformed about the progress or behavior of a student in other teachers' classrooms, such meetings can be difficult and unpleasant experiences for the teacher. When teachers work together on teams, however, they constantly exchange and pool information about the students they have in common. Their individual knowledge about the students on the team grows enormously. In a team conference with parents, this common knowledge of the student can be used in important, productive, and less defensive ways. By working with the counselor who has had proper training in conference skills, teachers and parents both extol the virtues of working together as a team.

Although many teams of teachers stop at this first organizational phase, in which the benefits are primarily for the faculty, other teams can be helped to recognize the virtues of creating a situation in which the students also believe that the team is theirs and that each is an important member of that group. In most middle-level schools, the counselor will be one of the few people who, naturally and without prompting, will be able to see the benefits of taking time and effort to create the sense of community that signifies the second phase of life on teams.

In one school where I observed the transition from departmental organization to team groups, the first phase (organizational) was markedly successful. Teachers developed common rules, held team conferences with parents, and had separate team conferences with individuals and small groups of students. The common procedures they worked out made life much simpler, and because students only had to go to the next door for their next class rather than across the building and back every 45 minutes, hall problems were nearly eliminated. Everything seemed about as good as it could be.

When I asked the students about team life, however, I was surprised to learn that they did not really view the team as theirs. According to the students, organization into teams meant that "the teachers are ganging up on us" or that "the teachers are unionizing against us!" The students did not object to this from the teachers, not at all; they were actually glad their teachers had decided to work together to make school improvements and seemed flattered by the attention. But the team meant little more than that to the students.

Inspired by the school counselor, the teachers on several teams in the school encouraged the students to become team members. With the counselor's help the teachers committed themselves to creating a learning community in which teacher and students could help each other realize the goals of the program. "We're in this together, on the same great team," became the watchwords. Team colors, logo, motto, song, newsletter, and special activities that enhanced the group feeling were developed. Soon students were answering the question "What is a team?" very differently than they had been before. They began to view the group as something small within the much larger school, a group small enough and important enough for them to belong to. It was a place where they could be known, and they liked it. Discipline problems decreased and achievement increased.

Most people think of team teaching when they hear the word "team" in connection with schools. Actually, this phase of team life is important and no less critical to school success than other components. It is, however, the area in which educators in middle-level schools have made the most mistakes and, therefore has a very negative connotation for many teachers. One of the reasons so many mistakes have been made in this area is that the skills and insights involved in small-group planning are often not well developed in teachers who have spent their lives in classrooms by themselves.

Who is the person in the school who is likely to possess those skills? The school counselor. If school counselors take an active role in training teachers in planning skills and in helping them to realize what they can do together instructionally, middle-level schools can be much more exciting environments in which to learn.

Belonging to a Spirited Leadership Team

Research in corporate productivity points to the skills of group management as the most critical component of modern leadership. It is not different in productive, middle-level schools. As modern business leaders are learning that employee involvement leads to considerably high productivity, educators are also moving toward a clearer understanding that middle-level schools are so complex that a one-person management process will be much less successful than will participatory decision making. Group planning and participation in decision making are, however, far from quick and easy ways to develop policy or solve school-wide problems. Management processes that are democratically oriented often take much longer and require considerably more attention to the affective side of the lives of those involved than do traditional approaches to management.

School administrators, even those eager to share their power and involve teachers in collaborative decision making, have rarely been trained to accomplish these difficult tasks. The consulting counselor can assist in the collaborative process in ways no one else in the school can. Without the guidance of a counselor skilled in managing groups, many administrators will retreat from the kind of management educators now know will move the school forward. Teachers, of course, also need help in learning how to participate in the decisions that affect their lives, usually even more than many administrators do. The counselor has to be the person in the middle.

Conclusion

Asking overburdened school counselors to consider new roles for today's middle-level schools will seem, to some, like the situation from the Old Testament when the Egyptian pharaoh commanded Moses to direct the Hebrews to make bricks without straw. Many counselors will say, and correctly, that with a counseling ratio of 500 or more to 1, new roles seem impossible and that counseling bricks have been made without straw for more years than the Hebrews made theirs. Abandoning the affective oasis will no doubt cause a significant number of problems, and donning the cloak of educational ombudsman will not automatically and immediately take up the slack. It is indeed, a difficult transition to make.

If counselors do not voluntarily assume this new persona, however, the consequences for school life in the near future will be ominous. The national obsession with testing, credit accumulation, tracking, and negative thinking as a way of life will move the schools closer and closer to institutions in which human beings are perceived as nothing more than products and in which all of the goals counselors espouse will be imperiled.

If not the counselor, then who?

References

Edmonds, R. (1979). Effective schools for urban poor. *Educational Leadership, 37,* 15–27.

George, P. (1982). Interdisciplinary team organization: Four operational phases. *Middle School Journal, 13*(3), 10–13.

George, P. (1983a). Confessions of a consultant: Middle school mistakes we made. *Middle School Journal, 14,* 3–6.

George P. (1983b). *The theory Z school.* Columbus, OH: National Middle School Association.

Lipsitz, J. (1984). *Successful schools for young adolescents.* New Brunswick, NJ: Transaction Books.

Naisbitt, J. (1982). *Megatrends: Ten new directions transforming our lives.* New York: Warner Books.

Ouchi, W. (1981). *Theory Z.* New York: Addison-Wesley.

Pascale, R. T., & Athos, A. (1981). *The art of Japanese management.* New York: Simon & Schuster.

Peters, T., & Waterman, R. J. (1982). *In search of excellence: Lessons from America's best-run companies*. New York: Harper & Row.

U.S. Department of Education. National Commission on Education. (1983). *A nation at risk: The imperative for educational reform*. Washington, DC: Author.

Teacher Based Guidance: The Advisor/Advisee Program

John Arnold

The most significant development in middle school guidance over the past decade has been the rapid emergence of teacher-based programs, usually referred to as advisor/advisee (A/A), home base, or advisory programs. Alexander and McEwin (1989) report that 39% of the grades 5–8 and 6–8 schools have such programs, and numerous other schools are planning them. Moreover, George and Oldnaker (1987), in a study of 130 schools widely recognized as exemplary, found that over 90% had substantive advisor/advisee programs. Virtually all authorities on early adolescent education regard A/A programs as a key component of schools which seek to be developmentally responsive.

A well-conceived advisory program consists of a teacher meeting with from 12 to 20 students on a regular basis to engage in activities that nurture social and emotional growth. It provides each middle schooler with an adult friend and guide, a small community who know each other well, and a forum for the issues and concerns of being an emerging adolescent.

Rationale

In the best of situations, most 11–14 year olds experience difficulties dealing with the rapid and highly variable physical, intellectual and socio-emotional changes that occur during early adolescence. Will I ever grow? Will my zits go away? How can I make friends? How do I get along with people in authority when I can't have my own way? How can I be part of a group and not lose my soul in the process? What's right and wrong? What's worth committing myself to? Am I really okay? These are but a few of the questions that emerge.

In contemporary society, the difficulty of dealing with these issues and questions is greatly exacerbated. The breakdown of the family, drugs and alcohol, child abuse, media exploitation, confused values, etc.—the whole litany of social problems—mightily work against healthy development. Frequently young adolescents have to make complex decisions from a bewildering array of choices with insufficient parental supervision.

Thus middle school students have profound need for continuing care, support, and guidance. School counselors cannot begin to meet this need by themselves. They are simply too few in number and have too many other duties. Further, most middle schoolers will not seek out a counselor for help under normal circumstances. They find it much more natural to talk to someone with whom they have daily contact. Thus, the teacher-based guidance provided by an advisor/advisee program is essential.

The need for advisory programs is not confined to students. Most adults enter teaching with the hope of getting close to kids, interacting meaningfully with them, and making a difference in their lives. Yet too often they become isolated from students and disillusioned, caught up in an impersonal bureaucracy. An effective advisor/advisee program has the potential to break down barriers and make meaningful student-teacher interaction more possible.

It should be noted that A/A programs are most often associated with houses and interdisciplinary teams in a school organization plan that seeks to create small personal communities within large institutions. For example, a middle school of 900 students might have three houses of 300 students each, three teams of 300 each, and six advisory groups of 16–17 students each. Each component has its own functions and activities; all seek to provide a sense of identity and belonging. Where the components exist in concert, they mutually strengthen one another. This interaction will be noted in several instances in this chapter.

Roles of the Advisor

When they first learn of A/A programs, some teachers are leery. "I'm no psychiatrist," or "I'm not an expert in moral development," are frequently voiced misunderstandings. While expertise in counseling and values education is of course helpful, it is not essential to becoming a good advisor. The fundamental role of an advisor is simply to be a friend to advisees, that is, someone who demonstrates interest, care, and concern for them.

Advisory sessions are different from regular classes. Respect and order must be maintained, but the atmosphere is more informal. No grades are given; discussions are more wide-ranging; student expression is especially fostered. In many ways, it is a time for teachers and students simply to be themselves and to get to know one another on a personal level. The spirit of being oneself is captured in the story Paul George, a noted scholar on middle schools, tells about an advisor who was an enthusiastic member of the Millard Fillmore Society. For several weeks, he managed to engage his advisees enthusiastically in activities related to Fillmore's birthday. Posters abounded, jingles were written, songs were sung, intercom announcements blared, "Only three more days until Millard Fillmore's birthday." Hokey? Yes. Real? Yes.

Closely related to the role of friend is that of being an advocate for each advisee. Being the adult who knows the student best, the advisor represents the advisee's interests to team members, other teachers, administrators, and parents. Sometimes this may simply require opening lines of communication. At other times it involves explaining or defending an advisee's behavior. On occasion it may necessitate prodding or chiding the advisee in an "I think better of you than that" vein. Above all, it entails providing recognition and support for the advisee. Because the advisor is an advocate, in schools with well developed A/A programs, discipline problems are routinely referred to the advisor.

Thirdly, the advisor serves as a guide for advisees. Academically, this role may involve helping the advisee make course selections, develop better study habits, or find assistance with classwork. Personally, it entails being a good listener, posing alternatives, and generally facilitating decision making. It is obviously crucial that advisors know when to refer advisees with personal problems to the counselor or to a professional in the community. Unless specifically trained, they are not expected to become involved in serious counseling relationships.

Fourthly, the advisor is a coordinator with parents. In elementary schools, parents deal directly with their child's self-contained classroom teacher. In middle level schools, parents too frequently "drop out" because there is no one teacher to whom they can talk who genuinely knows their child. The A/A program provides this missing link. A good advisor is proactive with parents by sending home positive notes, making positive phone calls, and setting up conferences. Also, the advisor is available for discussions initiated by the parent. Depending upon the nature of the issue, the advisee may well be involved in conferences also.

Fifth, the advisor acts as evaluation coordinator for advisees. This role, perhaps the least developed in most programs, has great potential. Because advisors have relatively few advisees, they can meet individually with them to assess progress. In addition, they can engage advisees in goal setting and self-evaluation, activities which are highly important yet so often neglected during early adolescence (Arnold, 1986). The small numbers also allow the advisor, after gathering grades and information from team members, to write narrative comments which address the advisee's total development to accompany report cards.

Finally, and highly importantly, the advisor serves as activity leader and community builder. Here the focus shifts from the individual to the group, with the advisor seeking to promote friendship, group identity, and a sense of belonging. In so doing, the advisor helps the group explore issues and feelings pertinent to adolescent development. The types of activities involved in these pursuits will be discussed in the following section.

A/A Group Activities

There is an almost limitless number of activities that can be used during A/A sessions. The types selected will depend upon the goals of the program, its structure and schedule, the experience of the advisor, and the specific needs of the students. The following sampling of activities from the Advisory Handbook (1988) of the Shoreham Wading–River Middle School, Shoreham, New York, one of the nation's very finest, illustrates the richness of the possibilities:

- Discuss feelings about being new in a new grade, a new building and with new teachers.
- Discuss current events, a TV show, movie, or event.
- Discuss school problems and student concerns.
- Plan A/A group activities, such as a camping trip, service project, dinner for parents, or outing.
- Discuss school procedures, policies, opportunities, mini-course registration, community service programs, independent study opportunities, getting involved with the artist in residence, report cards, etc.
- Keep group and individual journals.
- Read stories orally or discuss books read.
- Design, invent, and/or play games.

- Cook a group breakfast in home economics class first period.
- Have individual advisees tell of experiences and plans.
- Channel energy in positive ways: lobby for a specific mini-course, change lunch options, develop strategies for changing policies.
- Discuss progress reports with individual advisees.
- Explain and re-explain the what, when, where and how of middle school phenomena.

One of the keys to the long term viability of A/A programs is establishing a balance of activities between those which require considerable planning and those which do not. Already overloaded with five or six classes a day, many teachers feel, "The last thing I need is another daily preparation." Indeed, programs which require extensive daily preparation may be doomed from the start.

Alexander and George (1981) describe a number of worthwhile activities, most of which require relatively little preparation, that can be scheduled on a weekly basis. These include (1) It's Your Day, where the group focuses on an individual advisee's interests for a full session; (2) Uninterrupted Silent Sustained Reading; (3) Uninterrupted Silent Sustained Writing, with content focused upon issues of personal importance to advisees; (4) Academic Advisory, where advisees bring problem work to the group, or do short units on study habits or test taking skills; (5) Indoor/Outdoor Games; (6) Story Time, which involves oral reading and discussion; (7) Career Explo, where adults from the community speak to the group about their careers, and (8) Orientations relative to school policy and events.

Examples of activities which require more extensive preparation include teaching and discussing interpersonal skills, promoting self-esteem, and planning special projects, trips, or celebrations. A number of commercial or already prepared materials are available to help with developmental and interpersonal activities. Perhaps the single best source is *Quest: Skills for Adolescence*, developed by the International Lions Club. *Quest* is a substantive, three-year middle school curriculum whose effectiveness is well documented (Gerler, 1986). Some advantages of using *Quest* are that faculty are being specially trained before they may obtain the materials, and that the activities, designed for 45-minute periods, may be adapted to shorter A/A periods. Two other sources of materials are the *F.A.M.E.* (Finding Acceptance in the Middle School Environment) Program, developed by the Alachua County, Florida School System, and *Prime Times* available from the National Resource Center for Middle Grades Education.

The Public Broadcasting System (PBS) has produced two series of 15-minute, school oriented television programs, "Inside Out" and "Self Incorporated," which are particularly useful. Also, "DiGrassi Junior High" and "Wonderworks" are regular PBS productions which are geared to the needs and interests of young adolescents. Addresses for all these materials mentioned are listed at the end of the chapter.

Some advisors are "naturals" who need little external structure for their activities. The majority, however, especially when programs are just getting underway, can benefit from a set format. Thus many schools have found that a repeating weekly schedule that balances high and low preparation activities works best for them. Such a schedule might be structured as follows:

Monday	Current Events or School Issues
Tuesday	Development Issues
Wednesday	Silent Sustained Reading/Individual Conferences
Thursday	Academic Advisory
Friday	Group Projects or Developmental Issues

Other schools schedule activities on a thematic basis. One such example is from Tapp Middle School in Cobb County, GA. (Campbell, 1986).

Advisement Monthly Themes

	6th Grade	7th Grade	8th Grade
Aug./Sept.	Get Acquainted	Get Acquainted	Get Acquainted
Oct.	Test Taking	Study Skills	Study Skills
Nov.	Making/Keeping Friends	Decision Making	Caring
Dec.	Community Service	Community Service	Community Service
Jan.	Decision Making/ Peer Pressure	Substance Abuse	Decision Making
Feb.	Communication	Caring/Manners	Test Taking/Careers
March	Who Am I?	Careers	Creativity
April	Getting Along with Others	Creativity	Family Relationships
May/June	Georgia	Problem Solving	High School Preparations

This approach can provide a cohesive framework for activities and is appropriate for schools with mature programs.

There are also schools which periodically schedule a number of all-school activities, such as intramural sports, assembly programs, or special events during advisory time. While this strategy can be effective, care must be taken that the integrity of the advisor/advisee program is not violated. Repeated interruptions or breaks in routine can easily devastate a program. All-school events must be known about well in advance and built into the A/A schedule.

Grouping Advisor and Advisees

For an A/A program to function well, advisory groups need to be as small as possible. Thus virtually every teacher, including unified arts, foreign language, physical education, special education, and library staff serve as advisors in order to reduce the advisor/advisee ratio to under 20:1. Where appropriate, well-qualified aides can also become advisors.

Advisees must be placed carefully with advisors. In some schools, advisees have considerable say in their placement, though they cannot be guaranteed their first choice. In other schools, advisors exercise a choice of advisees. Administrators, counselors and/or an advisory committee usually make final placements, taking into account student, parent and teacher preference, friendship patterns, potential discipline problems, and space available.

In teamed schools, it is very important that advisors be assigned advisees who belong to their team. Thus a group of 100 students might be assigned to six team teachers, four core academic and two "special" teachers affiliated with the team. In this framework, the behavior, development, and progress of each advisee can be systematically discussed on an ongoing basis during team planning time by a group of teachers who instruct them daily (Arnold, 1981).

There are three basic patterns for grouping advisors and advisees over time, with the over-all structure of the school often determining which option is chosen. The most common pattern is to have grade level advisories which change advisors each year. The make-up of the group itself may or may not change. This grouping is advantageous in schools with grade-level teams, assuring that advisors teach their advisees. A second pattern is for the advisor to keep essentially the same advisory group for three years. This configuration has the potential for developing very strong advisor-advisee relationships and group cohesion. A third pattern is for the groups to have a multi-grade make-up, where an advisory might consist of an equal number of sixth, seventh and eighth graders who remain with the same advisor for three years. This approach also builds strong relationships and potentially reduces age-based pecking orders in schools. The last options are particularly appropriate for schools with multi-grade houses and/or teams.

Scheduling Options

It is essential that A/A periods be scheduled on a regular basis and be long enough for significant interaction to take place. Most successful programs have sessions of 25 minutes or longer; in those with shorter time allotments, the advisory tends to become a glorified homeroom/ study hall period.

There are a number of possible scheduling options, with the choice dependent upon program goals and over-all school organization, especially its master schedule. Among the four most prevalent are: (1) daily, full group meetings; (2) three times a week, full group meetings, with mini-courses or activities the other two periods; (3) a relatively short full group period daily, with individual advisor-advisee conferences scheduled during lunch, independent study time, study hall, or before or after school; (4) scheduling left to the discretion of teams, who have time added to their block schedule for advisory purposes (Alexander and George, 1981).

Combinations of scheduling options are of course possible. The building of Shoreham-Wading River Middle School, for example, was designed purposefully without a lunch room so that A/A groups could eat lunch together. The mixed-grade advisory groups also meet at the beginning of each day. In addition, at the instigation of the faculty, advisors meet individually with each advisee once a month for a 45-minute breakfast, usually at the McDonald's across from the school.

Time of day is another important consideration. An A/A program should not be scheduled at the end of the day unless it is an additional, brief "wrap up" time. Both advisors and advisees are tired at this time, and such scheduling conveys a negative message about the program's importance. Just before lunch is usually not a good time either, though combining A/A with part of the lunch recess can provide flexible time for intramurals and other all-school activities organized around advisories.

In the writer's experience, programs scheduled on a daily basis for 25-30 minutes the first thing in the morning tend to work best for most schools. This scheduling sets a tone and orients students for the day, deals immediately with out-of-school experiences students are eager to share, and emphasizes high priority for the program by using "prime time."

Schools just beginning advisor/advisee programs, especially those who are implementing other new programs as well, might consider starting with a three-times-a-week program, with a commitment to extend it to five times a week in a year or two. This transitional strategy can provide time to do the job well, thus building enthusiasm for the program.

Role of the Principal and Guidance Counselor

As is the case with most middle school programs, the commitment and support of the principal is paramount to the success of an A/A program. The principal must understand its importance and potential for both advisee and advisor, be knowledgeable about its structure and methods, and genuinely want it to work. Translated into practice, this means reading, visiting other schools, providing resources, allocating appropriate time in the schedule, working closely with the school counselor(s), assistant principals, and advisory committee, delegating responsibilities, and a host of other supportive behaviors.

The guidance counselor, ideally the resident expert on early adolescent development, is the person most often in charge of the A/A program. Like the principal, the counselor has to be knowledgeable, committed, work closely with others, and perform numerous duties. In schools with multiple counselors, these duties can of course be shared. It is crucial that the counselor feels "ownership" of the program, realizing that it can and should be the single most important component of an overall guidance program, not an intrusion or another "added duty." Wise principals find ways to relieve counselors of nonessential chores so they may have more time to facilitate the program.

There are a number of specific leadership roles the counselor may take in developing and maintaining substantive advisory programs. A chief role includes planning, usually in concert with a committee, the goals, objectives and structure of the program, as described in the next section. The counselor also helps to gather, design, and distribute appropriate A/A activities, and prepare faculty for their use. Conducting inservice sessions, in particular those which help faculty develop active listening and group facilitation skills, is especially helpful in this regard. Further, the counselor meets with teams or other groups of advisors on a regular basis to help with advisory session planning, and provides support and assistance to individual advisors who are having difficulties. Finally, the counselor may serve as public spokesperson for the program to parents or community groups.

Planning a Program

An advisor/advisee program seems relatively simple but is deceptively complex. Many authorities in fact regard it as the single most difficult middle school organizational component to implement. Lack of time, commitment, understanding, and preparation are some of the reasons for this assessment. Hence careful planning is in order. While the time required for effective planning varies, many schools have found one year in advance of program implementation to be workable. The following are some recommended steps for a district-wide planning process which can be adapted by individual schools.

1. Form a steering committee to oversee the planning. The committee might include a central office representative and board member in addition to building administrators, counselors, teachers, and in some instances, students. Obviously, the committee must become knowledgeable.
2. Write a short mission statement with goals and objectives, and seek board approval for it. A written, approved statement not only gives a program direction; it may establish and protect it from being eliminated by the idiosyncrasies of future principals or central office administrators.
3. Establish details of the overall program including grouping, schedules, and tie-ins with other programs.
4. Make a general curriculum plan that addresses topics to be covered, materials available, activities to be planned by staff, relation to teams, etc.

5. Formulate an implementation plan designating events, dates, and persons responsible.

6. Provide extensive staff development that addresses the nature of the program and roles to be performed, familiarizes faculty with curricular activities and options, and offers opportunity to learn skills and to "practice" activities.

7. Develop a building-level support committee, made up of administrators, counselors, and teachers, for ongoing program maintenance and improvement.

8. Implement the program.

9. Develop an evaluation plan. In addition to informal observations and discussions, formal surveys which ask teachers, students and parents to rate and comment upon specific aspects of the program, are recommended.

Conclusion

The considerable time and energy spent in developing an advisor/advisee program are decidedly worth the effort. If done well, an A/A program can transform the climate and relationships in a school, making other programs and activities more effective in the process. As Burkhardt and Fusco (1986) state, "Our advisory at Shoreham–Wading River functions as the heart of the school. It pumps life into the entire system. Everything flows from it, and its effect can be felt throughout the day" (p. 22). One of their eighth graders adds,

> Advisory means a lot to me. It's a time to talk and get ready for working. It's a time to share questions and some problems. But usually you talk to your advisor about problems. It is also a time to find out what's happening in school. Without an advisory I would be so confused about all my work and what's happening in school. (p. 29)

We live in a world that is often lonely and uncaring. We owe it to our students, as well as ourselves, to create an atmosphere of warmth and acceptance as best we can. Well conceived advisor/advisee programs can play a key role in this effort.

References

Advisory handbook. (1988). Shoreham–Wading River Middle School, Shoreham, New York. Unpublished document.

Alexander, W. M., & George, P. S. (1981). *The exemplary middle school.* New York: Holt, Rinehart & Winston.

Alexander, W. M., & McEwin, C. K. (1989). *Schools in the middle: Status and progress.* Columbus, OH: National Middle School Association.

Arnold, J. F. (1981). Guidelines for discussing students in team meetings. *Journal of the North Carolina League of Middle Level Schools, 3,* 25.

Arnold, J. F. (1985, October). *A four-fold process of middle school classroom evaluation.* Paper presented at the annual convention of the National Middle School Association, Atlanta, Georgia.

Burkhardt, R. M., & Fusco, E. (1986). Advisory: an advocacy program for students. In M. James (Ed.), *Advisor–advisee programs: Why, what and how* (pp. 21–39). Columbus, OH: National Middle School Association.

Campbell, M. (1986). The personal approach to development. In M. James (Ed.), *Advisor/advisee programs. Why, what and how* (pp. 30–34). Columbus, OH: National Middle School Association.

George, P. S., & Oldnaker, L. (1985). *Evidence for the middle school.* Columbus, OH: National Middle School Association.

Gerler, E. R. (1986). Skills for adolescence: A new program for young teenagers. *Phi Delta Kappan, 67,* 436–439.

Selected A/A Curriculum Resources

Printed Materials

QUEST: Skills for Adolescence. Quest International, 537 Jones Road, P.O. Box 566, Granville, OH 43203-0566. Full middle school program.

F.A.M.E. (Finding Acceptance in the Middle School Environment). School Board of Alachua County, 620 East University, Gainesville, Florida 32601. Separate activity booklets for grades, 6, 7, and 8.

Prime Time. National Resource Center for Middle Grades Education. University of South Florida, College of Education, EDU 115, Tampa, Florida 33620. Separate activities for grades 6, 7, and 8.

PBS Videotapes

"Inside Out." (Thirty 15-minute shows) and "Self Incorporated." (Fifteen 15-minute shows). Both available from some state departments of public instruction, or from Agency for Instructional Technology, Box A, Bloomington, IN 47402-0120.

"DiGrassi Junior High." Can be taped directly from PBS, or tapes available from: Direct Cinema Ltd, Box 69799, Los Angeles, CA, 90069. (213-652-8000). Discussion guides are available from Discussion Guide, Box 2222 DG, South Easton, MA 02375.

"Wonderworks." Can be taped directly from PBS, or tapes available from Wonderworks, 4802 5th Avenue, Pittsburgh, PA 15213

A Mentor Program for Beginning Middle School Counselors

Sandra DeAngelis Peace

Counselor mentor programs are underway in various parts of the United States. These programs facilitate counselor induction into the public school system by assigning experienced, successful educators, who are trained as mentors, to work with new counselors. The purpose of this article is to suggest a new induction model that addresses the concerns of middle school counselors during the first year of employment.

Introduction

There is a clear trend emerging in the majority of states to increase the number of school counselors. Paisley and Hubbard (1989) surveyed all 50 states and the District of Columbia. With a 100% response, they found that 28 states had increased school counseling positions in the last five years, and that 32 states plan an increase in the next ten years. The most prevalent reasons for the increases included: "rise in the number of elementary and middle school positions, increased student populations, recognition of benefits of school counseling for high risk students and state mandates" (Paisley & Hubbard, 1989, p. 66).

Along with large numbers of counselors entering school systems, there is a trend toward increased emphasis on evaluation of counselor competencies. Both of these factors have implications for counselor education programs, counselor supervisors, and for the professional and personal well-being of the novice counselor. These trends in public education provide an opportunity, and indeed create a responsibility, to offer an induction program for beginning counselors.

The Importance of an Induction Program

An individual faces certain inevitable development tasks during the initial phase of a career. Schein (1978) referred to "reality shock" as the period when a person experiences the differences between one's expectations and the reality of the job. He stressed the importance of accomplishing the task of becoming socialized in the organization by understanding the unique features of the organization and one's role in it. The individual's initial perceptions of this relationship have important consequences for the person's career (Schein, 1978). The issues of socialization and induction for teachers have received considerable recent attention. Driscoll, Peterson and Kauchak (1985) referred to this vulnerable time for teachers as a period when they "experience a number of psychological shocks, including frustration and feelings of isolation, lowered self-concept, lower aspirations for one's self in the teacher's role, and lowered expectations of pupils" (p. 108). After completing a study of two state-mandated teacher programs, Hoffman, Edwards, O'Neal, Barnes, and Paulissen (1986), strongly advocated formal teacher induction programs.

Middle School Counselor Induction

Even though educators have written about teacher induction programs, there is little in the literature about induction programs for middle school counselors or for school counselors generally. To highlight the dearth of information, Matthes (1987) noted that even a national report (The Commission on Pre-college Guidance and Counseling, 1986) calling for counselor reforms did not mention the process of counselor induction. Matthes stressed the need for counselor induction programs to address new counselor initial role ambivalence, professional isolation, and general difficulty in practicing new behaviors. A study by Matthes (1987) found that beginning counselors' concerns centered around interpersonal dynamics with clients, teachers and parents. Few efforts existed to assist with these concerns, particularly from professionals trained in counseling. Matthes' investigation concluded that the most common mode of induction was the "sink or swim" approach. The new counselors were expected to operate as experienced counselors and little was offered for assimilating new counselors into their new roles. The lack of attention to an induction phase implies that a counselor is a "finished product" and it ignores the importance of looking at counselor development as an ongoing process.

Beginning middle school counselors are by no means "finished products." The following are typical concerns expressed by the counselors early in the school year:

"How can I possibly do everything I'm expected to do? My principal expects me to keep good records. Teachers expect me to see troubled kids. Parents expect me to return their phone calls. How can I do it all?"

"Who is going to evaluate me as a counselor? The principal can't be in my office to see me counseling individually with youngsters. How will I possibly be judged fairly?

"Are the kids going to like me? I don't want them to see me as someone who doesn't care."

If these concerns of beginning middle school counselors' problems go unresolved, they can contribute heavily to counselor stress. Methods of coping have been addressed in numerous publications, but what about a comprehensive program to act as a preventive measure early in a counselors' career? Mentoring can provide extra support and assistance to middle school counselors during their induction period.

Mentoring as an Induction Strategy

The mentoring concept has historical roots from the time of Homer's *Odyssey*, where Mentor was responsible for nurturing the son, Telemachus. The benefits of mentoring in a variety of professions have been frequently documented (Gray & Gray, 1985; Kram, 1986; Levinson, Darrow, Klein, Levinson, & McKee, 1978). In the field of education, teacher mentor programs have appeared as a part of the effort to improve the quality of instruction (Glavez-Hjornevik, 1986) and are major components of the teacher induction process (Hawk & Robards, 1987; Reiman, McNair, McGee & Hines, 1988). Driscoll et al. (1985) contended that if a teacher mentor system is carefully designed, it can be of benefit to the beginning teacher, the mentor, the school district and to students. It seems reasonable to assume that beginning school counselors might also benefit from mentor programs.

A New Approach to Counselor Mentor Programs

Program Rationale

The goals of this new approach are based on cognitive-developmental research and theory, and recognize counselors and teachers as adult learners (Sprinthall & Thies-Sprinthall, 1983). Cognitive developmental theory is used as a framework because it recognizes that the task of helping another grow and develop is complex. Thies-Sprinthall (1986) cited studies indicating that "the helper (teacher, counselor, physician, nurse, principal) who can process experiences at higher-order stages of development performs more adequately as a supervisor" (p. 15). The focus of the cognitive-developmental model is to plan strategies to promote higher levels of thinking and problem-solving so as to enhance the performance of the complex tasks of teaching and mentoring. (Thies-Sprinthall, 1986). This model also uses a system (Joyce & Weil, 1980) to organize mentor skill training into training components. These training components are incorporated into the model along with conditions needed to promote psychological growth to form a Cognitive-Developmental, Teaching-Learning Framework, detailed in Thies-Sprinthall (1984).

The rationale for adopting this model in a teacher induction program can be applied to a mentoring program for middle school counselors. Just as in teaching, the tasks required for successful counseling require more complex functioning. Research has shown the significant relationship between a counselor's conceptual level and the level of a counselor's skills (Holloway & Wampold, 1986; Strohmer, Biggs, Haas, & Purcell, 1983). A cognitive-developmental mentor program emphasizes promoting growth and improving middle school counseling skills. The counselor mentor program offers technical assistance and support to middle school counselors during their first year of employment.

Counselor Mentor Training

From a developmental point of view, what is true for counseling is true for mentoring. The task of successful mentoring requires complex skills. Thies-Sprinthall (1986) explained that a teacher mentor needs to have the ability to break down the process of teaching into manageable parts and model the skills of teaching. It follows that this is true for a counselor mentor. The Cognitive-Developmental, Teaching-Learning

Framework (Thies-Sprinthall, 1984) is used in the counselor mentor program as a fundamental guide. Adaptations and changes in the training format have been made to accommodate the unique aspect of counselor skills and the counselor mentor role. Mentor training is preceded by an individual relationship building conference conducted by the trainer. The trainer's purpose for this conference is to listen to the prospective mentor's concerns and identify that person's overall learning style. The counselor mentor training program addresses the following topics:

1. Building and maintaining a helping relationship
2. Adult development theory
3. Using models of supervision according to the needs of the beginning counselor
4. Levels of counselor concerns
5. Roles and responsibilities of the mentor
6. Problem solving
7. Cycles of supervision

Role of the Mentor

The basic theoretical framework for the mentor training is used as the focus for the mentor's work with the beginning middle school counselor. The trainer models techniques that the mentor trainees can adopt when they begin as mentors for beginning counselors. The roles of the mentor, listed below, identify services that mentors provide to novice middle school counselor:

1. **Establish a helping relationship and maintain ongoing support.** The mentor conducts a relationship building conference with the new counselor using an adapted format from the conference conducted by the mentor trainer. The conference provides the mentor with information about the beginning middle school counselor's concerns, learning style and needs for assistance. An important purpose of the conference is to communicate empathy and support for the new counselor's concerns. Providing support is one of the key components to this model of supervision for promoting growth, along with experiencing challenge (Thies-Sprinthall, 1986).

2. **Provide individual assistance.** The mentor assists the novice middle school counselor with the planning and implementation of the school's guidance plan. The mentor acts as a consultant and provides ideas, materials and suggestions for resources. Support continues as an ongoing service throughout these contacts.

3. **Maintain relationships with other members of beginning counselor's support team** (principal guidance department chairperson, guidance supervisor). The main activity in this area is a Communication Conference arranged and facilitated by the mentor in the company of the beginning counselor and that person's principal. The purpose of this conference is to explain the mentoring activities, highlight the new counselor's school activities and discuss plans for the school's guidance program and ways the mentor can provide assistance.

4. **Conduct monthly meetings for all beginning counselors and mentors.** This service is a collegial approach to supervision and offers training about a specific counseling skill. Group support is another important goal of the meetings. The meetings provide networking opportunities and a chance for the beginning middle school counselors to offer their ideas and support, too.

5. **Provide assistance with specific counseling skills: Cycle of supervision.** A cycle of supervision includes a pre-conference, observation of a counseling activity, and a post-conference. Mentors often begin by conducting these cycles around one aspect of the middle school counselor's work (e.g., leading classroom guidance sessions or consulting with teachers and parents).

Questions about Mentor Programs

Questions about mentor programs have been raised about mentor selection, the mentor's role in the novice's evaluation, type of mentor training, and the matching of mentors with protégés (Kram, 1986; Patterson, 1989). Some of these issues have been addressed in cognitive-developmental models, resulting in the formation and revision of program policies, mentor training, and the kind of assistance rendered to beginning middle school counselors. As mentor programs grow, these issues require continual attention. The length, content and structure of the training, and program accountability measures should be scrutinized regularly. It is important that the trainers and administrative staff look to this model's theoretical framework as a guide for future implementation and evaluation of the program.

Implications for Supervisors

School system supervisors play an important role in a counselor mentor program. Supervisors are responsible for mentor recruitment and selection, and matching mentors with protégés. As a member of a beginning middle school counselor's support team, for instance, the supervisor serves as a liaison with the protégé's principal and mentor. Supervisors also supply administrative support to the mentor trainers and collaborate with them about program policies.

A counselor mentor program has advantages for the supervisors and a school system's counseling program. The mentor's technical assistance reinforces skills which supervisors acknowledge as needed to implement guidance program goals unique to a particular school system. Supervisors have observed that middle school counselors who are mentored move much more quickly through initial concerns than those without such services, and therefore, are seen as more effective counselors.

Conclusion

Cognitive-developmental mentor programs acknowledge that middle school counselors have needs for developmental beyond pre-service training, and especially during the critical induction period. The program recognizes that assistance can be provided by an experienced, successful peer who is trained to guide and support the novice counselor. There are, however, some issues that require ongoing attention. Formal evaluation of mentor programs is necessary to determine the degree of accomplishment of this program's goals. In the meantime, informal evaluations have pointed to the benefits to the beginning counselors and to a revitalizing experience for the mentors.

Middle school counselors reach out to a variety of audiences—students, parents and staff. With greater numbers of counselors expected to enter the field, it seems that it is time for experienced counselors to offer services to new counselors for their benefit and for the betterment of the profession.

References

Driscoll, A., Peter, K., & Kauchak, D. (1985). Designing a mentor system for beginning teachers. *The Journal of Staff Development, 6,* 108–116.

Glavez-Hjornevik, C. (1986). Mentoring among teachers: A review of the literature. *Journal of Teacher Education, 37,* 6–10.

Gray, W. A., & Gray, M. M. (1985). Synthesis of research on mentoring beginning teachers. *Educational Leadership, 43,* 6–10.

Hawk, P. P., & Robards, S. (1987). In D. M. Brooks (Ed.), *Teacher Induction—A New Beginning* (pp. 33–40). Reston, VA: Association of Teacher Educators.

Hoffman, J. V., Edwards, S. A., O'Neal, S., Barnes, S. B., & Paulissen, M. (1986). A study of state–mandated beginning teacher programs. *Journal of Teacher Education, 37,* 16–21.

Holloway, E. L., & Wampold, B. E. (1986). Relation between conceptual level and counseling-related tasks: A meta-analysis. *Journal of Counseling Psychology, 33,* 310–319.

Joyce, B., & Weil, M. (1980). *Models of teaching.* Englewood Cliffs, NJ: Prentice-Hall.

Kram, K. E. (1986). Mentoring in the workplace. In D. T. Hall (Ed.), *Career development in organizations* (pp. 160–201). San Francisco: Jossey-Bass.

Levinson, D. J., Darrow, C. N., Klein, E. B., Levinson, M. A., & McKee, B. (1978). *The seasons of a man's life.* New York: Knopf.

Matthes, W. A. (1987, April). *Induction of counselors to the profession.* Paper presented at the Annual Meeting of the American Education Research Association, Washington, DC.

Paisley, P. O., & Hubbard, G. T. (1989). School counseling: State official's perception of certification and employment trends. *Counselor Education and Supervision, 29*(2), 60–70.

Patterson, R. H. (1989). A counselor mentor program: A mentor's perspective. *The School Counselor, 36,* 167–172.

Reiman, A. J., McNair, V., McGee, N., Hines, J. (1988). Linking staff development and teacher induction. *Journal of Staff Development, 9,* 52–58.

Schein, E. H. (1978). *Career dynamics: Matching individual and organizational needs.* Reading, MA: Addison-Wesley.

Sprinthall, N. A., & Thies-Sprinthall, L. (1983). The teacher as an adult learner: A cognitive developmental view. In G. Griffin (Ed.), *Staff development: Eighty-second yearbook of the National Society for the Study of Education* (pp. 13–35). Chicago: University of Chicago Press.

Strohmer, D., Biggs, D., Haas, R., & Purcell, M. (1983). Training counselors to work with disabled clients: Cognitive and affective components. *Counselor Education and Supervision, 23,* 132–141.

Thies-Sprinthall, L. (1984). Promoting the developmental growth of supervising teachers: Theory, research, programs and implications. *Journal of Teacher Education, 35,* 329–336.

Thies-Sprinthall, L. (1986). A collaborative approach to mentor training: A working model. *Journal of Teacher Education, 37,* 13–20.

Focus on Improving Your Middle School Guidance Program

James W. Costar

Few disagree with the notion that the primary function of any school is to help children learn and that the core of this activity is the instructional program, including the classroom teacher. In recent years teachers have focused much of their attention directly upon the pupil—the learner—looking for more effective ways to enhance the learning process; and yet, there still appears to be a growing reluctance of young people to learn. The most common manifestation of this attitude is poor school attendance, something which has now become almost epidemic. Not only do many students continue to leave school permanently at the earliest possible age, but among middle school students, there is an increasing number who absent themselves for one day or one week at a time. They say school is boring.

Much time and energy has been devoted by all educators in attempts to overcome this growing problem. The middle school movement itself is, in part, an effort to create an atmosphere conducive to better learning. New classes and class materials have been developed, new ways of grouping pupils devised, instructional techniques were modified, the length of class periods and the school year changed. And yet, most of what has been tried seems to have done little more than to help students tolerate boredom rather than eliminate the cause of it.

Shocking as the fact may be, school work still does not seem relevant to most young people in spite of monumental efforts made in the 1960s and 70s. Gradually, educators at the K–12 levels have come to realize that a large part of "relevancy" is in the minds of students and that teachers cannot make things seem relevant to young people who do not have sufficient insight into their own present and future needs. Educational relevancy requires considerable personal planning; and in order to do this well students must first know "who they are" by coming to understand what things interest them the most, what aptitudes and skills they possess, and which direction in their life will be most profitable and satisfying for them. Helping them acquire these understandings is an important part of the guidance function of the middle school.

Thus, the primary goal of the middle school guidance program is to help students find meaning in their lives; and by this means, find relevancy in what schools have to offer them. A sense of relevancy is accompanied by higher motivation to learn and, as a consequence, greater achievement. Good teachers have always known this, and continually seek more effective ways of making the subject they teach meaningful to their students. An effective developmental guidance program helps them accomplish this important task.

Clarifying the Purpose

In the beginning, considerable confusion regarding the goals and structure of middle school guidance programs existed among those who were in charge of them. Fully aware of their responsibility to assist each pupil in "bridging the gap" between childhood and adolescence—between elementary school and high school—middle school staffs found it unwise to fully adopt the design of guidance programs at either of the other two levels. Nevertheless, because of insufficient research on and practical experience with middle school guidance, many did look to crisis-oriented high school programs for certain practices which were either adapted for the middle school or adopted without change. Often it was a serious mistake. Not only did such practices simply perpetuate some high school mistakes of the past but, in addition, failed to give sufficient consideration to the unique characteristics of 11–14 year-old children for whom the middle school was designed, not the least of which were the developmental needs of these emerging adolescents.

At the juncture between elementary school and high school, the middle school is in a position to combine the best of elementary school guidance (with its emphasis upon continuous developmental teacher-oriented activities) and the strengths of high school programs (characterized by highly trained guidance specialists who emphasize counseling with individuals and in small groups). Such combinations are more easily brought in line with the fundamental purpose of the middle school and have as their primary basis: 1) a developmental approach which stresses **prevention** of learning difficulties rather than **treatment** of disabling conditions, and 2) an organizational structure in which the classroom teacher is the focal point of guidance services for both pupils and their parents. Both points are supported in a *Policy and Position Paper on Comprehensive Guidance and Counseling Programs* adopted by the Michigan State Board of Education in 1987.

The Developmental Approach to Guidance

There are those who have advocated for years that more time and money be spent on the preventive aspects of guidance, never quite realizing that although developmental guidance is preventive, prevention alone does not necessarily result in human development. In fact, there are times in our schools when efforts at prevention may actually inhibit pupil development—e.g., student conduct regulations, required courses and rigidly scheduled activities. Regretfully, efforts to prevent problems from developing often prevent pupils from developing.

At the present time, there are several areas where discrepancies exist between what educators believe about good developmental guidance programs and what is typical in our secondary schools. For instance, it is commonly believed that:

1. **Developmental guidance programs are integrated with the total school program,** but most programs still operate, for the most part, as a separate department of the school consisting only of counselors.
2. **Developmental guidance programs provide every staff member with a guidance function to perform,** but the emphasis today is on the work of counselors. It is a common misconception in our secondary schools that the counselors are the guidance program.
3. **Developmental guidance programs stress self-understanding by the learner,** but our guidance activities center more often around the staff's understanding of pupils.
4. **Developmental guidance programs are long-term and continuous from the time children enter school until they leave,** but only little attention is given to the maintenance of strong programs at the middle and elementary school levels. Instead, help is directed to the high school where the need is greatest because problems are often more severe.

5. **Developmental guidance programs help students learn how to make wise decisions for themselves,** but insufficient effort is being made to help students develop in all areas needed for wise decision-making.
6. **Developmental guidance programs focus on preparation and planning,** but in many middle schools there is still little more than talk about collaborating with parents in helping children develop a sense of direction in their lives. Most programs are reactive (crisis oriented) rather than proactive (planned).
7. **Developmental guidance programs exist for all children,** but the limited resources available are usually directed more toward the needs of children with serious problems than those with normal developmental concerns.
8. **Developmental guidance programs enhance the total development of children,** but it has become popular to emphasize personal and social development while neglecting academic-vocational development.

Administrative Concepts

The term guidance has been used to describe many different processes, philosophies, and activities. Since it is often interpreted so loosely, it has given rise to many district formats in middle schools. However, there are a few widely accepted concepts related to the administration of an effective guidance program.

A Guidance Program is a Program of Services

Many definitions of guidance can be found in the related literature. Most of them refer to it as a process or as an activity which is concerned with the total development of students. This would seem to be the goal of all educational experiences. The difference then between guidance and the instructional function of the school is not always easy to discern—depending, to a large extent, upon the goal associated with an activity, i.e., the reason it is being performed.

For most it is easier to envision the guidance program as a program of services—services which are easily defined, administered and evaluated. It is then possible to describe a guidance program as those services specifically designed to facilitate the growth and development of pupils. A description of each guidance service will be found later in this booklet.

Guidance Services Are Facilitating Services

Frequently, the guidance program is thought of as something apart from the instructional and administrative functions of the school. As such it would be of doubtful merit. The primary role that a program of guidance services must play is that of making the instructional function more efficient and effective, i.e., facilitating the primary function of the school, helping children learn.

Guidance Services Are Not an Added Activity

Expanding guidance services should not be thought of as just an added responsibility, but rather, as a change in priorities if such a change is made, it should be judged on this basis: "Will this change make our efforts more meaningful to the individuals in my room?" It then becomes a question of which of the many things being done do the most to enhance the total development of every child?

Guidance Services Are Primarily Preventive in Nature

One important aspect of an effective guidance program is the prevention of problems before they arise. Finding and helping youngsters remove minor obstacles to their development before they create major problems is a high priority objective in all guidance programs. This does not mean that guidance workers in such programs avoid problems of severe maladjustment in some students; but rather, such cases become fewer in number and are handled primarily by other means inside or outside the school system, e.g., special education or community agencies.

Guidance Services Need Specialized Personnel

In spite of the unique position and qualifications for offering guidance services to their pupils held by classroom teachers, it is apparent that highly trained guidance specialists are also necessary. Staff members, including counselors, social workers, nurses, and psychologists, are always needed to provide the kind of remedial or therapeutic aid for some pupils which is beyond the training, experience or time allocation of a typical teacher.

Guidance Programs Require Coordination

If all pupils are to have an equal opportunity to use available guidance services and if such services are to be administered in an efficient manner, continuous coordination of the guidance activities of all persons within the school is necessary. In addition, the guidance program in each building must be carefully articulated on a system-wide basis with those in other elementary, middle and senior high schools as well as with agencies and referral persons outside the system.

The Guidance Services

Objectives

Many different organizational patterns are used in providing guidance services in middle schools. Because of differences from school to school in available resources, levels of staff development and need priorities of students, differences in program organization should be expected. However, the structures of most guidance programs reflect a desire to attain seven widely accepted operational objectives:

1. To collect from and interpret to all individual pupils personal data which will help them better understand themselves and, thus, to make more valid decisions related to personal growth and development.
2. To furnish to and interpret for pupils and their parents certain kinds of personal, social, educational and vocational information useful in making long-range plans.
3. To provide individuals and groups of students counseling assistance in acquiring insights and drawing conclusions.
4. To analyze and, when necessary, alter the home, school and community environment of pupils in order to improve their personal, social and academic adjustment.
5. To aid individual students in planning for and adjusting to post-school life.

6. To continually assess and evaluate the effectiveness of the guidance services offered for students and their parents.
7. And finally, to make certain that for every child there is an adult in the school who knows him or her well and carefully monitors that child's progress.

In order to reach these objectives, the following guidance services are provided.

Pupil-Inventory Service

The Pupil-Inventory Service is concerned with a careful and systematic study of each student in order to personalize his or her educational program as much as possible. It includes all the tools and techniques used to obtain various types of information about every pupil. Devices such as questionnaires, autobiographies, sociograms, standardized tests, anecdotes and procedures for recording and interpreting pupil data make up the major part of this aspect of a guidance program.

Information Service

The Information Service is composed of three very closely related areas. Each consists of a different type of information students need for personal growth, including educational, vocational, and personal-social information. Vocational information outlines the world of work; educational information describes educational programs inside and outside the school while personal-social information is that which will help children in understanding their own behavior and that of their peers and parents.

Counseling Service

The Counseling Service consists of competent personnel, facilities and time provided so that every pupil will have help in analyzing his or her concerns or plans for the future as the need arises. Because it is based on the notion that the counseling process is an individualized activity, this service emphasizes conversations with students on a one-to-one basis and in small homogeneous groups.

Placement Service

The Placement Service is an integral part of the total guidance program and includes both educational and vocational placement. Since few middle school children hold jobs, even on a part-time basis, vocational placement activities are seldom found at this level except on an informal basis. Educational placement gets more attention. It includes efforts made by the staff to place students in those classes of greatest benefit to them and where the teaching techniques used match their unique cognitive styles.

Follow-up Needs Assessment Service

The Follow-up Service is concerned with problems, successes, failures and suggestions of pupils after they have graduated or moved to a new grade level. Since the vast majority of middle school pupils go directly to the high school, formalized follow-up of a pupil's stay in the middle school is that done by individual classroom teachers keeping in touch informally with their former students. This service, however, should not be overlooked. A follow-up of former middle school students now in the high school can prove extremely helpful to the staff in improving educational programs for future students.

The accountability movement in education, with its emphasis upon management by objectives, has made the continual assessment of the needs of students an essential aspect of providing relevant educational programs and services for them. Assessment of the needs of the guidance program itself is also an important element in an effective follow-up service and is addressed more fully in the following section.

Designing an Effective Guidance Program

Current stress upon "accountability" in education is having a significant impact upon guidance programs at the middle school level. Widespread criticism of junior high school counseling has given impetus to efforts at developing new approaches to guidance services for pre-teenage pupils. These, in turn, have had a strong influence on the middle school movement itself.

Because of the uniqueness of their philosophy and their emphasis upon the social and psychological aspects of learning, middle schools

have provided fertile ground for the development of new and more effective delivery systems for counseling and guidance, including the teacher-
advisor concept mentioned earlier. Although the guidance program has
always had an important role to play in helping middle school students
reach the maximum of their potential as human beings, the relative
importance of this function has increased dramatically during the past
few years. As a result, middle schools have assumed a leadership role in
the design of many new aspects of this important area of education.

Revitalizing the Guidance Program

The press for better management in our nation's schools has caused both
parents and educators to give more attention to their guidance programs.
Many have concluded that it is the most neglected school program. For
those who wish to ensure that the guidance services of their school will
adequately meet the needs of the pupils they serve, the first question
often asked is: Which needs of students should our schools try to meet?
Followed by: What priority should be given to each need?

To the degree to which the goals and objectives of the school already
reflect the developmental needs of its pupils, guidance services have
only to facilitate their attainment. In that sense, the guidance program is,
as it should be, an integral part of the total school effort. Programs with
objectives that are not consistent with the general philosophy and goals
of the school are sooner or later judged to be a "fifth wheel" and are
either abandoned or severely restricted during periods of economic
crisis. Thus, the first and most important step in revitalizing a guidance
program is to assess the relative strength of the physical, psychological,
social, and intellectual needs of the students being served in order to
determine the highest and lowest priorities among them. With this
information about the basic needs of their students the staff can more
easily determine which services should receive the greatest emphasis
(strongest needs) and from which human and financial resources can be
diverted (weakest needs) if necessary.

Assessing Pupil Needs

It is not always essential to survey the entire student body. Most teachers
already have a fairly accurate perception of the needs of the pupils in
their classes. A ten percent sample of students may be all that is needed

to confirm beliefs already held by the staff or to indicate that a more extensive assessment should be made in a specific area. Some find it helpful to ask the teachers in a more systematic way what the priorities should be, and many means have been developed for collecting such data, the two most common being personal interviews and written questionnaires. Neither need to be elaborate nor time consuming to be helpful. With a few modifications the student questionnaire can be used with parents and teachers to assess their perceptions of pupil needs.

Agreeing on Goals and Priorities

Having collected the needs assessment data, the next step is to translate this information into a set of understandable goals for the guidance program, acceptable to the professional staff as well as students and parents. Typically there will only be seven or eight broad goals similar to those found later in this booklet. A means can then be easily devised for the staff, school board and parents to establish a system of priorities by which resources will be assigned to and time allocated for each of them. A form developed for this task can be found in Figure 1.

Implementing the Program

A serious effort to improve the guidance program of any school can be both costly and time-consuming; however, neither is rarely the case. Much is probably already being done well though the staff is not fully aware of it. Even so, it is hard to find a guidance program that cannot be improved if the staff is willing to make the effort. The following is a list of principles which are sufficiently valid for all guidance programs to serve as a basis for developing a sound administrative guidance structure in any middle school.

1. Guidance services, in some form, are in all schools though they may not be labeled as such.
2. Every guidance program must be individually tailored to fit the unique characteristics of the students and staff of the the school in which it operates.
3. Every staff member has a role to play in providing guidance services to pupils and their parents.
4. The effectiveness of the guidance program increases as fast as the development of the staff.

Figure 1
A Statement of Tentative Goals for the Guidance Program

Students should be assisted in:

	RANK 1 High 7 Low	RATE See Scale Below
1. Attaining an educational experience relevant to their needs and to the full limit of their interests and potentialities.		
2. Acquiring effective techniques in working with others, both peers, and adults.		
3. Becoming acquainted with ways of providing a livelihood, obtaining employment and succeeding in it.		
4. Developing an ability to assume civic responsibility, including acceptance of self and others.		
5. Developing fundamental behavior patterns conducive to good physical, mental and social health.		
6. Developing effective ways of using leisure time.		
7. Developing better self-understanding, self-direction and self-discipline.		

Programs Needs Assessment

To conduct a current assessment of the guidance program, rate each of the above goals on the following scale. Then calculate the average score for each goal. The lowest scores tell you where there is much to be done. The highest (13–14–15) tell you where you might get the resources and time to make improvements.

Extremely poor 1–2–3	Poor 4–5–6	Fair but needs improvement 7–8–9	OK leave as is 10–11–12	Too much being done 13–14–15

5. A guidance program develops to the extent that the school administration and Board encourages and supports it.
6. An effective guidance program requires trained leadership.
7. The guidance program must be evaluated against its ability to facilitate the work of both teachers and administrators.

Role of the Principal

Probably the most important person in the development of a good guidance program is the building principal. Without strong and continuous leadership from the principal, who is ultimately responsible for all programs in the building, little can be accomplished for the guidance program.

In the past, many building principals have ignored their role in the development of guidance services or, at least, have turned over that responsibility to the counselor. Although counselors can be of considerable help in organizing, administering and evaluating guidance services, principals cannot reassign these responsibilities entirely. It is through active personal participation by the principal that the staff becomes confident the priorities which have been established will be carried out and that it will be worthwhile for them to spend time and energy in an effort to improve the counseling and guidance program. Leadership by the principal is especially important in the following areas:

1. Establishing a written philosophy and related goals for the guidance program which are consistent with the overall philosophy and goals of the school.
2. Obtaining financial support for guidance staff and services.
3. Assigning competent and dedicated staff.
4. Acquiring suitable facilities, equipment and materials.
5. Providing certain counseling and guidance services for which he or she is personally most qualified.
6. Encouraging staff participation in regular in-service training for guidance activities.
7. Supporting continuous evaluation of the guidance program and related support services in the community.

Role of the Middle School Counselor

The most important and unique aspect of the guidance program is the counseling service. Because all guidance services, to be truly effective, must ultimately be tailored to meet the individual needs of each pupil, conversations on a one-to-one basis are essential. These require time set aside for talks with individual students, locations where uninterrupted discussions can be held in an atmosphere conducive to thinking, and adults with special skills who are able to assist counselees in analyzing their perceptions, attitudes, and feelings—particularly as they relate to decision-making and evolving valid plans for their own development. This is the main work of the counselor.

The middle school counselor is a staff member with specialized knowledge and ability who provides assistance to students in making decisions that ensure an orderly progression through the various stages of their personal growth. At certain periods in the life of all children they must accomplish corresponding developmental tasks in order to proceed to the next level of their total development: mental, physical, social, and vocational. Arriving at valid insights required for successful accomplishment of each task requires that children and their parents carefully identify, and weigh for their relative importance, the various factors associated with choices to be made. The school counselor possesses those skills and personal qualities which facilitate this decision-making process and spends the major portion of his or her time each day conferring with individual pupils about their unique concerns.

As is pointed out in a later section devoted to the guidance responsibilities of classroom teachers, counselors are not the only ones in the middle school who help students make plans and resolve problems or concerns. The level of skill that is needed depends upon the complexity of the problem. Teachers, administrators, secretaries, aides, peers of friends and parents may also help. However, no guidance program can be expected to reach its full potential without the services of a fully trained counselor.

Though all school counselors are expected to have many of the same basic skills, middle school counselors do have certain characteristics and abilities which make them especially adept at working with preadolescent youth. Just as guidance programs at the elementary, middle and high school levels all must vary somewhat in their emphasis in order to reflect the gradually changing needs of growing children, so must the role and function of the school counselor vary at each level. Variations in emphasis among the following primary responsibilities of school counselors will be found from school to school as well as grade level to grade level.

1. **Collecting Data About Pupils.** Gathering, analyzing, and recording information about students which is helpful to teachers, administrators, parents, and guidance specialists.
2. **Consulting with Teachers, Administrators and Other Specialists.** Discussing normal growth and development problems as well as problems of special concern to individual pupils.
3. **Collaborating with Parents.** Reviewing, from time to time, the long-range educational plans for their child and assisting them with problems of immediate concern to them.
4. **Counseling with Pupils.** Meeting with pupils, both individually and in groups in order to provide additional help to those who need the assistance of a staff member with more time and training for counseling than the typical classroom teacher and to make referrals both within and outside the school system.
5. **Conducting Research Studies Related to the Guidance Program.** Collecting and analyzing data describing the nature of the student body and the community served by the school that is useful in evaluating the degree to which the total school program meets the needs of all pupils.
6. **Coordinating all Guidance Services Available to Pupils in the School.** Making all services within the school and community easily accessible to every pupil who can profit from them.

Increasing the participation of teachers in the guidance program as described in a later section can have a significant effect on the role of the counselor. Where teachers are active guidance workers there is greater need for coordination, supervision and provision of in-service training by certified counselors. One can also expect that the number of referrals from the teaching staff will increase.

Models for Middle School Guidance Programs

When considering a suitable structure for delivery of guidance services to middle school youth, thought must first be given to the other student services available within the school district. Because of the relatively small number of pupils needing the help of a school psychologist, social worker, hearing and speech therapist, nurse or attendance worker, these pupil personnel specialists ordinarily spend only part of their time in a single building, and are usually housed in a more central location within the district. It is when the entire specialist team is joined with teachers and administrators that the guidance function of the school is carried out most effectively.

Of course, the simplest and oldest program arrangement is when the principal and teachers alone provide whatever guidance services they can through the curriculum and regular activities of the classroom. However, a guidance program of this nature does little to make certain that each child will be provided his or her fair share of continuous high-quality guidance assistance geared to their specific stage of development. This type of program only works when classes are small and homogeneous in their make-up.

A more common model today is similar to that found in Figure 2. Here the staff is assisted by one or more counselors working with other members of the pupil personnel team, especially when helping teachers with more difficult or time-consuming cases and the principal with administration and evaluation of the program. More often than not, the teachers in this approach assume less and less responsibility for guidance of their pupils over the years and the counselors eventually become the guidance program. In order to prevent this from happening and to

Figure 2
The Guidance Team

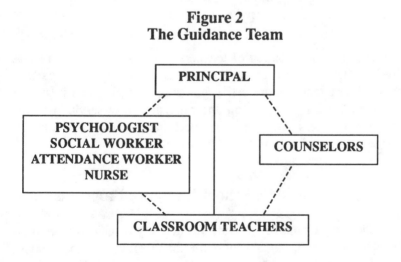

promote maximum efficiency as well as productivity, the teacher-advisor approach is now widely used in middle schools.

The Classroom Teacher in the Guidance Program

The press for better management of guidance programs has caused a return to greater use of classroom teachers as a primary source of guidance assistance for students in both elementary and secondary schools, and it is interesting to note that the leadership for this movement came from middle schools.

The teacher-counselor concept, now usually referred to as either the teacher-advisor or the teacher-guide system, is not entirely new. Its roots are firmly established in guidance programs of the past. As recently as a generation ago classroom teachers were expected to provide most of the guidance services for pupils in elementary and junior high schools. The main reason for their use at that time was a shortage of trained counselors. Because partially trained teachers were being asked to do the work of fully trained counselors, there was considerable dissatisfaction with the arrangement. Rapid steps were taken to change this condition as soon as a larger supply of qualified counselors became available during and following the National Defense Education Act of 1958.

Today, the practice of using classroom teachers as guidance workers is again increasing in popularity—but for a different reason. Hiring full-time counselors has not proved to be the best way of providing all the guidance services needed by every student. In short, the rush to hire counselors to do the counseling led many schools to discontinue utilization of teachers as guidance workers in any capacity. Now we realize that both teacher and counselors have distinct guidance roles to perform which each is in a better position to execute than the other.

Having recognized this mistake, more and more school systems across the nation are redefining the function of classroom teachers to include emphasis upon the provision of those guidance services which they can provide for their pupils. At that same time, both pre-service and in-service training programs are being developed to help teachers become fully qualified to offer them. The middle school movement, with its stress upon individualizing instruction, facilitating the total growth and development of pupils, and humanizing the learning process, has been a major force giving strength to this new trend.

Since the primary purpose of the middle school guidance program is to facilitate the learning process, it is natural for the classroom teacher to have an important part to play. Even in schools employing counselors, it is neither logical nor practical to exclude teachers from the guidance program for there are many aspects of guidance which can be carried out either more efficiently or more effectively by them.

There are several reasons why this is so. First, the teacher spends a great deal of time with certain children each day and is in a good position to develop the kind of personal relationship with his or her pupils that is essential for implementing sound guidance practices. Second, because teachers have the same students each day, they are in a better physical location to provide guidance on a regular systematic basis. Finally, many guidance activities are better carried out within the context of related subject matter and learning activities of the classroom. This is not to say that guidance and teaching are synonymous; but rather, that the unique function of each enhances the other.

The Teacher-Advisor Program

The teacher-advisor program is not intended to be a substitute for the school counselor. Nor is it designed as a replacement for guidance which has become a traditional part of regular classroom activities. Rather, it is intended to provide greater emphasis upon the guidance function of the school through a well-defined structure for group guidance activities which can be superficially defined, assigned, and evaluated, thus assuring that every child will be provided his or her fair share of guidance services at the time they are most needed. Without this more intensive organization guidance becomes an incidental part of the total school program and many children who need the help are overlooked.

The main objective of the teacher-advisor arrangement is to guarantee that for each child in the school there is an adult professional staff member who knows that pupil well and is in a position to continuously monitor his or her growth and development.

To accomplish this it is essential that only a small number of advisees be assigned to available staff members. It is easy to see that there can never be enough counselors *per se*. The whole student body must be divided among the entire staff, including administrators and counselors as well as classroom teachers. Such an arrangement usually makes it possible to limit each TA group to no more than twenty pupils, a reasonable number for each advisor to know and monitor. If all teachers cannot participate the first year, then the usual practice is to start with the lowest grade level and include the upper levels during the succeeding years.

Any guidance activity that is judged worthwhile must have time provided for it. The amount of time required depends upon how well the staff is prepared. As mentioned in a later section, teachers must have clearly understood objectives, related materials, and the necessary skills. Success in implementing the program is enhanced by starting with a minimum amount of time allocated for teacher-advisor meetings (say one-half hour per week) and increasing the allotted time as the demand for it by teachers and students increases. It pays to be cautious when starting the program. Assigned time without adequate preparation can cause the program to regress to the ineffective homerooms of decades ago. During the first year or so short weekly staff meetings to go over the objectives and materials to be used during the following week builds confidence in the teacher-advisors that they will do a good job and helps maintain the high morale necessary for success of the program.

As pointed out earlier, the teacher-advisor program does not reduce the need for qualified counselors. In fact, it is more likely to increase the demand for their services since the counseling needs of each pupil are being more carefully assessed. Obviously the duties of the counselors do change as the teacher-advisors assume more of the guidance tasks that require little additional training and refer to the counselors more complex and time-consuming cases which they have discovered. In addition, leadership and in-service training for the teacher-advisor program falls naturally into the domain of the counselor though all are not immediately comfortable with this role.

Teacher-Advisor Activities

The areas of guidance in which the classroom teachers and teacher-advisors have a significant role to play include: career development, educational planning, collaboration with parents, social development, and general school adjustment. In order to provide these, the teacher-advisor engages most often in the following activities:

1. Counseling in those cases where both the nature of the problem and the assistance required are within the training and experience of the teacher.

2. Collecting data about individual students useful in helping them overcome personal factors which hinder their ability to develop in a normal manner.

3. Modifying the classroom environment of a pupil when it has been determined that certain physical psychological, or social conditions are necessary to facilitate his or her growth and development.

4. Providing career information of all kinds, but particularly that which is related to the subject matter of the class being taught.

5. Adapting instructional procedures and techniques to meet the unique needs of individual pupils.

6. Providing educational information concerning school requirements and regulations, course offerings related to the teacher's instructional field, extra-curricular activities, and post-secondary education.

7. Assisting with placement in part-time jobs during the school year and summer as well as full-time employment after leaving school.

8. Influencing a given student with whom the teacher has somehow been able to establish a special personal relationship.

9. Participating in a continuous evaluation of the guidance services being offered by the school.

10. Helping with the organization and administration of the guidance program, particularly the coordination of guidance services for individual students within his or her classroom.

11. Collaborating with parents as they try to help their child with physical, social, emotional, academic and vocational development.

12. Referring students to counselors and other specialists when the help they need is beyond the ability of the teacher to provide it.

Guidance Skills Needed by Teacher-Advisors

In each of the twelve areas above, teachers are in an excellent position to help students in their classes. Whether they are helpful or not depends, for the most part, upon the skills they possess. Although teachers sometimes feel inadequate in the guidance area, many already have sufficient training to work effectively with students who are in need of limited assistance. Difficult time-consuming cases do appear in all schools so well-trained counselors are also needed. However, as pointed out earlier, counselors cannot be expected to do everything, even under the best conditions.

Thus, classroom teachers must possess a number of special skills in order to satisfactorily carry out their role as a guidance worker in the classroom. These skills include the following related to:

A. Learning about Pupils
1. Administering and interpreting standardized tests.
2. Administering and interpreting non-standardized techniques.
3. Recording data about pupils.
4. Sharing information with others in a legal and ethical manner.
5. Observing student behavior.

B. Providing Information to Pupils
1. Vocational information.
2. Educational information.
3. Personal information
4. Social information.

C. Counseling with Pupils and Parents
1. Individual interviewing techniques.
2. Group counseling techniques.
3. Collaborating with parents.

D. Using Consultants
1. Utilizing community resources.
2. Making referrals inside and outside the school system.

E. Administering Guidance Services
1. Assisting with the definition of guidance roles of staff.
2. Becoming familiar with evaluation procedures.
3. Providing helpful public relations activities.
4. Helping with scheduling and educational program planning.
5. Supervising para-professionals.

Guidance in Groups

A basic characteristic of developmental guidance programs is the utilization of student groups. Many guidance services can be offered by this means; thus, it is important that classroom teachers involve those groups of students already a natural part of the school structure to provide guidance services. There are several advantages. Better use can be made of time, physical facilities and school personnel. In addition, the group itself has characteristics which are helpful in nature. It can provide individual pupils with a supportive relationship based upon knowledge gained in the group sessions that many of their peers are concerned about the same problems and are using similar methods of resolving them. In the latter case, the group often provides an excellent means of facilitating individual counseling offered to participants. By this method, large numbers of pupils can also be made aware of the guidance services that are available to them and how they might make use of them. It should be pointed out, however, that group techniques are not a substitute for individual counseling. They are an excellent method of supplementing individual counseling and often increase the demand for such help.

Group Activities in the Guidance Program

Getting groups together during school time to discuss a common problem is not an easy task. Many class schedules make it difficult for either teachers or pupils to free themselves at a particular time for a special meeting. A teacher-advisor program provides regularly scheduled time for group meetings. In addition, there already exists within the present structure of most middle schools a number of opportunities for extending guidance services to pupils in groups beyond regular classes or teacher-advisor groups. Some of the more common ones are listed below.

1. **Special Clubs.** Clubs formed because of the expressed interest by pupils in such things as music, art and science are ready-made vehicles for providing guidance services to their members. Such groups are an excellent means of helping children acquire new knowledge and skills by capitalizing on the high degree of interest and motivation held by members.
2. **Student Government.** Student councils and other forms of governing bodies, whether they operate within a single classroom or throughout the entire building, provide the guidance worker with many opportunities for encouraging students to analyze and act upon social problems with which they are confronted in their daily lives.
3. **Special Classes.** Occasionally, special classes such as those in career education, health, techniques of studying, physical education or certain subject matter areas are offered for students who

have special interests or are seeking assistance in problem areas not ordinarily covered in the regular school program.

4. **School Assemblies.** Assembly meetings are accepted activities in most middle schools. They offer any number of opportunities for providing children with information about the school, themselves and the world of work.

5. **Camping Programs.** Some schools have their own camping programs maintained both during the summer and regular school year. In others, national organizations such as the Boy Scouts, Girl Scouts and Red Cross, have been instrumental in setting up group guidance programs that operate in conjunction with schools.

6. **School Newspaper.** Supporting a school newspaper published for and by the pupils has a number of guidance possibilities. Not only does it provide an opportunity to work closely with the students who are responsible for gathering and writing the news, but it furnishes the teacher or counselor with an effective means of distributing guidance information throughout the entire student body.

7. **School Library.** School librarians have many opportunities to work with children in small groups. When their activities are coordinated with those of the regular classroom teacher and the counselors, they can become one of the most important members of the guidance team.

Preparing the Teachers as Guidance Workers

Most classroom teachers like the idea of taking an active part in the guidance program. For them a major reason for choosing their profession was the satisfaction that comes from helping young people. However, a troublesome aspect of implementing a teacher-advisor program is the in-service training needed by the teachers.

The degree to which acquisition of the necessary knowledge and skills is of concern to teachers on the job is heightened by the fact that the skills must be applied at the very time they are being learned. However, it is also true that under these somewhat stressful conditions it is easier to identify the troublesome areas and to devise suitable in-service programs for correcting them. The four most common problem areas in the in-service training of classroom teachers for their role in the guidance program are helping them: (1) select a common approach (philosophy) to guidance for their school's program from among the many that currently exist, (2) balance their teaching activities with those devoted to guidance, (3) form an effective guidance team with the counselors in their school, and (4) overcome normal forms of personal resistance to implementing their new role.

Choosing a Philosophy

In order for teachers to adequately carry out their guidance role in a school, there must be agreement by the entire staff as to what the general goal of the guidance program itself will be. The overall aim must be consistent with both the stated goals of the school and expectations of the students and their parents. Selecting the most suitable approach for a middle school is usually not as easy as it may seem. There are currently at least four major categories to choose from: (1) those that stress selection and preparation for a vocation, (2) those that emphasize crisis intervention and problem solving, (3) those that stress humanism and humanitarian acts in all programs and activities of the school, and (4) those that promote a specific area of human development.

The task is made no less difficult by the fact that the best philosophy approach for a given school usually includes something from each of the four general areas. Thus, it is important that an in-service training program provide teachers not only with a comprehensive knowledge of the various philosophies of guidance found in middle schools today but, in addition, with preparation both to systematically assess the needs of their students and to reach agreement among themselves on the approach to guidance which is most appropriate for their school.

Balancing Teaching and Guidance

It is easy for some teachers to become too enthusiastic about their role as a guidance worker. They are often heard to say: "My job is to be a counselor for my children." If this is so, who will be the child's teacher?

The most suitable apportionment of time allocated by the classroom teacher to teaching and to guidance is as difficult to determine for a specific classroom or school as it is to maintain. Many forces are at work, sometimes encouraging the teacher to spend more time on instructional activities and sometimes more on guidance. For instance, the desires of individual students are often in conflict with those of society in general. The priorities of a local school are sometimes different from those of the larger governmental unit in which it operates. Children and their parents do not always agree; and finally, there is the question to be answered in every school as to whether students should be encouraged to make decisions regarding their life goals on the basis of reality as their elders see it or on their own dreams for the future. Support for the teachers in maintaining a satisfactory balance is provided by the underlying philosophy and organization of the guidance program in each school.

Forming an Effective Teacher-Counselor Team

All to often classroom teachers envy or even resent school counselors. This is because they can see the possibility that counselors will take from them that part of teaching which they enjoy the most—helping students grow and develop.

Throughout the United States another aspect has contributed to the teacher's envy of school counselors. Very rapid growth of guidance programs during the thirty-year period from 1958–1988 placed the counselors in the educational spotlight where attention was continually drawn to their concern for the welfare of individual students and away from the same concern held by teachers and administrators. The effect was that teachers were often left with the impression that they are to tend to the teaching of subject-matter while the counselors tend to the needs of students. Of course that is an impossible arrangement and, as a result, feelings of animosity developed which interfere with establishment of a good professional relationship between teachers and counselors essential for an effective guidance team.

Resisting a Guidance Role

Many teacher-advisor programs have failed simply because they were begun before the staff was ready. As was mentioned in an earlier section, most middle school teachers want a part to play in providing guidance services for pupils. However, they are naturally hesitant to participate when they are not adequately prepared. Experience with teacher-advisor programs in the United States has revealed several common causes for resistance on the part of teachers which are not unreasonable nor difficult to overcome. They usually form the basis for in-service training programs. Resistance may be the result of:

1. **Lack of Understanding.** Teachers are hesitant because they do not understand the difference between guidance and instruction, the changing needs of students, or the way in which the guidance program can be expected to have an impact upon students and the primary function of the middle school.

2. **Lack of Time for Guidance.** Most teachers already feel there is not enough time in the day even for teaching. Priorities must be realigned, and time must be set aside in the daily schedule so that all students and teachers can participate.

3. **Lack of Sufficient Skill.** Special skills are required for conducting guidance and counseling activities and most teachers do not feel confident that they are adequately prepared to assume an expanded guidance role. The most common teacher-advisor skills were listed in an earlier section of this report.

4. **Lack of Suitable Material.** Many guidance exercises require specific kinds of information and materials, e.g., occupational information and values clarification materials. These must be prepared well in advance of their use and special training sessions in their application may be required before teacher resistance is eliminated.

5. **Lack of Interest in Students.** A few teachers are just more interested in subject-matter than in students, and may always be. However, their reluctance to form a closer personal relationship with students often has other more subtle reasons such as the fear that such a relationship will cause the teacher to lose control of his or her class making it more difficult to teach.

6. **Resentment of Counselors.** Where counselors are already in the school differences between their role and that of the classroom teacher are often clearly established, usually with the counselors designated as the guidance person in the school. When the suggestion is made that the teachers should assume more of a guidance role they conclude that the counselor will have less to do and, of course, resent it.

7. **General Resistance to Change Itself.** All normal excuses for not accepting a new role can also be expected. Some will say there is too little time before retirement to make worthwhile the effort to acquire new knowledge and skills. Resistance to the person advocating the new role is also quite common. Others just feel guidance is not a part of teaching so they should not be expected to get involved.

8. **Fear that Students are Unprepared.** Many envision, and it is often so, that in the beginning middle school students will lack the necessary communication and problem-solving skills to successfully participate in teacher-advisor groups.

In the last analysis, guidance services are judged as worth the time, effort, and resources they require only to the degree to which they facilitate the main goal of the middle school, helping each child with all areas of their total growth and development—academic, physical, personal and social. Foremost attention must be given to the primary function of the classroom which is to help pupils learn. Over the years many forces have been operating to divert the main thrust of the guidance program for this central purpose of the school, and the teacher-advisor movement can be viewed as a successful effort to restore guidance and counseling as an effective component of all middle schools.

Selected References

American School Counselor Association Governing Board. (1978). The unique role of the middle/junior high school counselor (position paper). *Elementary School Guidance and Counseling, 12*(3), 203–205.

Cole, C. (1981). *Guidance in the middle school.* Columbus, OH: National Middle School Association.

Costar, J. W. (1980). Classroom teachers in the school guidance program. *International Journal for the Advancement of Counseling, 3*(1).

Georgiedy, N., Heald, J., & Romano, L. (1984). *A guide to an effective middle school.* New York: Irvington Publishers, Inc.

Godwin Heights Middle School. (1982). *Teacher-advisor.* Wyoming, MI: Author.

Heer, E. L. (1979). *Guidance and counseling in the schools: Perspectives on the past, present, and future.* Falls Church, VA: American Association for Counseling and Development.

Hubel, K. H. et al. (1974). *The teacher/advisor system.* Dubuque, IA: Kendall-Hunt Publishing Company.

James, M. (1986). *Advisor-advisee program: Why, what and how.* Columbus, OH: National Middle School Association.

Michigan Department of Education. (1987). *Policy and position paper on comprehensive guidance and counseling programs.* Lansing, MI: Author.

Page Middle School, The Lamphere Schools. (1984). *Student advisor guidance experience.* Madison Heights, MI: Author.

Stamm, M. L., & Nissman, B. S. (1979). *Improving middle school guidance.* Boston, MA: Allyn and Bacon, Inc.

A View From the "Right": Who Needs School Counseling and Guidance Programs, Anyway?

Sidney B. Simon

I am weary of those "bleeding heart" liberals who criticize "right" minded people for making it increasingly clear that they simply cannot justify spending money for counseling programs in public schools. Serious budget constraints demand that money be placed where it can best serve the youth of this nation, and counseling programs can only be judged as frills of the most frivolous kind. Schools are for learning; they are not places for dealing with emotional problems that students just might happen to bring with them on the school bus. There are other agencies set up to deal with children's problems: these are for those rare millions of children who just might have problems or find themselves in trouble.

The truth is that society is working quite well. Any emotional problems of youth that once might have justified counseling programs have vanished from this land. The real issue is that College Board scores are embarrassingly low, and this problem must be addressed—but not by counselors, of course.

With this in mind, I offer ten reasons, described below, for eliminating counseling programs in the schools.

Reason 1: The Healthy American Family

The American family has never been stronger. Students come to school from beautifully intact nuclear families where love, understanding, and abundant attentions of the most nourishing type are bestowed on each youngster. It is so fortunate that the "latchkey" youth of the past no longer exist; all children are now secure and come home from school to find both of their parents sitting together, cheerfully talking over the delights of their day, sipping hot cocoa with marshmallows in front of a cheery and cozy fireplace.

You ask about single parents? Where are they? Not sending children to our school. You ask about the impact of separation and divorce on the children? Not in our school. I will admit that at one time there were children who came to school bewildered, hurt, angry, and depressed because they were caught in the crossfire between two bewildered, hurt, angry, and depressed adults who did not have the resources to resolve conflicts and move on with their lives as a couple.

But with American families at the healthiest they have been in the nation's history, counseling programs that attempt to deal with dissonance in families and how it troubles children simply cannot be justified. Obviously, society must take the money that once went into such work and put it where it rightly belongs, into the basics, and must beef up homework and enforce stiffer grading systems.

Reason 2: The Demise of Drug and Alcohol Abuse by Teenagers

Counseling programs are not needed because alcohol and drug use among students is at an all-time low. The majority of youths are simply into healthy and uplifting recreational activities and have turned their backs on addictive substances and any of the forms of chemical dependency. These days educators witness party after party at which high school students abstain from alcohol and drugs. Instead, they sip lemonade, and their gatherings are dominated by quiet discussions of computer languages and the latest foreign films.

Naturally, there are a few exceptions. Those students who do imbibe or take drugs somehow equate the word party with getting "plastered," "wasted," "smashed," "ripped," "bombed," "burnt," "blown away," "crocked," "snookered," or more often just plain drunk. Such students are clearly a minority and not a concern of the schools. Let those immoral few get caught up by the social service network established by the state. It's just not an issue for schools.

Reason 3: The Absence of Suicide Among Youth

I can't find any reliable statistics that show that children are committing suicide or have suicidal tendencies. Although there has been some talk about the warning signals a potential suicide victim sends out, often while at school, this is simply not the concern of teachers and other school personnel. They are there to teach! Using tax money in the schools to prevent suicide cannot be justified. People who want to take their lives are probably those who would have ended up on the welfare rolls anyway.

Reason 4: Child Sexual Abuse Has Been Eliminated

No child I know of comes to school as a victim of child sexual abuse anymore. Of course, in the past I had heard the horrendous statistic: one out of four women would have experienced some form of sexual abuse by the time they reached the age of 18. That problem has been eliminated today.

All children now trip gaily to school, unscarred, unafraid, and completely relaxed about what goes on at home. There are no secrets that they can't tell anyone about.

Daddies don't molest their children. What an abominable idea! I just don't understand what all the fuss is about. It's probably a plot or a scheme to sell newspapers. No child comes to school with the secretive eyes, the avoidance behaviors, or that persistent, unexpressed guilt and rage that used to interfere with learning and growth. Who needs counselors for something that doesn't exist anymore?

Reason 5: Peer Group Pressure: A Thing of the Past

It has been a genuine pleasure to witness the decline of peer group pressure in the mid 1980s. Students increasingly refused to wear what other students wore or to say or think what other students said or thought. Somehow, automatically, they became their own persons. They moved toward an autonomy that was marked by mature decisions, careful reassigning on all kinds of tricky personal issues, and an abandonment of faddish behavior of any sort. Several striking features of this reduction in peer group pressure could be measured. It was difficult to ever find students hanging out at the malls. Because of a lack of viewers, Music Television (MTV) went bankrupt, and if students used their "Walkman" cassette players, it was to listen to inspirational messages from the leading pastors of the country. Strangest of all, the family telephone was free for hours at a time, because none of the kids needed to know what anyone else was going to wear the next day. Students worked hard at school and at home. Even the peer group language disappeared. Expletives went the way of those formerly ubiquitous expressions such as "Like, you know, right, you know, like." Without the problems generated by peer group pressure, who needs to pay salaries of counselors?

Reason 6: Unwanted Pregnancies Disappear

The forces that eliminated sex education from schools have also provided this reason to eliminate counseling programs. Boys and girls today do not even seem to be curious about sexuality, and with this curiosity gone, none of the girls get pregnant. Much counseling time used to be spent dealing with the heartbreak of unwanted pregnancies, but, fortunately, sexuality in all of its evil forms seems to have disappeared from the lives of school-age youths.

Not only are teenagers refraining from experimenting with sexual activity, they just do not seem to be thinking about it. It was so clear to me that sex education, although often nothing more than information about reproductive organs, had in the past encouraged students to experiment; but with the elimination of sex education, pregnancies miraculously disappeared and counselors were free to do the more significant work of getting students placed in Ivy League colleges. I must be frank here, however. College placement is work that can be done by well-tutored clerks, and thus I argue, once more, that counseling programs can be eliminated as easily as unwanted pregnancies have been. (I mean eliminated as an issue: I'm not for abortion, obviously.)

Reason 7: There Are No More Children of Alcoholics

Society has been so fortunate to have witnessed adults, who were formerly caught up in the problem of alcoholism, all marching off to join Alcoholics Anonymous. As a result, sobriety reigns in the country.

Consequently, the many children of alcoholics, with their shame, their secrets, and their social detachment, have also recovered. Why, you may ask, do I mention social detachment? It used to be that children of alcoholics were never able to bring a playmate home, so they became detached from their peers. Who would bring a playmate home if he or she were to be embarrassed by parents who mumbled, stumbled, or tumbled out of control?

With the problem under control, is there any justification for wasting counseling budgets to share information on the disease of alcoholism or time to help a child who must return each day to a home where there is violence, no predictability, or constantly impending financial disaster?

If there were any youths with that situation to go home to, I would be the first to vote for money for alcohol prevention programs in the schools. But the problem does not exist. All youths return each afternoon to homes where promises are kept, where there is quiet and order, and where there is a safe and nurturing atmosphere. Of course, there are exceptions, but I don't believe it is that horrible to have alcoholic parents. It might even develop character. It's not such a horrible thing to be forced to act like the adult in the family, and it's not so tragic to be a child who never had a childhood.

In any case, school is not the place to talk about problems like that, even if they do exist, which they don't. Furthermore, alcoholism is a private and personal matter, and it is an abuse of a parent's privacy for a child to have a forum to talk about such things in school.

But all of this is academic, because research has shown that children now come to school without any of the alleged problems that develop because of alcoholism. These are the kinds of problems that were once recognized as coating a life with psychic debris and damage that will last a lifetime for children of alcoholics. Because there are no more alcoholics, there cannot be any children of alcoholics in the schools, so why have counselors scurrying around trying to find some lost child to help? I say eliminate those counseling programs.

Reason 8: Children No Longer Drop Out of School

As standards for high school graduation went up, along with increased use of statewide achievement tests, demands for acquiring more knowledge spread to the lower grades. The focus on basics made school so much more fun, and the battle for grades made school more like an exciting game to go to; thus, absenteeism decreased astronomically.

Also, the emphasis on basics let students know exactly what was expected of them, so that they delighted in striving for higher achievement (like knowing the names of the Stuart kings in order or the eight major products of Pakistan). Although not everyone could make "A"s without lowering standards, students kept on working, learning, and pushing to memorize everything they could in every class.

The result, as educators rightly predicted, was that students no longer dropped out of school. Everyone stayed, and average daily attendance went off the charts. Each morning, eager, alert students came to school with the appropriate intrinsic motivation. These students were not frightened about failing, and all of them believed they fit in.

The holding power of the schools became so great that football players and other athletes neither felt better nor worse than the boys and girls who couldn't even do two push-ups. There was room for everyone, because each student believed that he or she was really invited to learn and each knew that school was the place to come early to and to stay late at.

One especially delightful fallout from all of this has been that there are no longer any students with learning disabilities. The youths who couldn't learn, whose tight little bodies grew rigid with failure, used to occupy so many counselor hours; well, they simply are not factors anymore. Everyone learns, everyone stays; so who needs counselors?

Reason 9: There Are No Children With Weight Problems

I have never understood this misplaced compassion for students who either eat too much or too little. Such "bleeding heart" people give overbloated names like bulimia or anorexia or obesity to something that could be corrected with a strong whack over the knuckles by a parent. But here I am talking as if there were a problem when there is none. Everyone is probably a few pounds overweight. What's the big deal? So what, if the chubby kids don't like themselves, and what if they do get teased and ridiculed? No wonder they want their doughnuts and pizza.

But now all of the children are just the right weight and always demonstrate, just like their teachers, the highest state of nutritional wisdom. There is no longer a need to support programs that waste time on weight awareness meetings or any other kind of frills based on coddling children.

Reason 10: All of the Adults Who Serve Children Work Together Cooperatively

This is the final justification for eliminating counseling programs. Counselors in the "good old days" were badly needed and spent much time and energy massaging wounded egos of staff and faculty, putting out brush fires among jealous, envious colleagues, and of course, protecting children from sometimes vicious teachers. But that is clearly a thing of the past.

Today, all school personnel work together in peace and harmony and express loving and nurturing support for each other. In such an environment, pettiness, backbiting, and gossip are rarely, if ever, heard. Thus, one more former role counselors might have had—peacemaking between warring factions in a school—is no longer a viable concern. Schools can now use the money that once supported those feeble efforts at parlor psychiatry for the real purposes of the school—learning, learning, and more learning.

Conclusion

I hope I have convinced you that eliminating counseling programs in the schools is essential. All ten of my reasons boil down to one basic observation, an observation that makes it abundantly clear that society can no longer support counseling programs: There are simply no wounded, hurting, needy, deprived, dejected, depressed, abandoned, scarred, scared, damaged, or bewildered children any more. No one comes to school afflicted with any social or emotional damage these days. The following are the facts (or myths, as the pro-counseling people would call them):

1. Self-esteem in every child soars higher than the tallest buildings society has built.
2. Put downs, ridicule, or killer statements are never heard in schools.
3. Every child comes to school with a strong, family-instilled set of values. They all know what is right and wrong and they all act accordingly. (That's one of the reasons the forces on the "right" have struggled to keep counselors from doing values clarification. It's not needed. All values are already clarified.)

4. All students live whole, rich lives; their lives are focused on positive love, and they are committed to justice and the removal of injustice in whatever form it takes (e.g., racism, sexism, ageism).

Does anyone reading this see it otherwise? There is nothing to worry about. Any problems children might have had are now figments of some sob sister's paranoia. So join me in supporting the dropping, or eliminating, of all counseling programs. The "right" minded among us will all feel better doing that. Just look at today's youth. My question is: Do students need counseling programs or not? Who in his "right" mind or conservative budget would say yes?

ERIC/CAPS

Educational Resources Information Center—ERIC

ERIC is a decentralized nationwide information system founded in 1966 and currently sponsored by the Office of Educational Research and Improvement within the U.S. Department of Education. It is the largest education related database in the world. ERIC is designed to collect educational documents and journal articles and to make them readily available through a number of products and services, e.g., the ERIC database, abstract journals, microfiche collections, online and CD-ROM computer searches, document reproductions, and information analysis publications. The ERIC audience is equally wideranging and includes teachers, counselors, administrators, supervisors, policy makers, librarians, media specialists, researchers, students, parents, and other educators and interested persons.

Counseling and Personnel Services Clearinghouse—CAPS

CAPS is one of the 16 subject-oriented clearinghouses of the ERIC system. CAPS' exceptionally broad coverage includes K–12 counseling and guidance, post-secondary and adult counseling services, and human resource development in business, industry and government. Among the topics addressed are:

- preparation, practice and supervision of counseling professionals
- development of theoretical constructs
- research on programs and practices
- interviewing and testing
- group work
- career planning and development

- employee assistance programs (EAPs)
- training and development
- marriage and family counseling
- student activities
- services to special populations (substance abusers, public offenders, students-at-risk)
- program evaluation

CAPS acquires literature in its subject area, processes the information into the ERIC database, and produces a variety of subject-specialized materials. It offers such products as monographs, special issues papers, state of the art studies, computer search analyses, bibliographies and digests. A quarterly newsletter (free upon request) features Clearinghouse activities, products, and articles on timely topics. CAPS' professional staff also offers question-answering services, computer searching of the ERIC database, on-site user services with a complete ERIC microfiche collection at the CAPS Resources Center, and national, state and local workshops on high-priority counseling and human services concerns. We welcome visitors and mail or phone inquiries.

ERIC/CAPS
2108 School of Education
The University of Michigan
Ann Arbor, MI 48109-1259
(313) 764-9492